'Wayne Duvenage has rallied citizens to become activists, who were excited about playing a role in changing a system they felt was unjust. He managed to unite typically opposing groups and keep the e-toll debacle top of mind. His unwavering commitment to a drawn-out legal battle has shown great leadership. The story of citizens standing up and speaking out is one that needs to be told more often. He was named Lead SA Hero in October 2013. Wayne is a great example of active citizenry.'

– **Yusuf Abramjee**, *Lead SA and anti-crime activist*

'The beauty of the South African Constitution is that it gives real protection and real power to the people. But it is a power we too infrequently use. In this sense *The E-Toll Saga* is a story and a lesson for all of us. It tells the tale of how every quest for justice must commence with an individual, sometimes an unlikely "activist" like Wayne Duvenage. But as this true tale unfolds we see how unlawful and unjust policies can be challenged by patient popular mobilisation, well-marshalled research, savvy media and use of the courts. Bravely, it is also an account of one of those rare occasions when civil disobedience is justified. These are the keys to a successful and accountable democracy. They are keys that should be held by everyone.'

– **Mark Heywood**, *director of Section27*

'Wayne Duvenage has achieved what politicians fear, he has educated a nation, accustomed to the abuse of the rule of law for the last six generations to favour the powerful, to the simple truth that laws badly formulated, without consultation, don't need mob violence, but simply for the people to ignore these laws. "Government by the people for the people" means just that. Arrest us all and who do you have left to tax, to spend on your private empires?'

– **Hugh Glenister**, *civil activist*

The E-Toll Saga

I dedicate this book to my wife, Helen and our three children.
For your support, understanding and personal courage.
With love
Wayne

The E-Toll Saga

- - - - - - - - - - - - - - - -

A Journey from CEO to Civil Activist

Wayne Duvenage

with

Angelique Serrao

MACMILLAN

First published in 2015
by Pan Macmillan South Africa
Private Bag x19
Northlands
Johannesburg
2116

www.panmacmillan.co.za

ISBN 978-1-77010-427-3
e-ISBN 978-1-77010-428-0

© 2015 Wayne Duvenage

Editing by Valda Strauss
Proofreading by Sally Hines
Design and typesetting by Triple M Design
Cover design by K4
Cover photographs: Protestors, including spokesperson for OUTA Wayne
Duvenage (centre), hold placards during a peaceful protest against e-tolls
organised by COSATU (Paballo Thekiso, *The Star*); e-toll gantry from
Gallo Images/Foto24/Felix Dlangamandla

Printed and bound by Paarl Media, Paarl

Contents

▬ ▬ ▬ ▬ ▬ ▬ ▬ ▬ ▬ ▬ ▬ ▬ ▬

Abbreviations

AA	Automobile Association
AARTO	Administrative Adjudication of Road Traffic Offences Act
ANC	African National Congress
ASA	Advertising Standards Authority
BEE	Black Economic Empowerment
BMF	Black Management Forum
BUSA	Business Unity South Africa
COSATU	Congress of South African Trade Unions
CSIR	Council for Scientific and Industrial Research
DA	Democratic Alliance
ETC	Electronic Toll Collection
GDP	gross domestic product
GFIP	Gauteng Freeway Improvement Project
GIBS	Gordon Institute of Business Science
IMC	Inter Ministerial Committee
ITS	Intelligent Transport Systems
JPSA	Justice Project South Africa
MEC	Member of the Executive Council
MPL	Member of the Provincial Legislature
NAAMSA	National Association of Automobile Manufacturers in South Africa
NADA	National Automobile Dealers Association
NGO	non-governmental organisation
NPA	National Prosecuting Authority
OECD	Organisation for Economic Co-operation and Development
OUTA	Opposition to Urban Tolling Alliance
POPI Act	Protection of Personal Information Act
QASA	QuadPara Association of South Africa
REDISA	Recycling and Economic Development Initiative of South Africa
RFA	Road Freight Association

SAA   South African Airways
SANCU   South African National Consumer Union
SANRAL   South African National Roads Agency Limited
SARS   South African Revenue Service
SATSA   Southern African Tourism Services Association
SAVRALA   South African Vehicle Renting and Leasing Association
SC   Senior Counsel
SCA   Supreme Court of Appeal
TCH   Transaction Clearing House
TNS   Taylor Nelson Sofres [global market research company]
VPC   Violations Processing Centre

Foreword

- - - - - - - - - - - - - - - -

Wayne Duvenage's book on the e-toll saga represents a fascinating and informative chronicle of a topic that has elicited massive public attention and discussion over the past four years. The issue of raising government revenue to help finance the construction of the Gauteng Freeway Improvement Project (GFIP) through e-tolls has been a fairly dominant subject of discourse in society, the motorist public at large, trade unions and the political environment more generally.

In many ways the e-toll saga ought to be a storm in a teacup, given the relatively modest financial magnitude of the issues at hand in relation to the broader macro-economy at large. It is all about government raising approximately R2.5 billion per annum to pay for certain road improvements, compared with a national budget approaching R1.2 trillion and government revenue collections of over R1.0 trillion. Despite this, the amount of attention the issue has drawn and the emotions it has evoked have been extraordinary. Arguably, the issue has united interest, cultural and income groups drawn from a wide variety of disparate causes, usually unrelated or even in opposition to one another. To this day the saga continues, with the latest pronouncement by the government that it still intends persisting with the system, despite acute protestation by the public at large.

There are several reasons for the emotions and frustrations generated by the system. The government persists in perceiving that the driving force for the opposition to e-tolls is the actual cost being borne by the consumer and therefore hopes that by reducing tariffs, this might appease the protests. However, it has been abundantly clear all along that there are several other factors surrounding the system that are causing frustration. There is an acknowledgement that the system involves devotion of a high proportion of revenue raised simply to finance the cost of running the system, administering it and ensuring compliance. It would be possible to raise the funds required so much more easily by simply increasing the fuel levy by about 5%, which would equate to raising the fuel price by just 1%. This would amount to less than 0.05% of people's incomes, with administration and compliance costs of negligible magnitude in comparison with the e-tolls. From a practical point of view, motorists would need to do little more than pay marginally more for their fuel at the pump station. Frustration with the additional practical compliance burden imposed on road users by the system would thereby be avoided. Indeed, had the fuel levy been increased to cover the costs of the construction of the GFIP four years ago when the rumblings about the system first began, the South African National Roads Agency Limited (SANRAL) would have already collected R10 billion towards the funding of the project.

The question is therefore raised as to why the government continues to be so obsessed with proceeding with a system that is threatened with continuing failure. This raises considerable suspicion as to who the financial beneficiaries of the project are and yet affirmative responses remain murky. With perceptions of corruption in the allocation of large projects throughout the economy at an all-time high, it is understandable why so many questions are being asked. We are told that the system is based on the user-pays principle and yet there are a multitude of exclusions being made that renders the system inequitable to begin with. Supposedly, these exclusions are aimed at helping the poorer sections of society, yet the fuel levy itself could have been used as a vehicle through which higher-income motorists, who could afford to buy fancier cars with higher fuel consumption, would end up shouldering a bigger proportion of the financial burden. Besides, does it not matter that such a high proportion of people using Gauteng's freeways are engaged in generating goods and services provided to the rest of the country?

At the forefront of asking these questions of government over the past four years has been the Opposition to Urban Tolling Alliance (OUTA) led by Wayne Duvenage. With the assistance of an able team of fellow travellers and colleagues, Duvenage has provided a huge service to society in fighting the imposition of a system to which so many are opposed. It has been a fight that has required considerable courage and came at enormous cost, in terms of time, stress and finance to those involved, none less than Duvenage himself. It has come out of an inner conviction of what is ethically and morally right.

Numerous obstacles were put in the way of the attempts at opposing the introduction of e-tolls, some even potentially life threatening. The cowardice of some corporate executives in sacrificing principles in abandoning the fight in order to pander to the wishes of the authorities as a means of ensuring that their corporations benefit financially is an all-too-frequent allegation levelled at the captains of industry in the capitalist world of today. Nowhere was this more evident than in the crusade undertaken by OUTA. It contrasted with the fairly generous support for the opposition's efforts provided by small businesses and various non-governmental organisations. This in itself tells us about one aspect of the fault lines currently facing the South African economy.

On the other side of this message is the countervailing trail of bullying tactics being used by some in authority in the public sector to try to scupper attempts at opposing an iniquitous system that might stand in their way. One of the arguments aimed at opponents of the e-toll system was that abandoning it would lead to fiscal Armageddon, with disastrous consequences for the country's credit ratings and, through this, for economic growth more generally. Despite this, four years have elapsed and South Africa's credit ratings continue to enjoy investment grade, principally because the magnitude of the financial issues concerned are relatively small in comparison with the country's overall debt burden.

There are clearly some far more pressing issues facing the economy, such as the industrial relations impasse, energy insecurity and a more general loss of business confidence, in part due to ambiguity in economic policy-making and uncertainty created by this. The issue of e-tolling should never have carried such attention as it did. It did so because of a feeling amongst so many that the government was not listening to them. Fortunately, the country possesses people of the ilk of Wayne Duvenage and his colleagues, who have had the courage to champion the frustrations of so many.

Whilst one acknowledges and recognises the dynamics of the arguments for and against e-tolls, the book provides a fascinating tale of the intrigue surrounding the issues at hand. From a historical perspective, it provides useful information that can be used to illustrate the type of dynamic that generates civil activism. What a pity that such a technologically advanced and sophisticated concept as e-tolls should have been so poorly communicated, introduced and implemented in a society that was clearly not ready for it.

Dr Azar Jammine
May 2015

Dr Azar Jammine is director and chief economist of Econometrix (Pty) Ltd, South Africa's leading independent economic research, consultancy and forecasting company, established in 1982. He has been in his current position since December 1985 and has established a significant profile in South Africa as an analyst and commentator on domestic and international economic affairs.

Preface

- - - - - - - - - - - - - - -

In the latter half of 2010, shortly after South Africa successfully hosted the Soccer World Cup, the citizens of Gauteng (South Africa's powerful economic region), learnt of a new road tax scheme that the government had hatched, to settle its debt for the upgrade of an existing freeway network.

The methodology chosen by the government, as advised by South African National Roads Agency Limited (SANRAL), a wholly owned government entity, was that of an internationally tried and tested electronic tolling mechanism, more commonly referred to as 'e-tolling'.

This book tells the story of the *e-toll saga*, which unfolded over five years in Gauteng. It is a personal reflection told from the perspective of Wayne Duvenage, the man who became the face of the public's e-toll defiance campaign. It traces his journey from chief executive of car rental company Avis in 2012, to becoming the head of a newly formed civil action movement, the Opposition to Urban Tolling Alliance (OUTA).

However, this is more than just a tale of one man's journey to tackle a government policy decision. It is an account of what gave rise to South Africa's biggest public funded legal challenge against its sovereign elected government since the dawn of democracy in 1994. It's a story of a small team of people who energised OUTA's civil action and litigation efforts. And it is, ultimately, a story of courage that gave rise to a civil disobedience campaign in which over 1.5 million road users participated in defiance of government legislation, and how the people won.

This saga reflects on the intricate connections between government, business, trade unions, churches, the media and the public, and exposes how government was tripped up by a newly awakened active citizenry.

Many groups of people conducted their own efforts and in their own way, adding significant impetus to challenge the e-toll decision. There is not one entity or group that can lay claim to the overall outcome of the e-toll story. But there is no doubt that the concerted efforts of OUTA became the spearhead and a catalyst towards defeating the unpopular and contentious e-toll scheme.

The e-toll saga breathed new life into the idea that people can defend their rights against unjust government policies. What this story will show is that, twenty years into South Africa's new democracy, a largely middle-class segment of society – who until now have been complacent in fighting for their rights – have behaved in a way they normally never would.

This was a campaign that would not have been possible in the absence of modern-day social media platforms, combined with an environment of freedom of speech and a strong free press. Good and factual knowledge is power and these healthy communication platforms enabled the flow of meaningful information, which in turn empowered the public with sufficient civil courage to successfully defy government's orders. This was a resounding triumph for the protection of citizens' rights.

One of the questions that has arisen from the e-toll saga and a number of other issues currently being challenged by society is: why now, some two decades into our new-found freedom, is South African civil society launching challenge after challenge against its democratically elected government? We live in a country with one of the most advanced constitutions in the world, with the freedom to resolve our problems learnt from the legacy of Nelson Mandela.

And yet, as this road tax revolt has shown, the people of our nation are becoming restless. Once more, it would seem, the people are having to stand up and fight to have their voices heard.

What this book is *not*

This book does not go into heavy and intricate detail of the legal challenges that OUTA undertook in 2012 and 2013. The pertinent and salient facts about the court challenges are in Part Two of the book, but we didn't want the reader to be lost in a barrage of heavy legal interpretation.

It is also not a book that goes into the complex economic toll modelling and costing scenarios related to road funding, although an overview is provided on the matter. What we have come to realise, however, is that the authorities can justify and find logic in a range of different funding models available to them. The complexity of social and economic infrastructure funding become enormous when one considers the dynamics of a state-owned entity (such as SANRAL) that treats the country's national roads as *its* assets, which are partially financed through general taxation and partly through public-private concessions that are allowed to cross-subsidise other toll road projects.

It is also not a story that speaks of long forensic audits and investigations in an attempt to follow the money, to expose corruption that might lie behind the scheme. While concerns about corrupt practices and the undue flow of money are expressed on occasion (most certainly during the road construction phase of the project), we never had the luxury of time or money to conduct such an investigation. Our view was that we didn't need to expose corrupt practices to halt the scheme. We only needed to empower the public by providing them with sufficient evidence that the scheme was unjust and irrational enough to defy.

*

Told from Wayne Duvenage's view, his journey follows a range of emotions, from frustration, anxiety, anger and fear, on the one hand, to elation, surprise, courage and relief, on the other hand, all of which come with challenges of this nature. He shares his first-hand experience of how corporate South Africa has become both paralysed and inept in its need to cross swords with government. Civil activist Hugh Glenister's description is probably most apt when he says, 'Big business is just too busy tendering to make the rope to hang this country with.'

The book closes on a reflection of the political and institutional dynamics that are currently at play in South Africa, and which, if not addressed and attended to by a stronger and more organised civil society, will see the slow economic demise and erosion of prosperity for the country.

Martin Luther King once said, 'The arc of the moral universe is long, but it bends towards justice.' This is so true for the e-toll saga.

In Wayne's words, 'This journey and challenge have taken a lot longer and consumed far more effort, and at a much higher personal price, than I ever imagined it would.'

Wayne Duvenage and Angelique Serrao
June 2015

Summary of e-toll events

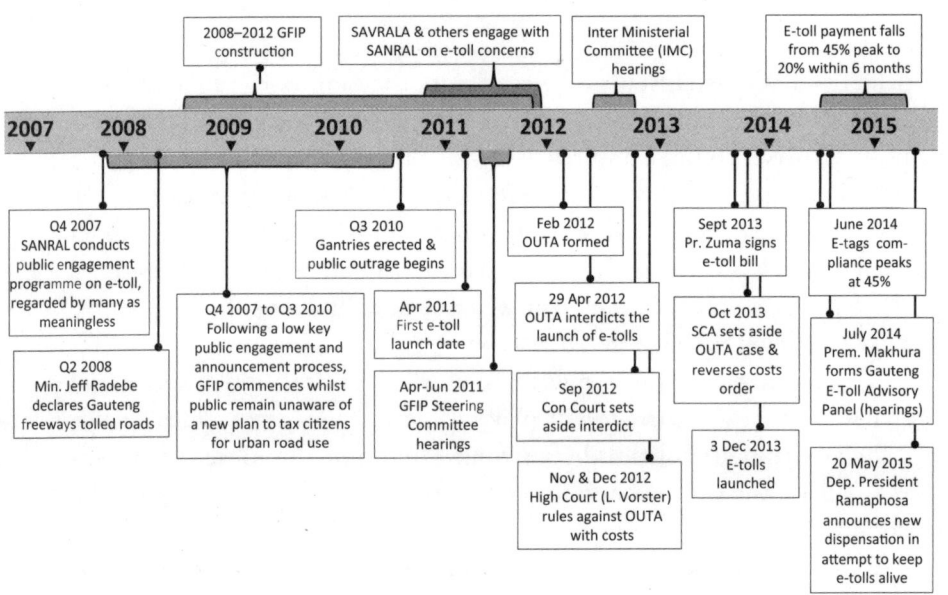

PART ONE

- - - - - - - - - - - - - -

The need for change bulldozed a road down the center of my mind.
   – Maya Angelou

CHAPTER 1

How the hell did I get here?

- - - - - - - - - - - - - - - - -

My mind was reeling in a profusion of thoughts and imaginary questions as I rehearsed the answers over and over again.

I pictured them: the journalists, the cameras and TV crews.

I wondered whether I would be able to cover accurately all the salient points and issues we were challenging about the e-toll decision.

I couldn't sleep as I lay in bed, staring at the ceiling, dimly lit by the streetlight that leaked in through a gap in the curtains.

Two hours passed before I nodded off. But dawn broke too soon and I hadn't got the sleep that my body and mind longed for. It had been weeks since I'd had a good, solid night's sleep.

It was 5.30 am, Friday, 23 March 2012. The day the world would learn about the Opposition to Urban Tolling Alliance, or OUTA as it became commonly known. It was the day we were to announce what it was we stood for, and just how far we were willing to go to oppose a system we believed was fundamentally wrong.

This was the day we were to announce to society and, I guess, to the world, our legal and civil action challenge to oppose an unjust government-approved project.

Once showered and dressed, I read our prepared speech for the umpteenth time over breakfast with my wife Helen:

> *The calls to oppose e-tolling of Gauteng's Freeway Improvements (GFIP) are loud, filled with anger and a growing resentment towards this unnecessary burden.*
>
> *It is a sad day when a nation's government develops a tense and threatening relationship with its people, when trying to force an unjust and unpopular decision into being …*[1]

It all seemed right, but I began to question and doubt my involvement. Was this decision the right one to take? What was I doing here? Would my participation and actions bring pressure to bear from government on my employer? My mind was churning.

The Opposition to Urban Tolling Alliance was recently formed out of a necessity for business organisations and people of similar mind to coordinate their efforts and consider a legal challenge to the e-tolling matter.

Our investigation has unpacked a number of issues and transgressions that highlights a disregard for protecting the interests of the public.[2]

Ever cautious, I started to worry about what could or might go wrong. What if I couldn't answer the questions? What if, what if …

'Relax, Wayne,' Helen reassured me, reminding me that we had done all the necessary preparation as best we could. 'What will be will be, let it take the road you have planned.' She is my rock.

Negative thoughts weren't going to help. I tried to mask my anxiety from Helen, but after eighteen years, she could read me like the back of her hand. My mind was far away as she wished me luck.

Here we go, then, I thought as I climbed into my car. No turning back now. I drove towards the Sandton skyline.

By 8.30 am, I was on the eighth floor of the wallpapered and plush-carpeted floors of Cliffe Dekker Hofmeyr, our attorneys responsible for managing our legal affairs.

Marc 'the Irish Terrier' Corcoran, head of the South African Vehicle Renting and Leasing Association's (SAVRALA's) e-toll working committee and an integral member of OUTA's team, was in Boardroom #10 next door, with our senior counsel, putting the final touches to our founding affidavit and other legal papers, which were about to be lodged with the North Gauteng High Court.

I was in Boardroom #12 with Paul Pauwen (a director and the secretary of OUTA) and attorney Owen Blumberg. We sat around the high-gloss, white table and went over the press statement for what felt like the hundredth time.

We needed to be sure we had an answer to every probable question. My night-time worries were suddenly alive again, and zigzagging between us:

Challenging the actions of one's government in court is a most unpleasant stance to take and in this case, it is our last and very necessary resort. Our application to interdict the decision to toll Gauteng's Freeways was issued from the Pretoria High Court (today).[3]

By 9.00 am, there was nothing more we could do. We were ready and Owen was smiling. He was eager and expressed confidence that the case would pan out in our favour. I needed to hear this. It was uplifting, but in reality they were only words of prediction.

Owen has that straight-faced humour thing down to a tee. The type of man who is so frustratingly good at it, you find yourself wondering if he is joking or serious about half the things he says.

'It will be over in a few months,' he enthused.

The earlier worries had ebbed away. The energy in the room was high, concerned emotion giving way to a sense of eagerness to embark on what we were about to do.

I noted it, watched it, wondered why I was watching it fade. I began to drift.

There was a voice in my ear.

'My God, Wayne, you've turned whiter than a cue ball,' remarked Owen.

Really? I tried to stand up. My legs refused to cooperate. I fell back into the chair.

Oh shit, something is wrong.

I was dizzy. I picked up the press statement and tried to read it. The words were floating. My speech was slurred. My head swayed.

'Hey, Paul, I'm not sure what's going on here, but I can't read this statement feeling like this. You may have to do it.'

'Don't panic,' said Paul, a constant voice of calmness and reason. 'You just relax.' He picked up a copy of the speech from the journalists' packs on the desk and began to read it through. Just in case.

I was getting worried now.

'Wayne, I have the number of a good doctor on call. Should I get him?' Owen asked.

A doctor? But we were leaving in 30 minutes. Surely not? What was happening?

'Look, for all we know you could be having a heart attack, a stroke, or whatever. Let's not take a chance,' Owen said, assuring me that the doctor could be at the offices in ten minutes.

9.45 am: Doctor Josselsohn arrived with his large, brown bag of tricks. I barely registered his presence in my light-headed and dizzy state.

He asked a few questions and, in a jiffy, my shirt was off. After a few minutes of prodding and stethoscoping, the diagnosis was delivered.

Vital signs were good and I was in top shape. 'Well, you could be fitter,' he hinted, and after a few more questions informed me, 'You are having an anxiety attack.'

Thank God. I breathed in deeply. I needed air.

How embarrassing, I thought.

'It's been a hectic month of late nights, Wayne.' Paul was again at my side reassuring me.

He reminded me of the many hours we had put in over the past three weeks, working flat out and into the early hours of every morning as we researched, helped and directed Adrian d'Oliveira, our junior counsel advocate, in the preparation of our founding affidavit.

From the day Minister of Finance Pravin Gordhan had announced in his budget speech of 27 February 2012 that e-tolls were here to stay, we had just three weeks to put the case together. During this time, we needed to prepare and file our founding affidavit in order to allow the legal process to flow if we were to have any chance of interdicting the launch of e-tolls on 30 April 2012. It was a hectic, torrid period for us.

Adrian was a genius at preparing and writing affidavits in a concise way that drove and directed our arguments in court. I learnt over the next year and a half just how brilliant he is at his job. He was also a hard task master and requested input and information from us at all hours of the day. Together Marc, Paul and I became his slaves, digging into archives, searching for documents and trawling the Internet, seven days a week. We were compiling a comprehensive and multifaceted argument with supporting references that filled boxes of lever-arch files. We had little time for our paying jobs, let alone our families and friends.

This isn't the type of thing you do on a whim. Instituting a legal challenge against government on behalf of society is a serious matter. The arguments we presented had to be strong and valid.

We support the government when its actions are for the betterment of society and believe it should be challenged when this is not so...[4]

Owen handed me a glass of sugar water, which started to calm my nerves. My mind and senses began to return to normal. I got up and walked around, breathing in deeply.

By 10.00 am we were in Paul's car. I was boosting my energy levels by chewing on wine gums and drinking an Energade from the local Engen Garage, as we headed south to the Gordon Institute of Business

Science (GIBS), where our press conference, which had been so efficiently arranged by the Press Club, was to be held.

As we turned into the parking lot at GIBS, it dawned on me how big this challenge might become, but even then I had no idea of how truly enormous it would turn out to be.

By 12.00 am, the OUTA panel was seated in the front of the auditorium. It consisted of OUTA members: Dr Clif Johnston of the South African National Consumer Union (SANCU), Pieter Conradie of Cliffe Dekker Hofmeyr, myself, Michael Tatalias of the Southern African Tourism Services Association (SATSA) and Joseph Machwe from the QuadPara Association of South Africa (QASA). Antoinette Slabbert from the Press Club sat in the middle to facilitate and field the questions.

The auditorium of the GIBS Classroom #10 was packed with journalists who fell silent as Antoinette welcomed all present to witness OUTA's announcement. Question time would follow thereafter. Antoinette then turned to me and formally announced, 'You may proceed now, Mr Duvenage.'

Cameras blazed away and pens scribbled as I read our press statement, announcing through the media, to society and our government, that a new civil action organisation had recently been formed and today it was filing legal papers to challenge SANRAL, the Ministry of Transport, the Department of Water and Environmental Affairs, the Gauteng MEC for Roads and Transport and the National Consumer Commission. We were challenging their decision to subject Gauteng motorists to a complex, irrational, inefficient, costly, unworkable and unjust tolling system on the existing, but recently upgraded, freeway network within the province of Gauteng.

At the time, it seemed to us that the case was a slam dunk and would be quick and easy. I sincerely believed it would be one that would have the authorities reassessing their decision as a result of our court challenge, and possibly even cancelling their e-toll plans.

How wrong I was. That day was the beginning of a long and costly fight. A fight that fundamentally changed the course of my life. It was a decision that brought many moments of joy and frustration, enlightenment and angst. But it was a decision and experience that I will never regret.

CHAPTER 2

Unbearable congestion and the World Cup looming

▬ ▬ ▬ ▬ ▬ ▬ ▬ ▬ ▬ ▬ ▬ ▬ ▬ ▬ ▬ ▬

It all started in 2010, around eighteen months prior to the filing of our founding affidavit in March 2012.

Ke Nako. Feel it. After years of waiting, our moment in the international football sun had arrived. It seemed to have happened so fast and was gone in a flash.

It was mid-July 2010 and South Africa was on a high. The nation had just successfully hosted the world's biggest sporting event. We had danced the 'Waka Waka', and shown the world how much noise we could make with a plastic horn. Danny Jordaan was our hero back then. However, recent controversy surrounding corruption, linked to FIFA's host country bid-rigging scandals, suggests there is a lot that he, the South African Football Association and government officials might have to answer to.

It didn't matter that our home team, Bafana Bafana, had been knocked out in the opening round, despite a draw against Mexico and a 2–1 win against France on 22 June 2010, our last game in the competition. Our disappointment was brief and we remained proud of our team as we moved on to enjoy the rest of the spectacular event. Our national pride was on stage and we had all become football fundis.

South Africa had defied the critics who predicted that the event would be a flop, that tourists would be mugged and murdered and that the stadiums would not be built on time.

We shook our heads and clicked our tongues at the sensationalist opportunists who sold stab-proof vests online.

By the time August of that year had rolled around, the last of the estimated 309 554 tourists,[5] who had come to enjoy our unique heritage and generous hospitality, had departed. The nation sat back and wallowed in a collective soccer fever afterglow.

Many businesses counted their profits while others reeled from their losses, wondering how they had got the attendance numbers and short-term business plans so wrong. Many, particularly in the hospitality industry, had predicted almost double the actual number of visitors who would turn up for one of the greatest sporting spectaculars the world has to offer.

Happy with our new freeways

Joburgers had become used to seemingly endless roadside construction. We were being urged by radio station DJs and newspaper columnists to be patient while our freeways were being improved for the onset of the Soccer World Cup. Besides, we had no choice. It was the honourable thing to do, a matter of World Cup national pride.

For the previous two years, since 2008, the existing freeway network around Gauteng had undergone a major upgrade, known as the Gauteng Freeway Improvement Project – or GFIP for short.

The South African National Roads Agency Limited, otherwise known as SANRAL, was the state-owned entity responsible for our national freeway network. It was in charge of this multibillion-rand project and kept society up to date with the upgrade, flighting a series of advertisements and press statements to reassure everyone that it was hard at work to have most of the construction completed by June 2010. Adverts featured people travelling with jet packs to work, but until that sci-fi future arrived, we needed good roads and a wider freeway network around the nation's economic hub. SANRAL was our congestion saviour in the here and now.

By the time kick-off to FIFA arrived on 11 June 2012, as promised, most of our Gauteng freeway upgrade had been completed and building had ceased on those parts that were not yet complete while the games were on. The public had been patient and understanding about the lane restrictions. SANRAL was the hero of the day, keeping its suppliers and construction companies working day and night to meet the deadlines. Any poll done on SANRAL's brand equity at that time would have come out close to an 8 or 9 out of 10.

The need for the freeway upgrade

Prior to the 2008 start of construction, the state of Gauteng's freeway network had become a long-standing gripe among residents. Everyone who lived in the economic heartland of Africa knew without a doubt that something big had to happen. Given the poor performance by Gauteng's provincial government and metros to provide a reliable public transport network, the residents of Gauteng had become largely trapped into making use of road-based vehicles in order to commute. The widening of our freeways was probably the only thing the authorities could do to ease the congestion at the time. It was most welcome.

Most of the region's freeway network consisted of three lanes in either direction. Another lane, along with some upgrading of the intersections and off-ramps, would go a long way towards easing the congestion. Our nation's obsessive reliance on cars as a primary means of transport was a legacy of the apartheid system, which gave rise to our cities' spatial development into racially segregated areas, sprawling outwards as opposed to being concentrated. Besides a few rail links between the city's commercial zones and the poorer areas where the mass labour force for industry resided, roads became the main commuter arteries. Today, 10% of the region's workforce commute by train while 84% make use of cars and minibus taxis (roughly 42% each), and the remaining 6% either walk or cycle to work. We have essentially become a society with little option but to use road-based transportation.

Following a decade of a rapid average annual gross domestic product (GDP) growth of 3.3% per annum between 1995 and 2005,[6] sadly not much had happened with the region's road network, the congestion turning the freeways into an effective car park. South Africa had slipped into a general era of short-term leadership thinking that preferred not to spend tax revenues on long-term infrastructural, needs or planning. Maintenance programmes also took a back seat so that the nation began to witness a degradation of its vital social and economic infrastructure, which was not confined to roads, but extended to energy generation, water reticulation, rail networks, electricity supply and so on.

Municipalities were hardest hit. Necessary engineering skills were lost, while local authorities exhausted the ratepayers' coffers to service other matters to redress and right the wrongs of under-spending in the impoverished areas of society. More and more was emerging about the problem of corruption, which had weaved its way into the tender processes. This created an imbalance where service delivery was not always put first and services as well as infrastructure projects were starting to suffer as a consequence.

Needless to say, by 2008, a 50-kilometre drive between the two major city nodes of Johannesburg and Pretoria could take you up to two hours. And while the public welcomed the announced commencement of the freeway upgrade in 2008, SANRAL and the Gauteng provincial government were engaged in behind the scenes bargaining for provincial roads to be transferred under SANRAL's jurisdiction. No meaningful or serious attempt was made by SANRAL to notify the road users of its plans to impose a 45-gantry and electronic tolling system as a means to extricate funds from society to finance the project.

Gauteng, a powerful concentrated economic hub

Gauteng is South Africa's smallest and most concentrated province. Its 18 000 square kilometres covers only 1.42% of the total land area of the country, housing 12.3 million[7] of South Africa's 52 million people. Yet, it contributes roughly 37% to the country's trillion-rand GDP. It is a thriving place, thumping with the energy of people who both work hard and play hard. From its early start as a dusty mining town in 1886 when gold was discovered on the Witwatersrand, the region has attracted almost all the nation's business headquarters and commercial decision-making over the past century.

The people of Gauteng get far less back than what they put into the national Treasury's coffers. In fact, it receives R95 billion[8] to spend on its own regional infrastructure, having contributed around R375 billion.[9] But the people who make this frenetic megalopolis home know this. They are aware that their wealth and prosperity assists with the socio-economic needs of the rest of the country and they do not bemoan this fact. They simply put their heads down and get on with their fast-paced lives and with making a positive difference to the lives of millions of others around the country.

Most economic hubs around the world tend to grow very quickly. The opportunities that emerge from these environments are social magnets to people from rural and neighbouring countries in search of wealth or, as often turns out to be the case for millions, a meagre survival. Since the birth of South Africa's democracy in 1994, the Gauteng urban landscape has flourished.

During this period, the freeway infrastructure consisted of a ring road with tentacle-like feeder routes reaching out to the neighbouring satellite metros and municipalities around Johannesburg, and the Ben Schoeman Highway that linked Johannesburg to Pretoria (see the map on page 12). Five years into the new century and this road network began to groan under the pressure of a growing commuter base.

The use of the road network had expanded by 1.6 million registered

Gauteng Freeway Network

vehicles in 2000[10] to around 3.6 million by 2008. Added to this, roughly 140 kilometres of the 185-kilometre freeway network was in need of resurfacing, but like the inhabitants of any growing city in a thriving economy, its people generally believed that behind the scenes, the urban planners and government authorities had made the necessary provisions in advance to ease the congestion.

Congestion relief arrives

It was against this backdrop that SANRAL came in with its 'please be patient, we are improving your roads' media campaign directed at Gauteng residents in early 2008. It was music to motorists' ears and we were patient as the three-laned freeways were largely reduced to two lanes in each direction to allow for the upgrade and widening of the network. On the R21 eastern carriageway the road would be expanded from two to four lanes in each direction. This alternative link between the two cities of Pretoria and Johannesburg had become very popular and extremely busy since the turn of the century.

All in all, 185 kilometres of the urban freeway backbone to the region was labelled as Phase 1 of the bigger 350-kilometre project. Congested interchanges and off-ramps were being improved and median lighting was being installed.

A civil engineering feat of note and certainly the largest single road infrastructure project undertaken on the continent – and a much welcomed one at that, I recalled thinking after hearing the news of the upgrades.

At the time, I was the chief executive of Avis South Africa's car rental division, a position I had filled since May 2007.

'This temporary congested situation and construction works will probably push up our car rental accident damages, with more windscreen damage from stones,' said one of my Avis executive colleagues at the time, 'but it will certainly be worth the frustration in the long run.' There was no doubt the upgrade was necessary and overdue.

What emerged, however, was not only the matter of the road upgrade, but the immense controversy that would unfold a few years later: on how this project was to be funded. The Gauteng open road tolling system was, in fact, conceived in tightly closed channels of communication between SANRAL, the big construction companies and government leaders at both regional and national level. The first reference to the scheme that I have been able to find is a *Financial Mail* report dating back to June 2003, written by the late Ian Fife. What is remarkable is that his focus is not on the merits of tolling but rather the stifling blanket of secrecy that surrounded the idea. The headline said it all: 'Poor visibility on Toll Road Plan makes debate difficult: No one will comment on project for fear of victimisation.'

Contrast that with the unambiguous wording of the Constitution, which obliges the government and state-owned entities to be governed by 'democratic values and principles',[11] and one begins to understand a serious issue that would become problematic for the e-toll decision, namely, a lack of transparency and public participation.

CHAPTER 3

Growing up with change

■ ■ ■ ■ ■ ■ ■ ■ ■ ■ ■ ■ ■ ■ ■ ■ ■

Looking back on my early years, I realise there were key moments that nurtured my growing attitude towards fighting injustice and inequality.

I was born in Harare in 1960, and remember very little of my early life in Zimbabwe. My parents had moved to Natal when my sister (3) and I (5) were very young. Our parents, Arthur and Bertha, were divorced a year later and my first real memories were of my early school days at Pinetown Primary. When I was ten, we moved with my father who relocated to Newcastle in northern KwaZulu-Natal where he was appointed as a factory manager at Hume, a concrete pipe manufacturer. Newcastle in those days was undergoing massive industrial growth. Iscor, the state-owned iron and steel manufacturing corporation (since privatised as ArcelorMittal) was being expanded and the town was booming.

I performed at the bottom half of my class during my school days until matric when for some reason my neurons kicked up a gear and I managed a top-ten placement, but was never an ace student. I played hockey and cricket for the second team and just enjoyed every minute of the sports I played, my mates and the outdoor fun we had during and after school.

As children growing up in the 1960s and 1970s in an all-white, middle-class neighbourhood, we were oblivious to apartheid. The government propaganda machine was hard at work to ensure the evil realities of racially segregated living were kept hidden from us.

There were odd occasions during my youth that presented encounters that triggered questions and raised my curiosity about racially based inequalities. I recall clearly, at the age of fifteen while attempting to weld the framework of a go-cart at my father's factory, meeting a kind man named Said. He was softly spoken and helpful, and we spent the afternoon chatting about soccer, pellet guns and go-carts.

Apartheid social engineering did not make it easy for anyone to befriend anyone else who was not of the same racial classification as themselves, but I asked Said where he stayed and said I'd come and visit him one day. A few months later, I rode my bicycle across town from our new, leafy, all-white suburb, Arbour Park, across to Lennoxton – a poorer suburb just west of the town centre – to meet with Said who had recently left his job at the factory my father managed.

I pushed my bike up the driveway to his red-painted porch. He had no idea I was coming and was surprised when he opened the door to my light knock. 'Come in, come in,' he said, looking up and down the street to see if anyone had seen me. I had lunch with Said and his family, my first encounter with Muslim traditions, and after two hours I realised I had to get back home. I was fifteen and was already swimming against the official stream, although I was not doing so with any political protest in mind. I liked the guy. We had common interests. It was just natural.

My father, Arthur, has always been a gentle, deeply religious and hard-working man. He provided my sister and I with a great start in life, strong values and a grounded outlook, as best as any single parent could do. I love him dearly and know that I don't spend enough time with him. He worked off a student loan to ensure I went to university, a stance he was not prepared to compromise on. What a gift and what a mentor.

At university in 1978, I was exposed to the evils of our ruling government and alternative theories of the origin of humankind. My indoctrinated paradigms of religion and racially segregated living were being rocked and my enquiring mind triggered many a long and often-heated debate over family dinners. Despite our opposing views on these subjects, my father and I were close and spent many good times playing chess and golf together.

Debbie, my younger sister, was a weekly boarder at St Dominic's school, not far from where Said lived. She was beautiful and a magnet for all my school friends, which meant that on weekends my brotherly protective instincts kicked in to keep the testosterone-filled teenagers outside the gates. Sadly, Debbie passed away at the young age of 43 from a massive stroke at a time when she needed her family more than ever before to cope with personal stress in her life.

As kids, Debbie and I spent many of our holidays in Durban with our mother, Bertha, or Bee as she was known to her close friends. It was Bee who planted the seed of awareness of how wrong racism and apartheid were in my young mind. One statement she made summed it all up for me. 'Wayne, do you understand how privileged you are because of one thing only?' she asked. I didn't quite catch what she meant. So she hinted a tad further, 'If you had been born with one thing different, your whole life would have been significantly less privileged. You wouldn't be able to go to good schools, catch nice buses, go to the best beaches, and play in well-maintained parks.' While I was still pondering on whether this was a trick question, she responded, 'Your skin colour, my boy. If your skin colour was black instead of white and for no other reason, the many privileges you take for granted would vanish overnight.'

Her description was profound for me and I will never forget how this discussion sensitised me to the shocking absurdity of apartheid. My mom always challenged us and pushed the envelope, making us see the other side of everything.

As I neared my final days at school, I'd set my sights on architecture as a career, but after being reminded of how the feast-or-famine fluctuations of the building industry could make this career a less lucrative one, I switched to Geology instead and signed up at Durban's University of Natal for a science degree, with a penchant for regional and town planning. After a year of studying dissected rocks and minerals, I realised Geology was not for me. I had no desire to work in the mines or prospecting out in the countryside or building roads, where most of the bearded and sun-baked geologists appeared to spend their careers. My heart lay in the hustle and bustle of the city, so I changed tack to Industrial Psychology and graduated with a BSc in December 1982.

The question of challenging and defying my call-up for compulsory national service did cross my mind in 1982. My moral conscience was awake and I contemplated the call to civil disobedience. But I was too young and not mentally courageous enough to go through with this call. I worried about my patriotic father's views and his toiling to pay for my university education. Would this be the right way to treat him?

But it was my life, I thought. On learning that my degree in Psychology would earn me an officer's rank and my time in military service would not be spent in the killing fields of the questionable war, I went ahead with the call-up. In hindsight, nothing could justify the participation in a senseless war to defend a criminal policy, except for the evil impact and threats of incarceration, humiliation and coerced hell. But hindsight is an exact science and while the moral conscience of many a white South African male has since been stirred, it became something we learnt to live with.

I guess it might have also heightened my resolve to challenge the coercive and threatening behaviour of a future government action that would unfold later in my life.

On entering the working environment, I really had no idea of what my career path should be. The thrust of my studies pointed in a human resources direction, but somehow that didn't really grab me.

So it was no surprise that I was sceptical about the trainee manager position at a car rental company that I had applied for in December 1983. But a-job-is-a-job and with not much to choose from, I couldn't afford to be fussy. After two interviews with Sharon Jensen, the Avis airport manager and her boss Pat O'Brien, the Natal regional manager, the personnel agent phoned me with good news: R900 per month and I would supervise a team of eight staff who cleaned, prepared and drove cars between the Durban airport parking lot and the muddy vehicle preparation yard across the highway.

'I sure hope it's a temporary situation, as this is hardly what you got your degree for,' my father commented. But with no responses from the other two applications I had submitted, washing and cleaning rental cars was as good as any other job out there. Stepping stone or not, I was in there like the proverbial robber's dog.

Nothing can describe the freedom of independence and feeling of security you get from that first salary cheque. It's awesome and, quite frankly, any job would have felt right then for me. The joy of signing my first rent agreement for a one-bedroom flat in Stamford Hill Road (aka the Bronx) was bliss. Throw in a girlfriend from across the Umgeni River in upmarket Durban North, and a happier 24-year-old man was nowhere to be found.

My independence was taking shape. 'I promise I'll search for better opportunities, Dad,' I assured him, but more importantly, I was comforted by the fact that I wasn't returning to the stinky industrial town of Newcastle where my dad had indicated he could find me a better paying job. The lure of the city of Durban was strong and that was where I wanted to be.

A happy career

The job at Avis wasn't the stepping stone it was intended to be. The company was full of energy and growth opportunities. The car rental industry was relatively new and expanding as a form of travel for both business and tourism, especially at airports. New branches were being opened, providing opportunities for growth to an eager 24 year old hoping to be given the chance of promotion.

Three months into the job at Durban's airport, I was offered the opportunity to take up my first real branch manager assignment. Wow, that soon? I was blown away, until I heard the catch – it was based in Umtata in the Transkei.

'When do I start?' The second catch was about to be revealed. 'On Monday,' Sharon said.

'But it's Saturday today; you obviously mean next month?' I replied on the telephone, nursing a hangover from a long night at the Warehouse nightclub.

'No, in two days' time,' Sharon said in a stern voice, 'and if you want the job, you'd better get your ass down to the depot by noon to discuss the plan.'

It turned out that the previous licensee operator had terminated his services with little notice to the Transkei government and the daily flights into and out of the airport were left without a car rental operator.

The next 48 hours were sheer chaos, but I managed to pack my bags, said cheers to a friend down the corridor, received tears and a goodbye kiss from my girlfriend of two months, notified my landlord, met seven drivers at the Durban airport depot on the Sunday, grabbed a box of stationery and relocated to this so-called foreign homeland country, some four hours' drive away.

What a great year it turned out to be! Making ends meet under extraordinary and trying conditions are character-building experiences you can't buy. 'Nothing like a baptism of fire on your first rung of the corporate ladder,' my regional manager, Richard Anderson, reflected some months later.

It was the start of seven years of moving around the country. Five branch and regional management promotions culminated in a posting as the Gauteng regional manager based at Isando by 1992, where I planted my roots in Johannesburg, my home town ever since. Well, the Sharks rugby team remained in my blood and for some unknown reason I couldn't come around to supporting the Lions. It all happened so fast, but you don't notice time passing when you're having fun.

My silent mentor

All the while, unbeknown to him, the company's co-founder, Glenn van Heerden, played the role of a silent mentor to me. I met Glenn for the first time when I got my initial promotion to Umtata. About two months into my new role, Glenn phoned to say he was coming to meet a senior goverment official in the Transkei and I was to accompany him.

Meeting a foreign dignatory, even in a false economy and stooge country like the Transkei was back then, was a feat for me at 24. But it was watching Glenn in operation that taught me valuable leadership lessons in life. It later reminded me of the concealed impact and influence that leaders have on their young subordinates in business. Leaders seldom realise how much is observed and taken in by their junior staff.

The lesson I learnt that day was how to handle the request for a bribe, tip, payout, call it what you like. There I was sitting in the office of the official observing Glenn's approach to political protocol and banter. Towards the end of the meeting, the official asked Glenn: 'So where's my gift?'

Gift? Was I hearing an open request for a bribe? Surely not that blatant, I wondered.

Glenn pushed it aside and said, 'What we will do is bring to your region the *gift* of good car rental services to all the visitors who come to the Transkei. That's the gift we have for you.'

The official smiled. 'Yes, but don't forget, when we open these doors for business here, we expect something in return,' he said.

Glenn replied: 'Don't worry. I'll send you something.'

I was intrigued at first, thinking that Glenn had fallen prey to the corporate-government corruption trap. But I chuckled aloud when the official's gift arrived for me to hand deliver to him: it was an Avis golf shirt and a sleeve of three Titleist golf balls with the red Avis logo printed on each ball. After all, the official was an avid golfer, or so he had told Glenn that day.

I cannot describe the pain I endured trying to control my mirth, watching the official open the large brown envelope and peering deep into its emptiness for a cheque or something more valuable than the shirt and balls he had hastily removed.

'Is that it?' He looked at me, puzzled. Then he smiled having felt a piece of paper between the folds of the golf shirt, only to frown again when he revealed a card on which Glenn had scribed, 'Thank you for your faith in Avis. We won't let you or your visitors down.' The expression of sheer disappointment was priceless.

'Maybe another car rental company would have appreciated my help and generosity more?' he mumbled as he led me to the door of his office. I think we'd ruined his month or maybe even his year.

This was a great reference point for a young manager on how to deal with bribery – boldly and direct. No half measures. Years later Glenn told me that even the gesture of giving him the golf balls and shirt was pushing it a bit far. Unbeknown to him, Glenn was my hero.

Looking back, rare moments like these, in combination with my parents' values and a caring upbringing, somehow planted the seeds that strengthened my moral courage to challenge the e-toll matter that would loom large in my life in my early fifties.

Meeting my best friend

It was October 1994 and Woodski, a likeable, jovial and portly work colleague at Avis, introduced me to a friend of a friend, Helen, who had recently moved up from Durban with her two young boys, Darren (4) and Brett (2), to take up a position at a freight forwarding company. Our chemistry was right, and from our first introduction we connected and have been together ever since.

Helen has become my pillar and rock of support. A more supportive woman I couldn't have asked for. Although stubborn at times, a mutual trait we bear and which drives a lot of debate between us, Helen is an amazing, protective and caring mother to our children. Her value of family tradition and support has been immense and a relief when making life-changing decisions, such as the move we made to build and start a country hotel in the Magaliesberg in 2001 and later again, in 2012, when I resigned from the security of corporate life a second time to challenge government's e-toll decision. Helen's encouragement, understanding and love have been nothing short of incredible to me.

We married in 1997 and in the spring of 1999, our daughter bellowed her arrival down the corridors of the Sandton Clinic maternity section. The proudest moment of my life. The boys were eight and ten by then and their new sister got all the attention she demanded. Ours is a happy family.

On being tempted back into the corporate trap

In early 2006, having spent five years outside corporate life, I received a phone call from Keith Rankin, the recently appointed CEO of Avis. He was checking my appetite to return to Avis as the operations director, a role I had occupied for a few years prior to my resignation from Avis in 2001.

It was not a difficult decision to make. The little country hotel that

Helen and I had developed in the Magaliesberg was running well, so we appointed a manager and moved back to the city where our young boys could enjoy a better schooling environment with friends and sport. A new chapter in our life unfolded.

The recent purchase of Avis by Barloworld made the return even more exciting as it brought the prospect of capital for much-needed facility expansion. This would help undo years of constrained resources and congested facilities that had hampered Avis's operational efficiency and expansion throughout the 1990s. As the company's operations director in the late 1990s, I had become frustrated by the lack of capital investment for the sake of short-term balance-sheet and profit motives, which made the business more attractive for the shareholders to capitalise on. This factor, combined with a fallout over other leadership issues, triggered my decision to leave Avis in 2001, and with those impediments removed from the equation, returning was an easy choice to make.

After a year in the operations director seat, Keith extended the chief executive baton my way in 2007 as he took up bigger responsibilities in a group role.

Surrounded by a highly competent executive team, I set out to do things slightly differently and to seek the real work and fun in my new role with this fantastic brand that I had come to know so well.

It was a case of balancing the responsibilities of the corporate owner's strategies with those of the international guidelines from Avis Incorporated, and throwing in my own ideas of corporate responsibility to customers, staff and the environment. Fortunately, both Barloworld and the Avis International Licensor interfered very little in what they deemed was an extremely successful operation. Keith was very supportive and our highly competent team was keen.

To my mind, leading organisations and brands needed to do more than simply be good at what they did to earn revenue. In our case at Avis, we were competent at renting and selling cars, but I sincerely believed that our responsibilities had to go beyond mere profit returns for the shareholders. The conventional boundaries of 'business as usual' needed to be pushed and I wanted Avis to become more responsible as a corporate citizen.

Beyond profit-driven business motives

Over the next few years, Avis spent around R260 million on facility expansion projects and became a leader in business sustainability programmes. We recycled 90% of the water we used to wash our cars and became South Africa's first carbon neutral company in 2009.

The most exciting time we had as an executive committee was entrenching a service excellence culture change programme that placed significant distance between Avis and its competitors. It was an amazing journey and drove new-found energy, fun and incentive programmes into the business. Customers loved the results and Avis began to receive a number of service awards, on top of acknowledgement for our environmental efforts.

On driving a thought leadership process

In 2008, the topic of thought leadership was mooted by Ogilvy public relations executive Joanna Oosthuizen and placed on the agenda of our monthly meetings with them. We set out with an industry leadership hat firmly placed on our head and listed initiatives and actions that we needed to tackle or stimulate debate on and drive leadership behaviour beyond the boundaries of conventional business thinking. I loved it and grasped the belief that businesses simply cannot play a leading role within their respective industries by playing it safe and remaining within their cosy limitations of maximised short-term profits in a 'business as usual' way.

It was during these discussions that we decided it was time to do more for the environment. We linked up with leaders in the field such as Kevin James of Global Carbon Exchange and Professor Owen Skae, the director of Rhodes Business School which emphasised Leadership for Sustainability, who decided to record and document the Avis Green Journey as a case study for his students.

I recall at the time that Jessecca Perumal, our energised general manager of marketing, ran a fresh, cheeky advertising campaign with the headline, 'The "Greenest" Car Rental Company is the Red One'. It was a dig at Europcar, which was trying to claim green credentials by identifying its green brand colour with its efforts in the space of environmental responsibility at the time. To our surprise, Europcar's management took offence and laid a complaint with the Advertising Standards Authority (ASA), claiming it was the green brand, and our campaign was raining on its 'brand colour' parade. The ASA ruled in our favour on all four counts. I smiled when Jessecca brought me our next advert to sign off, which read: 'The Greenest Car Rental Company is *Still* the Red One'.

The next thought leadership space we decided to provide comment on was the government's recently published Carbon Tax Green Paper in 2010. After reading the document, I realised that government's intentions of this proposed policy had little to do with environmental matters and everything to do with revenue generation. It was money for the national fiscus and nothing more.

To check my concerns, I asked the London-based Carbon Neutral Company – which managed our carbon offset programme – to share its opinion of the South African Carbon Tax Green Paper document with us.

The Carbon Neutral Company concurred by saying that while some parts of the proposed carbon tax policy had merit, the entire plan would not amount to much change in business behaviour. Instead, the tax would merely push up the price of doing business and swell the coffers of government's tax pot. So it was that I entered into discussions and debate on the issue and decided to write an open letter to then Environmental Affairs Minister Edna Molewa (see Appendix 1).

What peeved me most about the proposed carbon tax policy was that despite the fact that our company was carbon neutral and in accordance with the United Nations Climate Change Convention, we would receive very little reprieve from paying carbon taxes. A carbon neutral company paying carbon tax. 'What utter bullshit,' I remarked.

In late 2010, the next thought leadership issue we looked at tackling was closer to home: the growing problem of faulty traffic lights in Johannesburg. It was getting worse by the day with a massive impact on the region's productivity and something needed to be done. But, before we could get deeper into the traffic light challenge, the recent erection of SANRAL's e-toll gantries loomed larger than any other issue and became the central topic of our thought leadership discussions into 2011.

Our fight was about to begin and a new chapter in my life was about to unfold.

Looking back, I guess there were many signs of a latent corporate activist stirring deep within my soul, and by mid-2011 it raised its head in no uncertain terms.

CHAPTER 4

A rude awakening to a new tax

▬ ▬ ▬ ▬ ▬ ▬ ▬ ▬ ▬ ▬ ▬ ▬ ▬ ▬ ▬

By late August 2010, the early signs of a southern hemisphere spring were poking their heads into the treeline. It was the best time of the year for me as the warm summer days lay ahead. I was on schedule for another weekday commute to the office, noticing the unfurling of the Highveld's spring blanket that had started to transform the city's forest into the new season's luminous green.

Travelling to work that day, I came out of my reverie to notice strange roadside buildings being constructed, every 10 kilometres or so, alongside our recently resurfaced and widened freeways. They'd obviously been building these for a few weeks and I hadn't noticed them until now; they were surprisingly close to the edge of the road.

Must be some kind of new emergency breakdown stage post, I thought.

I soon learnt from the region's morning talk show host – John Robbie on Talk Radio 702 – that my inquisitive mind was not alone. Robbie and other radio and newspaper journalists began to receive questions from the public about the purpose of the freeway structures. As the weeks rolled on, the roadside buildings took on a new shape with mega metal columns reaching up to support the arched beams that straddled the freeway like futuristic billboard structures. It wasn't long before the SANRAL CEO, Nazir Alli, was invited to explain the presence of the monolithic contraptions.

What the vast majority of Gauteng residents then learnt for the first time was a new plan to tax road users for travel on urban commuter freeways. The new gantries, erected at intervals on the freeway, formed part of a new, free-flowing electronic tolling system designed to charge you for driving on the road. The more you used it, the more you would pay. I recall Alli explaining that it was quite a simple process, one that had been successfully applied in other parts of the world. He described the process along these lines:

- It was an ingenious scheme in that it allowed users of the freeway to pay electronically at point of use, without having to stop at traditional 'boom down' toll plazas.

- All that was needed was for everyone who owned or drove a car on the new e-toll freeway to trundle off to one of the many e-toll centres scattered around the region, or to one of many supermarkets and newsagent outlets, to purchase a R50.00 e-tag (otherwise known as a RFID or Radio Frequency Identification Device).
- Prior to fitting the e-tag to the windshield of their vehicle(s), the owner needed to register the tag with SANRAL's e-toll system, linking it to their specific vehicle licence number. This could be done by telephone, the Internet or at one of their customer service centres.
- Then motorists were required to put money into their e-tag account with SANRAL, or they could choose to settle their account within seven days of each transaction, to qualify for the e-tag holders' discounted rate, still to be determined.

It all appeared to be straightforward and simple – well, at least by Alli's account thereof. Or was it?

My mind was spinning. I couldn't believe what I'd just heard. At the time, Avis had some 7 000 vehicles in and around the Gauteng region and another 13 000 around the country. The e-tag and tolling process would be a relatively complex process for our industry to manage, not to mention the administration and reconciliation of accounts. There was no doubt this scheme would have a profound impact on the business of fleet owners. We needed to find out more about it.

The e-tolling matter was placed at the top of the agenda on our Monday morning executive committee meeting, at which we decided to rally the industry for a task team to engage with SANRAL on the matter. There were too many questions that we needed answers to.

By October 2010, at our quarterly South African Vehicle Renting and Leasing Association (SAVRALA) meeting, the e-toll task team was formed and headed up by Marc Corcoran, a man who was fast becoming known in the industry for his strategic prowess. The SAVRALA e-toll technical committee was tasked to meet with SANRAL to establish the extent of the system's ability to manage our industry's needs and to understand the complexities and detailed workings of the system.

We needed to know how bulk vehicle uploading would work and the speed of tolled information flow from SANRAL's e-toll computer system to ours for live billing purposes. We also wanted to know how vehicle licence plate cloning would be dealt with and how we were to address billing disputes and query management. The seven-day payment term was also a worry for us, as we were never paid within seven days by our corporate clients or government for that matter. Our list of concerns was growing.

Following several engagements with SANRAL, the technical committee reported back to the industry's respective operations executives and CEOs to reflect on the complexities and onerous nature of the system. It became evident to the car rental leadership that SANRAL hadn't paid much attention to the needs and requirements of fleet owners and, in particular, the car rental industry.

We discovered that not one CEO of the large fleet operators, from car rental to leasing to logistics companies, was aware of the e-tolling scheme for the Gauteng freeway upgrade. How was it possible that SANRAL had slipped this plan into place without proactively engaging with large fleet and logistics companies? I wondered. This generated even more suspicion and anger amongst the industry leadership as it appeared SANRAL had flown this decision below the radar screen until the last minute, when it was ready to be introduced.

I recalled thinking that, were I in Alli's shoes when contemplating such a venture, I'd have invited the major fleet-based organisations and associations to a workshop, at which I'd explain the plan with a view to seeking input on how the system might impact on their respective industries. From this engagement, I would task my engineers and process people to find solutions to the concerns raised, the very concerns that the public might also have. Alas, it was not to be. But I guess one could ask, who am I to speculate on how Alli ought to behave?

Over the next few months and into 2011, groupings in society began to express their frustration at how complicated and unnecessary the entire scheme was. It was certainly going to introduce additional costs and changes to the way we conducted our car rental business, and, in my opinion, anything that impacts negatively on business efficiency is a curse and should be interrogated.

We asked basic questions, such as: 'Why was SANRAL forcing a complicated process onto society, when the easy-to-apply, tried-and-tested fuel levy funding mechanism was available to them or their masters?'

The concept of tolling new long-distance intercity freeway connections, new tunnels or bridges, was not foreign to us in South Africa. Many of our intercity arterial routes had been constructed through toll-revenue-generation mechanisms. These tolling projects alleviated the need for government to fund such costly infrastructural necessities, used more as economic veins and during the occasional holiday journey by the public.

What became more concerning to us was: 'Why the need to toll an urban road network that was necessary for daily commuter purposes?' These were routes used to access places of work, school, sports, religious and community events. Surely this kind of social infrastructure ought to be financed using the taxes collected from society? Something was fundamentally wrong and, personally, I became angrier every day, cursing under every gantry I passed.

A technical committee was set up by SANRAL to meet with SAVRALA and throughout the first half of 2011 our respective teams worked hard to seek solutions for our members. When we asked why they had not sought input from the public and business through a public consultation process, SANRAL replied that it had met the necessary public engagement requirements in November 2007 and April 2008 for the R21 portion of the project. It was also pointed out to us that our SAVRALA general manager, Val van den Berg, had attended a stakeholder discussion on the matter in May 2008. Both of these facts were news to us, prompting a look at how and why we had missed the engagement opportunities to question the e-toll decision.

It became clear to us that while SANRAL may have conducted what it deemed a public engagement process, the fact was that its efforts had been inadequate to say the least. The SAVRALA committee became incensed at how SANRAL had made a mockery of the public consultation process and was getting away with it.

Val was quite taken aback at Alli's claims that he (SANRAL) had engaged with her on the matter. Val said that the essence of that meeting was merely to explain what SANRAL was doing with regard to the freeway upgrade and to give those present a very brief heads up as to a new proposed funding mechanism referred to as electronic tolling. Alli was in command of that meeting and it was a charm offensive that was more about the long overdue freeway development plan. Heaven knows how frustrated business and society were becoming with the growing freeway congestion problems, so the project was a welcome one indeed.

At this meeting attended by Val, the brief mention of the proposed new electronic tolling mechanism was quickly described as an easy, internationally tested mechanism that would require no formal 'boom down' toll booths, but rather a seamless process that would not be onerous on the users. When asked for more detail on the e-tolling mechanism, Alli responded that SANRAL would get in touch with the various industry players to explain how it works in due course. No pamphlets or brochures were provided to the small audience to explain the e-toll mechanism or SANRAL's elaborate plans. That was it and Val left it at that, as there was not much she could talk to the SAVRALA members about, expecting to receive a call from SANRAL in the next few weeks to set up industrywide engagement sessions.

Nothing more happened on the explanation of the e-toll matter until the gantries were erected.

The public outrage over the e-toll plan rose to new heights at the end of 2010 and spilt over into the opening months of 2011. E-toll tariffs of R0.66 per kilometre and the scheme's launch period of April 2011 were announced by SANRAL. The public debate heated up as Alli took to the airwaves and tried in vain to placate the growing protest. The public debates on radio attracted much heated discussion and a common picture of total lack of awareness by the public was evident. Most believed the freeway upgrades were a legacy from the Soccer World Cup event.

Government brought out more ammunition in an attempt to reason with the public. Pravin Gordhan, the popular and ever-logical finance minister, came on air to soften the noise and gave several interviews during which he lightly apologised on behalf of government for the seeming lack of discussion, and explained that it was a policy that government had adopted and it could not turn back the clock. The roads were built and had to be paid for. The Treasury's coffers were tight and being spent in other pressing areas.

Other proponents and friends of SANRAL 'in favour' of the scheme were thrust into the debate to rationalise a positive logic of e-tolls. Dr Roelof Botha, a renowned economist from GIBS, provided an explanation of the 'benefit to cost' ratio that the public could expect. Botha explained that for every R1.00 the public spent on the e-toll bill, the motorist or vehicle owner would receive in return a benefit of R8.40 in the form of less time on the roads, less wear and tear on tyres and savings from less fuel consumption while vehicles stood idling on the congested freeways. Details of how this figure was arrived at were called for, but SANRAL never shared the actual calculations of the model with the public. We just had to accept it as being the truth.

The management of e-tags on our car rental fleets was always going to be a mission. Damaged windscreens would have to be replaced and tags would go missing. We expected that customers might also steal the tags, erroneously thinking that they might be able to use our tags to offset their vehicle payments. The fact that we can process hundreds of new vehicles on a daily basis for rental to our customers was the result of a process that was refined and extremely efficient. E-tagging all our vehicles would now throw unnecessary delays into our processes, costing us millions of rands in lost vehicle utilisation each year.

A 'flat daily rate' for our industry member's vehicles was proposed to SANRAL. Our suggestion was that car rental members would upload their registration details into SANRAL's database and the gantry movements would be tracked and supplied to each vehicle's owner, on a monthly or weekly basis, to track the average freeway use by our members' vehicles. A solution along these lines would be a massive relief for our industry. It would mean that we didn't have to tag each vehicle and could simply add an agreed daily e-toll rate to all rentals in the Gauteng region, estimated at around R10 to R20 per day. The administrative requirements would certainly be significantly reduced for our members and SANRAL alike, but naturally we were also concerned about other unintended consequences of this option as well and it needed to be explored, with SANRAL's consent.

Remaining true to the approach it had adopted to date, the idea was shot down by SANRAL and it became a case of 'its way or no highway' for the car rental companies. The arrogance that radiated from the SANRAL technical team was strong.

In January 2011, SANRAL announced that its planned e-toll launch for April would be postponed and a statement of the new launch date with tariffs and greater clarity on matters would be made in due course. 'Thank goodness,' we said and breathed a sigh of relief as the car rental industry was far from ready for the system's launch. We had no e-tags on our vehicles and our systems were not yet integrated with SANRAL's to receive the billing information.

CHAPTER 5

Good people making it possible

■ ■ ■ ■ ■ ■ ■ ■ ■ ■ ■ ■ ■

Any attempt to challenge an issue of the magnitude of government policy decisions doesn't happen without a team of committed people. As the famous quote by Margaret Mead goes: 'Never doubt that a small group of thoughtful, committed citizens can change the world. Indeed, it is the only thing that ever has.'

Mead's statement is very true in the case of OUTA's challenge against the e-toll scheme.

Every cause needs a champion, someone at the helm who steers the initiative and becomes the voice or face of the effort. Yet this person's energy and effort are reduced to nothing without the dedication and passionate resolve of people behind the scenes. These are the people who are the cogs and flywheels of the entire drive and without such a team OUTA would never have achieved what it did. Our committee comprised a team of between six and ten people at any one time, and while all played meaningful roles at various intervals, it was the input, work and effort of four people who were predominant in driving OUTA's energy.

The committee members of OUTA were:

Wayne Duvenage – OUTA director and chairperson and SAVRALA chairperson (2012)

Paul Pauwen – OUTA director and secretary and SAVRALA general manager (2012)

Michael Tatalias – OUTA director (2012/13) and CEO of SATSA (2012)

Jeff Osborne – OUTA director (2014/15) and CEO of the Retail Motor Industry (2013)

Clif Johnston – OUTA committee member and SANCU vice chairperson

Ari Seirlis – OUTA committee member and QASA CEO

Marc Corcoran – OUTA committee member and SAVRALA president 2013/14/15

Nick Tselentis – OUTA committee member (2012)

Rob Handfield Jones – OUTA committee member
Tracey McKay – OUTA committee member (2014/15)
Mokesh Morar – OUTA committee member (2014/15)
Howard Dembovsky – OUTA committee member (2014/15)
Rob Hutchinson – OUTA committee member and social media consultant to OUTA
John Clarke – OUTA committee member, joint spokesperson and consultant to OUTA

Aside from our two part-time consultants who joined OUTA in the latter part of 2013, none of the committee members or directors received a cent in payment for their services.

Any organisation's existence and success lie purely in the energy generated by its people. OUTA's initial energy was largely generated by Marc Corcoran, Paul Pauwen, Michael Tatalias and myself, without whom the entity's early efforts and successful court interdict in 2012 would not have been possible. I sincerely believe that it was this interdict of the initial launch of e-tolls, which was the bold step and catalyst to society's heightened energy and a strengthened sense of civil courage, that ultimately prevented the e-toll scheme from achieving the heights of compliance it needed. Naturally, there were others on our team, such as Ari Seirlis and Jeff Osborne, who were consistent with input and positive energy and were crucial to the work of OUTA, as were the paid lawyers and advocates who added to OUTA's success.

Almost two years into the battle, OUTA's efforts were buoyed by John Clarke and Rob Hutchinson who breathed new energy into the organisation at a time when OUTA evolved from an entity focused on litigation to one dedicated to civil activism.

It is important to note that OUTA's work could not have been as prominent or successful had it not been for many other groups, individuals and entities that played their own roles and added to the dynamics of the anti-toll lobby. Here I list organisations such as the Congress of South African Trade Unions (COSATU) and, in particular, Zwelinzima Vavi and Patrick Craven. Father Mike Deeb of the Justice and Peace Department of the Southern African Catholic Bishops' Conference provided a significant boost to our cause when that organisation came out with a strong statement denouncing e-tolls in no uncertain terms. Father Deeb was recorded at one of our press conferences in 2012 speaking frankly about his concerns related to the 'smell' that surrounds the entire e-toll issue.[12]

There were the Bikers Against Tolls and the many individual citizens who comprised the Bridge Banner Brigade, a self-motivated grouping of active citizens who took to the freeways every morning for months, hanging banners across bridges at a time when the need to boost the motorists' civil courage was at an all-time high. And then there were the individuals whose efforts drove awareness through the social and mainstream media from the early days, such as the Automobile Association's (AA's) Gary Ronald, Howard Dembovsky and Rob Handfield Jones (who were later seconded onto OUTA's committee in 2013), Rob Hutchinson, Jason Fivas, Ali Gule and many others, all of whom added fuel to the challenge that SANRAL and the authorities had to contend with.

Enter the Irish Terrier

There is something compelling about Marc Corcoran. To me it is a combination of his boundless energy and endless enthusiasm, combined with his keen intellect, dry Irish humour and smiling eyes that draw you in.

Marc was one of OUTA's pivotal cogs in the engine room. A strategist and information junkie of note with a Master's in 'Googlelitics', Marc had an amazing ability to surf cyberspace and his laptop's hard drive in search of pertinent information. Without Marc, I can categorically say that OUTA would more than likely not have achieved the success it did. For it was his tenacity, endless research, hard work and tireless support as a sounding board and confidant since 2010 that I found simply magnanimous. A pillar of strength and rational thinking. A man I would go to war with.

The hours of work and input required to compile OUTA's affidavits for the successful interdict in April 2012 was largely attributable to the efforts of Marc, Paul and myself (more about Paul below).

Marc is an immigrant from Ireland who came to South Africa in 1993 on holiday with a school friend. He loved the political dynamic of a country at the height of its historic transition and decided to make South Africa his new home. There is little time to relax and chill with Marc. His positive thinking and ever-enquiring mind, always eager to find meaning and motive behind every development, decision or outcome is tireless, and yet contagious.

I first met Marc in 2006 at a SAVRALA meeting shortly after my return to the industry. SAVRALA was the car rental body that met on a quarterly basis at the Johannesburg Country Club in Auckland Park. At these meetings the industry tackled matters related to crime and vehicle damage trends, along with industry education and training initiatives, government policy and other pertinent matters, but without transgressing or falling foul of the Competition Commission and the Competition Act of 1999.

When I met Marc he was the operations director for Tempest Car Hire, number five in the pecking order of brand size in the industry. He was a very active member at SAVRALA's meetings, asking probing questions and posing constructive suggestions to the executive committee on how we should be tackling whatever issue or challenge there was at the time.

People with such energy quickly become co-opted into the technical and working committees of an organisation and Marc heeded that call with gusto and energy at SAVRALA. He was a tornado of fresh air to the industry's membership.

Towards the end of 2006, I was seated alongside Marc at a Toyota vehicle launch luncheon to which the car rental industry leadership had been invited. Our discussion was exploratory as we kept our competitive cards close to our chests while our conversation parried and danced around broader issues that plagued our industry. Marc was on the ball. An astute elastic band of a mind, stretching his thoughtful conversation one way and then bouncing back to another matter within two sentences.

A minefield of strategic thinking, I recall pondering before I commented quietly to him, 'Have you ever considered that you might be far happier and more productive if you came to work wearing a red jacket?' Avis was the red brand in the industry and for a brief moment he looked surprised at my obvious suggestion. He knew in an instant what I was hinting at, but being the true poker face, he just smiled and quickly changed the topic of conversation. The lunch and speeches were over and we parted ways. I wondered if I had planted the seed deep enough to germinate.

Avis had a strict policy never to employ people who were or had worked for any one of our competitors. For a few reasons it was a good and fairly rigid policy that had lived with us for decades and had been passed down the line from our founder Glenn van Heerden's days. The occasional exception to the rule had to be approved by the chief executive officer.

As it turned out, a few months later I received a call from Marc. We had met a few times during SAVRALA meetings since the Toyota lunch, but no hint of eagerness emanated from the Terrier until the call came through, which went something like this:

Marc: 'Hi Wayne, do you have a minute?'

Wayne: 'For you, Marc, I have an hour, possibly a day.'

Marc: 'Do you recall a comment you made at the Toyota lunch, about how good I would look in a red jacket?'

Wayne: 'Absolutely.'

Marc: 'Well, I have in mind to enter the wild world of consulting and I thought that Avis may be wise to make use of my services.'

I had thoughts that he might do better wearing a red jacket as opposed to part-time consulting for us. We agreed to meet for a pint and a chat at the Baron in Sandton. I realised that we had no vacancies or opportunities at his level at the time and were also working hard to correct our imbalanced ratio of white to black middle and senior management. Adding another white male to the upper echelons of management would merely make matters worse for us. But Marc is exceptional and an exception has to be made, I recall thinking.

Two months later, I was pleased to hand Marc his red Avis jacket after he was appointed as the manager of our new Special Projects and Six Sigma initiative. What a find he was, executing logical thinking and challenges to existing processes, finding the answers to queries that drove our BEE (Black Economic Empowerment) Scorecard to a better level. Just when we thought we had exhausted all avenues to get the extra points that had become vital in the chain of procurement, Marc would find them. He worked long hours with operations managers to successfully implement and entrench behaviour change into new processes. How Tempest or the Imperial group let him go was beyond my imagination.

Naturally, Marc's hand went up when SAVRALA needed to coordinate the industry's efforts on the e-toll debacle and it made sense that he was appointed to do the same research for Avis. His efforts kept the industry united on the decision and reinforced its determination not to be bullied by SANRAL into signing its agreements until all our issues had been addressed. True to his terrier ways, he never let go of a good bone.

Enter Mr 'P'

Aside from Marc, Paul Pauwen was another person who was pivotal to OUTA's formation and who added his voice to our debates and kept the ideas flowing as we developed SAVRALA's (and later OUTA's) challenge against the e-toll decision.

Paul was an immigrant from Belgium who had travelled the world and worked in a number of countries in Africa. He is the ultimate entrepreneur and owned a small car rental company 080 Car Hire when I met him in 2003. At that time, I filled the part-time role of general manager for SAVRALA while running our family hotel near Magaliesburg. Paul had joined SAVRALA in 2001 and was a fast learner.

What struck me about Paul was his likeability, his keen interest in learning and his helpful and courteous demeanour. Paul was and remains the ultimate gentleman. Everybody loves Paul and Paul loves everybody, except for a few folk at SANRAL, I imagine.

It takes a giving person to offer one's time to take up meaningful portfolios on industry committees. Because of Paul's generous nature he was quickly co-opted into the role of chairperson of the Car Rental section and later the president of SAVRALA for three years from 2007 to 2009. It was also inspirational to see the shareholder of a small car rental operator in the seat as president for the entire industry. This was the nature of SAVRALA, with the big players making room for the smaller members to flourish and play a meaningful role in the industry.

In 2007 Paul merged his small car rental company with U-Drive, which was later sold to Europcar in 2009, whereafter Paul and his partner opted to move on after their one-year 'lock-in period' was up. Paul enjoyed the industry and was happy to take up the general manager role for SAVRALA, which was vacated by Val van den Berg in 2010.

Having Paul in the role of general manager of SAVRALA was a good thing for OUTA. He provided continuity to the association and became actively involved in the e-toll technical committee, working alongside the Irish Terrier. As SAVRALA was the founding member of OUTA, Paul was there in the thick of it and was happy to be the signatory to the founding affidavit. Like Marc and myself, he toiled into the night and over weekends, formulating court affidavit papers throughout March and April 2012.

Paul did this while he was going through a difficult time in his own life. His wife Gill was extremely ill and suffering from the ravages of terminal cancer. The disease had riddled her body after a relapse from an onset a decade earlier.

Paul's support, the use of his office in Highlands and his effort in helping with the court paper content played a pivotal role. His actions and generosity made a massive contribution to OUTA's success.

I recall many an occasion as we toiled to formulate our arguments for the founding affidavit, when Paul would respond to e-mails at 2.00 or 3.00 am. When I asked him about his nocturnal working habits, he reminded me that this was the time he could work, when his wife was asleep and out of pain. Paul is a tough character, a fighter, an emotionally strong and passionate man. A leader in the OUTA trenches.

I can only thank these two men for their tireless support, which I leaned on heavily at times. More about the other special people later on.

CHAPTER 6

Outrage and early signs of falter as the truth emerges

▬ ▬ ▬ ▬ ▬ ▬ ▬ ▬ ▬ ▬ ▬ ▬ ▬ ▬ ▬

When we first projected that it would cost 50c a kilometre, those were not thorough figures. Now we have considered the actual costs.
If you travel on a good road the savings that you get through maintenance are greater than if you travelled on a bad road ...
— SANRAL CEO Nazir Alli, 4 February 2011 (*The Saturday Star*)

Since the emergence of the gantries, the social talk of SANRAL's e-toll scheme was directionless, as the tariffs, the tenders and the costs were unknown, along with other pertinent matters related to the scheme. But that was about to end. If Nazir Alli thought his headaches were about to subside, he got it completely wrong as he sat at the head of the press conference on Friday, 4 February 2011, to announce the latest on the e-toll saga.

In what came to be known as its usual slick professional public relations campaign, SANRAL announced that on 23 June of that year motorists would be paying 66 cents per kilometre to travel on Gauteng's freeways.

The content of Alli's announcement was a no-brainer for the next day's headlines in *The Saturday Star*: 'Toll Road outrage. You will pay 66c/km to get to work.'

During the press conference Alli and Alex van Niekerk, senior GFIP project manager, explained:

- Road users would pay 66 cents per kilometre – before discounts – if travelling in light motor vehicles.
- For heavy vehicles they would pay R3.96 per kilometre.
- Motorcyclists would be charged 40 cents per kilometre.
- Registered public transport would be offered a 50% discount.

Van Niekerk estimated that a commuter travelling between Pretoria and the Johannesburg inner city would pay R418 in toll fees a month, after the e-tag discounts.

The AA was quick on the ball, condemning the system, while most other organisations were still trying to absorb the news. 'The announcement of SANRAL's 66 cents a kilometre means horrific implications for the motorist, not to mention the nasty dent it will put in the freight industry's pocket,' said the AA's Gary Ronald. Ronald had become a highly vocal opponent of the e-toll scheme, which provided significant courage to the public and industry bodies, such as SAVRALA, the Retail Motor Industry and others, to investigate the impact on their respective industries and add their concerns to the debate.

Over the next week the news began to be absorbed by the media, transport organisations and the public. As fate would have it for SANRAL, its timing was not good for the announcement of a massive urban toll road scheme. It coincided with Eskom's electricity tariff increase of 24.8% and the price of petrol was then R1 per litre more expensive than it had been the previous year. The knock-on price escalation on other goods, particularly food, was certainly not going to make the e-toll entrance an easy one.

'There is concern that the toll fees will come into force at the same time as a lot of these prices are going up, and that the e-tolling will make it even worse,' said Clif Johnston of the South African National Consumer Union. 'When those [food] prices go up, everyone will blame it on tolling. SANRAL really didn't think this through – there's going to be a huge consumer outcry.'

The public outcry became loud and the e-toll topic was on everyone's lips over the next few weeks. The Freedom Front Plus had set up an online petition to demand the e-toll tariff be reduced to 5 cents per kilometre. In five days 60 000 people had added their signatures to the petition.

On 11 February 2011 the *Financial Mail*'s Barney Mthombothi wrote an opinion piece on the e-toll saga titled 'Highway Robbery':

> *There is something particularly offensive and utterly distasteful about the manner in which roads authorities seem intent on mugging motorists on the country's motorways. It is extortion of the worst kind, and it has major implications not only for individual motorists, but for business and the economy as a whole.*

Mthombothi went on to say that the upgrading of the freeway and the introduction of the Gautrain were sold to the people as some of the benefits of hosting the Soccer World Cup.

'We bought into it. But there was a sting in the tail. Suddenly freeways aren't free anymore. Overhead structures started appearing on freeways. We now know that this structure is called a gantry. It's something we'll come to hate with a passion.' With foresight he predicted that a class action on the matter stood a good chance of success.

The anger and disbelief was piling up. Something was clearly wrong, with so many expressing their disdain for the plan. What had happened to SANRAL's formal public engagement programme required in our nation's Constitution for decisions of this nature? The scene was clearly being set for a civil action campaign.

The Star's Angelique Serrao was immersed in the furore that had the public's attention. By Valentine's Day of 2011, a new twist started to unfold as she unpacked the costs of the e-toll collection process. Johannesburg's biggest daily broadsheet newspaper, *The Star*, was emblazoned with the following headline: 'R4bn toll contract fury'.

The report, written by Serrao and Louise Flanagan, revealed that a large chunk of the money that motorists would be paying for Gauteng's e-tolls would not be used to finance the upgraded freeway. Instead, billions of rands would be spent on the e-toll collection process managed by Electronic Toll Collection (Pty) Ltd, 85% owned by Austrian-based Kapsch TrafficCom. Their profits would be flowing straight out of the country. The figure given at the time was that the tender was worth R4.56 billion for a five-year period.

The information surrounding the tender for the project had been so shrouded in secrecy that the reporters for the paper had only been able to find the information on Kapsch's Austrian websites, which expressed the lucrative nature of its new South African operations.

Civil society organisations were spitting mad. Thami Bolani, chairperson of the National Consumer Forum called the new tolls 'anti-people' and COSATU's Patrick Craven said that a company would be making money from something that would adversely affect the economy. 'Roads are a public service, and not for anyone to make a profit from,' Craven said.

E-tolling was on everyone's lips. Radio shows were inundated with calls and usually quiet people began to comment on social media. The general sentiment was reflected by one woman's comment of 'No bloody way, will I ever pay'.

Every week for the next month, one or more papers carried a headline story on the e-toll saga. The public could not get enough and it seemed that everyone wanted to know more about e-tolling:

'Highway robbery anger Joburg'
(*The Mercury*, 15 February 2011)
'Two faces of ANC. If you don't like it, take a hike'
(*The Star*, 16 February 2011)
'You try public transport, angry readers tell minister'
(*The Star*, 17 February 2011)
'R91 million. Cost of a kilometre of Gauteng toll road'
(*The Star*, 18 February 2011)
'Toll road fat cats'
(*City Press*, 20 February 2011)
'Mashishi: Why I sold my shares'
(*City Press*, 20 February 2011)
'While government battles public outcry over
gantries fat cats coin it'
(*The Sunday Independent*, 13 March 2011)

The barrage of media reports dissected every angle possible, pulling apart a project that had never sought the prior support of the public. The high construction costs of the road upgrade was the next issue that began to attract the attention of the people, rising from an estimated R6.8 billion in SANRAL's 2006 publications to almost three times that within five years.

The normal rhythm of news – headline today, gone tomorrow – didn't apply in the case of e-tolls. The more reporters delved, the angrier the Gauteng public became. It was an emotive topic. Trawling through the social media comments on each story painted a picture of citizens fuming with anger. Nothing good was said about e-tolls and when the occasional person posted a comment even slightly in favour of the scheme, the barrage of responses thereto was derogatory. Gauteng was buzzing like an angry beehive. SANRAL's Alli and his cohorts were about to don their beekeeping suits.

A slick PR campaign becomes a PR nightmare

SANRAL's management became shell-shocked, devoting many hours to responding to questions from the media. They decided to go to ground for a few weeks to gather their thoughts and strategise on how to make sense of and respond to the furore, turning to their bosses in the Department of Transport to say something. True to form, the arrogance was echoed by the higher authority and on 16 February 2011 Transport Minister Sibusiso (S'bu) Ndebele made headline news with his comment in the *Pretoria News* that 'if they didn't like the price of a toll road they should hop on a taxi, a bus or a train instead'.

With the minister now having put his foot down, SANRAL's Alli popped his head back up again and held a press conference at the National Press Club in Pretoria. Seething and barely able to contain his anger at what appeared to him as one-sided reporting, Alli scolded the journalists for writing stories about foreign companies doing business in South Africa in a negative way as this could be construed as being 'xeno-phobic' and dangerous.

Alli also stated that while he had faith in the public transport system, he would not use it. 'We need to engage in a responsible manner. These reports concern me, especially the hype around foreign investment and the underlying trend to say that we have been robbed.'

'Tomorrow when Somalis are attacked we all throw up our hands. Do we have a different agenda now that we are saying we have been robbed?' Alli said in the *Pretoria News* on 17 February 2011.

Alli handed journalists a document that claimed the consortium that had been awarded the contract had, in fact, been given the tender for R6.22 billion for the five-year operating period. It was one of many variations relating to numbers linked to the scheme. Alli clearly hadn't read the book on 'how to engage constructively with the media and gain their trust'.

The e-toll buzz grew louder. The leaders became authoritarian and their comments were seen as antagonistic, autocratic and uncaring. 'Get used to it, e-tolls is going to happen,' was the comment by government spokesperson Jimmy Manyi published by one newspaper, and later S'bu Ndebele would be quoted as saying: 'Plan A is e-tolling and Plan B is Plan A'.

The arrogance that emanated from government and its agency's leadership poked the ire of the citizen ribcage. Their behaviour defied every rule in the book of leadership and they did not display the caring and empathetic approach that permeated the earlier leadership of the African National Congress (ANC) under Nelson Mandela and Thabo Mbeki. The textbooks on good public leadership tell us that when the people become agitated, you placate them by listening and engaging while extending logical reasons and facts to calm things down. You most certainly do not become an autocrat and speak from a position of power, ordering the angry masses simply to comply. The signs of an agitated government leadership were beginning to show.

The social media comment pages poured out the hearts and minds from all sectors of society. The message was loud and clear – the people were having nothing to do with the e-toll decision. And the authorities were having nothing to do with the people's views. The country's biggest stand-off between a government and its citizens in our new democracy was about to unfold. Who would blink first?

Enter the GFIP Steering Committee

The first blink was about to take place. Within a few weeks, on 8 March 2011, Minister Ndebele announced that the e-toll project would be put on hold so that a stakeholder consultation process could be completed. In his speech, Ndebele outlined that the GFIP Steering Committee was to include representation from both government and business.[13] From government's side, the committee would be made up of representatives of the Gauteng Office of the Premier, the Gauteng Department of Roads and Transport and the (national) Department of Transport. These officials included:

- George Mahlalela, director-general of the Department of Transport (chairperson);
- Kgaugelo Lekgoro, from the Office of the Premier;
- Benny Monama, head of the Gauteng Department of Transport; and
- Nazir Alli, CEO of SANRAL.

Announcements would follow on the other panel members.

The furore died down overnight, and like the pressure valve on the cooker kicking in, the heat subsided. Had the people been heard? Had they convinced the authorities this was a bad plan? Time would tell.

By now, the SAVRALA members had come to know Alli a lot better and became familiar with his controlling style of leadership. He was a man who didn't like his plans being interfered with and we were very aware of his passionate desire to get the e-toll scheme underway. Alli was the mastermind and 'architect' of the project and was not going to roll over and allow the scheme to be whipped out from under his feet. Certainly not after all the work he and his team had put into it. With his inclusion on the GFIP Steering Committee panel, we saw little chance that it would enjoy meaningful engagement and input from business representation. But we gave him and the process the benefit of the doubt, and the Irish Terrier seized the opportunity of presenting SAVRALA's concerns to the GFIP Steering Committee.

To cut a long story short, in my opinion, the GFIP Steering Committee was a farce. It never appointed people from business onto the panel, as was suggested would happen by the minister. The final panel consisted solely of members from government departments. It was a one-sided affair that was never going to be impartial towards the suggestions and input from those opposed to the decision.

During the stakeholder engagement process, the committee received input from a number of bodies, including COSATU, the Road Freight Association, the AA, SAVRALA and others, but nothing as extensive as Gauteng Premier David Makhura's advisory panel, which looked into the e-tolls' socio-economic impact on the region some three years later in 2014.

Two months later, on 7 May 2011, it was announced that the consolidated report would be finalised by the Steering Committee on Friday, 13 May 2011 and a follow-up meeting with the stakeholders would be arranged soon thereafter.

The GFIP Steering Committee report of 110 pages was written to motivate the reader (most certainly government officials) that the e-tolling decision was the right one to pursue, and any suggestion to undo what had transpired to date would be a futile one. From the outset, the report provided a background of the tolling strategy and an in-depth thirteen-page overview of the freeway upgrade project along with its socio-economic impact studies, the infamous 8.4:1 benefit-to-cost analysis, micro- and macro-economic analysis reports, and so on.

By page 23 of the report, the statement is made that the 'tolling of the GFIP cannot be cancelled'. Up until this stage in the report, there is no mention of input and arguments made by business and other groups. The committee's recommendation was based on the fact that the benefits of better roads are being accrued to the motorists and that since the fuel levy is not ring-fenced for specific projects, therefore the fuel levy argument does not apply. The report then postulated on the fuel levy income levels, compared to what was required for all road infrastructure at the time, and concluded that there was not enough to pay the GFIP and the road maintenance backlog over eight years and, if so, the fuel levy would need to be increased by an absurd amount of R1.53 per litre, something no minister could ever suggest or agree to.

Furthermore, the GFIP Steering Committee report went into lengthy explanations about existing public transport such as bus routes, train routes and the recently introduced high-speed Gautrain service, suggesting that there are sufficient public transport alternatives for the motorist. While not everyone read the Steering Committee's report, it was statements like this that highlight SANRAL's blindness to the reality of the situation and why people don't take them seriously. Even the president, who conducted a personal inspection of the public transport system in Gauteng a year later (on 14 June 2012), expressed concern about the complaints he had received related to the unreliability, poor security and shocking safety issues of the public transport system. And again, two years later, Makhura's advisory panel in 2014 reflected on the serious inadequacies in the Gauteng public transport system, which effectively denounced the GFIP Steering Committee's statements on the matter. The input relating to the viable public transport system as an alternative for motorists was simply not worth the paper it was written on.

The GFIP Steering Committee was clearly a one-sided report and the committee appeared to have made up its mind on the outcome before the end of the process. The committee fobbed off the queries about VAT being applied to tolls (the tax-on-tax argument) by simply stating that the payment of tolls was not a form of tax and therefore could not be exempt from normal tax regulations like VAT.

On 30 June 2011 the GFIP Steering Committee announced its decision to continue with the e-toll project, but at a reduced tariff from 49 cents to 40 cents for cars with tags, thinking that this reduction in the tariff would placate the outraged public. The Steering Committee had not cottoned on to the fact that it was not the tariff, but rather the idea and concept of an irrational and cumbersome scheme that lacked society's support, which made it problematic. Lowering the tariff merely raised questions such as 'so where was the money at the higher rate going to in the first place?'

Nonetheless, the Department of Transport informed the media that a new e-toll launch date would be announced shortly and the public was informed that as far as the GFIP Steering Committee's research was concerned, the 'user-pays' system of e-tolling was here to stay. A case of 'Right, thank you, Mr and Mrs Joe Soap, we've heard your concerns and lowered the rate as a compromise, for which you ought to be grateful. As far as we're concerned, e-tolling remains the best option and it is here to stay.' The lid on the pressure cooker was shut tight again, and public anger began to stew once more. The pressure began to build.

The fact that the committee was an all-government affair added further mistrust to an already tarnished image of its e-toll facade, but this appeared to be of no concern to the authorities. The arrogance of government's attitude suggesting 'it knew what was best for society and the public should just accept it' came through loud and clear.

CHAPTER 7

The day I became a corporate activist
■ ■ ■ ■ ■ ■ ■ ■ ■ ■ ■ ■ ■ ■ ■ ■ ■ ■

It was 2 June 2011. A work colleague commented on the headline article in *The Times* newspaper – 'E-tolling: An inefficient farce' – which quoted me as the author of the content therein. I was taken aback as a few days earlier Ogilvy had submitted the article generated from our thought leadership discussion. I was expecting it to feature, if at all, as an opinion piece or in the letters column of one of the papers.

Instead, it featured as a headline news story in a major newspaper, a rather daunting situation as it thrust me into the space of someone who is assumed to be knowledgeable on the issue. I knew I now had to become more prepared for a higher level of challenging responses that could possibly emanate from SANRAL and enquiring media minds. The newspaper story sucked me deeper into the debate and my input or opinion on the e-toll scheme were regularly requested from that day on.

And so began a journey that would set my life on a new course: a path of civil activism in which I had very little prior interest, knowledge or experience. I quickly began to follow with greater interest the content of the debates that COSATU, the Democratic Alliance (DA) and the AA were presenting as they were the main commentators on the e-toll issue in 2011 and theirs was a constructive and thoughtful approach.

What amused many was how the two entities of COSATU and the DA, which were generally very opposed to each other's opinions and ideologies, were now sitting side by side and shooting arrows at a new common enemy, the ANC, its government leadership and, in particular, its state-owned entity, SANRAL.

I recalled a televised session in mid-2011 at which Zwelinzima Vavi (the secretary general of COSATU) and Jack Bloom (the head of the DA in Gauteng) were to receive copies of the e-toll contracts from Nazir Alli. Within minutes of flipping through the pages in a few of the files, Vavi pointed out that many of the pages or paragraphs were blacked out and accused Alli of a cover-up. Alli was hard pressed to explain the need for secrecy and the outcome of this debacle further heightened suspicion and caused another of many media frenzies on the topic. SANRAL had just scored another own-goal, and there were more to come.

At that time, Marc, Paul and I began to liaise intensively with the fleet-based industry leaders, from which we developed collective opinion based on the irrationality of the matter: 'It simply made no sense to spend a billion plus rand per annum to administer the process of raising another estimated two billion each year to finance the freeway upgrade, especially when there were easier and cheaper ways to extract these funds from society through a fuel levy or general taxation.' This position remained one of our fundamental issues throughout the campaign. As the weeks and months unfolded, so new issues and elements of the argument began to unfold, filling our anti-e-toll quiver with new ammunition to denounce the scheme. The picture of a shockingly poor decision sold to the cabinet by SANRAL began to unfold. As our junior advocate was to describe it in a few months time, 'it was a scheme that was born in sin'.

Throughout the remainder of 2011, we became increasingly convinced that the e-toll system was fundamentally flawed and wrong for this country. To control my frustration and anger as I drove under the gantries day after day, I constructed mental visions of the gantries being dismantled and the huge 'Register and pay for e-tolls' notice boards being taken down and removed from the freeways. I guess it was a case of my thoughts driving my actions, and at that time my energy was highly focused on seeing an end to the e-toll system. There was no way I was going to pay to drive on our freeways. But the challenge that began to worry me most was how to apply this position at Avis, a private entity that owned South Africa's largest fleet of vehicles.

On a spring morning in 2011 I recall walking into Keith Rankin's (my boss's) office, to discuss the idea of an industrywide challenge to thwart the e-toll system. Lance Smith, our erstwhile executive for strategy and a well-respected leader in the industry, was just finishing off a discussion with Keith and I asked him to stay, so that he could offer his opinion on what I had to say.

Keith was always present and willing to listen, an ever-calm gentleman whose unflappable leadership style was always relaxed. In all the time I'd got to know Keith, I don't think I ever saw him lose his cool. By now both Keith and Lance were well aware of the industry's frustrations, along with the public outcry and my strong opinion, which was featured in *The Times*. But it was on the view that our industry seriously needed to contemplate a legal challenge to halt the scheme, that I sought Keith's blessing. In my opinion, SANRAL and the government had erred significantly and so seriously in their decision and conduct on the e-toll matter that I felt it would be remiss of our industry not to challenge the scheme. The intention was either to have the scheme ruled unlawful or to convince the authorities to contemplate the reversal of the decision.

Lance was surprised at my stance and expressed a view that cases of this nature against government were generally unsuccessful and a waste of time. Of course, I knew it would not be a walk in the park, but I was adamant that we couldn't sit back and do nothing. The scheme would impact negatively on our business at Avis. The industry would suffer from the system's inefficiencies if left unchallenged or allowed to proceed in its current format. Either the scheme should change its complicated processes or be scrapped. I explained the logic of the fuel levy option and that I sincerely felt that government might change its mind on e-tolls, if indeed they witnessed that business bodies such as SAVRALA, along with the unions and others political bodies, were serious about bringing an end to the scheme.

Keith indicated his support for my views on condition that the matter was driven under the industry banner with a united opinion from the other leaders in the industry. 'Absolutely,' I said. 'There is no way this should ever develop into a case of a one business brand versus government affair.' At the time, I was the chairperson of the car rental section of SAVRALA, and so I set out to broach the matter with the industry leaders.

Industry dynamics and signs of corporate fear

At our September 2011 meeting I first met with the SAVRALA national executive committee to convince the team that we needed to contemplate an industrywide challenge to halt the e-toll scheme. The Irish Terrier had conducted discussions with the leadership of the AA and the Road Freight Association to gauge their appetite for a possible legal opinion and challenge to the e-toll scheme. They indicated potential support and, using the input we had gathered to date on the ills of the scheme, Marc was tasked to seek senior counsel opinion (which was obtained from Roelof du Plessis, through Strauss Daly Attorneys) on the strength and possibility of litigation to halt the e-toll scheme.

Over the last quarter of 2011, the message was unanimous from the car rental and leasing industry members of SAVRALA. They didn't agree with the e-toll mechanism and were happy to support litigation, agreeing on the necessity to stand together as an industry and challenge the government on its decision. The decision and opinions expressed by the SAVRALA national executive committee were supported by all the car rental company leaders. All they needed to do was obtain approval from their respective boards – a matter easier said than done.

I soon learnt that simply because the heads of Avis, Budget, Europcar and the other brands felt it was right to challenge government in court didn't necessarily mean their owners and the boards of their respective holding companies agreed with their car rental executives. The main shareholders of Avis, Europcar/Tempest, Budget and First Car Rental were Barloworld, Imperial, Bidvest and Combined Motor Holdings respectively. These were large conglomerates with big business ventures throughout other industries and many of them enjoyed revenues from managing national and regional government fleets, along with numerous other contracts and tenders. Furthermore, seated at some of their respective boardroom tables were highly connected government cadres.

As things would pan out, it would be pressure brought to bear from the higher echelons of the corporate power base that would exert force on the SAVRALA members to pull back on the litigation stance we had taken. There were clear signs that government officials had sought to express their not-so-favourable views on business's position on the e-toll matter.

Europcar's Dawn Jones informed me early in 2012 that the Imperial board was the first to exert pressure on its car rental company to pull out of the anti-toll issue. While Dawn convinced her board of the need to remain part of SAVRALA, she and her other executives pulled back from participating in SAVRALA's position on the e-toll matter. Instead, in what appeared to be a complete turnaround from its initial position of supporting the call to challenge SANRAL's e-toll decision at the end of 2011, Europcar began to work with SANRAL, by fitting e-tags into its Gauteng-based vehicles. This development gave SANRAL a significant boost as it had the effect of fragmenting the industry and assisted with testing the e-tag system in the car rental and fleet management environment. The senior managers within the rest of the industry called me to express their anger at this situation and signs of a weakening in the industry's challenge against SANRAL began to emerge.

I guess I was partially aware that driving this challenge would take a lot of my time, but I did not imagine the scale of work, effort and determination that this case would demand of us. The extent and dynamics of the legal and political beast within the e-toll saga were immense and I had no idea where it was going to take me. At the time, I sincerely imagined it all to be cut-and-dried stuff, naively thinking that government might come to its senses about the decision and possibly back down prior to launching the scheme.

Instead, what we would learn about government's resolve over the next three years would open our eyes to the reality of a political system that was not intent on serving the best interests of its citizens. There were signs of underlying currents and forces with long tentacles that ran much deeper than we would ever imagine. These forces were very similar to those that ran deep into the problems that were surfacing in areas such as the country's energy crisis developing within the Eskom debacle as well as South African Airways, the South African Post Office and other critical sectors of our country's economy.

PART TWO

The activist is not the man who says the river is dirty. The activist is the man who cleans up the river.

   – Ross Perot

CHAPTER 8

A new civil movement is born

I was on holiday in January 2012 on the Wild Coast when I got a phone call from Jack Bloom from the DA.

'I believe you guys [SAVRALA] are looking at court action on the e-toll matter. The DA is also contemplating court action. Let's combine our efforts.' That is the shortened version because anyone who knows Jack knows there is no such thing as a short discussion on a topic that excites him.

We agreed to meet on 13 January 2012. Jack brought along his colleague from the legislature, Neil Campbell, and his legal adviser, Owen Blumberg.

I asked Paul Pauwen and Marc Corcoran to join me to ensure a broader perspective was attained and to keep my challenging nature in check and met at the City Lodge Hotel at O.R. Tambo International Airport.

We shared our opinions and views on the e-toll matter and Marc provided Jack, Neil and Owen with insight into the legal opinion we had obtained from Strauss Daly Attorneys in October 2011. Jack informed us that the DA had also sought legal advice and we agreed that it would be wise to combine our efforts and proceed with one court challenge.

At that stage, by mid-January 2012, OUTA hadn't yet been formed, but we had already held discussions with the Road Freight Association (RFA), the Retail Motor Industry, the AA and one or two other entities, sharing our concerns and frustrations about SANRAL's e-toll scheme. There was a common view that SANRAL's e-toll plans were questionable, sincerely lacking in consultation and would be problematic and costly for fleet-based industries, let alone the person in the street.

We knew that if there was going to be any legal action it would be better that SAVRALA did not go it alone. A collaborative effort with other entities would always be better.

During an unrelated meeting I mentioned our potential legal plans against SANRAL to Ari Seirlis, the CEO of QASA (QuadPara Association of South Africa). He informed me that his organisation had also expressed dissatisfaction about the e-toll decision on behalf of the disabled community.

Enter Ari Seirlis

Until 2012, I had met Ari on several occasions, mostly business related, in our attempt to ensure that Avis catered for the needs of people with physical disabilities who wanted to rent vehicles. Avis had recently assisted QASA to launch South Africa's first driving school dedicated to catering for the physically disabled. I enjoyed Ari's direct approach to matters along with his business acumen and logic.

However, it was over the next two years that I got to learn more about the strength and character of this special person.

Ari is an incredibly courageous champion for the disabled community of South Africa and has fulfilled the role of CEO of QASA for the past decade. His leadership has taken QASA to new heights in its efforts to champion the rights of people with disabilities.

Ari is a paraplegic as a result of an accident during a water-sport activity, which rendered him paralysed from his waist down. I have watched how Ari operates and gets around at a pace that would put most able-bodied people to shame. He is simply the hardest-working person I know and never lets his wheelchair-bound disability get in the way of his travel and work schedule. And he does so with tenacity and a good sense of humour. Ari is a true inspiration to me.

Naturally, Marc, Paul and I were delighted when Ari announced that the QASA board had approved its association's participation in OUTA's efforts to challenge the e-toll decision.

With SAVRALA and the DA now having been joined by QASA, the formation of OUTA (the name still unknown at the time), started to gain momentum. Soon thereafter, a discussion with Michael Tatalias, the CEO of SATSA (Southern African Tourism Services Association), led to his board also approving the organisation's decision to join the anti-toll lobby group as his members believed the e-toll scheme would have a detrimental impact on tourism and its businesses. OUTA was growing bigger than we had imagined.

Marc and Paul set out to gather more associations' support and between them had rounded up the Retail Motor Industry headed up by Jeff Osborne, as well as the South African National Consumer Union (SANCU), whose vice chairperson Clif Johnston – also came on board.

By now it was mid-February 2012 and OUTA had become a sizeble organisation that represented multiple industry sectors. Marc was working hard on one more big player – the RFA – to join us, for it too had signalled possible legal action against SANRAL's plan.

The general consensus among the first 'gathering of the clan' was to wait and see if the authorities would come to their senses, the signs of which might be displayed at the end of February 2012, in a couple of weeks' time, when the Minister of Finance Pravin Gordhan would be delivering the nation's budget speech. The e-toll scheme had been postponed a few times and with the current public outcry, there was a reasonable possibility that sanity would prevail and that Gordhan might announce the Gauteng Freeway Improvement Project (GFIP) to be largely or completely funded through the fiscus.

Our minds were set on launching a legal challenge to halt the introduction of e-tolling in an effort to seek a judicial review of government's decision. But this next step hung on what Gordhan would tell the nation on 22 February 2012. Gordhan was known to be a sensible and reasonable minister, and had recently voiced his concerns about the growing public anger towards the e-toll saga. Our hope was that he would gather that the system was too unpopular and relatively unworkable to launch. We sincerely believed that he might see the rationality of servicing the freeway upgrade finance bonds through the national fiscus, thereby removing the need to subject society to an expensive and seemingly inefficient e-toll collection system.

On 22 February 2012, Marc, Paul and I sat watching the televised announcement of Minister Gordhan's budget speech, listening carefully to every word he said, knowing that his message would either trigger or defuse a massive amount of energy within a small team of people who were poised to challenge government on its new electronic urban tolling policy.

Having dealt with the formalities and normal allocations during his speech to the nation, Gordhan eventually got to the part that we were waiting for:

> *Mister Speaker, I am mindful that the introduction of tolling to finance the Gauteng Freeway Improvement Programme has caused considerable public reaction. We have listened carefully to the various suggestions and appreciate the difficulties that might be faced.*

Marc, Paul and I couldn't move. What would Gordhan say next?

If he decided against the unpopular road-payment scheme we could relax and get back to our daily grind.

If, however, he announced the e-toll decision would remain in place, the past few weeks we had spent planning and networking for the launch of OUTA would set in motion a new chapter in our lives.

> It is important to remember that road-user charges also serve an important demand management function on roads that are heavily congested. Users benefit through lower vehicle operating costs, time savings and improved safety. In addition, improved maintenance of regional and provincial roads is made possible by the additional revenue that our toll roads generate.

His words provoked us. They were not what we wanted to hear.

The minister then announced that government would contribute R5.8 billion to reduce the R20-billion debt of the GFIP. This would enable a further discount for Gauteng freeway users, from 40 cents (as indicated by the GFIP Steering Committee in mid-2011), down to 30 cents per kilometre. He also said there would be a monthly cap of R550 for frequent users and that taxis and other forms of public transport would be exempt from toll fees.

> Going forward, government will carefully evaluate future road infrastructure funding. In addition, the further development of efficient and cost-effective public transport systems will receive the urgent attention of the Department of Transport.

A new launch date was announced: 30 April 2012. This was a mere nine weeks away and Gordhan's words triggered the starting gun of our challenge. 'BANG' and OUTA's formation was set in motion.

By the end of February 2012, the public's negative reaction and noise against e-tolls grew louder than ever before. There were even threats of physical damage to the gantries but, in reality, nothing was happening. Hot air was not swaying the decision-makers minds and Nazir Alli was swatting off the concerns during every interview with his candid demeanour, quoting the user-pays principle at every turn.

No one was taking action and it was now clear that SANRAL was going to get away with a scheme that was poorly planned and lacked the necessary consultation required to seek society's approval, without which, SANRAL was warned, the scheme stood the chance of serious failure.[14] The courts were our last resort to halt the planned launch of e-tolls on 30 April 2012. Following the minister's budget speech, OUTA's newly constituted body unanimously agreed to set the wheels in motion to pursue litigation.

The decision to be politically non-aligned

During the formation of OUTA and at its first committee discussion in February 2012, the question of politics and the DA's participation within OUTA was raised. Consensus was reached that despite the DA's long-standing anti-e-toll stance, along with its political clout and potential to fund much of the case, the inclusion of a political party in OUTA's affairs would muddy the waters for the civil action group. The presence of a political party would have the effect of removing the case from being fought as a public and civil society matter to one that would become a political football. OUTA would be seen as a front for the DA and this might alienate many ANC anti-e-toll citizens from our cause. OUTA needed to be an apolitical entity.

We decided to ask Jack Bloom and Neil Campbell if they wouldn't mind pulling the DA out of the civil action legal challenge altogether.

Initially, I could see that Jack really wanted to be a part of this fight, but he had a very mature approach and agreed that the DA's inclusion would possibly have a diminishing impact on the nature of the challenge. He decided that the DA should gracefully withdraw, but would continue to raise its concerns and resistance against the e-toll scheme in Parliament. We were grateful for its stance.

Despite there being no formal link with the DA, throughout OUTA's campaign, SANRAL made repeated comments that OUTA was backed by – and was a front for – the DA. Unfortunately, as a result of these claims, we were labelled as a 'pale male front for the DA'. This was a stigma that we struggled to shake off and learnt not only to live with, but to turn to our advantage to forge cross-cutting interests between members of different political parties.

Setting up the legal team

Owen Blumberg, whom we had been introduced to by Jack Bloom, decided to introduce us to Pieter Conradie of Cliffe Dekker Hofmeyr attorneys, believing they were best suited to handle a public action case of this size and nature.

It was on a warm summer's morning, shortly after the finance minister's budget speech, that Paul, Marc, Michael Tatalias and I held our first meeting with the legal team, seated in Boardroom #12 on the eighth floor of Cliffe Dekker Hofmeyr's plush Sandton offices. Pieter Conradie walked in, followed by a team of five stern legal-eagle-looking folk, and began to introduce us to the people who would be working closely with us on our case.

Senior Counsel Alistair Franklin was to head up the case. A second senior counsel member of the team, Alfred Cockrell, was to support Alistair, and seated to Alfred's right a tall, younger member of the team was advocate Adrian d'Oliveira, the junior counsel who would be responsible for drafting the papers and arguments. The other two people were Kelvin Buchanan and Rebecca Thomson of Cliffe Dekker Hofmeyr who would fulfil outstanding roles as administrators during the case.

Our intial meeting of these legal minds was certainly intriguing. My first reaction to Adrian d'Oliveira, this tall, thinner and younger looking version of Arnold Schwarzenegger, was 'not impressed'. He had no expression on his face and seemed far too serious. But I soon learnt the true meaning of 'looks can be deceiving' when it came to Adrian, for it was he who would become an immense pillar of support to the case and cause. Adrian is the most direct and hardest working person I have ever known and had become extremely influential in OUTA's legal and advisory efforts.

After the pleasantries were exchanged, Alistair Franklin said: 'So, tell us your story.'

And tell them we did.

When we had finished talking, and after answering a couple of questions for clarity's sake, it appeared that Alfred Cockrell took pleasure in tearing our entire argument apart. It was so frustrating to hear him challenge us the way he did. There we were, gung-ho, believing our case against SANRAL was watertight, and he was shooting us down.

Upfront Alfred said, 'Guys, let me tell you something. There are some serious concerns about certain elements of your case, and you need to know that the chances of winning cases against government are much lower than losing.'

His words took the wind out of our sails. What did he mean? Was he not listening to our earlier input?

'Enthusiasm is one thing, but facts and strength of argument are what are needed to win this case, which is one that appears might have some strong administrative hurdles to clear,' Alfred added. 'As much as you may think you have a good case, government has made a policy decision and the courts will query your right to question this.'

Alistair further explained: 'Government has been democratically elected to rule, which means policy-making. This is their decision and society has little right to challenge this unless gross negligence and disregard for the Constitution can be proven. Secondly, this case may not be condoned on the basis that it has been brought too late after the declaration of e-tolls.'

He explained the action of 'condonation' whereby legal challenges to halt an approved decision must be raised within 180 days of that decision being taken, or knowledge of the decision being known, failing which the matter may be struck out of court before it can be heard. He then asked when we had become aware of the e-tolling decision.

'It was towards the end of 2010, at the same time as everyone else, when the gantries were erected.'

'Well', said Alfred, 'that was over a year ago and the condonation argument comes into play.'

Alistair explained that because we had been engaging with SANRAL for over a year and were only now deciding on court action, SANRAL could accuse OUTA of bad faith.

'But what about the fact that SANRAL flatly refused to accommodate our needs and had not acted within the bounds of the Constitution when implementing its plan?' I protested.

The members of the legal team sat opposite us and summarised their concerns about the weaknesses in our case.

We were deflated by this news, but remained resolute that something had to be done. 'What should we do then?' we enquired.

'You need to convince us why you believe your case is a strong one. Go through your story again,' Alistair said.

We then categorised and explained in greater detail the main arguments of our case, summarised as follows:

- SANRAL's public engagement process was meaningless in that it failed to give proper notice of the intention to toll. Neither any of the large fleet industries nor big business was made aware of the e-toll decision. We were not invited to participate and it would appear the same applied to the general public.

- Furthermore, judging from what we had now learnt of SANRAL's flimsy consultation process, there was insufficient information provided in its few newspaper adverts for the public to form a clear understanding of the e-toll scheme or to draw any reasonable deductions about its implications. Therefore society was not able to participate meaningfully in the public consultation process or to lodge objections. This was surely a transgression of our constitutional rights.
- The cost of collection was disproportionate to the recovery costs, making the scheme an irrational one. At that stage, based on a steering committee report, it appeared that the system would cost R1.00 for every R3.00 it collected. At a roughly 30% cost of collection, this appeared excessive and irrational in our books.
- The volume of gantry transactions was estimated at over two million per day and a mere 10% non-compliance would be too large for the scheme to be practically enforced, making it largely unworkable.
- We believed that the minister of transport in 2008, Jeff Radebe, might not (or could not) have sufficiently considered all the facts and information pertaining to the true cost of e-toll collections and possible problems, when approving the scheme.
- There was inadequate alternative public transport to offer the public a choice.
- The e-toll terms and conditions were out of line with the Consumer Protection Act.
- Finally, we were concerned about possible transgressions in the Environmental Impact Assessment process, as was highlighted by the Strauss Daly opinion provided to us.

As we delved deeper into each point our case came together as the merits of our arguments became stronger. In substance the case was convincing, but we were haunted by the procedural question of 'administrative justice'. How would the court exercise the discretion it had to condone the lateness of the application? The 180-day window for lodging an application for judicial review of an executive decision had long lapsed. How far would the judiciary venture to overrule a government executive decision?

Alistair Franklin indicated that the strength of our merits and the sensitive nature of the case in the eyes of the public could very well be enough for the judge to rule that a review was necessary and, therefore, the possibility of a successful interdict of the launch of e-tolls was relatively strong. This was the first hurdle we needed to cross.

The 'flip-flopping' Road Freight Association

With the legal team's nod to proceed, we were hoping the RFA would join us in our litigation. It was a powerful body and on record as being opposed to the e-toll scheme. We contacted Gavin Kelly, technical and operations manager of the RFA, to apprise him of our litigation developments and asked if instead of running a separate legal challenge against the e-toll scheme, the RFA might want to consider joining our effort. This way, we could also share the costs with more players, fighting the matter on one larger front.

Gavin was very clearly with us on this entire matter, but the decision was not his to make. It was up to the RFA's members and the board's to decide. We were surprised that after expressing their members' views about being strongly opposed to the scheme, the RFA decided not to join OUTA's efforts. We could only assume the decision had something to do with their larger logistics company members who managed big business contracts with government. Perhaps there was concern about the consequences this action might have on its members' dealings with government. We would have to do without the RFA.

Despite this, the RFA sought to join as *amicus curiae* (a friend of the court), in Part A of our case during the interdict arguments. Later in the year, even more astounding to us, was the RFA's decision to change its mind and give the e-toll scheme its blessing, with conditions. Then, two years later in 2014, the large logistics companies which made up the bulk of the RFA's membership, expressed their disdain for the e-toll system. This put pressure on the RFA to change its stance once again on the e-toll matter, when it announced the RFA as being opposed to the e-toll decision during its submission to the GFIP E-Toll Advisory Panel (appointed by Gauteng Premier David Makhura) in September 2014. I hadn't seen this many flip-flops than when I was last on Durban's beachfront.

At the time of its first about-turn in 2012, when the RFA announced its acceptance of e-tolling, this was a massive blow to OUTA and our cause took a serious dent. SANRAL made a meal of this development, publishing several media releases to give the impression that big business was on board and acceptance of e-tolls.

The formation and naming of OUTA

The gathering of a collective anti-toll energy from various organisations required that we form an alliance of associations opposed to the e-toll issue with a common opinion on the matter.

Paul, Marc, Michael Tatalias and I sat in the lounge area of the Balalaika Hotel, prior to our next meeting with our lawyers, to decide on a name of the new grouping of associations. Our attorney had asked us to inform him of the name of the litigant that would be lodging the challenge.

We started bouncing names around the coffee table. The Opposition To Tolling (OTT) was the first suggestion raised. Tolling was too broad, Marc said, as we were not opposing the tolling of existing long-distance rural routes. This was an urban tolling issue, so we added the word 'urban' to the mix. Opposition to Urban Tolling (OUT). Knowing that we needed to set up a website, I quickly Googled 'OUT' and deflated the discussion by telling the group that www.OUT.co.za was already taken by the highly visible insurance company – Outsurance.

We had to tweak it slightly by adding an extra word. 'Let's add the word *alliance* at the end; we would have OUTA,' said Paul. The Internet indicated that OUTA was available, and presto – OUTA was the acronym and brand name chosen to unify its members for the challenge.

The work of appointing a digital agency to help us register the acronym was paramount. I quickly phoned Yoav Techlet, an ex-colleague and MD of J. Walter Thompson, to register the web address and social media names for Facebook and Twitter on our behalf. Paul agreed to draft the entity's constitution as a not-for-profit, public benefit organisation. The alliance's various members would be asked to help fund the association's core operating and legal costs.

In search of the e-toll interdict

There were two ways to approach the court action. We could have let the launch of e-tolls take place on 30 April 2012 and then pushed for a judicial review of the e-toll decision some eight months down the line. Or we could urgently attempt to halt the launch until the judicial review had taken place.

We believed that allowing the scheme to launch would have jeopardised the review, as there are several cases that have displayed the difficulty in halting a process that is already in place, even if it has been attained unlawfully or comes with warts and oversights. Our view was that SANRAL hadn't followed due legal process, and, in this regard, they should not be allowed to launch the scheme until a judicial review was undertaken.

We agreed to go for the urgent interdict, but time was short. It was now the beginning of March, and the interdict would have to be heard in court for at least three days before the e-toll launch date of 30 April 2012. During this period we had to file our founding affidavits, allowing SANRAL at least two weeks to respond, and then we would need to file our replying papers.

This meant we had to lodge our papers in the Gauteng North High Court by 23 March 2012. We literally had three weeks to compile our case. Three weeks might have appeared to be ample time, but little did I know what was needed to build a legal case of this magnitude. Our advocate, Adrian d'Oliveira, was an avid taskmaster and Marc, Paul and I became his slaves. He wanted to know everything and more. All the facts, the history, past statements made by SANRAL, transport economists' models of the tariffs, and so on. The more we could use to expose the irrationality and unlawfulness of the e-toll decision, the stronger our case would be. It took Adrian a while to get the enormity of the situation into our minds, but once he did, we worked around the clock.

The flurry of the next three weeks exploded and all I can say is that I've never worked so hard in all my life. I attended to my leadership requirements as a chief executive of Avis by day, and the requests for mountains of information, sought by Adrian, at night and over weekends. Life was a blur and sleep was scarce for the four of us.

The time of day mattered not and our respective families saw little of us as we toiled non-stop. One Sunday morning at 2.45 am, as I was about to shut my laptop down, an e-mail from Adrian popped into my in-box seeking some input to the case. A minute later, Marc responded that he'd have it back to Adrian within 30 minutes and Paul replied a minute later with his opinion. What crazy energy is this? I thought and closed my laptop, stumbling towards the bedroom in dire need of sleep.

A week into March, I decided to chat to my boss and our team of executives, explaining that I might be missing in action for the next three weeks. Marc and I needed to give the necessary time and effort to this crucial period of the e-toll challenge if we were to do this properly. They were extremely obliging and supportive.

I was convinced that Adrian was not human. Surely one had to possess robotic qualities to put in the number of hours and churn out the quantity of pages he did as he toiled away at compiling our founding affidavit. Within a week, the initial perception I had of a quiet, stern advocate had dissipated and transformed into that of the 'Terminator' of case compilation. Keeping Adrian waiting for information was always followed up by a terse mail or SMS. He was the epitome of *thorough* and *productive*, and it was ultimately Adrian's work and drive that enabled OUTA to achieve the urgent interdict we sought.

If there is a PhD in Google, the Irish Terrier has earned it. Just like the four-legged Terrier, Marc would do most of the finding and fetching while Paul would do the thorough reading and grammatical corrections to maximise the message's impact. Together, we gelled and produced 166 pages of scintillating arguments that would give Nazir Alli and SANRAL's lawyers a lot of head-scratching moments.

Three weeks later, 23 March had arrived and we had made it. The last few corrections were being made to the founding affidavit and it was time to tell the world what we were doing. The realisation that the moment had come dawned on me. I had no idea what to expect from that morning's press conference and was about to be smacked with the anxiety attack mentioned in the opening chapter.

OUTA's first press conference – 23 March 2012

11.00 am had arrived. The press were all seated and Antoinette Slabbert of the Press Club had introduced the OUTA panel. Today, right now, we were: '… launching an application against SANRAL, as well as the Department of Transport, the Department of Environmental Affairs and the Gauteng MEC for Transport'. We were doing so 'to halt what we perceived as the launch of an irrational, ill-conceived and very expensive scheme that had been introduced without the necessary transparency and public consultation that is required in our Constitution'.

The statement continued to reflect on the many aspects that highlighted our views, position and the strengths of our argument.

By 1.00 pm the press conference was over. Relief, I thought, naively believing it was over until the court case transpired.

How wrong I was. In two weeks, I had caught up with my work mails and meetings at the office, only to be called by Adrian who said, 'Right, we now have SANRAL's responding affidavits and we have a week to compile and file our replying papers.'

No way, I thought, this can't be real.

SANRAL's papers gave an in-depth view of its decision to go ahead with e-tolling. It was an infrastructure plan approved at the highest level, it argued, and one that would boost the economy, where toll fees would finance the bonds borrowed to upgrade the freeway and provide a benefit-to-cost return of 8.4:1 to the road users.

SANRAL's reply had based its case heavily on denouncing urgency and highlighting the condonation argument.

The manner in which SANRAL had dealt with many of the merits, i.e., the actual grounds for unlawfulness that we had laid out in our founding affidavit, was very poor. I recall Alfred Cockrell saying to me that the first 50 pages of SANRAL's case was very strong and might be tough for us, but then it was downhill from there. What came after its arguments on urgency and condonation was very weak, surprisingly so, and if we could steer our way around these two elements, we would have a strong chance of interdicting the e-toll launch.

SANRAL argued that our application was not urgent because government had made known its intentions to toll since 2007 and that an interdict to stop the project would have far-reaching consequences.

'SANRAL would then have to incur the expense of financing the bonds and the tolling network without any of the planned income accruing thereto. This would place SANRAL in breach of its contracts with ETC joint venture which would have a devastating impact on the credit ratings of the entity and the country as a whole,' was the argument made in its papers.

The importance of the whole responding and replying affidavit process was starting to make sense to me.

When the decision to toll the Gauteng freeways was made in 2008, the minister of transport was led to understand that it would promote ride-sharing through park-and-ride facilities, high-occupancy vehicle lanes and integration of public transport services, such as the Bus Rapid Transit, Gautrain, and an upgraded metro-rail system, which would all be operational.

By the final hour, with tolling about to commence, it was very obvious that besides the limited influence of the Gautrain, the majority of these original plans by government had not been implemented and nor were they about to be. The public had virtually no alternative but to use their vehicles or the informal taxi industry to commute to work, school, sports, places of worship, and so on.

The mad rush to file our replying papers was on and I disappeared from my chief executive duties at Avis and family life for another brief period in time.

By 21 April we had filed our replying affidavits.

It was clear to us that even at this late stage, with or without an interdict, SANRAL was not ready to launch its e-toll scheme. Exemption notices recently announced by SANRAL required the public to respond by 9 May, yet e-tolls were set to commence on 30 April 2012.

'How on earth could SANRAL claim to be ready to launch e-tolling?' we commented in our press release as we prepared for the courtroom showdown.

Our replying papers made it clear that e-tolling at the current rates, with expected escalations, would generate in excess of R102 billion over the next twenty years, this for an infrastructure that cost only R32 billion to finance over the same period, including interest. We argued that R70 billion would be overpaid by the public.

'This is not a matter of a few unhappy people who are opposed to e-tolling. This is a matter of the vast majority of citizens from all segments of the population who are opposed to what can only be described as an unjust, unnecessary and costly taxation which has been thrust upon them,' we said. Our arguments were having a positive impact on the public debate.

It was 26 April 2012 and we were ready to face off in court.

CHAPTER 9

The court interdict

▬ ▬ ▬ ▬ ▬ ▬ ▬ ▬ ▬ ▬ ▬ ▬ ▬ ▬ ▬

It was the final hour. Just a day before one of the country's biggest court challenges against a government policy decision in our new-found democracy was set to get under way.

The topic of OUTA's court challenge had generated a surge of discussion in the media, social and mainstream. Everyone was talking and seemed to have an opinion on the matter.

The debate was intense, some in favour of the scheme, but the vast majority against SANRAL's e-toll decision, as was revealed by global marketing research companies Ipsos and TNS (Taylor Nelson Sofres), which had conducted public sentiment research on the matter at the time. There was also a large section of the Gauteng population that was simply confused about the entire process at that stage. They would become wiser to the issue as the debates unfolded in the media and around dinner table discussions in time.

While distancing itself from being part of OUTA, the Road Freight Association announced it would join OUTA's case as a friend of the court in the interdict. Technical and Operations Manager Gavin Kelly said OUTA's application did not cover two points related to the tariffs and the extended powers granted to SANRAL's peace officers, which they wanted to raise in the court challenge.

Late in April 2012, just days before the court challenge, the Department of Transport had published the e-toll tariffs, which showed that non-registered, non-e-tag users of the road would pay double the e-tagged rate per kilometre to use the road. Motorists would also only have seven days to pay their e-toll bill or suffer further penalties and charges for late payment. This was another red rag to the bullish citizens who were becoming very vocal and vowing not to pay the e-toll.

But when the court case started, the RFA withdrew as a friend of the court.

COSATU, the giant trade union confederation, also added its voice to the court process in opposition to e-tolls, putting its own lawyer, Paul Kennedy SC, in court on a watching brief, 'just in case there is a need to intervene legally at a later stage', said their spokesperson Patrick Craven. The union group had also expressed a plan to commence nationwide mass protests against the system on the same day court was to begin.

Government upped its rhetoric, chanting that the user-pays principle was here to stay and that it would defend itself in court.

The battle lines were drawn.

OUTA had not cited the Treasury as a respondent in the case. Nonetheless the Treasury announced its application for leave to intervene shortly before the case got under way. Initially, we did not see this as a big issue, but as the case dragged on and went into the appeal stages several months later, it was the Treasury that drove the legal challenge against OUTA the hardest.

This was 'in view of the significance of this matter for the state's financing of road infrastructure and integrity and sustainability of the public's finances', the Treasury announced.

The Treasury's Director-General Andrew Donaldson said that if e-tolling did not begin on the Monday [30 April 2012], government may have to pay off the full R19 billion it had guaranteed in Gauteng freeway upgrade debt immediately. In its court papers it said that if SANRAL failed to implement the GFIP this would effectively constitute a default on the loan, triggering an immediate repayment of the entire loan, a consequence that never materialised, despite the fact that e-tolls were not launched for another nineteen months. Donaldson also said at the time that SANRAL's credit rating would be affected, which would, in turn, lower the country's credit rating, negatively affecting its ability to raise debt. As it would turn out, over the following two years, SANRAL's credit rating did take a knock as a result of a failed e-toll collection process.

At the time, however, this was government's emotional grip on the case, and it was being used in an attempt to persuade the judge that his decision could have dire financial consequences for the country. What made this rather farcical was that it was government's own Civil Service Pension Scheme, through the Public Investment Corporation, that had made most of the investment finance available for the freeway upgrade project, so in effect this meant that one government body would hold another government body to account for the road repayment default and thereby jeopardise the country's credit rating. Hardly likely, we thought.

'There is so much resentment and anger building up against the Department of Transport. We are hoping this [application] will force government into having an open discussion about the tolls,' I told the media one day before the case was set to start.

OUTA at this stage consisted of SAVRALA (the South African Vehicle Renting and Leasing Association), the Southern African Tourist Service Association (SATSA), the Retail Motor Industry, the QuadPara Association of South Africa (QASA) and the South African National Consumer Union (SANCU).

The long-awaited day began on a sunny morning on Tuesday, 24 April 2012.

At least twenty legal representatives dressed in black robes and carrying boxes of files filled two benches of the court, ready for battle. This was administrative case law battleground Utopia for all the robed silks present.

The DA had organised an array of blue-T-shirted protesters outside the Pretoria High Court, adding a vociferous 'no e-tolls' battle cry to the mix. Their placards asked motorists passing by the courts to 'hoot for a toll-free Gauteng'. A cacophony of hooting ensued.

Nazir Alli arrived at the court quietly, accompanied by the GFIP Project Manager Alex van Niekerk. Heads down, they said nothing as they strode quickly past a barrage of press photographers and into the courtroom.

Marc Corcoran and Paul Pauwen greeted the DA's Neil Campbell warmly, smiling as they entered court.

Legal representative for OUTA Owen Blumberg arrived with Hilda Maphoroma, who had brought an affidavit before the court as a member of civil society's argument included in OUTA's arguments. She had to travel from Leondale to Norwood every day with her husband. She said the couple had calculated, prior to the recent e-toll cap announcement, that they would have to pay roughly R1 000 a month in e-toll fees, which they simply could not afford.

On the left side of the court, in dark suits and with serious faces, sat SANRAL representatives and employees from the various government departments. On the right sat OUTA and all its alliance members, whispering among themselves, at this stage jovial and excited that the case was starting. The energy in the OUTA camp was high as the experience of litigation in business matters was a first for its members. This was not the case with Alli and his people who had significant experience of being hauled to court to defend themselves on various matters over the years.

The last two back benches were filled with journalists, complaining about the court's inability to provide much-needed plug points to keep their laptops and cellular phones powered throughout the day. The old-fashioned pens and notepads were at hand as back-up for the dreaded 'flat battery' situation.

In the front of the court sat the four main players of the quick-witted oral show that lay ahead.

Three teams sat on the left side of the courtroom, appearing on behalf of the respondents. Representing SANRAL was David Unterhalter SC, a tall, solemn-looking man with a traditional English barrister style of enunciation. One row back sat Jeremy Gauntlett SC, a more theatrical orator and seasoned advocate with a quick mind, appearing on behalf of the Treasury. To his right sat Vincent Maleka SC, an older, serious orator whose demeanour paled somewhat when compared to his loudly debating colleagues. He would be appearing on behalf of the Department of Transport.

On the other side of the court sat one man, Alistair Franklin SC, on behalf of OUTA. He was a quieter, gentle-looking man with kind eyes who stuck to his guns. Behind Alistair sat the other members of his legal team: Alfred Cockrell SC and Adrian D'Oliveira, their junior counsel.

Hearing the case was Judge Bill Prinsloo, a very astute and well-seasoned judge who commanded high respect among the legal fraternity. He had a larger-than-life presence in the courtroom, and from time to time during the proceedings he displayed an unusual sense of humour.

The first order of the day was whether the interdict application should be considered urgent and heard at all. This was the weakest part of our case and if we got past this hurdle we knew we would be in a good position.

Unterhalter handed in all the state's notices since 2006 showing the process it had used to declare the roads as toll roads and its subsequent public consultation. He said that in the past year the government had made it clear during all the e-toll commencement postponements that it was interrogating the tariffs and not the concept of road tolling.

Gauntlett said that in its application OUTA had expressed hopes that e-tolling would be scrapped, showing it had knowledge earlier than February of that year that tolling would happen. Therefore, he said, the application should have been brought before the court a lot earlier, and this late and urgent application was therefore unwarranted.

'Even on the alliance's website it says "after months of consultation with our legal team",' Gauntlett said in his argument that the case could not be considered urgent.

Franklin countered this saying that because e-tolling was about to commence in less than a week the matter was urgent. He asked Judge Prinsloo to consider the enormous public interest in the case. 'Don't close the door in the face of the public,' he said.

He also said tolling could not be considered formal until tariffs were announced, which only happened earlier that month. If e-tolling were allowed to start, the 'horse would have bolted' on a scheme that could very well be illegal, he added.

He set out his two main arguments for the day regarding the illegality of the system, which were that the collection costs were almost as high as the cost of building the roads, which made the scheme impractical and irrational. He said that collection costs of over R20 billion were estimated over the twenty-year period, and that both SANRAL and the transport minister refused to divulge the true costs of the collection process.

As for the impracticality of the system, Franklin argued that even if SANRAL's estimation of 7% of road users not being compliant was accurate, it would encounter the equivalent of 70 000 transgressions a day as each gantry movement must be treated as a separate transgression. This, in turn, would equate to 70 000 summonses per day after the payment period had lapsed. On top of that, 7% non-compliance was in itself a tall order and non-compliance was expected to be much higher than 7%.

We think what attracted the court's mind, which Franklin was careful to show, was all the steps that had been taken to try to change SANRAL's mind about going ahead with e-tolling, following the announcement of the toll rates. There were stages when government indicated it was still consulting (in 2011) and the scheme was put on hold on several occasions.

There was this ambivalence and uncertainty around e-tolls. The court seemed to understand that. It seemed able to look at it from the perspective of the people who were never sure if this scheme was ever going to go ahead.

Franklin was also good at giving the court a taste for the merits of the case, showing the judge there was a real case here – there was a strong case for unlawfulness and SANRAL had provided no strong answer to it in their responding affidavit.

I was kept apprised of the opening day's proceedings in court through telephonic conversations with Marc and Paul, as I was unable to attend the first day on Tuesday, 24 April 2012. I happened to be facilitating one of our Avis Brand Ambassador programmes at a conference centre in Benoni. It was a fascinating interactive programme at which each executive took a turn in hosting around 30 staff members for two days.

I thoroughly enjoyed these two-day sessions with our staff, where we discussed people engagement and alignment with our brand promise of 'People will always be more important than cars'. However, this particular session was heavily interrupted by press interviews over tea and lunch breaks and I struggled to remain present and connected to the group.

I was caught between being present at the programme and giving the media (and therefore the public) the much-required input of our challenge to the e-toll matter. One of OUTA's strengths throughout the entire challenge was our accessibility to the media. We needed to seize every opportunity to get our messages, arguments and reasoning into the debate and top of the public's mind. By doing so we believed we could empower the public with sufficient information to make up their minds about the irrationality of the scheme, along with their rights to challenge it. We took every opportunity we were given by the media to put our case forward.

After a long and exhausting day, I met with Marc and Paul to get an overview of the first day's arguments in court.

'What a lovely day,' said Paul and Marc, as they articulated OUTA's arguments and the strength of Franklin's approach on the opening day as being exceptional.

They were so positive and it made me feel good.

Court – day 2

With the Avis Brand Ambassador programme over, together we drove through to Pretoria for the second day of arguments in court. I could sense Marc's frustration that the first day had been consumed by the urgency issue. He so much wanted the interdict part of the hearing to get underway.

With the mass excitement of day one in court over, there were no protestors outside and no cars hooting in support. Today the faces were grim, with determined looks and last-minute talks between the numerous legal representatives present.

During the proceedings, Unterhalter articulated that the urgency of postponing the start of e-tolling was unnecessary because the alliance's legal review on the legality of e-tolls was set to go ahead in a few months, regardless of the interdict or not. He remarked that OUTA's claim that R20 billion would be needed to operate the tolls was excessive. But Franklin countered this by asking SANRAL to come forward with the true cost of operation. Unterhalter said the figure depended on the levels of non-compliance.

In a dry sarcastic tone Judge Prinsloo asked: 'The way things are going, what do you think the rate of non-compliance will be?'

Less than an hour into the second court day of hearings, Judge Prinsloo had made his decision: he decided the interdict was indeed a matter of urgency. He said it was in the public's interest to rule before the end of the week as to whether tolling would go ahead or not.

'It seems to me that the immense and widespread public interest in this matter and the ongoing protest from many quarters should also persuade me to exercise my discretion in hearing this matter as one of urgency,' Judge Prinsloo said.

Just before lunch AfriForum's legal representative, Greta Engelbrecht SC, attempted to become a friend of the court wanting to bring the matter of the tariffs before the court, an argument that Judge Prinsloo had dismissed the day before. Two hours later an agitated judge dismissed their application, saying he had so little time to hear all the arguments for and against the interdict.

'We have to finish this matter tomorrow,' said Prinsloo. 'We may have to work through lunch.'

Franklin began by presenting OUTA's arguments, which rested on five main points: the cost collection of the tolls was disproportionate to the amount spent on upgrading the roads; the system was unreasonable because law enforcement was practically impossible; there was a procedural error in the decision to toll because the public was not properly consulted; there was no alternative integrated public transport as promised; and the environmental authorisation was irregular.

Franklin said R21.56 billion would be spent to collect tolls over the period of twenty years, equal to the costs of the freeway upgrade. Additionally, if one million vehicles use the road daily, at a 7% non-compliance, an estimated 70 000 summonses would have to be issued daily. He said this alone would make e-tolling a practical impossibility.

The second day in court also marked the same day that Transport Minister S'bu Ndebele made his R39-billion budget speech in Parliament. In his speech Ndebele said that South Africa had a responsibility to service the R20-billion debt that the Gauteng freeway upgrade had incurred.

He warned: 'Failure to honour this obligation will adversely affect our country's credit rating. This is important to note, particularly because as a country we borrow at least R10 billion a week to service our budget deficit and state debt and to meet the financial obligations of state-owned companies.'

But Opposition MPs were having none of Ndebele's rhetoric and fired their own warning to the minister. They said government faced a massive civil disobedience campaign and described the way e-tolling had been handled as a public relations disaster.

'This tolling system is in essence nothing but a government-induced cancer introduced into South Africa's economic system,' said Freedom Front Plus MP, Anton Alberts.

During my first day in court, I was emotionally lifted by Franklin's sterling work and arguments.

Court – day 3

On the third and final day at the Pretoria High Court, the government's lawyers described in detail why they believed that if e-tolling were suspended it would spell disaster for the economy.

For two hours Unterhalter and Gauntlett described the possibility of 'economic Armageddon' if the e-toll system was not turned on, likening our credit rating decline to something that could plunge the country into junk status.

'South Africa would become another Greece,' Gauntlett said in his theatrical way to the judge. I was totally amused.

I thought to myself, how is a R2 billion additional cost per annum to cover the GFIP bonds, within a trillion-rand budget, supposed to spark an economic Armageddon?'

Unterhalter said the granting of the interdict would cause SANRAL to suffer irreparable harm because it would be unable to raise funds on the international market.

'This will reverberate through the financial markets. Damage that is done in months will take years to rehabilitate. Greece knows about this,' he said, adding that for every month e-tolling was delayed, SANRAL would lose R220 million.

'My client considers that a massive amount of money,' Unterhalter said. 'They are asking us to close the shop door and that is a very serious thing to ask a court to do.'

Gauntlett added his voice: 'These are decisions [of tolling] that were made nobly, and it does not rest with campaigners who are not successful politically to question that.' He said other projects would suffer and that the country faced high financial instability.

Listening to such arguments in court, where you cannot interject or comment, works up one's frustration levels. The blatant over-dramatisation of certain points and issues made me angry. Unterhalter painted a picture of SANRAL being ready to launch a very workable system, with high e-tag compliance levels expected and at reasonable costs of collection. 'What complete and utter crap,' I muttered softly to Marc. I was agitated and found it difficult to sit quietly and listen to Unterhalter's and Gauntlett's attempts to shred our case.

There were distractions during the court hearings. Finance Minister Pravin Gordhan quietly slipped into the court at one point. He sat and listened for a bit before slipping out again. We read Gordhan's appearance as government sending a clear message to the judge as to the level of political attention this case was attracting.

By midday on day three, a group of theatre dancers outside the court stripped to their underpants, saying they were taking an 'e-shower'. When police showed up, they quickly dressed and said they were there to add their voices to the anti-e-toll debate.

In response to the arguments presented by government's legal teams, our second senior counsel team member, Alfred Cockrell, took up the fight on behalf of OUTA in our closing arguments.

His was our final attempt to convince Judge Prinsloo that an interdict of the e-toll scheme was a just and right decision.

Cockrell argued that the wool had been pulled over the South African public's eyes by SANRAL, as well as the eyes of Transport Minister Jeff Radebe at the time.

Cockrell said SANRAL had failed to outline to Radebe just how much it would cost to collect toll fees – and that they had used a 'thumb-suck' estimate of R200 million as being the annual collection and operational costs to convince him. Cockrell also showed how exorbitant the cost of the whole system was. The GFIP Steering Committee report said the tender that had been awarded was R5 billion for five years of toll collection. Extrapolated simply, we worked out that the cost over twenty years would be R20 billion – being the same amount as the capital cost to upgrade and widen the freeway network. This appeared not only to be exorbitantly expensive, but irrational.

As the tendered costs of collection were out there, SANRAL had not refuted our point on this matter. Nor could they refute the fact that Radebe was presented with the estimated cost of e-toll collection at around R200 million, as this was in their papers. Our argument on this point was strong and Cockrell pointed out that if the scheme is irrational, then a court can't save it.

We expected SANRAL to come in thick there, but its answer was dismal. In fact they said the figures were correct. There was some mention by SANRAL that these high costs were calculated to apply at a high level of 60% non-compliance. But we denounced that statement, saying this was nowhere to be found in the GFIP Steering Committee Report, written some ten months earlier in June 2011.

Then Cockrell pulled out another smoking gun from this report, which had the impact of blowing SANRAL's arguments out of the water. In SANRAL's court arguments, which made reference to the GFIP Steering Committee Report, they had conveniently left out the warnings related to the impact of default payments from non-compliance, which were contained in the recommendations of the report. Fortunately for us, SANRAL's co-defendant, the Transport Ministry, had kept the entire GFIP Steering Committee's Report, including the recommendations in their affidavit, and Alfred Cockrell was quick to point this out.

'Non-compliance [in paying e-tolls] is indeed a reason not to use e-tolls to recover costs. That would be practically unworkable. SANRAL was warned about that by the steering committee and ignored it,' said Cockrell. 'SANRAL's omission of these recommendations in their affidavit has painted a bad picture of their credibility,' argued Cockrell.

Cockrell's argument capped a legal battle that involved just over 2 500 pages of founding and answering affidavits. Nineteen eminent counsels appeared before the court, ten of whom were senior counsel, two for OUTA and the rest for government.

While Cockrell was speaking, Alli and SANRAL manager Alex van Niekerk kept on leaving the courtroom.

Just as Cockrell finished, COSATU's Zwelinzima Vavi tweeted: 'ANC and COSATU leadership agreed to postpone implementation date for e-tolls by month to allow task team more time to explore alternative funding.'

It was the fifth e-toll postponement announced by SANRAL in just over a year.

The court was abuzz. What did this mean and would it impact Judge

Prinsloo's judgment? Was the interdict no longer urgent or even required? And what about government's argument that any delay in the payment of the system would result in financial instability for both SANRAL and the country?

The disconnect between the delay and what the lawyers had been arguing in court could not be explained by the Department of Transport.

Transport Director-General George Mahlalela attributed the delay to the need to finalise administrative and regulatory issues rising from a court challenge to the system.

But we knew the postponement was more of a political move, an attempt by the ANC to appease its angry alliance partners. On top of this, it was not ready to launch the scheme, as we would later establish. Even if given the green light to do so, the scheme was unable to launch.

As it turned out, the ANC's announcement of a delay made no impact on the judge. It was Thursday and Judge Prinsloo announced he would need two days to make a decision. He decided to open the court on Saturday, 28 April, to deliver his judgment at 11.00 am. A court opening on a Saturday is a very rare occurrence indeed. Clearly he was taking this case very seriously. Was this a good thing or a bad thing for us? we wondered.

The judgment

Judge Prinsloo wasted no time. He made it clear that while he realised SANRAL would suffer financial losses, the public would also suffer hardship if e-tolling went ahead. The judge said people were being held captive by toll roads and the alternatives were dismal.

'Tens of thousands of motorists, businesses and ordinary men and women, including family members of these affected motorists and business people, will suffer ongoing financial hardship if the interim relief is not granted,' said Prinsloo.

He ruled that SANRAL was forbidden from levying or collecting e-tolls until a full judicial review of the project could be heard in court.

'Quite apart from any other consideration I have a sense that this exceptional case, with its particular characteristics, and the public interest that it had evoked, should be afforded the attention and consideration of a court of final instance,' Prinsloo said.

The reaction was immediate. On Twitter Vavi said: 'There is no replacement to principle and truth – congratulations!!!'

He later tweeted, 'Biggest lesson is that people united will never be defeated. Well done for uniting irrespective of other usual differences.'

Saturday, 28 April 2012, was a lovely day indeed. To describe listening to a winning judgment is difficult. It felt like a tsunami of emotion welling up inside as the slant of the decision started to flow in our direction. I was consumed. It was simply powerful and all the stress over the last two months was finally released.

Tears of relief and joy welled up in my eyes as the final words of the judgment were being read. Paul, Marc and I jumped up and hugged each other in the courtroom. It was sheer elation.

I had prepared two speeches. One for a loss and the other for a win. I had struggled while preparing the 'loss speech' the night before. It made no sense losing such a rational argument, but write it I did. Both speeches were circulated between Paul, Marc and I, to ensure we got the message of a victory for the people across.

Within seconds of the judgment awarding the interdict, the media scurried over to the SANRAL side of the court to get comment, knowing that the winners of court challenges tend to hang around rejoicing in the verdict for a lot longer than the losers. A few minutes later, the media surrounded us. We had anticipated that a win would require a more organised press conference to not only deliver our speech, but to give input and answers to more questions. We then invited the press to join us at the Court Classique Hotel in Hatfield at 2.00 pm that afternoon where we would respond to the outcome of the case and explain our plans that lay ahead.

Yusuf Abramjee, the head of Prime Media's broadcasting arm and a vocal citizens' rights campaigner, assisted us in arranging the press conference. We met for a brief discussion with him at the hotel and prepared our feedback for the media.

I took the speech marked 'win' out of my folder as the OUTA panel sat down in the crowded meeting room, packed with camera operators and journalists eager to hear what we had to say.

'OUTA remains adamant that much could have been done by both SANRAL and the Department of Transport to have averted this legal action,' I read out from my speech. 'One senses that this may well be the start of new consciousness within South Africa where its citizens have been vindicated and their voices heard.'

The rest of the speech covered how irrational the e-toll decision was and the wrongfulness of government's attempt to defend its actions and decision on e-tolling, which could only be regarded as indefensible.

After the OUTA panel had fielded the myriad questions and expressed our gratitude to the team and the public, the conference was over. The media moved off to file their stories and suddenly it was quiet. It was the end of a torrid and most stressful period of my life and we all needed a good rest.

By Monday, 30 April, the extent of what we had achieved started to sink in. We received calls and interview requests from media houses both from around the country and even far enough afield to include Al Jazeera and the BBC. The world was interested in what we were doing. This was not just a South African civil action campaign, but one that attracted world attention to our democracy, and how active citizenry could challenge and alter government's policies and decision-making processes.

But we also knew that the interdict was only the start of what would be a fierce battle in court to prove that e-tolling was unjustified, irrational and an unnecessary punitive tax on the citizens of South Africa. The court review still lay ahead.

'We remain hopeful that all parties will find each other prior to the court review,' I had told journalists at the press briefing.

But for now it was a victory and I booked a table at the Grill House in Rosebank for the team and all our legal representatives and their partners to celebrate. There were seventeen of us and we paid tribute to all the hard work by an excellent team.

Paul's wife Gill joined him at this dinner. I was very surprised as we were aware of the advanced stage of her battle with cancer. She was very ill but very, very brave. It was the last time I would see Gill.

CHAPTER 10

The aftermath of the interdict

After the interdict was granted we were convinced that government would come to its senses and call a halt to the e-tolling decision, once and for all. One got the impression from a few remarks made in the media and Parliament that the minister of transport, S'bu Ndebele, and his deputy, Jeremy Cronin, were not all that convinced about the e-toll decision. It was a highly questionable project they had inherited from the previous minister of transport, Jeff Radebe.

As the CEO of Avis, I was relieved that we may have got one step closer to not wasting our company's time and money by e-tagging all our vehicles. Well, for the moment at least. Business was complicated enough and we certainly didn't need this added cost and complexity on our hands.

Preparing for the court case meant it had been months since I had spent some quality time with my wife and family. A few days after the interdict, I suggested to Helen that we get out of the house for a night and do a movie, dinner and stay at the Pallazzo Hotel at Montecasino in Fourways. It was a night to relax and reconnect after the stress of the past few months.

The next Monday, my boss Keith Rankin called me into his office.

'I don't want you to panic or anything, Wayne, but we have some feed-back from our security division that you are being followed,' he said to me.

Avis has a security team that works relentlessly recovering and inter-cepting stolen vehicles. Armour Gittings was the manager of this depart-ment and he is well connected in the security and surveillance industry. The head of one of our supplier companies (I'll call him Jo), who works in the surveillance business, called Armour and informed him that I was being followed. The story went as follows:

Jo was sitting upstairs at Coco Bongo restaurant inside the Montecasino complex when he happened to see my wife and me walking past. He was very aware of the e-toll court case and he thought, Wayne has probably made many enemies. I bet he is being followed.

Jo scouted around and soon noticed two men attempting to behave inconspicuously, walking apart but keeping pace, at a distance, with Helen and me. To me they were inconspicuous, but not to the trained eye of someone like Jo who described how they were clearly following us. The stalkers walked apart and never spoke to each other in the centre, but they remained on our tail.

To be sure, Jo kept an eye out for us and said that ten minutes later, he spotted Helen and me walking back to the restaurant area (from the movie theatre complex where we had purchased our tickets for a later show). We were on our way to our favourite Portuguese restaurant and Jo looked to see if the two men were still on our trail. Sure enough, they were not far behind us, keeping their distance and remaining apart.

Jo was concerned, but didn't want to alarm us. He could see we were trying to enjoy some private time together and so, unbeknown to us, he stalked the stalkers to see if his hunch was correct. An hour later, Jo saw us walking back to the movie theatre area of the complex, once again being followed by the two stalkers. He watched them watch us go into the movie theatre, whereafter they walked off to the car park, still separated, where Jo saw them meet up and have a conversation over a cigarette. They then left the complex.

His full description of the evening gave me no reason to doubt his claim. He knew where we had been the whole evening. Jo's opinion of the two lurkers was that they had been instructed to follow me and see who it was that I might be meeting. His description was that these two men were professionals and knew what they were doing. There did not appear to be any threat to our lives. In his view, someone probably wanted to know who was backing OUTA, and by following me they thought they could uncover some information.

I was told my phone probably would be tapped. It wasn't inconceivable.

'These are very obvious tactics by the intelligence authorities. They will want to know your every strategy and who you are talking to. They will want to listen into your conversations to pre-empt what you are doing so that they can circumvent your tactics,' I was told.

That day my mind was preoccupied by the concern that my family's privacy was potentially being violated. Strangely enough, I felt no fear, but was very angry. I contemplated whether I should tell Helen and my family. This had already been a stressful period in all of our lives and I didn't want to complicate matters any further.

I decided to tell Helen and we called our children together to inform them. While Helen was angry, she maturely contained her emotions as we discussed the matter with our children. Our sons, who were in their early twenties, were unbelieving at first, then angry and I could see the concern in our thirteen-year-old daughter's expression. She needed reassuring that all would be fine.

Helen had spent some time working for a security and surveillance company shortly after she left school, so she was very aware of the issues and concerns related to this development. She began to notice on a couple of occasions that there were unknown cars, suspiciously parked across the road from our home. Were we being watched? Helen became very concerned, not so much for us but for our children. 'Please, Wayne, never speak of our children during press interviews,' Helen would remind me. There had been several interviews during which journalists had asked about my background and family and it made sense to keep those details out of the media. We made the decision that the e-toll saga should never feature or include our family in public.

I didn't think anyone would try to take us out, although you hear of stories of staged hijackings or house breakings where innocent people are 'removed'. These were the thoughts that kept on running through my head. Who could be following me? I wondered. Was it government? SANRAL? Electronic Toll Collection (ETC)? Or was it some contractor who stood to lose money if the e-toll project never saw the light of day? Were the other chaps on the OUTA team being followed?

I was very aware that the e-toll scheme involved billions of rands and when projects of this magnitude become threatened, greedy people become desperate and angry. Perhaps it was just unnecessary paranoia, but for weeks we felt uneasy.

As much as I worried, I knew that fear was the last thing that should stop us from challenging this policy. I have always held the view that death is a pointless fear, because when you die, you don't know it. What matters is the people you leave behind and that they need to be looked after and so I checked to ensure that my affairs were in order and my family would be cared for.

The road of civil action has had many scary moments, but I knew that if you allow the fear of all the things that can go wrong to get to you, then your opponents win. Government institutions don't tend to be fans of being challenged. I kept reminding myself of how the might of apartheid was brought down by courageous people with a strong will to fight for their rights. If no one had taken up the challenge against apartheid, we would still be living with an evil system.

I resolved that no matter what happened I would think positively about this challenge from now on, and continue to fight.

The fight goes on

For two weeks after the interdict was granted government remained silent about whether it would appeal or not. The Treasury was unhappy with the decision made between the ANC leadership at Luthuli House and COSATU to delay e-tolling by a month. Its legal team was arguing in court that delays would cause an economic emergency and this kind of behaviour was not good for their case.

Treasury officials commented to the media that they had been made to look like fools and had been undermined by Luthuli House. The Department of Transport said its officials were studying the judgment, while SANRAL remained silent.

As the days went by, we became more and more confident that an appeal of the interdict would not happen. What cemented this belief further was a letter from Werksmans Attorneys that indicated the Department of Transport would not appeal the interdict. It didn't mean they weren't going to fight the judicial review, planned for later in the year, but in the meantime e-tolling would be halted.

Our legal team told us government had ten court days to lodge an appeal. The tenth day came and went and there was no appeal. We were relieved. I just wanted to get back to work and my family and I knew the same was true for Marc, Paul and others on our team like Michael Tatalias who had stayed close to us and provided significant input and support at the time.

In May 2012, SANRAL was given its first black mark by Moody's Investors Service since the e-toll debacle raised its head.

Moody's senior analyst Francesco Soldi and analyst Kenneth Morare said that SANRAL was one of the biggest borrowers in the country and had raised more than R33.5 billion from local investors. The agency gave SANRAL a negative outlook saying that any final pronouncement against e-tolls would have severe negative credit rating repercussions for the roads agency and would exert pressure on the finances of the government.

Nazir Alli resigns

The biggest bombshell in the wake of the interdict was the resignation of Nazir Alli just ten days after the court ruled in OUTA's favour.

'It's goodbye to Nazir Alli, chief executive of SANRAL, who resigned from his post this morning,' *The Star* announced on its front page on 8 May 2012.

'Where his casual laugh at difficult questions was once found to be endearing, he became increasingly known as arrogant,' the article said.

The more the media asked of the Department of Transport why Alli had resigned, the fainter the response grew. SANRAL staff said the agency was in a state of chaos following the announcement. Most were surprised at what had happened. They speculated that Alli had been forced to hand in his resignation – the fall guy in the e-tolling fiasco.

Alli had headed up the formation of SANRAL after leaving the Department of Transport as a director to become the CEO of the new agency in 1998.

My boss Keith popped into my office the day Nazir resigned and asked what we were planning to say about Nazir's resignation. I responded that this was not a personal challenge; while we were against the e-toll system and SANRAL's despicable behaviour, we would not be celebrating his resignation openly in public. We certainly couldn't gloat about this development. Keith was happy with this response, reminding me of one of our company's key leadership behaviours of always playing the ball and not the man.

OUTA's press statement spoke of our concern that SANRAL had lost a good engineer and road builder and Alli's leaving was not our issue. The demise of the e-toll decision was what we were aiming for.

It was just a few days later that news leaked of Alli's run-ins with Minister of Transport S'bu Ndebele.

In the *Sunday Independent* on 13 May 2012, Alli was being accused of keeping crucial details of the e-toll contract secret, even from his transport bosses.

The paper said that Ndebele wanted to force Alli to hand over the full details of the e-toll deal, in particular the contract entered into with ETC joint venture, headed by Austrian company Kapsch TrafficCom.

One source told the paper that even the SANRAL board was in the dark about the full details of the contract.

Previous requests to get information on the contract by various organisations had failed. Alli had blanked out large parts of the document, which he handed to Zwelinzima and Jack Bloom during a live television debate. Even in court, government failed to submit the signed contract with ETC to substantiate its argument that further delays of the e-toll project would have an adverse effect on the country's economy.

Alli denied keeping the contract secret. 'That is a blatant lie,' he told the *Sunday Independent*. 'Awarding of tenders is a decision of the board's contracts committee. These things are all audited by the auditor general and SANRAL has had clean audits from the auditor general for many years,' he said.

And Alli returns

But it was clear something political was going on behind the scenes in the Transport Department. The mutterings of political in-fighting grew louder. Then, within two weeks of Alli's resignation, he was back again, reinstated by Deputy President Kgalema Motlanthe. Not by his boss, the minister of transport. Something was odd. And, within a few weeks of Alli's return on 12 June 2012, both the minister of transport, S'bu Ndebele, and his deputy, Jeremy Cronin, were moved out of their roles in transport. Wow, I thought, Nazir sure has connections to have this kind of impact on the president. Surely these moves could not be coincidental. I can't think of when last a minister and the deputy were moved mid-term from their positions in one fell swoop.

In one of Ndebele's last speeches in his role as minister of transport he announced that Alli had offered to step down if it was felt he was part of the problem. Ndebele said this was not the case and Alli was returning to his previous role.

In President Jacob Zuma's mid-term cabinet reshuffle, Ndebele was moved to head up the Department of Correctional Services while Cronin ended up as the deputy minister of public works, and the new minister of transport, Ben Martins, was brought in. Who is this new chap? we wondered at our next committee meeting. No one had really heard of him. He certainly was not outspoken in public and it soon became evident he was there to toe the line on the executive decision on e-tolls. He was clearly not there to find an alternative solution to the e-toll debacle.

Enter John Clarke

In 2010, I had met with John Clarke at the Wilderness Leadership School in Durban where we were discussing the topic of sustainability at one of Dr Ian McCallum's workshops. John was a relentless campaigner against SANRAL's plans to build a new tolled route through the Wild

Coast, which the community believed was being planned to assist a proposed titanium mining project on the dunes of Xolobeni.

I had agreed to extend Avis's corporate social investment sponsorship programme to help John and the local Amadiba community with the occasional short-term vehicle requirements to attend to their travelling affairs in their fight against the authorities on this decision. John and I had met a few times since 2010 and he was about to become a significant participant and help to the OUTA committee.

John called me in mid-May of 2012, a few days after Alli's resignation. He had told me that he knew S'bu Ndebele and asked if I would be amenable to a meeting with the minister if he was able to set this up. I was keen and indicated that we would be pleased if this meeting could be brokered by John.

Sadly, that meeting never happened, with Ndebele being redeployed too quickly. John had already made contact and the minister had indicated his interest to meet, but the reshuffle put paid to that development. It was a meeting that Marc, Paul and I were keen to have, as we had noticed on numerous occasions that both Ndebele and Cronin were not quite sold on the e-toll decision. They were both making the right noises and raising concerns about the choice of e-tolling being the best mechanism to charge citizens for road upgrades, a matter that we announced in a press statement at the time.

We never had the proof, but during our committee meetings we speculated that Mac Maharaj, the spokesperson for the president and the same person who appointed Alli to SANRAL in 1998, may have had something to do with Alli's return and Ndebele's departure. In our speculative opinion Alli's return to head up SANRAL came with conditions that his current unsupportive bosses in the department be removed. He needed people who would support him, which raised our speculation that something didn't smell right about what had happened regarding the redeployment of the minister of transport and his deputy.

The Treasury appeals the e-toll interdict

On the fifteenth working day after the interdict, we received a call from our lawyers telling us that the Treasury had lodged an appeal against the interdict. I was confused. 'I thought the final date for an appeal to be lodged was by day ten?' I asked Pieter Conradie, our attorney. There appeared to have been a mix-up. Ten days applies at one level of the courts while it is fifteen days in others. I was livid.

Then, we heard that the Treasury was bypassing the Supreme Court of Appeal and was going straight to the Constitutional Court with its appeal. It was to be another huge court case and an extra cost to deal with. 'Attrition through lawfare' was the statement that came to mind.

'It's disappointing that the state would choose to fight this out in the courts instead of meeting us to try to solve this constructively,' we told the media. It was the end of May and we met with our legal team to strategise over this latest development.

Clearly, now that Alli was re-ensconced and his questioning old bosses removed, government had changed tack. It was no longer the minister of transport speaking about e-tolling. Instead, Jimmy Manyi, the spokesperson and CEO of Government Communication and Information Systems, began to make controversial statements about e-tolls, which landed him in hot water. By August 2012 he had been moved out of the position. But during his last few months, he announced that a committee of ministers (the Inter Ministerial Committee – IMC), chaired by Deputy President Kgalema Motlanthe had been formed to look into the e-tolling issue. Another wave of public and political outcry was triggered and the media were having a field day.

Motlanthe made a speech at the end of May 2012 in which he said that cabinet had examined a number of options on how best to fund infrastructure and they had come to the conclusion that user-pays was the 'most viable, fair and equitable'.

He said open road tolling was being used successfully elsewhere in the world in countries such as China, Chile and Singapore and that the IMC would coordinate all work on the implementation of the project, respond to the legal dispute, consult stakeholders and propose short-term funding solutions for SANRAL in the meantime.

Motlanthe said that throughout the process government had shown a willingness to consult, engage and listen to the views of the people, and the committee would carry on with this process.

'While we continue to consult, we must bear in mind that there is a public debt that needs to be repaid and the longer we take to resolve this impasse the worse the country's financial position becomes,' he concluded.

It was clear his voice was there to placate the people, to calm the anger and insinuate that government had heard the people.

But the deputy president's words didn't quite have the effect that government was hoping for. In particular, Motlanthe had referred to Moody's estimates that SANRAL would be losing between R270 million and R500 million a month. We asked why Motlanthe was relying on an estimate from a ratings agency. Surely SANRAL itself could have given more detail about the nature and extent of its monthly commitments?

In June 2012, marketing research company Ipsos revealed that two-thirds of drivers in Gauteng did not have and had no intention of buying an e-tag. The survey also revealed that 72% of drivers in the province disagreed with the entire concept of e-tolling. SANRAL's ignorance of these significant numbers would become the scheme's undoing in time.

In the meantime, invited organisations were preparing submissions for their presentations to the IMC at the Union Buildings.

In August 2012, I attended three presentations on behalf of SAVRALA and OUTA and on all three occasions, in my opinion, the entire process was a farce. Here was this high-powered delegation from government, attended by the deputy president to the ministers and director-generals of transport, the Treasury and other departments and one could tell this was a waste of time.

Each session began with input from the Department of Transport, telling us their view of why e-tolling was the right decision. When it came our turn to present, it was a case of going through the motions. We were expecting them to ask questions and seek additional clarity on the points and arguments we put forward, but they remained very silent throughout our input.

Each time, after the talks, their spin doctors would call us over to agree on a joint press statement, which they had prepared during our presentations. They loved to include a slant that might indicate that we were on board with them. Deep in the statement, a sentence read: 'Both parties agree with the user-pays principle,' which was an inaccurate reflection of the situation.

In the end we could not agree with the statement compiled by the Government Communication and Information Systems, so we decided to draft our own separate press statements.

As it turned out, despite the input from those against e-tolls, be it SAVRALA, OUTA, COSATU and other entities, government's position on e-tolls remained unchanged. What made the entire six-month exercise appear even more farcical to us was that the IMC never released a report on how it arrived at its findings and conclusion. It merely released a statement expressing support for the e-toll decision.

We were not surprised and put the exercise down to just another monumental governmental waste of time. The mere act of consultation isn't enough; there needs to be a genuine approach and display of hearing and acting on the people's concerns.

CHAPTER 11

Corporate cowardice, funding challenges and my resignation

Trying to determine the expected costs of this legal challenge was a constant difficulty for the OUTA committe. We needed to know how much money we needed to raise and the initial estimate provided to us by Cliffe Dekker Hofmeyr was just under R500 000. That figure was based on an assumption that all would go according to plan on the interdict and that government would come to its senses by recalling its decision on the matter. But then again, in litigation, nothing ever goes according to plan and we never anticipated SANRAL's 'lawfare' strategy.

When discussing our need to raise the initial funding from the SAVRALA members, Paul Pauwen was wide awake and suggested that instead of seeking the indicated amount of R500 000, we should seek to raise a million rand, doubling the R500 000 that was initially suggested, as he had been aware of how legal expenses tend to rise well beyond their original estimations.

And a million rand we got from our members in no time. Pronto, that was the finances taken care of. Or so we thought.

By the time the interdict was over and our celebration thereof had died down, we had run up a bill of R3.5 million. 'How crazy was that?' we asked at our committee meeting in May 2012. We still had the court review ahead us and here we were, a month into our case, and we were R2.5 million in the red. With additional funds now needed to defend the interdict appeal in the Constitutional Court, we started to sweat and fund-raising was moved up to point number one on our agenda.

We asked for an explanation of the costs from our lawyers and reviewed the accounts. All was above board. 'It was just a situation of much more time on compilation of the founding and responding affidavits than we had envisaged,' we were told. In addition, the first estimate was based on one silk and a junior. We had an extra SC and additional expertise was commissioned on some of the environmental law arguments. We were rapidly learning a new skill of 'how to read and anticipate the true costs of litigation'. Not a pleasant skill to have to develop when you're on the paying end.

At our next committee meeting in June 2012, we discussed a more concerted fund-raising drive, one that consisted of approaching captains of industry, high net worth individuals and other associations, along with an appeal to the public. We also decided to go back to the SAVRALA members for another tranche of R1 million, which they duly agreed to. 'Thank goodness,' I breathed after the meeting, but it was still not enough and we were probably at the threshold of what we could expect the car rental industry to hand out.

By August 2012, government had started to unpack who these various members of OUTA were. SAVRALA members, for a start, were servicing national and regional government fleet management contracts and word started to filter through to us about pressure being applied at their respective company board meetings.

Despite the fact that we had achieved full support from all the SAVRALA leasing and rental members to proceed with the legal challenge to the e-toll decision (barring a couple of banks in the leasing division), I started to receive a few calls from MDs and CEOs to indicate that since then board pressure had indeed been applied to distance their respective companies from the e-toll challenge.

By the fourth quarter of 2012, the political pressure was becoming too much to bear and one sensed that SAVRALA's car rental and leasing company members were under severe pressure to resign from the 40-year-old association, unless of course, SAVRALA pulled its support from OUTA.

I was livid and spent hours on the telephone to a number of the CEOs and MDs of SAVRALA members to remind them of why we started this challenge and how important it was to stay strong. Sadly, they were under immense pressure and for as long as their jobs depended on it, there was a clear change of heart. As one CEO put it to me, 'Wayne, this is not my decision to make any longer and I'm not prepared to stake my job on the matter.'

Two of SAVRALA's leasing members who were connected to the banking industry refused to join the majority of the other members in supporting the e-toll court challenge, right from the start. Even personal visits to their senior managers couldn't get them to change their minds. They were extremely uncomfortable with being linked to the challenge, expressing that while personal sentiment was in favour of the challenge, their corporate psyche (and big bosses) had cautioned them to back off. 'It was not worth facing the wrath of government officials,' was the message that came through loud and clear. Naturally, I was disappointed in these attitudes expressed by corporate South Africa and while I knew there would always be some degree of trepidation, I never realised that the general moral courage of corporate leadership equated to having balls the size of raisins.

Then, in the short space of the three months between November 2012 and January 2013, four of the large leasing members of SAVRALA resigned. I decided to call one of the 'capitulators' and he had the audacity to say that e-tolls were actually seen as a lucrative revenue stream. He stated that his company was able to make up to R0.09 per gantry charged, due to a discounted 'key account' rate from SANRAL and an administration fee placed on the corporate fleet accounts to manage their respective e-toll bills.

My blood began to boil and I nearly lost my cool when I heard this crass logic. 'So what do you believe is the right thing to do? Profiteer or stand up against something you personally voted as worth challenging just a few months ago?' I asked, seething under my breath. It was no use. When the chips were down, their bonuses and jobs weighed heavily in their skewed decisions. Disappointed and angry, I decided to suggest to the committee that it was not worth pursuing further support from big business unless opportunities that made sense came to light.

It became blatantly obvious that government pressure had created all sorts of reasons why tolling was suddenly a good idea to support, as expressed by some of OUTA's members. This was corporate schizophrenia at its best, or was it? Let's face it, in the capitalist world of business, 'profits trump principle'. Business leadership has no difficulty in finding reasons to capitulate on a rightful societal agenda when their business volumes and share of the market depends on them doing so. This is when moral courage and decisions that offer best outcomes for the people as a whole tend to quickly drown in the cesspool of corporate bullshit.

It was time to find other ways of seeking the funds we so desperately needed. Our committee meeting time was taken up by this challenge and the mounting legal bills. My stress levels as the chairperson were rising.

The obvious choice was to heighten our call to the public to assist us in funding the campaign. Business, it would seem, did not have the determination that the people would have. It would simply pass the cost on to the consumer. It was the public who would pay for the roads twice in the goods they purchased and if indeed they travelled on the roads.

At the end of the day we were fighting this battle on behalf of society as a whole, and with the rising vociferous public outrage against the e-toll scheme, we were confident that once we put our plea for funds out there, money would be the least of our worries.

We did the following calculations and made some high-level assumptions:

1. There were 2.5 million Gauteng motorists using the freeways in Gauteng, of which roughly a million were daily commuters traversing the tolled routes.
2. We figured that if just 33%, or 300 000, of the one million regular freeway users had heard of OUTA's initiative and agreed it was right to challenge the e-toll scheme in court and that ...
3. If just one third of that number, i.e., around 100 000, took the time to donate an average of R100, i.e., one month's e-toll savings as a once-off payment, we would raise a further R10 million towards our mounting legal costs.

This would more than suffice and would also cover our marketing and operational costs.

In our minds, it appeared to be so easy. We knew the motorists of Gauteng were angry with the e-toll decision and we were confident they would support us in fighting the scheme on their behalf. After all, we had shown our worth by interdicting the scheme's launch and every day the motorists were saving money from the non-existent e-tolls as a result of our actions. Surely this would justify their passing some of their savings on to us. In effect, we believed they owed it to us and were confident of their funding support.

Our appeal to society took on many forms, from a concerted media PR campaign to our new Facebook pages and our website, which was attracting a lot of interest. We created an easy donation process to facilitate direct deposits and a PayFast credit card link. With the campaign all lined up, we set out to express our plea via the media, including the valuable airtime interviews we received on many occasions, often during prime drive-time radio programmes.

We also continued to call on businesses to assist us. The committee apportioned names and company lists between the members who hit the road, explaining our cause with hat in hand. OUTA was well known by now and initially we received a lot of time from business leaders who wanted to know more about our cause, but did not really assist us with funds.

The money we were raising was constantly in arrears of our legal bills. What made this so infuriating in our opinion was that a number of large corporates that we could count on two hands could have, and should have, given us R1 million each to solve our funding headache. These were companies with massive fleets, from courier companies to large trucking and logistics outfits. They were all going to save millions and more each year if indeed we were to succeed with our court challenge to halt the scheme.

Meeting these business leaders and listening to their excuses, or their hollow promises that never materialised, became the biggest disappointment for me during the entire campaign. FOGoB was clearly evident – the Fear of Government Backlash.

Their boards, some of them populated with non-executive directors connected to government, clearly did not want to cross swords with the authorities. Despite our offer of complete anonymity, they were not prepared to take the risk. Any link to corporate support for OUTA could mean lost contracts or a loss of favourable trading and regulatory environments that may cost them in lost profits. This would 'not be good for business' was the response I was often given and shown the door.

On the other hand, though, there were the heroes and some organisations that gave generously. They took the risk. They were often the medium-sized and smaller businesses. They gave R10 000 here, R20 000 there, with several depositing over R100 000 into our bank account and a few even more.

On a couple of occasions we received calls from the executives of large corporations who offered their assistance of their own accord. This was mind-blowing stuff. When one financial director asked me, 'So how much do you want from us?' I had to quickly check my thoughts. On the one hand, I'd have liked to have said R1 million, but then realised that might frighten them off. I was about to say R500 000 when that also seemed too large a sum, so I said, 'We were thinking that R300 000 for large organisations would be a reasonable donation.' Without blinking, he agreed and I kicked myself for not requesting more, but then again, a greedy approach might have backfired. I was content and shared the good news with our committee. We were elated. We needed a few more of these active corporate citizens.

After many appeals for appointments with large organisations, an association of large businesses answered our call to present our request for assistance to their board at a monthly board meeting. Paul Pauwen joined me, and just before we were called in, we were told the agenda was tight and our 30-minute time slot had been reduced to ten minutes to present our case. We decided not to waste time on doing our normal PowerPoint presentation and kept the laptop closed. I chose my words carefully and explained why the e-toll decision was irrational, unlawful and how their industry would be impacted by the scheme. We provided our views on the questionable legality of SANRAL's decision and then took questions, after which we were thanked and asked to leave.

I never even had time to put an amount in their heads, besides mentioning that we were R3 million shy of settling our legal debts at the time.

Paul and I left feeling deflated. We felt as if we had wasted our time and that the association would probably not help us. 'Who knows?' said Paul. 'We just can't stop trying.' I was constantly moved by his enthusiasm.

A few hours later we received a call from the CEO of the association to say its board had agreed to donate R1 million to OUTA. We couldn't believe it and jumped for joy. What a massive relief. He then said, 'I must tell you, Wayne, that before you came in we had decided this was not a cause we could support, but were prepared to listen. Your story convinced the chairman and when one of our board members suggested we donate R500 000, the chairman said no, let's do a million.' I thanked him profusely but he reminded me that this decision had to remain anonymous.

As much as I wanted the public to know who these great and courageous organisations were, we couldn't and still can't say a word. I know the public would love to support these organisations for their high moral courage, but government might also want to harass them for their respective decisions to help OUTA.

On another occasion, our hopes and faith in the corporate world were dashed yet again. I had presented OUTA's challenge to the executive committee of NADA (the National Automobile Dealers Association). At this meeting, their entire team was empathetic to our cause and needs. Together, they agreed to raise a substantial amount towards our legal fees. The order of between R300 000 and R500 000 was given as an indicative figure. Bearing in mind that the members of NADA included the large automotive dealer groups controlled by the big business conglomerates of Imperial, Unitrans, Combined Motor Holdings, Barloworld, Bidvest, etc., this would have been small change for them. However, I was also cautiously optimistic that if their higher boards got involved, these funds might not be forthcoming. That's exactly what transpired. They chickened out and never donated a cent, despite a second appeal to their board a few months later.

The Retail Motor Industry, on the other hand, under whom NADA was one entity, canvassed their other members who comprised of the windscreen associations, tyres industries, accessory fitment bodies and many others related to the automobile world. They gratefully managed to donate R220 000 to OUTA. Jeff Osborne, the CEO of the Retail Motor Industry, was unwavering in his support for the cause and dearly wanted his association to contribute more.

During the first twelve months of our fund-raising campaign until May 2013, just over 200 businesses gave us the equivalent of 82% of the R7.7 million raised, while 3 283 individuals had passed R1.4 million of their personal money our way. By the end of April 2015, a total of 413 businesses had given us R8.13 million, while 12 891 individuals (less than 1% of the Gauteng freeway users) had helped us to raise a further R3.36 million. An additional R1 million donation was made by the DA political party. In total, we managed to raise R12.5 million from society to fund the legal, marketing, administrative and other minor operational expenses, but even so, by the fourth quarter of 2013 we were still some R2 million short of the total amount we needed.

Of all the donations made, it was the R1 million from the DA that needed a lot of explaining. It was given to us at a time when our lawyers gave us a week to come up with R1 million in order to proceed with the appeal to the Supreme Court Appeal (SCA). We couldn't blame Cliffe Dekker Hofmeyr for this call, as we were around R4 million in the red with it and were asking it to take the shocking judgment of Louis Vorster on appeal to the SCA. A down payment was essential.

Accepting money from a political party was, however, always going to be tricky for us. It somehow turned our cause into a political one and, this being a year before the upcoming elections, this opportunity presented the DA with fair game to score some points.

'But what do you do when your back is against the wall?' I asked a journalist who questioned our action. It was not as if the DA had suddenly jumped on the e-toll bandwagon. The party had been very vocal in vehemently opposing the scheme from the outset. So we took the money gracefully and thanked the DA for their generosity. We were not wrong to do so, but it certainly tarred us with a political brush, one that we had worked hard to avoid, especially with the moral support we were receiving from COSATU at the time.

The action of accepting funds from the DA also came close to severing a few positive links and connections we had formed with entities and people who were close to the ANC. I had some answering and explaining to do to people like Kay Sexwale and Zwelinzima Vavi, both of whom had been with us every step of the way until then. Thankfully, they gave us the time to explain ourselves and accepted our reasons and intentions. All was forgiven and the collaborative fight continued.

The most disappointing aspect of our fund-raising campaign was the many examples of public apathy we encountered at a time when this ought not to have been the case. This attitude was evident during a number of calls made on air, often during prime-time listenership slots.

You can imagine our expectation after one such interview on Talk Radio 702 when I shared our plight of the massive funding shortfall. I said to over 100 000 prime evening drive-time listeners that without their financial support, we might have to pull back on litigation (this was after the successful interdict). I added, 'If just 10% of your listeners take five minutes to log onto the OUTA.co.za website when they get home tonight, and donate just one month's e-toll savings, we would have the money we need to fight this case.'

Lo and behold, a meagre R34 437 found its way into our coffers from some 145 people. We were getting desperate and wondered what more we had to do to light the fire of active participation and funding support from the public.

Then I realised the flaw in our plea – by suggesting that 10% of the listeners should donate, this probably gave the public enough reason to say, 'I'll be part of the 90% that won't donate.' In hindsight, what we needed to suggest was that *all* listeners and motorists should donate. But then we became paranoid in case we should be accused of trying to raise more than we needed. We were between a rock and a hard place.

All the while, SANRAL listened to our calls and pleas for funds, and was aware of our struggle to pay our lawyers, while it had the fortunate situation of being able to access public funds to settle its expensive legal bills.

Looking back, the fund-raising for this civil action campaign was one of the hardest challenges I have ever been involved in. I really feel sorry for the other entities that do great work, such as Section27, which works tirelessly for the good of the citizens of this country and is constantly short of much-needed funds.

We decided to be transparent about our fund-raising and put the numbers in a graph on our website, which we updated each month. There were some months that it never moved. Weeks would go by and it would show another R10 000, not enough to show any movement on the screen.

It was a difficult time. The first few months of 2013 were particularly slow and the constant trickle of daily donations appeared to have died down substantially. This was probably to be expected after the December judgment from Vorster had been a massive blow to OUTA, and the people believed the fight was over. The first quarter of 2013 was a most difficult period; working hard to get the revenues up, dealing with the media on a regular basis and preparing our efforts to appeal Vorster's shocking judgment. A normal life was far removed from us.

We then decided to tackle the high net worth individuals, the multimillionaires and billionaires who might just see this as a worthwhile cause to support. Unfortunately, most never entertained the courtesy of a meeting. Many of them lived in Cape Town and the e-toll cause for them was too far away to notice. A couple did meet with us and we managed to get R100 000 from each of them.

At the end of 2012, we decided to flight a *Sunday Times* full-page advert. Having received it at a good rate, we sincerely thought it would be R100 000 well spent. Once again, nothing. R5 350 for our efforts. What a waste. This was becoming exhausting. What were we to do? Telethons? We discussed this with a local radio station and it was decided this was not the right forum for our needs. We would open this door only as a last resort.

I once gave a talk at a black-tie function. There must have been 150 people at dinner that night. Seemingly wealthy people. I shared interesting insights about the case, our stance and challenges, and at the end spoke of our biggest challenge – citizen apathy and the difficulty we had in raising funds.

I explained that we couldn't understand that while nobody wanted to pay tolls (for one reason or another) and most people were in support of our work, we were struggling to get donations from the public. Something was wrong. I then ended my talk, my voice quavering with emotional stress over the saga, by requesting all present to do one thing before going to bed that night – to simply log onto the OUTA website

Accumulated donations to OUTA

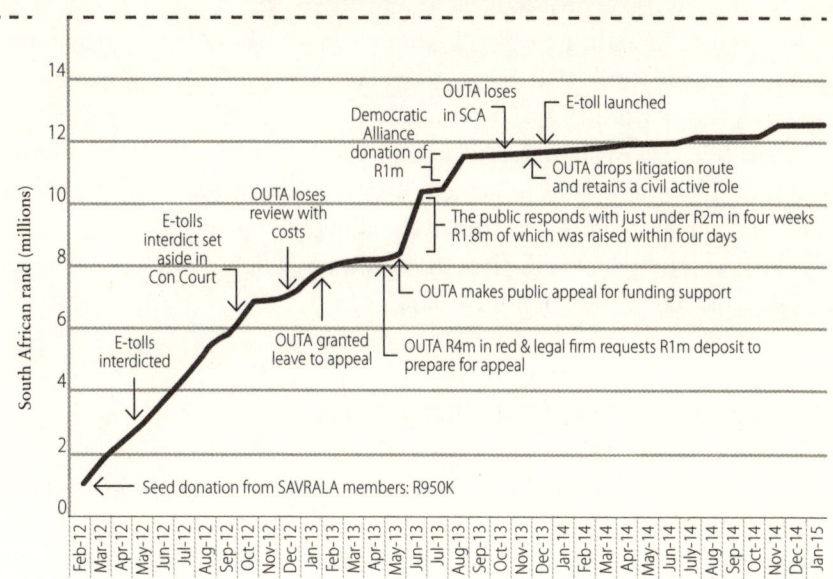

and donate towards this worthy fight. On the way home I did the mental arithmetic with my wife Helen and estimated that if an average of R500 were donated by only 60% of the 70 couples present, OUTA might see around R20 000 in donations made over the next couple of days. Alas, we received a mere R2 300.

I was convinced that virtually all those people would have donated, but only four people did. This was the heartbreaking essence of civil activism – citizen apathy – and it was beginning to frustrate me immensely. I was fast realising that South Africans who rightly bemoan the real and evil issues that must be tackled in our country tend to have an attitude of 'someone else will sort it out'.

And yet, throughout our challenge, despite this glaring apathy, we could not ignore the fact that over R12 million was raised as a result of many generous donations. The OUTA legal challenge was the biggest public-funded court case in the history of our new democracy and that was a fact not to be sneezed at. But it should never have been so difficult to achieve and we should never have been in arrears with our legal bills.

In one breath I wanted to express frustration at the public and say, 'It is not fair to call for the demise of tolling and then do little to help. You have a group of people fighting this case for you, going to court, giving up their personal time and jobs to challenge the irrationality of the scheme, and you give so little in return?'

In the next breath, however, I want to thank those who participated and gave us the funds that got us to where we were. Thank goodness for them, without whom OUTA would have disappeared a long time ago and SANRAL may just have been successful enough with its marketing and intimidation tactics, to achieve a sufficient ratio of tagged-up road users to keep the contested scheme chugging merrily along.

The graph on page 99 depicts the continuous flow of donations made to OUTA since its launch in February 2012.

Meeting and learning from other activists

We then made a call to meet with Mark Heywood of Section27. He was a renowned activist from the Treatment Action Campaign and had recently fought the much-televised 'Missing Limpopo School Books' matter. Perhaps Mark would have some tips for us. Perhaps his organisation was better positioned to take over this case on behalf of society. The response: 'You can never stop working on raising funds. It is a slog and requires full-time effort,' Mark told us. He also made it clear that this was not his fight, it was ours. Causes are taken up by people who are passionate about the reasons why they entered the challenge in the first place. They cannot simply be handed over to someone else. 'We were on this train and could not jump off until it had reached its destination, no matter where that might be,' he told us. The message from Mark was valuable. We had to change our tactics and simply do more to raise the money we needed.

I also made a call to meet up with Hugh Glenister of the 'challenge against disbanding the Scorpions court case' hall of fame. Hugh, or Bob as he prefers to be known, let out a wry smile and said, 'Good luck'. I discovered during our first meeting that he had put a few million rands of his own money into this case against the government's decision to disband the Scorpions. Despite the fact that he won in three of the five hearings at the Constitutional Court, the authorities in power simply amended the clauses on which the courts ruled against them. By doing so, the government pretty much ignored the thrust of Hugh's case, which was to reinstate the independent Directorate of Special Operations, more commonly referred to as the Scorpions. Sadly for him and the nation, this entity that did good work to uncover and expose organised crime began to cross swords with the politically connected, and the future of the Scorpions was history. Its replacement entity, the Hawks, has been mired in controversy related to leadership and political interference, ever since the demise of the Scorpions.

Hugh provided me with great insight into the journey ahead and the underlying problems facing our nation, which were largely built on a corrupt government leadership who had sucked big business into its trap. It was Hugh who shared the phrase of 'business being too busy tendering to make the rope to hang the country with' and also cautioned me on not setting high expectations for public donations towards our cause. 'Yes, they will cheer you from their armchairs, but don't expect them to get up and march, or even donate much in the way of funds,' he said.

While I cherished and agreed with his wise words, I was a little more positive on the public's supportive funding aspect of the drive, despite the fact that we had significant experience of citizen apathy.

In mid-2013, I had a brief meeting with Terry Crawford-Brown of the arms deal saga. Again, this involved more learning about challenging government on unjust decisions, but there was one highlight that I took away from this meeting. After many years of fighting the government on the arms deal challenge, Terry was tired and the issue had cost him a lot of personal time and money. I could sense things going in the same direction and vowed to myself that as soon as the time was right, I would extricate myself from this challenge, without jeopardising the cause, as I needed to get on with the constructive, entrepreneurial and family aspects of my life.

The personal toll and my decision to leave Avis

By June 2012, I was feeling the pressure. We had decided to fight the appeal at the Constitutional Court and a challenge that I thought would be over by now felt as if it had just begun.

I started to give thought to resigning from my job as the chief executive of Avis.

I got the impression that government would start to place pressure on Barloworld who were the shareholders of Avis. I sensed that while my boss Keith Rankin was fully behind the challenge and my efforts, there was discomfort in the attention the case was bringing to our brand and group as a whole. I recall that in May 2012, a newspaper ran an article on the 'Avis man behind OUTA'. They found a picture of me in my red

Avis jacket on the Internet and published an article without formally interviewing me. I had no idea the article was being featured.

This obviously annoyed Keith, as it did me, as it appeared that I was conducting the challenge against e-tolls from a brand position as opposed to an industry one. Keith reminded me that the challenge must be fought from a SAVRALA platform and that articles of this nature are not good for the brand. I agreed, but commented that I couldn't help it when journalists did their own thing. Incidents like this are unfortunately among the unintended consequences of such a challenge.

I got the impression that some pressure was being brought to bear on Keith from higher up in the organisation as a result of my involvement in this matter, but at that stage it wasn't intense enough to be unpleasant. Keith was level-headed and always fair. He realised the attention was out of my control, but asked me to be very careful going forward.

How does one exercise caution in a case like this? Look at what happened when Reuel Khoza of Nedbank and Nigel Harris of First National Bank stuck their heads above the parapet to condemn government on valid issues. Their brands got it in the neck from government. There was bound to be pressure brought to bear on Barloworld and Avis, despite this being challenged as an industry issue. Later on I would learn about how real this undue pressure was.

I knew inside of me that I couldn't give up on this e-toll challenge. Perhaps I had become fixated on seeing the matter through to the end, which didn't seem further than a year off at the time. But I also knew that I couldn't do my job as effectively as I wanted to, if indeed I were to put in the time and energy required to head up OUTA's work. My personal and family life was also being put on hold for too long. I had to make a decision.

Being the chief executive of any business is demanding, but more so when it is a leading brand in its industry. The pressure becomes greater when the role operates in a highly competitive and commoditised environment, requiring innovation and continuous energy to stay ahead. And I loved it.

Fortunately, the Avis executive management team was brilliant, every one of them a leader in their own right. For the first six months of the e-toll and OUTA initiative, the team's strength allowed me to spend around a third of my time on OUTA's work. But the pressure was weighing on me. They could sense it, and as much as they extended assurances that my back was covered and I need not worry, the more uncomfortable I felt.

I was working for Avis by day and OUTA by night. But OUTA demanded my daytime energy as well. Mainstream and social media demands increased. My family saw little of me for around five months. I left for work at 5:30, got home at 7.00 pm and buried myself in my home office until midnight. Not good, and something had to change.

Most of the questions on the social media platforms of Facebook and Twitter were of a technical nature, which related to the case and rationale of OUTA's stance. It wasn't stuff we could leave to a junior social media appointment at our digital marketing company. Paul, Marc and I had to get involved and interact with the public on a daily basis through Facebook and Twitter. We had no OUTA offices with administrators, media liaison officers and so forth.

I remember getting home in mid-June and suggesting to Helen that I felt it was time for me to resign from Avis and move on. My rationale was that I had been in the role of chief executive for five years and I had achieved what I wanted to during this period. I enjoyed developing and driving the company's sustainability programme, our facilities expansion project, the service excellence project and other initiatives. I had also indicated to Keith, several months earlier and long before the e-toll court challenge, that I was looking for a new challenge. I needed change despite the fact that I was having a lot of fun in my role. I am a firm believer in not staying too long in one place. Five to seven years is about when leaders need to move on, make space and reinvent themselves.

OUTA had become the catalyst for the change I was seeking. We all felt we had a winnable case. However, without full-time attention and accessibility to the media, we stood a real chance of jeopardising the cause. I decided that if my exit package were reasonable, I would take it up and resign from Avis.

Even though I knew my decision to resign felt so right, it was a tough one to make. I had spent a total of 23 years with the brand.

On 31 July 2012 I packed my box and said farewell to what had been a big part of my life, and hung up my red jacket for the last time.

CHAPTER 12

Off to the Constitutional Court

In May 2012 Finance Minister Pravin Gordhan came out guns blazing. He had become the loudest voice in the pro-e-toll camp in government and was not going to stand back and let society smack government in the face with an interdict. If the Department of Transport was reluctant to appeal the interdict, he was going to make sure it happened.

The Treasury was so determined to have its case heard that, according to *Beeld* newspaper, it handed the appeal papers directly to Chief Justice Mogoeng Mogoeng and Gordhan said he considered the case so urgent that he asked the court to convene during the annual July recess to hear the application.

Forget the Supreme Court of Appeal (SCA). The Treasury's appeal against the court interdict granted in the Pretoria High Court to halt e-tolling, bypassed the SCA and went straight to the Constitutional Court.

It was an appeal against an interim order, which in itself was an extraordinary challenge. The traditional legal position on that is that interim orders are not usually appealed because the matter will be sorted out in the review process of the case.

In June 2012, the chief justice decided that the Treasury's leave to appeal would be heard on 15 August. The date had been set and, as had been the case in the days leading up to the High Court interdict, there was a mad rush by government to get e-toll regulations ready.

But the Treasury played its cards just right because it didn't choose just anybody to depose the affidavit. It approached Minister of Finance Pravin Gordhan to fulfil this task.

Pravin Gordhan had a lot of gravitas. He had credibility and clout.

He told the whole Constitutional Court, under oath, that there would be economic catastrophe. He said that South Africa would have to brace itself for negative international credit ratings and that institutions providing essential services, such as schools and hospitals, would be adversely affected if the temporary court order remained in place, implying that funding to keep the e-toll bonds serviced would extract revenues from other essential services.

How could anyone really contradict that? If it was coming from the minister of finance himself it was therefore always going to weigh heavily against us in the Constitutional Court.

Gordhan's main argument was one that sought to uphold the 'separation of powers' between the judiciary and cabinet. In this argument he stated that the courts do not have the power to make decisions about the validity of government policy or how the government generates revenue. Gordhan said his department would not be able to make any long-term plans if the courts issued orders derailing the planning process.

Our opinion, however, as I told the *Mail & Guardian* at the time, was: 'Government cannot introduce policies that are oppressive on the country's people. Policies need to be reasonable. While government was elected to do its job of introducing policies, at all times these need to be rational and in the best interests of society at large.'

Along with the papers filed before the Constitutional Court were documents provided by SANRAL, which revealed a different figure on the e-toll revenue to be generated (to fund the Gauteng Freeway Improvement Project), from that produced during the interdict hearing.

Nazir Alli indicated to the Constitutional Court that e-tolls would generate R90 billion over a 24-year loan period.

This was a very important argument in our defence. At the High Court our papers had reflected that this was an exorbitantly expensive scheme in that R120 billion was to be generated by e-toll charges over a 24-year period, this being SANRAL's initial figure filed in its April 2012 affidavit. This, we argued, was irrational as the bonds raised for the capital expenditure only totalled R20 billion.

Furthermore, there was nothing that indicated in the record before us that the fuel levy was properly considered as an alternative. Thus, failure to consider alternative funding mechanisms was another real issue in our argument.

In the Constitutional Court papers, government started to fill in the holes that we had glaringly exposed during the interdict hearing. In essence, it was changing the arguments from its original papers. So, not only did Gordhan's lawyers claim there would be 'fiscal Armageddon', they also set out this whole chapter and verse about how the fuel levy was specifically considered and rejected at cabinet level.

This was apparently just the governement's say-so as no proof was provided to this effect. We were aghast at how this was portrayed and not challenged by the court.

SANRAL filed a supporting affidavit in which, for the first time, it entered evidence that watered down the power of our R20 billion 'cost of e-toll collections' point. This point added to the irrationality of the scheme in that, over twenty years, collection costs would amount to in excess of R20 billion, which was equal to the R20 billion needed to build the roads.

Now SANRAL said that wasn't the full picture on the costs. The organisation attached its first schedule, which gave the capital costs, the costs of maintenance over twenty years, interest over twenty years, and all of a sudden the collection-cost figures were down to R17 billion.

The clear facts that had been in front of Judge Prinsloo were R20 billion bond cost and R20 billion to collect, and that was irrational.

In front of the Constitutional Court, the cost of collection relative to all these other costs, which had now been increased by SANRAL, made e-tolling look very expensive but the cost of collection less irrational.

The reason why this matter, and the new figures that were being presented by Minister Gordhan's lawyers, was significant is that ordinarily when one appeals a prior judgment, the appeal must be made against a decision and the facts that were before the earlier court in reaching its decision. But here we now had a situation where government had come along and introduced revised figures to the Constitutional Court. Essentially, it was providing the court with a different set of facts on the basis of which this court needed to decide on the appeal. Effectively, the Constitutional Court wasn't faced with R20 billion capital cost versus R20 billion cost to collect. It was faced with SANRAL's schedule, which looked like R17 billion to collect over 24 years of a total income of e-tolls being R90 billion.

The questions the court then directed to OUTA's Alistair Franklin were: 'Where is the authority that something is unlawful merely with the fact that it is expensive? Or wasteful expenditure? Where is the authority for that?' We were dumbfounded at how this twist panned out and how the Constitutional Court seemingly ignored this change in strategy by government.

OUTA replied to the Treasury's and SANRAL's application in the Constitutional Court saying that SANRAL was not yet ready to launch the project. The alliance also listed the same key elements that were argued during the application for the interdict:

■ That the true costs of collection had not been considered by the minister of transport when approving the decision.

- That the system was unworkable because enforcement was practically impossible.
- That the public was not given proper notice of the decision to toll, nor the tariffs, as required by the Constitution.
- It was also argued that the dire financial consequences highlighted by the applicants if e-tolling did not go ahead were not substantiated in their papers, especially in light of the alternatives available in existing government policies, such as the fuel levy.

Days before the 15 August 2012 court date, the DA also applied to join the Constitutional Court case as a friend of the court.

'The DA has an interest in the key issue in this case, namely the extent to which courts can and should exercise their powers to interdict government,' said DA MPL Jack Bloom. 'If government wins, then expect to see more decisions like the e-tolls pushed through without proper consultation.'

AfriForum and the Road Freight Association also applied to be friends of the court. But all three were turned down the day arguments for and against the appeal would be heard.

The Constitutional Court is situated at the top of a hill in Braamfontein and has to be one of the most beautiful court buildings in the country. A long, thin, horizontal window cuts through the right side of the court, which looks out onto the roadside pavement so that those inside can see the feet of passing pedestrians. Each of the eight chief justices sits behind a cowhide, giving a sense of solemnity to each court hearing.

The sombre atmosphere of the court was broken by the noise of a loud protest outside and the chatter of over a dozen lawyers who were preparing for the day.

About 50 DA supporters were outside singing and waving banners asking motorists to 'hoot for a toll-free GP'.

At least thirteen advocates, half of them senior counsel, were appearing before the court, along with their various instructing attorneys.

Nazir Alli took the front seat in the public gallery.

'No comment,' he quickly told any journalist who approached.

OUTA's team sat across the court. I felt positive, but cautiously so. We had never planned to be in the Constitutional Court responding to an appeal and we weren't sure what to expect.

One of the first things revealed during the court proceedings was that the Treasury had gone out of its way to allocate R5.57 billion to

SANRAL in February to reduce the burden on society by bringing the vehicle e-tag tariff down by 25%, from 40 cents per kilometre to 30 cents.

Advocate Jeremy Gauntlett SC, appearing on behalf of the Treasury, said that at the end of July cabinet had approved a special appropriation bill for SANRAL. He hinted that the new bailout was R2.7 billion.

David Unterhalter SC, appearing on behalf of SANRAL, said it was ready to launch e-tolling immediately and that if the interdict was overturned SANRAL would start e-tolling within two weeks. It was ready to launch and every day was costing them millions in lost revenue, which they urgently needed to service the debt.

Franklin argued this was nonsense, that with the recent withdrawal of the regulations it was obvious they were not ready. SANRAL was unable to launch until the toll fee tariffs, enforcement and exemption regulations were in place.

Unlike in the lower courts where attorneys present their entire arguments, the justices at the Constitutional Court prefer to ask questions, seeking clarity from the legal representatives in front of them. The afternoon was spent in this toing and froing manner. A question was asked and an answer given, with never a hint in which direction the justices would choose to go. It seemed so disjointed to me and I was quickly learning the ways of the higher courts.

Listening to how the judges grilled our senior counsel for much longer than those of government, plus the types of questions posed to us, gave me a strong feeling that the ruling would not be in our favour.

Nobody knew how long it would take for the court to arrive at a decision.

In our case it was just over a month. We were called back to the court on 20 September 2012 and Deputy Chief Justice Dikgang Moseneke read out the unanimous judgment.

In the judgment Moseneke said there was no doubt the temporary restraining order on SANRAL was immediate, ongoing and substantial.

'The immediate and ongoing result of the interdict is that the National Treasury, the Executive Government and the National Legislature will have to allocate R270 million per month to SANRAL in order to meet its ongoing capital and interest repayments in respect of the GFIP. Thus the order has wide-ranging consequences for rational finances and the management of our country's sovereign debt,' the judgment read.

The deputy chief justice said there was no doubt that OUTA had every right to approach the courts for a review of the system, and it was up to the review court to make the final decision on whether e-tolling should go ahead or not.

Moseneke said, however, that he did not consider it irreparable harm if motorists paid e-tolls, only for the courts to set aside the system later on, because motorists could claim their money back from SANRAL. But this was not the case with SANRAL whose credit rating had been downgraded two notches and who needed to be funded by the Treasury in the interim.

He added that the duty of determining how public resources are spent lies in the heartland of the Executive Government, and how policy is implemented is the exclusive domain of the National Executive.

'The High Court's deafening silence on the over-arching consideration of separation of powers, taken together with other factors that go to where the balance of convenience rests, entitles this court to intervene,' said Moseneke. 'It should have held that the prejudice that will confront motorists in Gauteng if the interim interdict is not granted does not exceed the prejudice that the National Executive Government, National Treasury and SANRAL will have to endure should the temporary restraining order be granted.'

The deputy chief justice set aside the High Court interdict on that day, 20 September 2012.

SANRAL was now free to implement the system immediately. But, of course, as we predicted, it didn't. It simply couldn't and did not do so for the next fifteen months. And fiscal Armageddon did not poke his nose into SANRAL's or the Treasury's or the nation's affairs. Their theatrical statements were just that – theatre.

We had somewhat expected this outcome from the Constitutional Court and initially I was not phased by it, knowing that we still had our judicial review in a few months' time. But that would change as we began to examine the impact this judgment might have on our case.

We were slightly concerned that this Constitutional Court ruling would interfere with the High Court process, in that it would be a brave judge to rule in our favour, given that he would effectively be ruling against the Constitutional Court judges' thinking about the separation of powers. However, our attorneys indicated to us that the Constitutional Court had not heard and ruled on the unlawfulness of the e-tolling decision. Its ruling was merely one that indicated the executive powers of government must be free to apply their policies, while these may or may not be tested under full judicial review in a court of law.

What the Constitutional Court said in its decision was specifically implied in the context of how a court should approach interim orders, not final reviews. The judges said a court should be careful about interdicting huge government projects like this at the last minute, unless there are clear incidents of illegal or fraudulent behaviour, of which none was presented.

In our view, the one serious transgression of illegality was the failure of SANRAL to consult meaningfully with the public. But this was getting back into the merits of the case, which would be reviewed in November.

The case was an emotionally battering process. The hearing was hard; the court's judgment was very categorical in its tenure. It was vitriolic. I felt the judges were also unjust to Judge Prinsloo. Why? Because Judge Prinsloo had a materially different case in front of him.

The facts that were before the Constitutional Court were not the facts that were before Prinsloo.

The Constitutional Court was faced with this massive government project. There was the sheer physical presence of the gantries that had been built. The purple lights were shining. The court said you can't just come at the last minute and set it aside. The minister of finance, whose position carried a high level of integrity, was not like other members of the cabinet, and he was in charge of the nation's purse.

But the Constitutional Court was very clear in its judgment that it was not entertaining the merits of the case. It was not going to trample on the review. It asserted, very powerfully, that if it is found to be unlawful then e-tolling must be stopped.

But unfortunately, later on, that aspect of the judgment was lost and future cases on this matter interpreted the outcome that the Constitutional Court was clearly in support of the decision to toll. The message from this court was clear: 'Don't judge government and don't interfere with government's efforts at raising money for the building of infrastructure.'

The context of the decision that it was only an appeal of an interim order was lost, and looking forward, this ruling had dealt our case a serious blow.

At the time, however, the review was still to take place and we believed that the judge, who would hear our multiple arguments as to the apparent irrationality and meaningless public engagement programme undertaken by SANRAL in 2007 and 2008, would be hard pressed to give the system the thumbs up. We were still buoyed by the content of Judge Prinsloo's interdict ruling in April earlier in the year, the decision of which contained the merits of our arguments, and we were confident that we would again succeed.

OUTA believed that the facts presented showed that any minister of transport who was guided by reason and rationality would never have approved e-tolling. We were hoping by this stage, prior to Part B of the court challenge, due to be heard in November 2012, that someone in authority with courage, such as the finance minister, would now take a step back and from a position of strength advise Nazir Alli to make peace with the system's critics. He might also have cautioned him against mistakenly concluding that the Constitutional Court victory was sufficient to ensure success.

There is a very apt quote by the ancient and wise Marcus Tullius Cicero (born 3 January 106 BC), which describes our thinking in this space:

> *For there is but one essential justice which cements society, and one law which establishes this justice. This law is right reason, which is the true rule of all commandments and prohibitions. Whoever neglects this law, whether written or unwritten, is necessarily unjust and wicked.*

CHAPTER 13

Entering the political arena

As frustrating as it was to lose at the Constitutional Court, we didn't have time to dwell on the loss too intently. We were far behind in funds and needed to pay our mounting legal bills, but more so, we were committed to Part B of our application, which was the full review of the merits of our case. We remained confident that our arguments were sound and strong, and that we would win when we faced the court review of e-tolling set down for the Pretoria High Court in November 2012. As much as we were aware of the Constitutional Court's ruling and the possible damage it had done to our case, we had to remain positive and stick to our grounds.

Condolences for our loss in the Constitutional Court started to pour in on our Facebook site. People were reading this judgment as if it were the end of our case and the talk was that e-tolls was a done deal. 'It will forge ahead and the fight is surely over,' someone surmised to me. Unfortunately, this situation dampened the appetite for the public to continue their funding of OUTA.

We had to do a lot of damage control by convincing the public that Part B of the judicial review still lay ahead and that we were confident of the merits of our case. E-tolls was not a done deal and the fight was far from over.

The recently appointed new minister of transport, Ben Martins, was uplifted by the Constitutional Court ruling and under the direction of SANRAL started to talk the system up, speaking of 500 000 e-tags sold to the public and the system's launch that was about to happen.

So much was happening behind the scenes. Meetings were taking place beyond the public eye, all of which kept Marc, Paul and I very busy. We sought to engage again in meetings with the leading captains of South Africa's business industry and gave presentations to a number of boards about why the e-toll decision was flawed and why we needed their funds to continue with our legal challenge.

Foraging in political territory

There were also a few meetings that had nothing to do with the business world, and instead delved into something completely new for me: politics.

In early May 2012, our foray into the political arena began with a very pleasant meeting, facilitated by the DA and held at the Gautrain HQ, courtesy of Jack van der Merwe, at which Paul and I had the pleasure of meeting MEC for Transport in Gauteng Ismail Vadi.

It was a fascinating meeting with a lot of debate. The ultimate aim was to discuss possible solutions. Vadi was an interesting man. I liked his approach. It was conciliatory and exploratory. Vadi said he supported e-tolling because it was government policy. He did, however, say that he had questioned Nazir Alli as to the workability and practical implementation of the system, and Alli had convinced him that it would work very well as it has done in other parts of the world.

Vadi reflected his views along these lines: he was ... not sure he was totally sold on the plan. It was Nazir's baby and he guessed that if Nazir says the system will work, then he believed him. It is government policy after all ...

I got the impression from Vadi that he was not absolutely convinced by Nazir's explanation, but that he had no option but to support him. I surmised that doing otherwise would be political suicide.

Vadi spoke about the public transport plans for Gauteng and hinted that the ANC in Gauteng might contemplate other funding options for the freeway bonds. There was mention of an additional R0.15 on the fuel levy to lighten the load, but in combination with e-tolling – a hybrid model of part tolling and part fuel levy.

It was a positive meeting for us in that we had a sense that Vadi knew the issues and was prepared to listen and explore options. We responded that we were pleased the fuel levy was being mentioned, but that one couldn't be 'half pregnant' on e-tolling. It must either be implemented in full or scrapped as the costs of e-tolls were too exorbitant in its current format and reducing the e-toll tariff would increase the irrationality of the high cost of toll collections.

It was Vadi who suggested we should also meet with ANC Secretary General Gwede Mantashe. We agreed and Vadi duly arranged for us to meet with Mantashe a few weeks later.

Enter the unimaginable – Gwede Mantashe

The pleasantries of our foray into the politics of this matter came to an abrupt end.

Paul, Marc and I went to Luthuli House on 18 May 2012 and were ushered into the boardroom. I must say I had expected something more plush, but then realised that we were probably sitting in boardroom number 3 or 4. There were the remnants of a laid-out lunchtime meal and cold drinks on the side table, probably from a meeting that had ended around midday.

This was something I had noticed about meetings at all levels of government – the food laid on, be it sandwiches at tea time or a full lunch spread at noon. I imagined how the catering tenders were divvied out in the back rooms of the corridors of power. I couldn't get my mind around this habit of the provision of meals for meetings, which seemed to have become a norm in the public sector. It appeared to be an unwritten rule that if you were in a meeting, lunch would be laid on.

In came Gwede Mantashe, the secretary general of the ANC, and alongside him the premier of the Gauteng province, Nomvula Mokonyane.

This is going to be interesting, I thought, and the tone of the meeting was set from the outset. It was certainly not going to be conducted in the manner and tone that we had experienced with Vadi.

Mantashe allowed us to have our say first, and we explained the rationale of our case and concerns, providing him with input about the system's inefficiencies, its expenses, the sheer arrogance of SANRAL and its shocking public engagement process. Moreover, we highlighted the lack of reasonable alternatives, be they road options or public transport.

'But there are alternatives,' said Premier Mokonyane.

'With all due respect, Madame Premier,' Paul said, 'have you tried travelling through the suburbs during peak-hour traffic, with the faulty traffic lights and potholes? The highways were built to manage the congestion, not the suburban roads.'

'Well, then, you must pay for the highways,' Mokonyane intimated.

We were going nowhere quickly when Mantashe took over in his rather inevitably condescending manner.

'You businessmen. You want to use the nice new roads. You make a profit off those roads. And then you don't want to pay for them'

'This is not true. We do want to pay for the roads. What we don't want to do is pay double the price when there is a cheaper and easier way of doing it,' I said.

It was clear to us that Mantashe was not there to hear our views. He was there to lecture us. He questioned OUTA's right to question a government policy, which he clearly believed we had no right to do.

He said government had decided on the user-pays principle and why should some businessmen question that?

We managed to get our points across again and explained the irrationality of paying R1 in fees to collect R2 for the tarmac and that the system would be faced with massive administrative burdens, and that the people were angry because of a lack of consultation and transparency.

But Mantashe and Mokonyane weren't interested.

Mokonyane's logic that 'every other road off the freeway is an alternative road' was infuriating. I struggled to keep cool and knew she could see my facial expression of frustration.

I reiterated that these routes were not practical alternatives and the public transport alternatives were also non-existent for millions of freeway users.

'Have you ever tried to get from Roodepoort to Woodmead or the airport on a Tuesday morning without using the freeway?' I asked the premier. 'It would take you an extra two hours. That's if the traffic lights are working.'

'But that is still an alternative,' Mokonyane responded. 'It may take you longer, but it is an alternative.'

'Diverting traffic through the suburbs is not a wise thing to suggest. It will push up the accident rate and will place more pressure on these roads,' said Paul.

We explained that not only cars but heavy duty trucks would then be driven through the suburbs. This would lead to a faster degradation of the provincial and municipal roads and more people could be killed. Surely, as the premier of the province, this should concern her.

We cited the Spanish example of an overloaded propylene tanker that ploughed through a suburban campsite killing 220 people, all because the driver was told to avoid using the tolled routes. We also quoted the example of Premier Foods, a company whose management had in 2011 issued an instruction to their drivers that if they used the tolled roads, the company would not pay their toll fees. Obviously, the Premier Foods management quickly retracted this statement when they realised the story had broken on the news, attracting a lot of negative media attention.

But Premier Mokonyane disagreed with us. It was turning out to be one of those nonsensical debates that went round and round. It was best to cut the argument short and jump off the merry-go-round.

Then Mantashe changed tactic. He became more bullying and suggested that OUTA should back off. He implied that we should focus our efforts on running our businesses and leave government to run the country.

Then he looked straight at me and hinted that he might see fit to have a chat with Avis's principal, Barloworld, to see what they felt about my meddling in the affairs of government's business.

He made it clear that he had done his research and knew who Avis's owners were. I read this as a direct threat that pressure might be brought to bear against those organisations that support OUTA.

At the time I kept calm, but when we got into the car after the meeting I expressed my anger at this shocking behaviour. 'Stuff him,' I said to Paul. It gave me even greater resolve to go and fight this case.

I don't know if Mantashe ever did speak to my bosses. They never mentioned anything along these lines, but I wouldn't have been surprised if he or some other official within the upper echelons of government did.

However, even though that meeting didn't go well, we didn't want to give up on our quest to approach other government officials, hoping someone close to the top would lend a logical ear and understand our reasoning.

If you had asked anyone who they believed to be the most rational man in government at the time, the answer would more than likely have been Pravin Gordhan, the minister of finance.

Despite the fact that he had launched the Constitutional case against us, I believed that if we could just meet with him, we could explain how and why we had arrived at this situation. He was surely a reasonable man and if he heard the stark realities of our viewpoint, outside of the legal interpretations, we believed he might just understand both the irrationality and unworkability of the scheme.

About two months after the interdict, around late July 2012, I bumped into Imtiaz Patel, the head of Multichoice. I had got to know Imtiaz through Alistair Roper of Sun International. Avis was a long-time sponsor of the Nedbank Golf Challenge for which Supersport had the television rights. We'd met at a strategic planning discussion about the forthcoming golfing event, arranged by Sun International.

That day in July, Imtiaz and I chatted in brief and got onto the subject of e-tolls, which he explained he was dead against. He mentioned that he was a close friend of Pravin Gordhan and that during a recent dinner he had expressed his strong and principled views that he would never pay e-tolls to Gordhan. He reflected that it was an interesting evening during which a heated debate was generated on the matter.

I asked Imtiaz if he would try to set up an off-the-record, informal meeting with Gordhan, as I was sure he would be very understanding of our approach and reasoning. He said he would see what he could do.

Eight weeks and our appearance in the Constitutional Court went by with no response to the request. I sent an SMS to Imtiaz to check whether he had suggested the meeting to Pravin. He replied that he had done so twice and had not received any response to his request.

About six weeks later I got a call from Minister Gordhan's office. He came on the line and said, 'I hear you want to have a chat with me,' and proceeded to invite me to his offices in Pretoria to discuss the matter. Well, this is good, I thought, confident that Pravin would lend a logical ear and hear our side of the issues. Pravin had influence and maybe we could convince him to set up a series of meaningful engagement sessions with SANRAL and others, in search of a solution that would negate the need for litigation. Our debt was climbing and a halt to the mounting legal bills was top of mind for the committee. Surely Gordhan would see the impracticalities and unworkability of the scheme.

Two days before our meeting with Gordhan, I was chatting on the phone with Ari Seirlis from QASA and I told him I had a meeting with Gordhan at his offices. 'What a coincidence,' remarked Ari. 'So have I.' Or was it a coincidence? Was Gordhan planning to meet with OUTA's constituents on a separate basis in an attempt to divide us?

It turned out that Ari's meeting was scheduled for an hour before ours, also at Gordhan's offices at the Department of Finance in Church Street, Pretoria.

This was clearly not turning out to be the informal chat I had thought it would be. I checked with Marc and Paul and suggested the tentative arrangement for them to join me was now real. This was no coffee chat, it was business, and it was best I did not go alone.

Ari suggested that we meet in the corridors after his meeting with Gordhan for him to give us a sense of what we could expect.

But when Marc, Paul and I arrived at the offices of the Finance Ministry in Pretoria we were ushered into a meeting room, which is where we believed our meeting would take place. The door was closed and there we waited, not saying much for fear that our conversation was being overheard.

It was ten minutes after the scheduled start of our 11.00 am meeting when the facilitator entered and instructed us to move through to another room where the meeting would take place.

Ari could see what was happening. The officials clearly didn't want us to meet in the corridors, but he stalled his departure and we did bump into each other. We were ushered through, leaving us no time to chat. 'I'll call you after the meeting,' Ari said and I could hear there was concern in his voice that we were being played. 'Be cautious, Wayne,' was all he could say.

When we entered the main boardroom of the Ministry of Finance, all thoughts of an off-the-record coffee chat with the minister dissipated in a flash. There were eight people sitting around the table waiting for us, including Minister of Transport Ben Martins, Director-General of Transport George Mahlalela and other officials.

Thank goodness I had asked Marc and Paul to join me. It was all rather daunting and over-powering. Not in the least informal.

After the usual introductory pleasantries, Gordhan got into highlighting the issues at hand, explaining that government's role was to upgrade the infrastructure and address the need for integrated public transport systems. It also had a challenge to increase the country's credit ratings and ensure the sustainability of SANRAL. For these reasons the introduction of user charges and other revenue sources were required to prioritise public transport development.

He also made it clear that government realised the need for optimal levels of compliance and that e-tolling was not about behaviour change, but rather about the need to finance the freeway upgrade.

After he had laid down his rationale for government's view on the matter, he went straight to the point. 'So, what's your price?' he asked us.

I was taken aback. For a second I thought, is this a bribery discussion? But I quickly learnt that the discussion he was trying to have was about a negotiation on the tariffs, not on how much we were prepared to accept to back off.

'What is the level of the e-toll tariff that you will accept?' Gordhan asked. He came from a position of flexibility and asked that we should try to find each other at an e-toll tariff that was reasonable. He indicated that government was happy to look at reducing the rate and perhaps offsetting some of the reduction with other funding. 'But let's be reasonable,' he said, adding 'a figure of 10 cents would be too low, for example.'

'Our figure is zero,' I replied, adding, 'This is not about the rate. Our concern is the exorbitant costs of collection in relation to the capital costs of the scheme. In addition, we are concerned that the scheme is grossly inefficient and that in the context of the environment it will become unworkable. There are more efficient and existing policies to finance bonds, such as the fuel levy, and for these reasons, we will not accept e-tolls at any tariff.'

Paul joined the discussion. 'If you lower the tariff, the whole scheme becomes even more unsustainable because your cost of collection would become an even bigger proportion of your toll revenue,' Paul explained. 'It would take SANRAL much longer to pay off the bonds. This approach does not make any sense,' he said.

We explained to Gordhan that we weren't there to discuss a toll tariff reduction. We believed the e-toll scheme should be scrapped and the bonds should be serviced by the Treasury through the fuel levy collections. We explained that R0.10 additional to the fuel levy would raise the R2.2 billion required per annum to service the bonds and maintenance.

'We are fully aware that the e-toll tariffs of today will not be the price tomorrow,' I added. 'Increases slightly ahead of the Consumer Price Index [CPI of general inflation] will inflate the e-toll charges to extremely high levels over time.'

My days of chairing many a wage negotiation came to mind. I could see that Pravin was going to start at the current level of 30 cents, or even the prior 40 cents (which was the tariff before the R5.7 billion reallocation of funds) and that we might start at 5 cents and then whittle away from either position until we reached a figure that was acceptable to both parties. But that was never going to happen as our mandate to the public and our members was to not move one cent above zero cents per kilometre.

How foolish does he think we are? I thought.

'This is not about the e-toll tariff,' we reminded Gordhan. 'This is about the irrationality of the high costs of collection and a number of elements that make its implementation unlawful, unjust and extremely unpopular, which is why we are not prepared to accept a rate of one cent.'

He got the message – we were not going to be lured into this game.

We asked why the fuel levy could not be used to pay for the freeway upgrade, and Gordhan explained that government does not ring-fence money for specific projects that brought along other ramifications.

'Why not?' we asked. 'The road accident fund has money ring-fenced from the fuel levy, as has the inland pipeline. It's been done before. Why not for the GFIP? Even if you don't want to ring-fence the money you could easily give SANRAL an extra R2 billion a year to pay for the roads.' He was the finance minister after all. He made the decisions and motivations to reallocate funds to where the country needed these to be.

I recall Marc suggesting other options, one being 'Shadow Tolling', which is a combination of fuel levy funding channelled to an outsourced company (tendered) for road maintenance, accident reaction and bond repayment. It was far cheaper and negated the need for tags and all the inefficiencies that come along with it.

The tone of the discussion became condescending towards OUTA, with an attempt to discredit us and implications that we knew nothing about the figures and the costs of road financing, which was so wrong because we had exposed our understanding of these costs in our court papers.

We weren't 30 minutes into the discussion when Gordhan realised his strategy was not going to get traction. He indicated this in words along the lines of, 'Well then, we are wasting our time here. The e-tolling user-pays mechanism is government's chosen policy and if you don't want to work with us along these lines, this discussion is over.'

We agreed that we were not making any headway and the meeting was adjourned. As we left the building, I called Ari to find out how his discussion had gone. I put on the speaker phone and he proceeded to tell us that the minister had indicated that if he (QASA) resigned from OUTA, SANRAL would ensure that all the disabled members of society would be exempt from e-toll payments. He had been put under pressure to sign the agreement there and then, with the formalities to be dealt with in a few weeks.

Fortunately, Ari did not sign as the government officials had wished him to. He indicated to them that he wanted his lawyers to read through the agreement they had drafted and that he needed his board to also be convinced that the solution would be a practical and workable one for people with disabilities.

Ari told us that Gordhan was of the belief that the solution was an easy one to achieve and that QASA should trust them to resolve the matter with speed. It was clear that the disabled community's stance against government had become an embarrassment for it and it wanted nothing more at that stage than to see QASA break away from OUTA. I envisaged the media headline government would love to see: 'Disabled community turns its back on OUTA' – which would have been manna from heaven for SANRAL and a blow to OUTA.

Fortunately, Ari's years of wisdom and cautious approach paid off. As it turned out, SANRAL was unable to provide an exemption solution for individuals with disabilities, and some two years after this meeting with Gordhan, it was no closer to being able to implement acceptable solutions for the various categories of people with disabilities. In fact, QASA had to ask the human rights commissioner to summon SANRAL to its offices in order to seek its commitment to finding a solution.

SANRAL's problem was that the system was designed to have e-tags linked to vehicles and their respective licence plates. It could not be applied in the case of individuals, which was QASA's need. Most disabled members of society relied on the goodwill of others to transport them around and their exemption status could only be achieved if the disabled individual's tag could be used to override a tag that was allocated to a vehicle. SANRAL's scheme simply couldn't accommodate this requirement.

A few days after our session at Minister Gordhan's office, on 2 October 2012, OUTA met with Kgalema Motlanthe's Inter Ministerial Committee (IMC) once again at the Union Buildings. OUTA's entire membership was present, except for Ari Seirlis. Clif Johnston of SANCU was there, as was Jeff Osborne from the Retail Motor Industry, Michael Tatalias from SATSA, Gary Ronald from the AA, who was listed as a supporting member of OUTA, along with Marc, Paul and I. George Corbett, the operations director of Europcar and Mike Sherwood from Standard Bank were also in attendance in their capacity as national executive committee members of SAVRALA.

Gordhan quickly assumed control of the meeting and attempted to apply his strategy of getting one or more of our members to agree to coming in at a low price. There were more members of OUTA present and Gordhan probably thought that we hadn't filled them in on our earlier meeting with him.

After explaining his rationale that e-tolling was government's selected mechanism, he believed that our members were being unreasonable to reject it. He then proceeded to ask every member of OUTA, 'What price would you be prepared to introduce e-tolling at?'

After I had said 'zero' and began to explain why, he cut me short and moved on to the others. Looking at Gary Ronald from the AA, he asked the same question and Gary replied 'nothing'. This was repeated by all our members.

Gordhan expressed his frustration and, turning to the deputy president, he indicated that OUTA's presence in the IMC process was taking them nowhere. We were wasting his time.

This was the third IMC meeting I had attended. Nazir Alli, the CEO of SANRAL, was conspicuously absent from our previous meetings, but this time he was present.

The deputy president allowed us to explain our rationale again. One of our main gripes expressed was that one of our members, SAVRALA, had negotiated with SANRAL throughout 2011 to seek solutions to the many administrative problems the system would impose on our members. We believed there had to be a more effective and efficient alternative for our members. The e-toll model was too cumbersome, inefficient and costly to implement and came with many negative consequences to the industry. Motlanthe sensed that a more conciliatory and inclusive approach by SANRAL at the time might have helped and sincerely believed that a solution could still be sought with SANRAL. He then suggested that the SAVRALA members have an urgent meeting with Alli to once again seek a solution. With all the recent court action, he suggested that SANRAL might be better positioned to address our concerns by meeting with us to discuss a way around the matters that had frustrated the SAVRALA members.

We agreed to meet. Alli said he was a busy man and the only time he had was that same afternoon. It was a case of us having to fit in with him and his schedule and the meeting would also have to be at his offices. What arrogance, I thought, but we were obliged to indicate our willingness to cooperate. For Alli it seemed it was a case of asserting his power over the situation.

Strange as it was, Alli and I had never actually met in person until that day in his offices at Val-de-Grace, east of Pretoria. We certainly knew of each other and had seen each other across the courtrooms and in media sessions, but we had never actually spoken and been formally introduced.

Only the SAVRALA car rental members attended this meeting, Mark Corcoran, Keri Kirsten (who was the recently elected president of SAVRALA since I had vacated the chair after my resignation from Avis in July), Mike Sherwood and George Corbet.

On arrival at SANRAL's offices that afternoon, we were directed to sit in one of their boardrooms where Alli proceeded to assert more of his power over us by keeping us waiting for over an hour. After enquiring where he was, I was about to leave when he decided to grace us with his presence.

Alli was angry with us and for the first time, I was able to witness how he expressed and managed his anger and frustration. The team that sat in front of him was largely responsible for his e-toll headaches, having interdicted his launch and generated so much negative exposure to the scheme.

He started by asking all OUTA members present why we had turned down his out-of-court settlement offer, which was extended to us a week previously.

Yes, it was true that Pieter Conradie, our attorney at Cliffe Dekker Hofmeyr had received a letter from Werksmans, SANRAL's attorneys at noon on Friday, 21 September 2012. It was a short and straightforward offer of a refund of OUTA's full legal costs incurred to date if we agreed to withdraw in full from litigation against SANRAL on the e-toll matter. An answer had to be provided within three days, by noon on Monday, 24 September, which was a public holiday – Heritage Day – failing which the offer was off the table.

The offer was discussed with Marc, Paul and our lawyers and was deemed as not being sincere in that it gave us no time to consider it or call a meeting to discuss this with our committee members, most of whom were away for the long weekend break.

We notified SANRAL's attorneys, Werksmans, that we would need more time to discuss and consider the offer with our members, and if indeed SANRAL was sincere about this offer, it would grant this extension. It was not granted, so we never pursued the matter further.

We sensed Alli was trying to create dissension among the OUTA ranks on that day of 2 October 2012 by informing our members of a matter that he had gathered was not shared with all. I was having none of it and explained to our team the nature of the offer, which our attorneys advised us against. I looked at Alli and indicated that if the offer were genuine, would SANRAL extend the offer so that we could thoroughly consider it with the team? 'No,' replied Alli, it was too late. Discussion closed.

Then Alli started to hand out pamphlets that were printed by Avis in Portugal, explaining how they were working with the Portuguese National Roads Agency to implement their new e-tolling system into the car rental industry. Again, he was trying to imply that this system was being accepted around the world by car rental companies. So why is this industry here in South Africa fighting the scheme?

I responded that the conditions of implementation, the administrative process, vehicle licensing conditions, public consultation and other factors applied in the Portuguese situation had no bearing on or similarity to ours here in South Africa. Just because something works in Europe doesn't mean it will operate with the same efficiency under our different conditions at home.

As it turned out, we learnt some six months later that the Portuguese system was in trouble. Some eighteen months after its launch this scheme was fraught with impractical processes that made the collection process too costly and onerous. It was also rejected by a high percentage of the population and compliance could not be enforced.[15]

I couldn't help but think that it was quite strange that Alli and I had never connected face to face prior to this day, and we never connected or spoke to each other again thereafter (or not, at least, until the time of writing of this book). I would have imagined that the leader of an organisation under attack by its critics would have picked up the phone and said, 'Hey, Wayne, Paul, Marc, let's meet somewhere neutral and see if we can understand each other better and find a solution to our differences.' But it never happened.

It seemed to me that Alli always came from a position and attitude that said SANRAL had the power of government behind it and that it would wear us down. Attrition through law-fare appeared to be their strategy and they knew very well we were struggling with funds to pay our lawyers. There was no constructive or conciliatory approach to our differences.

We refused to be bulldozed or threatened out of this challenge. As it turned out, we were unable to find any solution on that Tuesday afternoon at SANRAL's offices. The Tolplan representative sent us a one-page summary of the meeting notes, which highlighted some of the rehashed technical difficulties discussed over the last two years, and no follow-up meetings were set.

This was another stalemate session with no real attempt to find each other. Neither party was willing to back down on its main issues and we left a seething Alli behind at his plush SANRAL offices. My impression was that he intended to do all he could to see the demise of OUTA.

CHAPTER 14

Changing dynamics and mounting public anger

■ ■ ■ ■ ■ ■ ■ ■ ■ ■ ■ ■ ■

It was October 2012. Over a month had passed since the Constitutional Court had set aside the interdict. SANRAL's lawyers had sworn that tolling would go ahead two weeks after the Constitutional Court judgment. Nothing happened.

We had no time to dwell on the delay, as Part B of our application for the court to review the e-toll decision was around the corner. This was the big case, the one that we hoped would decide whether the process that was followed by SANRAL and the Department of Transport in initiating e-tolling was legal or not.

Just like the period leading up to the interdict, there was another scramble by government to rectify, amend and push through new regulations and clean up the legislation for e-tolls to commence. It was quite astounding to us that even at this late stage, nearly two years after SANRAL had announced the first of a few launch dates in early 2011, the regulatory environment for e-tolling was still not in place.

Once again the atmosphere and debate on the e-toll in Gauteng (and around the country) was becoming heated. The amended Transport Laws and Related Matters Amendment Bill was tabled before Parliament in October 2012.

Problems with the bill were obvious and the South African National Consumer Commission raised concerns that it appeared to be giving SANRAL permission to sidestep the National Credit Act.

DA's transport spokesperson, Ian Ollis, called for an investigation. He said the legislation did not comply with the requirement that draft versions must first be sent to Parliament for input. Transport portfolio chairperson Ruth Bhengu said she would investigate the regulations for the seeming non-compliance with legislative requirements.

A few weeks later, the bill was withdrawn. Without the bill in place e-tolling could not begin.

Then, on 26 October 2012, new tariffs were announced. Allowing two weeks for the public to comment on them, a rather complicated array of five different tariff structures, which had within them additional discounts for time of day use and new capped tariffs for the previously uncapped larger vehicle categories (trucks), were introduced. The gazette also included previously unpublished e-toll exemptions for registered taxis, public transport, scholar transport and emergency vehicles belonging to the Gauteng provincial government, the city of Johannesburg, city of Tshwane and Ekurhuleni.

The Road Freight Association (RFA) represented the major trucking and logistics companies, many of which were owned by the main conglomerates in South Africa. They had been opposed to e-tolling and it was important for SANRAL to win them over. Their respective boards decided to find some middle ground and SANRAL's win came when they agreed to apply a cap to the tariffs for trucks. The RFA announced they would now accept the e-toll decision as they believed the new tariff structure would be cheaper for them in terms of conducting their business than if an increase to the fuel levy were introduced.

Naturally, SANRAL seized on the RFA's decision and published press statements that gave the impression that business was coming around to the idea that e-tolling was the right way to go.

The RFA's agreement came with conditions that an independent Transport Regulator would be appointed and that no future freeways planned for Gauteng would be tolled. The Department of Transport agreed.

At the time of publishing of this book, nearly three years after the RFA agreed to the Department of Transport's conditions, the authorities were still no closer to the appointment of a Transport Regulator. This was often typical of government negotiations, agreeing to do something and then not carrying out its commitments. As things would pan out, two years after agreement to the e-toll conditions, the RFA would renounce its support for the e-toll scheme at Premier Makhura's e-toll panel engagement sessions in September 2014.

By the final quarter of 2012, COSATU's Zwelinzima Vavi came out even more strongly in his opposition to the system.

'There won't be an easy ride for government. We're consulting Nedlac (National Economic Development and Labour Council) for our notice to be still used for the purpose of protesting,' Vavi said in the *Saturday Star* on 27 October 2012.

Vavi was talking of strikes and a 'drive slow' on the highway where even bicycles and tractors would take part. Government realised that this time around, it could not get away with publishing the e-toll tariffs for comment without holding public hearings on the matter.

The Department of Transport then published the dates for three meetings, one in Kempton Park on the East Rand, one in Pretoria at the CSIR (Council for Scientific and Industrial Research) and the final session in Sunninghill. Why the Department of Transport and SANRAL had neglected to include Soweto and Tembisa when scheduling these meetings was strange to us.

Marc and I attended all three sessions to observe the dynamics and were impressed that the Department of Transport, along with the Treasury and SANRAL, were all represented at the highest levels.

On Tuesday, 13 November 2012, in Kempton Park the 60 or so people who attended the first public hearings expressed in no uncertain terms that they were angry. The discussions got out of hand and half the room walked out. When the facilitator said that people were not allowed to voice objections to e-tolling and could only comment on the tariffs, tempers boiled over. I leant over to Marc and said, 'There is nothing wrong with people expressing that the tariffs are too high, by 100%.'

By the next day, the radio news broadcasts had featured the Kempton Park meeting and more people became aware of the final two public hearings. We featured the venue and times of the next two meetings on our website and in our discussion with the media, encouraging the public to attend these sessions. The number of public attendees increased substantially, with over 400 at each and only standing room available. The heat against SANRAL had been turned up.

These meetings in Pretoria and Sunninghill went on for nearly four hours as person after person stood up to have their say. Virtually every statement made was an expression of disgust, outrage, anger or frustration at SANRAL and the government about the e-toll scheme.

At the Pretoria meeting held at the CSIR conference centre, Yusuf Abramjee, the station manager at 702 Talk Radio, gave his input early into the public feedback session. It was a moving overview of his opinion that e-tolling was a bad choice and that he could never subscribe to the scheme.

To me the most touching statement that night was made by a young man who stood up and simply said, 'Mr Alli, I want you to know that I am poor. Yes, I own a car which I have worked hard to earn and I have to travel on these freeways to get to work. I am also a law-abiding citizen, but I will never, ever pay these e-tolls. It is a principle that I will stand by and am prepared to go to jail for.' The hair stood up on my arms. I was moved and the crowd cheered him. I went in search of him to thank him for expressing his civil courage after the session but I couldn't find him.

'It really feels like they have made up their minds. It feels like we are fighting a losing battle,' Pretoria resident Cornelius Parkin told a journalist from the South African Press Association.

On the third evening of these engagement sessions in Sunninghill, the officials from SANRAL and the national Treasury were drowned out by the crowd who heckled them.

One man shouted out: 'This government does not listen. Government listens to violence,' suggesting that maybe it was time to destroy the gantries.

A few months later, in early 2013, I met with a supplier to the e-toll system who was present at an internal SANRAL management meeting shortly after the Sunninghill public engagement session. He said that one of the SANRAL managers commented on the hearings, saying, 'If those meetings are an expression of how the public feel about e-toll, then we are in big trouble.' How right he was.

SANRAL decided it needed to get some positive spin and media coverage on the issue, as it was being drowned by volumes of negative talk on virtually all media platforms. It thus decided to hold a media conference and tour at its state-of-the-art e-toll Central Operations Centre in Midrand to demonstrate how the system would work.

Project Manager Alex van Niekerk said that in the past few months more than two million vehicles had been monitored on the highways as part of a live testing phase and over 500 000 e-tags had been distributed.

While all of this was happening we were furiously preparing for the upcoming case to be heard in the North Gauteng High Court by Acting Judge Louis Vorster from 26 to 28 November 2012.

CHAPTER 15

The Judicial Review – Part B of OUTA's application

▬ ▬ ▬ ▬ ▬ ▬ ▬ ▬ ▬ ▬ ▬ ▬ ▬ ▬ ▬ ▬

*As one judge said to another judge: be just. And if you can't be just,
be arbitrary.*
  – William S. Burroughs, novelist

Right from the beginning of our legal journey we had called for SANRAL
to disclose its contract with Electronic Toll Collection (ETC) so that
we could see the real figures of toll collection. Our request was simply
ignored by SANRAL.

By the time we filed our supplementary affidavit in July 2012 we had
been provided with SANRAL's and the minister of transport's record of
its e-toll decision-making process.

At that point we had this immense pressure to respond to the
Constitutional Court appeal while at the same time reading through all
this documentation to find new information.

SANRAL had sent us 5 280 pages of information in sixteen lever-arch
files. A further five lever-arch files came from the minister of transport.
I imagined Nazir Alli saying, 'Let's drown them in paper,' as they compiled the files for us, probably thinking that we would never take the time
to scour the thousands of pages. It was an overly pressured time for us,
and SANRAL's seemingly clear strategy of attrition through 'lawfare'
was taking its toll on us.

We tried to see the fuller picture behind government's decision. The
documents showed a few things, including that SANRAL and the minister of transport had allowed the 2010 Soccer World Cup to become an
overarching factor that forced the public participation processes to be
conducted hastily, in our view rendering it meaningless and inadequate.
What was interesting about the tolling proposal initially laid before
Minister of Transport Jeff Radebe at the time was that SANRAL had
attached some briefing notes on a presentation it was going to give the

next day in September 2006. The notes sent to us indicated that there were three pages in all but we only received pages marked 'one of three' and 'two of three'. Page three of three was missing.

The two pages we did have sketched out a need for road upgrades, the road congestion and traffic counts. The notes went on to cover Intelligent Transport Systems, the need to have electronic billboards on the side of the highways to inform people about traffic conditions, as well as electronic monitoring.

There was no mention in this document of how the upgrade was meant to be funded. Following the briefing notes was a presentation to the minister, which contained 14 pages out of the 27 in the original record. None of the pages in the presentation we had disclosed any information relating to how the freeway upgrade would be paid for.

We requested that page three of three of the briefing notes be provided to us, as well as the rest of the presentation.

Some weeks later, pages 15 to 27 were sent to us. These contained details of a tolling proposal, which now implied that the decision to toll was punted from an early stage, as far back as September 2006. There was no mention of other funding methods considered for the road upgrades, and only reflected that e-tolling was the method of funding to be used. We found this strange as we believed that all alternative funding mechanisms needed to be presented in order for the minister to apply his mind to the decision.

We were also told that 'page three of three' did not exist and SANRAL sent back to us a new document, which contained the same briefing notes, but this time they were numbered as 'page one of two' and 'page two of two'. Clearly, the numbering of the pages had suddenly been changed. This was not the format of the original three-page document. I thought at the time, how blatantly arrogant is this behaviour, to simply modify the documents and expect us to sit back and accept this nonsense. Our ailing trust in SANRAL was becoming more justified by the day.

What these documents showed us was that government had for years been hiding from the public the fact that this upgrade was always going to be a tolling project for SANRAL. There was never going to be a genuine approach to consider the fuel levy or any other funding mechanism. The documents raised serious questions and gave a completely different picture to what was presented to the Constitutional Court about the fuel levy having been seriously considered.

From that initial contact with the minister of transport in 2006, all the way through to the so-called public participation process in October

2007, there were a series of communications between Minister Radebe and SANRAL, which spoke almost solely about the pressures of the 2010 Soccer World Cup. They mentioned time being tight and that it was imperative that the freeway upgrade project got underway. It was clear that time for the public participation process was limited and there was little chance it was going to be done meaningfully.

The newspapers showed the objective facts of this 'public consultation': a notice to toll the N1, N3, N4 and N12 was published in a single edition of five newspapers on one day in October 2007. Some of these advertisements were placed in the business section of the newspaper and one was even *hidden* in the international business section. Normally, if one were to attempt to reach a wide section of the public, adverts of this nature would be placed in the general and most widely read sections of the newspaper. A government gazette was also issued.

However, there was nothing in these notifications of SANRAL's intent to toll the Gauteng freeways, which indicated the cost of the project as a whole. Neither did SANRAL provide the indicative tariff of tolling.

We also discovered that there were only 30 (yes, *thirty*) responses from the public to these notices, of which one was a petition that contained 54 signatures. SANRAL seemed to take pleasure in reflecting that it had received 84 responses from the public, as if to imply that this was a lot and that these were dealt with meaningfully.

The notice to toll the R21 was only published four months later, in April 2008, as it took time to transfer this important road linking Tshwane and the East Rand from the Gauteng Regional Authority to SANRAL.

This notification was only published in two newspapers, to which only *two* responses were received. It was in every respect an abject public participation process.

From this information we claimed in our supplementary founding affidavits that SANRAL had no intention of properly or meaningfully engaging with the public as it was supposed to do in accordance with the Constitution of the Republic of South Africa, most notably section 195 in Chapter 10, which reads:

195. Basic values and principles governing public administration
1. Public administration must be governed by the democratic values and principles enshrined in the Constitution, including the following principles:

a. **A high standard of professional ethics must be promoted and maintained.**
b. **Efficient, economic and effective use of resources must be promoted.**
c. Public administration must be development-oriented.
d. Services must be provided impartially, fairly, equitably and without bias.
e. **People's needs must be responded to, and the public must be encouraged to participate in policy-making.**
f. **Public administration must be accountable.**
g. **Transparency must be fostered by providing the public with timely, accessible and accurate information.**
h. Good human-resource management and career-development practices, to maximise human potential, must be cultivated.
i. Public administration must be broadly representative of the South African people, with employment and personnel management practices based on ability, objectivity, fairness, and the need to redress the imbalances of the past to achieve broad representation.

The bold clauses above are those we strongly believe have not been lived up to by SANRAL and the authorities during the e-toll process. It was also clear to us that SANRAL was left with no time to draw out the public participation process as it was necessary to begin with the construction of the project to be ready in time for the Soccer World Cup.

Another extremely important aspect to our case was that the record showed the failure of Minister Radebe to consider the costs of e-toll collection, which we had alleged in the interdict application. He had never replied to these allegations. We could find nothing in the record that suggested what the costs of the e-toll collection process of this project would be. We maintained that this record had never been placed in front of the minister for him to consider. Nor had he asked for it and therefore he hadn't considered it.

SANRAL and the Treasury had stated in the Constitutional Court hearings that e-tolling was conceived because they wanted to relieve congestion on the Gauteng freeway network. But through the papers we discovered the company hired as toll consultants had also said that the GFIP network upgrade would only ease congestion for a few years at most.

This was due to a well-researched phenomenon known as 'induced congestion', which happens when there are insufficient and unattractive alternatives to road use for commuting. This in turn merely induces more people to commute by road over time, and so the original state of congestion arises again in a few years' time. We made very telling points about this matter in our papers.

Despite the fact that we had asked SANRAL in our applying affidavit to provide us with a full copy of the tendered contracts with ETC, this was not provided to us. We again asked for the original ETC contract and again our request was ignored.

We continued preparing our papers with great hope and confidence for the review in November 2012.

Eventually, we had to bring an urgent application to compel SANRAL to deliver the ETC contract and their dry run of the system, which Alex van Niekerk had referred to during the recent media tour of their system.

We wanted access to that information as it would enable us to see how many cars were really making use of the freeway, from which we could work out how much revenue SANRAL planned to generate from the public. But of course they weren't going to give us that information despite the fact that it was not sensitive or secret by nature at all. To us it seemed that SANRAL just loved being difficult since it never acceded to many of our requests and certainly wasn't going to make our lives easy.

Instead of proceeding to oppose our application SANRAL offered us the ETC contract on the basis that we would sign a non-disclosure agreement to keep the contract from being shared with the public or any third party.

We only had a few days to answer and were faced with the decision: do we now go into another urgent court interdict process to try to get an order to compel SANRAL to disclose the contract, taking the risk that we lose that application and not get it at all? Or, do we get the contract into our hands, but with a compromise on our side that we could not disclose it to third parties?

We made the call to obtain the contract and agreed to sign the confidentiality agreement. Besides, we were out of money and had no funds for further litigation.

We decided, though, that a third party didn't mean the courts. We believe SANRAL wanted us to get the contract, take a look at it, but not use it in our court papers. We decided to include the pertinent findings in our papers, which did not impress them. They sent us letters saying we had given an undertaking not to disclose the findings to third parties, and asking why we had now included these in our court papers. In our opinion, we had every right to do so and nothing we had included was that sensitive to suggest that it should remain a secret. Irrespective of what SANRAL wanted, we were going to use them in court.

What the ETC contract showed was that the cost of toll collection, rather than being R17 billion over 24 years, as disclosed in the Constitutional Court, would be closer to R30.5 billion. It showed that the contract was much more expensive than SANRAL was making it out to be and it gave new impetus to our argument that it was an irrational scheme. It was, in our opinion, so expensive that it should never have been chosen. Had these costs seriously been explained to and considered by the minister, he would have been hard pressed to clarify how he could rationally believe this made sense.

It is important to note that these discoveries were going down in our preparation for the review after the Constitutional Court decision and judgment was made on 20 September 2012 to set aside our interdict. The content of that judgment indicated to us that we were going to have a hard time convincing the High Court of our argument that the high costs of collection showed the scheme to be irrational. Well, now we had that information, but it was provided to us too late to be raised in the Constitutional Court hearing.

We needed to focus heavily on this point in our papers, as it was now a serious matter that ought to sit in appointed Acting Judge Louis Vorster's mind when weighing up his decision.

We certainly couldn't believe that R30.5 billion out of an estimated R110 billion e-toll revenue at today's tariffs (i.e., 27%) could be construed as rational. This was a big point for us. In addition, when compared to the R17.9 billion capital costs of the freeway upgrade, excluding the e-toll system capital costs, the toll collection costs were outrageously high.

The input we provided, using the content of the ETC contract in our replying affidavit, had clearly embarrassed SANRAL. As a result, it had to act fast and decided to file an additional affidavit, which basically said that we were interpreting the information in the contract incorrectly. 'A mathematical error,' as SANRAL put it. But the calculations and explanations provided in its additional affidavit still did not measure up with what was in the contract provided to us.

We prepared our arguments for the review and remained confident that we also had a compelling case on the merits of SANRAL's inadequate public consultation for such a huge scheme. It had therefore failed in its constitutional obligations to the public and this, in turn, made the scheme unlawful.

We remained concerned that the 'condonation' issue relating to the lateness of our application was going to be a problem, but felt that our case on the unlawfulness of SANRAL's conduct was so compelling that this would override the condonation argument, as we had done with Judge Prinsloo in the interdict hearings.

Furthermore, after all the affidavits had been filed, Minister Radebe had still not indicated to us that he had considered the costs of collection. That matter was a slam dunk and when one weighed up all the facts and arguments we had prepared for the judge, we were confident leading up to our court review date of 26 November 2012. Then, four days before the review itself, suddenly an affidavit signed by Minister Radebe, saying that he had considered the costs of e-tolling before signing the declaration of the intent to toll, was given to us. We believed their legal team had read our arguments and realised they were in trouble on that point. So, hey presto, all of a sudden, they were able to produce an affidavit saying that in fact he had considered the costs.

Radebe said that he did consider the costs in the 2006 proposal. But when one reads the proposal, the costs of e-toll collection are incomprehensible. It was impossible to tell what the toll collections would be from what he read. All this proposal stated was that toll collection costs and maintenance would be R200 million per year.

There was no indication of what budget would go towards maintenance and what would go towards the collection process. The maintenance implied road repairs, potholes, barriers, etc. Yet the toll collection costs had little to do with road maintenance and everything to do with the management of the entire e-toll system.

After all the papers were filed, the date of the review rolled in. Once again it was an impressive list of legal minds. Eight senior counsel made up the sixteen advocates who walked into the Pretoria High Court. David Unterhalter still represented SANRAL, Jeremy Gauntlett appeared for the Treasury and Vincent Malaka appeared for the Department of Transport.

Our original senior counsel, Alistair Franklin, had notified us of a previous case booked in his diary some months earlier, which he could not escape and therefore he could not represent us in this Part B of our application. Our attorney replaced Franklin with Advocate Mike Maritz SC, whom we had met on a few occasions in preparation for the court review.

On the first day in court Maritz had the stage. He highlighted all of our key points – the lack of public consultation, the Soccer World Cup pressures, the irrational costs of the collection process and the minister's lack of consideration of these costs.

Day two and Unterhalter stepped forward. He said it was too late to put a stop to the system.

'Tolling can't be undone. People drive on the upgraded roads every day. We are going to fund it through tolls. It has been decided,' he said.

He claimed the public knew the roads would be tolled, and they only protested once tariffs had been published. He said there had been 132 media reports since 2007 discussing e-tolling. What he didn't say, though, was that these media reports made references to the road upgrade and not to the fact that these roads were being financed by means of an elaborate electronic tolling and gantry scheme that would cost billions of rands to administer.

On the final day in court Unterhalter kept on interrupting Maritz, threatening him and OUTA with punitive costs if he did not stop saying that SANRAL had acted dishonestly in its dismal public engagement process. Maritz responded heatedly saying he would not be intimidated.

Maritz finished off by insisting that the notices to toll published in the newspapers were so fragmented that you would have had to put them all together like a puzzle to understand the magnitude of what was happening.

Judge Vorster reserved judgment, not giving a date when it would be delivered.

One day after court hearings were concluded on 28 November, COSATU announced its decision to proceed with its 'drive-slow' protests. Among the hundreds of marchers who moved through the Johannesburg CBD were a number of business owners who felt the roads would cost them far too much money. COSATU said it wanted to show that it could be a thorn in the side of government on this issue, which would have a devastating impact on the poor.

A week later the 'drive-slow' took place on the highways, with vehicles moving at less than 20 kilometres per hour. Passengers and drivers hung out of car windows, hooting and holding up banners. The traffic congestion was horrendous.

Judge Vorster's judgment

Just three days after the drive-slow protests, in the middle of December 2012, Acting Judge Louis Vorster was ready to give his judgment.

I recall sitting at my computer on the evening of 12 December, typing the two press statements we needed to have. One for the win and one in case we lost, just as I had done for the interdict judgment.

I wrote the speech for the 'win' scenario. It was quick and easy to write, including excerpts from the interdict media statement, from which similar sentiments and feelings would be expressed.

Then, as I began to lay down the thoughts and expressions for the 'lose' speech scenario, I found it more difficult to write. It was almost impossible to rationalise a scenario of losing on each and every argument we had put forward. I thought it would be very unlikely for a judge to rule against us. It was late, I was tired and thought to myself, there is no need to prepare this speech. We simply can't lose.

How wrong I was. It was bad news for OUTA. In an eighteen-page judgment Vorster dismissed our argument that SANRAL had not consulted with the public, saying that the notices in the newspapers and the *Government Gazette* were adequate enough to inform people.

Vorster said: 'It is clear from the Constitutional Court judgment that the capital costs of the proposed toll scheme as well as the operating costs and likely tariff to be imposed are matters which are not open for public participation by potential interested or affected persons, as those matters fall within the domain of the executive government as a matter of financial policy.'

We were shocked to hear Judge Vorster making reference to the Constitutional Court's findings. Judge Vorster seemed to read the Constitutional Court decision to mean that when you come to the question of revenue raising for infrastructure projects, the court cannot go there. His judgment implies that decisions like these are reserved solely for the executive.

Vorster interpreted the Constitutional Court to mean that it's the government, its executive and it alone, that decides and considers matters of cost.

However, our interpretation of the Constitutional Court judgment was that it had only been made in reference to interim orders. The Constitutional Court judges had been looking at the court interdict that had been granted and specifically said they were not going to make a decision on the issues that the court review would be addressing.

In our view, it was a shocking judgment, but what made it worse was that Vorster slapped OUTA with all the full costs of the case, effectively saying that this civil action organisation must not only pay its own legal expenses but also those of the government departments that it was challenging.

I was gobsmacked. Marc, Paul and I looked at each other in amazement, checking with each other to see if we had all heard the same thing. We were utterly shocked.

When a civil action group or individual comes to the court to press for a ruling on a constitutional matter and citizens' rights against the state and loses, there is strong legal authority that each party should be ordered to pay its own costs. In some cases the government has even been ordered to pick up both parties' costs. The reason why courts will hesitate to award the state's legal bills against a civil society entity in a constitutional litigation matter is because this tends to have a chilling effect on people and civil action groups who are very necessary in society to ensure that the public's rights are protected.

Judge Vorster just said 'costs against'. His understanding of the Constitutional Court judgment on costs seems to have been that he had no discretion in the matter and that the moment he ruled against OUTA, he was compelled to order us to pay the costs. We believe this interpretation was wrong. The Constitutional Court judgment, in our view, indicated that the costs of Part A (the interdict) and the Constitutional Court appeal would follow the costs order of the review. In other words, whatever the costs order in the review matter would apply also to the two earlier court hearings. The Constitutional Court tends to bend over backwards to say that in a constitutional matter each party pays its own costs. Thus we believe that Judge Vorster retained the discretion to order that each party had to pick up its own costs, which then would have applied to all court case costs from inception.

I was still sifting through the words of the harsh judgment in my mind when the entire courtroom of journalists moved towards us, seeking our comments and thoughts on the blow that had been dealt to us by Judge Vorster. I was hoping they would first go over and get comment from Nazir Alli and his team, but not so. The unwritten rule was to seek input from the losing side first, knowing that the winners would linger on and give them all the airtime they needed. They scrambled over without giving me a chance to gather my thoughts.

The blow had been hard. I had no time to move out into the corridor of the courtroom and was literally surrounded by the journalists. Pinned against the wood-panelled wall inside the courtroom with microphones and recorders jammed in front of me, the 30 or so journalists wanted to capture the sensation of the moment.

I reflected that it was a sad day for South Africa's democracy and we would need to study the judgment in greater detail before we could respond. 'What about the costs order?' a journalist asked me. I responded to the effect that we had no idea where we would get the money to pay their legal fees when we hadn't sufficient funds to settle our own legal costs.

'Will you appeal this judgment?' was the next question. 'I'm not sure,' I replied. 'We will have to take a view as a committee and speak to our legal team first.' After deflecting a few more questions into the 'let's await our full and detailed assessment of the judgement', I was given some space to leave the courtroom. Of all the emotions I had experienced throughout this challenge to date, at this stage I was at an all-time emotional low and was simply drained of all energy and thoughts about the case.

On my way out I glanced over to the other side of the courtroom to witness the government team celebrating its victory with hugs and cheers as Alli, his deportment victorious, waited for the journalists to come over. I read the next day of how he lauded the good judgment of Vorster, throwing it in our faces, and that of the DA's Jack Bloom, saying we had no respect for the Constitutional Court. He then pushed aside journalists, refusing to say when the system would launch when asked to indicate a date.

Marc and Paul were waiting in the corridor outside for me. We were miffed and still in shock as we walked down the stairs and out of the North Gauteng High Court, trying to understand and digest what had just happened.

In the court passages, our legal team expressed disgust with the judgment and said we must try to relax and not get too hung up on the ruling for now. Let's take the weekend off and meet the following week to digest the judgement, they suggested. Relax? Easier said than done. It was the most disheartening weekend of my life.

We met the following week as a committee to decide on the way forward. We all wanted to walk away and not appeal. We were 'e-tolled out' and broke. On top of that, our SAVRALA members were being placed under immense pressure by their various government-linked board members to let this matter go. With the Constitutional Court ruling and now Vorster's shocking judgment against us, we all agreed, if we can get out now, we should.

But, there was one problem. We had government's massive costs order slapped against us. We estimated that if our costs were in the R10 million range, the cost of its three legal teams with multiple senior counsel was in the range of between R20 million and R30 million. Some said much more.

We also knew that it would be extremely difficult to convince the public to continue donating to our legal costs, now that our case was defeated, unless of course we decided to appeal and gave compelling reasons for our need to appeal. Our debate and discussion with our committee and legal team also highlighted that it was right to appeal the judgment for two reasons: the first being that there were a number of shocking misrepresentations and rulings passed by Vorster; and, secondly, the costs order was a gross oversight on his part. Our backs were against the wall and we had no option but to appeal.

Ironically, had Judge Vorster not slapped the costs order against us, or if SANRAL had stood up and said it believed that each party should pick up its own legal expenses, OUTA would more than likely have packed up and closed its offices by Christmas of 2012. Clearly, SANRAL could never bring itself to such conciliatory thinking. Neither did it contemplate that our fight would have to continue on the basis of having Judge Vorster's costs order overturned.

With no option but to fight on, we remained a thorn in SANRAL's side, one that would fester and our challenge would become a bigger problem for it in the future, not so much in the area of litigation, but rather to become more civilly active in our drive of a civil courage campaign that would give rise to South Africa's biggest tax revolt to date.

We indicated our intention to appeal the judgment just inside the allotted period required to do so and we appeared before Vorster one month later, in early January 2013.

Judge Vorster walked into the courtroom and carried with him the mindset that the Constitutional Court had largely decided on the matter. 'So, if I'm not with you on the public participation point then you are not going to get leave to appeal,' was his message to our SC, Mike Maritz.

During the course of the appeal hearing, he had made a comment to Maritz that if the South African Revenue Service wants to raise taxes, or government wants to raise taxes, they don't give the public a right to participate.

Maritz in his reply said, 'You are mixing up two things here. When it comes to taxes, that goes through Parliament through a specific act. It goes through the parliamentary process and public participation takes place there. With regard to tolling, the only public participation that takes place is through the SANRAL Act.' Vorster's demeanour suddenly changed as he took note of this input and said, 'Oh right, you have answered that question.' At that moment, we knew that we had won the application for leave to appeal. He must have realised that there was a strong chance that another court may come to a different conclusion.

Leave to appeal his judgment in the Supreme Court of Appeal in Bloemfontein was granted.

Hope had set in once again. OUTA lived on.

CHAPTER 16

The Supreme Court of Appeal

We sincerely believed the Supreme Court of Appeal (SCA) would provide us with a very strong chance of winning this case. We would get experienced judges who shouldn't be scared to make difficult decisions. Instead of one judge, there would be five judges presiding over the case.

So we prepared to go to Bloemfontein for what would turn out to be the last stage of our legal journey on the e-toll matter to be heard in the Supreme Court on Wednesday, 25 September 2013.

'Five places set aside on the bench: Brand, Petse, Swain, Nugent and Van der Merwe,' Alex Eliseev from Eye Witness News tweeted before court was due to start.

We were forewarned by OUTA's attorneys not to be alarmed by the anticipated grilling from the bench. 'The judges have all read the heads of argument and probably drafted their judgment already,' the young attorney Kelvin Buchanan explained while we shopped around Bloemfontein for bottles of water to keep the team's thirst at bay. 'They want to test how convinced each legal team is in defence of its argument,' Kelvin told us, 'and you will probably get a sense of where their hearts lie on the matter, by the questions and demeanour of their approach during the hearing.'

Paul Pauwen, John Clarke, Ari Seirlis and I had taken our seats to the right side of the courtroom, with Alli and company to the left. Mmusi Maimane, the up and coming politician (and future head) from the DA was also present in the court.

In our heads of argument for the appeal we again pressed very hard on the public participation angle – SANRAL's failure to conduct proper public participation. We pressed the minister's failure to consider costs. Even what he said he considered, was not proper decision-making. We believed that Minister Radebe's affidavit, which claimed he had considered the costs, was hopeless.

By this stage we also had the strong decision in the Constitutional Court on *The Democratic Alliance versus the President of South Africa* in the Menzi Simelane case. In this case the president's decision to appoint

Simelane as the head of the National Prosecuting Authority (NPA) had been set aside on the basis that it had been irrational in the process of the decision-making in view of the power to be exercised by the president. This was the appointment of the head of the prosecuting authority and the decision-making on an important position like this must be faultless. The court decided the decision was irrational because the president had failed to consider material evidence that Simelane had lied under oath. He was not a fit and proper person to be in that role.

The executive powers of the president could not fail to consider that. He had to have followed a proper process in his decision-making. This was close to our views on the e-toll matter.

Thus, in our case we argued that if Minister Jeff Radebe was going to unleash this exorbitantly expensive tolling system on the public, he had a responsibility to find out what impact the real costs of the scheme would have on the public.

There was also another court case, in the context of tolling, where the court said the minister stands like a bulwark in protection of the public when it comes to tolling. It is his job to look after the public and ask: what is this expense that the public is going to bear? This is the power and responsibility that a minister has to exercise.

Our senior counsel, Mike Maritz thus argued that in view of this power, the minister of transport had to carefully consider the costs of toll collection. Yet it was clear to us that he had failed to do so. What he said he considered was incomprehensible and it was an estimate that was some six times less than the actual costs. This, we believed, was a strong point in our argument.

We had earlier said that the system was unenforceable in terms of implementation. We didn't argue that point now, however, because the court had been given statements under oath that e-tolling was possible to implement. Government said it would put people in jail.

We still included it in our heads of argument because we believed the court would look at it and say, 'Jeepers, we can't let this behaviour of criminalising the public for non-payment of e-tolls happen.' How many thousands of people would be facing the prospect of a jail cell? Would the courts even be able to cope with the numbers?

The issue of 'condonation' was still a problem for us. SANRAL had strongly argued through every legal step that we had left our court battle too late, that it should have come years ago when it was decided the roads would be tolled. At every challenge we retorted that nobody had been

fully aware of tolling until the tariffs were announced, and then government had prevaricated so much that nobody knew what was happening.

To support us in our argument, we looked strongly at another case:
The State versus Smit decision (2006). We saw in this case that if something unlawful is not set aside by the court, then it will still remain
unlawful.

In our case this would mean that if people are then prosecuted for failing to pay their tolls, they can raise the objection, a collateral challenge,
and say 'we will not pay because it's unlawful'. And, as was the case with
The State versus Smit, the objection would be valid. We pressed this fact
in the SCA appeal. We told the court that it must set aside condonation
because if it is not set aside, it's still going to be brought to its knees
at a later date by the fact that the decision to introduce the tolling of
Gauteng's freeways was introduced unlawfully.

But the SCA ducked that by saying, 'It's not the collateral challenge yet,
so we will leave that for another day.' They just excluded our argument.

In the hearing itself it seemed as if the judges were with us on the public participation point, asking biting questions of SANRAL. But they
were otherwise completely against us on the condonation issue.

Maritz was pummelled mercilessly, first by Judge Brand who would
pose a question, and then his reply would be interrupted by Judge Nugent
with another question. Hardly a single sentence could be completed. He
was thus forced to circle around the one question that seemed to bother
the bench most: why are you attacking the lawfulness of SANRAL's
implementation of a cabinet decision instead of the cabinet decision that
empowered it?

Maritz stayed on the two rails that he had chosen to carry OUTA's case:
the lack of procedural fairness in the minister's declaration of the roads
as toll roads; and the substantive illegality of SANRAL's imposition of
e-tolling as a revenue collection system. He argued that the process of
declaring the tolls was flawed and riddled with 'unlawful decisions'.

Coming eventually to one of his 'traps' Advocate Maritz bravely reiterated his accusation that SANRAL had misled the public and avoided
effective consultation with the users who were then expected to fund
the construction of the roads by means of electronic tolling. It placed
a hugely costly overhead on the scheme, without adequate disclosure of
the beneficiaries of that overhead, which in consequence left the users
disinclined to enrol in the system by purchasing e-tags. To enforce penalties against non-compliance added a further overhead cost to develop the

capacity of the law enforcement systems. Perfectly reasonable concerns, but in the judges' minds, the horse had already bolted. The freeways had been constructed, the gantries erected, the computer hardware installed and the software programmes ready to roll. Why had OUTA, SANRAL and the minister of transport not sat down together to iron out their differences before resorting to such an adversarial and hostile contest?

As the exchanges went on, it seemed the judges were reluctant to overrule a cabinet decision, even if it was a bad one, especially in the light of the Constitutional Court having told the judiciary off for trespassing on executive prerogatives.

Just before the morning tea break, Maritz was allowed to rest his tall frame after finishing with an impassioned plea to the court to at least reverse the punitive costs order against OUTA. The judges appeared better disposed to that approach and I heaved an audible sigh of relief.

David Unterhalter SC, representing SANRAL, took the podium. With customary exactitude and verbal felicity, he argued that no illegality existed and that the publicity was extensive.

'Notices in the business pages of newspapers?' Nugent sarcastically observed. Brand added, 'Sports pages might have been more helpful,' injecting some levity. 'But the exorbitant cost. Were the public not entitled to know how much they would have to pay?'

Unterhalter was also subjected to disconcerting interrogation.

My spirits were heightened.

However, Unterhalter was as able as Maritz in staying on his chosen track, insisting that the public were not entitled to know all the final cost details at the point that the minister declared the roads as toll roads, and that public participation had been 'extensive'.

Unterhalter (and our numb posteriors) were greatly helped by the necessity of a lunch break, after which he was able to recap some of his responses, which seemed to placate the bench. They eased up on their derailing tactics. Perhaps the lunch break had given the bench the opportunity to discuss and to perhaps agree that their preconceived draft judgment that we assumed they had was sound enough, and that the proceedings could be brought to conclusion.

The only further mercy from the justices was for them to appear unswayed by Unterhalter's argument that I and OUTA had 'vexatious motives' and that a punitive costs award against OUTA was just desserts for daring to impugn the integrity of his client.

It was hard for the judges to ignore the presence of Ari Seirlis, seated behind the black berobed OUTA lawyers in his wheelchair, especially since he was right among them in the business end of the courthouse. Ari told me afterwards that the wheelchair-unfriendliness of the venerable courthouse extends to inaccessible ablution facilities. 'I always try to look on the bright side of my disability,' Ari cheerfully told us afterwards. 'Sometimes being stuck in a wheelchair has its advantages. There were no accessible toilets either. I had to go and relieve myself in the advocates' robing rooms by peeing in a bottle and pouring the contents down the basin.' This gave Ari the chance to peep into the inner sanctum of the venerable courthouse, the judge's chambers.

Consequently Ari's well-defined presence seemed to take the edge off Unterhalter's conviction that a crippling costs order against the OUTA members would be just. There had been much back-and-forth discourse between bench and podium about 'water under the bridge', 'in the real world' and 'collateral consequences' with respect to the fact that the Gauteng freeways and 42 e-tolling gantries were there for all to see. Whether the 'child' had been conceived in sin or a misarranged marriage, and even if it was now a loveless union between road user and road provider, Ari Seirlis's real-world presence, in a wheelchair alongside bench and podium, was there for the judges to see.

It appeared to us that in the judges' minds, it may have been too late to unscramble the soufflé omelette even if the ingredients were overly expensive imports, the recipe dubious and the price exorbitant. However, to expect OUTA's alliance members and the motorists of Gauteng to pay SANRAL's legal costs was outrageous in our minds. Unterhalter's tactic to argue for crippling costs had become their folly and served a reverse purpose, in that, ironically, the judgment that the SCA would later read paid what John Clarke had dubbed as a 'backhand compliment' to OUTA's case.

The Treasury, through Jeremy Gauntlett SC, took the proceedings through to the end of the court day. He argued in favour of division of powers between the judiciary and executive and about cost of delays. Gauntlett asked how the Treasury can plan when attacks come four or five years later?

Advocate Maritz rose at 5.15 pm to ask for an adjournment till the following morning before commencing his rebuttal.

'No, carry on, Mr Maritz,' Justice Brand insisted, 'let's see how you go.' It seemed cruel to expect Maritz to have to proceed with his rebuttal after all he had had to endure already.

Maritz returned to the grindstone to try as best he could to derail the preconceived judgment that he felt the court had brought into the argument some eight hours earlier. 'The minister must comply with the law …' he began.

'But we don't want the minister to comply with the law,' Judge Brand interrupted. 'We want the minister to change his mind.' As things were winding down, a totally unexpected tweet vibrated into the courtroom at 6.28 pm, to startle those of us glancing with half an eye at our smartphones: 'President Jacob Zuma has signed the e-tolls legislation, the Transport Laws and Related Matters Amendment Bill, into being.'

What?

There was something bizarrely Humpty Dumpty-ish about President Zuma's action. Apparently even Nazir Alli had been completely taken by surprise. Alex Eliseev had to show him the media release to confirm it. He reserved comment until he had studied it.

Paradoxically, it gave me something to talk about other than the 'tough day in the office' when journalists approached us for comment after Judge Brand finally rose to declare the proceedings over, and judgment reserved.

We were surprised by President Zuma's actions to sign the much-contested bill into law at this stage. When we had arrived in Bloemfontein, I was still expecting the ANC-led government to take advantage of the fact that the case was still in the throws of litigation, and thereby justify its action to 'kick the e-toll can down the road' until after the elections, due in the month of May 2014. Technical confusion still abounds over the Transport and Related Matters Amendment Bill and, in all respects, the regulatory framework and questions around enforcement painted the picture of a scheme that was unenforceable and inundated with controversy.

Furthermore, it was eighteen months after SANRAL and the Treasury were sounding dire warnings of 'severe consequences' if the judiciary interfered with the power of executive powers by granting OUTA's interdict to halt the e-tolling, and a year after SANRAL had been granted the powers to turn on the system by the Constitutional Court, and yet they could not do so.

We left the SCA not hopeful at all. The judges' questioning, as with the Constitutional Court case, pointed to a dissatisfaction with our arguments on the technical aspect of being unable to condone the lateness of our case, and their unwillingness to apply a collateral challenge on the merits of our case.

This came out in the judgment, which once again went government's way. The judgment read:

> Some five years have now elapsed since the impugned decisions were taken. During that period, vast and significant upgrades to the GFIP highways and related infrastructures had been completed. By all accounts these upgraded roads are truly magnificent.
>
> The advantages are enjoyed primarily by the motorists of Gauteng, but they also benefit the economy of the country as a whole. The downside is that this came at a cost of R20 billion. This amount had been borrowed by SANRAL with borrowed money. The interest on the loan is running at an alarming rate.

The judges said that time could not be turned back and history could not be rewritten and so they refused OUTA's case because of the rule of condonation, which applies in administrative law.

The judgment said that if they had chosen to set aside the e-tolling decision, it would not only affect GFIP, but it would have a detrimental impact on the countrywide network of national roads as a whole, with a clear knock-on effect on the economy. They described this as a spider's web where the pulling of one strand would cause tension in the entire web and would have an impact elsewhere.

It felt as if they were going to look for ways to find against us.

It appeared to us that the Constitutional Court's ruling had the impact of endorsing the High Court and the SCA's judgment and thinking. The entire system was up and in place. The money had been spent. The debt was waiting to be repaid. It couldn't be stopped now.

And still the minister of finance's fiscal Armageddon if the debt is not paid was a heavy weight on the Supreme Court judges' minds.

On 9 October 2013, a short two weeks after the hearing, the Supreme Court of Appeal handed down its judgment.

As we had feared, the SCA found against OUTA, but, as we had hoped, they overturned the crippling costs order against us.

The state media machine, quoting Tiyani Rikhotso, proclaimed that the 'Supreme Court's ruling further vindicates Government's long-held position that we have sufficiently consulted the public before the introduction of the electronic tolling project'.

However, Rikhotso was wrong in his remarks, as the SCA side-stepped the issue of lawfulness entirely and this was a very interesting development in the case. The judgment had completely avoided dealing with the merits of the case, as had been ruled on by Judge Vorster in the High Court.

'I believe that despite the appellants' various arguments to the contrary, we are not authorised to enter into the merits of the review application,' the judgment said.

By ducking the merits, the SCA didn't have to get into whether SANRAL's public participation process was adequate or not. It didn't have to rule on whether Minister Radebe had properly considered the costs or nor. It essentially also tweaked the law of condonation. The SCA referred to an earlier case, the *Beweging vir Christelik Volkseie Onderwys and others v Minister of Education and others*, and said in that case, it showed the courts could decide on condonation without reaching the merits of the case.

However, we maintained that in that case it referred to, the merits had become mute. That case was looking at an education policy, but by the time it came to the SCA the policy had changed, so there was no purpose in going into the merits of the case. What the appellants wanted had already been granted. However, in our case, the SCA refused our condonation arguments in the context of a judgment, thereby rescinding the merits of the case as being purely academic.

'The court failed to grasp the nettle of our argument,' an angry Mike Maritz said when the OUTA team met with the legal team to unpack the judgment. 'It didn't consider the consequences of the deception by SANRAL and the minister when the toll roads were publicly proclaimed in 2008.' Maritz was still bravely thumping the tub that SANRAL had misled the public by only publishing the regulatory notice (inviting public comment on the proposed decision) in six newspapers. Hardly in keeping with SANRAL's legal obligation to ensure effective public participation. As a consequence, there was indeed a long delay before the public cottoned onto the tactic. Objections could only come way beyond the normal 180-day period allowed for comment, when the public became truly apprised of the issue. 'Yet the Supreme Court simply dismissed our argument for condonation of the delayed response. The public have become victims of deception. The delay was due to SANRAL's [and the minister of transport's] failure to comply,' he fumed. 'The judgment has entitled SANRAL to reap the benefits of their own deception.

'Until the dispute over lawfulness of the ministerial decision has been decided, it is just postponing the inevitable,' Maritz concluded, sounding more like a prophet than a lawyer.

'The inevitability of what?' I asked.

'That a collateral challenge will be brought by somebody who is prosecuted for not paying e-tolls.'

The term 'collateral challenge' means something. Because the SCA judgment had been mute on the lawfulness of e-tolling, Adrian d'Oliveira, our junior counsel, explained, 'The situation remains open to any citizen to lawfully decide not to pay e-tolls and defend his/her prosecution on the basis that the toll declarations and the approval by the minister of transport of e-tolling were unlawful. This is called a collateral challenge in which the technical arguments of delay become totally irrelevant.'

We now understood why Maritz had kept nagging the Supreme Court to rule on the merits of the 'lawfulness' argument made by OUTA. He wanted it to act pre-emptively (even if it felt unable to condone the delay in the OUTA application) so that the state would be better able to set the table for any would-be objector who refused to pay a toll fee for the use of the roads in question. Judge Nugent seemed to clearly understand what OUTA's silk was angling to achieve, but was unmoved. He was seemingly resigned to the inevitability that the SCA had not heard the last on the e-tolling matter. However, that would come into the venerable courtroom in the form of a collateral challenge framed in terms of the precepts of criminal rather than administrative law, if indeed it ever came to that.

The testing autopsy of the judgment with our legal team left us in a dark mood and the lawyers left us to craft a statement in preparation for a planned media conference the following day.

There were those who believed the courts had made the right decision in not involving themselves in government's e-toll decision. In a *Mail & Guardian* opinion article by Sergeant at the Bar (1 November 2013), he said that the judgment 'served as a clear warning to litigants and judges to be careful about becoming involved in cases that are not suitable for judicial determination.

'Increasingly, South African courts are approached to solve political disputes, which are the subject matter of political contest, but are not suitable for adjudication. Judges should not be running the country,' he said.

However, we believed the judgment was sad for the country because this approach to dealing with condonation can never really stand in a constitutional democracy. The proper approach when deciding on con-donation is to decide on all the factors and all the prejudice that the public might suffer as a result of the policy. It is important for the courts to consider the prospects of success and the merits of a case.

In our case, the courts never answered as to whether there was a clear example of unlawfulness or not. By following this reasoning, an irra-tional system could come into being in future with no questions asked.

We have strong views on why the Supreme Court didn't want to deal with the merits. It's because when we sat and argued, especially on the failure of the minister to consider the costs of collection, the lights came on and the judges couldn't find a way around this. The judges seemed to be trying to offer arguments to the other side on how to deal with this. They appeared to be trying to help them yet without crushing the public by allowing the space for a collateral challenge to ensue if indeed SANRAL tried to prosecute for non-payment.

This case was just too big and with the Constitutional Court ruling weighing on their minds, the Supreme Court, as with the High Court under Vorster, just did not want to deal with real and serious issues of this case. There was too much water under the bridge. The amount of money that had been spent and needed to be paid was too big and they had the government, SANRAL and the Treasury telling them there would be irreparable harm to SANRAL and the fiscus if they couldn't toll.

Infuriated and dejected we had a decision to make. Should we appeal to the Constitutional Court, which had already set aside the interdict, but had not ruled on the merits? Would the Constitutional Court just go the same way again?

The advice we were given was a mixture of legal realism and practical reality. The practical reality being that OUTA had run out of funds.

Thank goodness the Supreme Court had overturned the costs order and ruled that each party pay its own costs. The Treasury admitted later in Parliament that its fees alone, excluding those of SANRAL and the Department of Transport, came to R6 million. We were still R2 million in the red with our legal expenses, despite having recently raised R2.9 million through our plea to the public (including R1 million from the DA) in April 2013.

We just didn't have the money to appeal the Supreme Court's judg-ment to the Constitutional Court. There was no petrol in our tank to drive the litigation car any further down the road. We'd actually run out of fuel a few months prior and were coasting under the gravity of a supportive attorneys in Cliffe Dekker Hofmeyr. And here I must thank Brent Williams and the executive team of Cliffe Dekker Hofmeyr, who were patient and ever supportive of our difficulties in paying the bills, essentially writing off a substantial amount, in recognition of OUTA's role in relation to society.

The legal realism was that given the treatment we had received from the Constitutional Court the first time around, and given the treatment we had received from the Supreme Court with this easy way out by using the condonation argument, we had lost our confidence in the courts to rule on the merits of this case. We also believed that had we approached the Constitutional Court itself, it too would probably have refused relief on the basis of condonation because this was an easy avenue open to it.

What remained very much alive was the fact that because the Supreme Court had not made a finding on the merits of the case, it was still open to the public to contest this in the event of being summonsed to court for the non-payment of tolls. In such an instance, a member of the public will be able to fight his or her prosecution on the basis that e-tolling was introduced unlawfully. In such a fight the court can't look at the technical arguments of delay. It will have to deal with the merits and make a decision on whether the person in the dock is guilty of a criminal offence against the backdrop of the many issues raised by OUTA's court challenge, which highlighted the unlawfulness of the e-tolling decision.

The venue that the National Press Club hired for OUTA's much-awaited press conference on our response to the judgment and our way forward was fittingly at the Gordon Institute of Business Science.

John Clarke and I were bleary-eyed after our late night crafting the statement. It broke many of the conventions of good media releases.

I was flanked by Ari Seirlis on my left and Mike Roussos of the Catholic Church on my right.

After I had spoken, Ari wheeled himself forward to speak of how people with disabilities like himself rely on help from others to drive them around. 'We cannot get out and about without using the freeways. E-tolling has "paralysed" us again.'

Mike Roussos then read a statement drafted by Moss Ntlha on behalf of concerned church leaders. It was a crisp page leaving no doubt that, even though the Supreme Court may have failed to deliver on a promise of justice, the promise was nevertheless still valid and would be fulfilled.

In the view of the churches, the outcome of the OUTA court case yesterday, 9th October, in which the case was dismissed due to its falling outside of the 180 day period required for such appeals, is merely a matter of legal technicalities.

It does not address the crucial matter of the moral injustice of the e-tolls. As churches, we remain of the view that:

• E-tolls are an injustice to the people of Gauteng and (due to its knock-on effects on the cost of living) to the rest of the country. The fact that they intend to extend this system to other parts of the country makes this compelling.
• Credible alternatives exist that would allow for the raising of money to pay for these roads, without incurring the large costs of collection entailed by e-tolling. Despite this, without setting forth any convincing reasons, government has preferred to ignore alternatives and forge ahead with e-tolling. This continues to provoke deep suspicion about the real reasons for the insistence on e-tolls.

While government reserves the right to ignore popular protests and govern in the way it sees fit, it is up to the people of South Africa to hold them accountable for such decisions in ways they see fit – including the freedom to decide whether or not to participate in this scheme – and via the ballot box. Thankfully, 'the people shall govern' remains a core value of our democracy.

Forging ahead with this method of funding the roads, regardless of the outcry that this has occasioned, is likely to generate a wide range of responses from the people of our country.

As always, Christians should make their decisions after careful thought and prayer, and on moral grounds like the pursuit of justice and the common good – rather than deciding on the basis of what suits our pockets. We will be told that Christians should obey their government and pay taxes, but that presumes that our government is governing righteously. In this case that is exactly the problem we face.

We continue to encourage all our people to focus on peaceful ways of demonstrating their resistance and refusal to participate in such schemes – rather than allowing our frustrations and concerns to result in any violence or destruction of public property.

Even at this late stage we, as leaders from a wide variety of churches, urge the government to re-think their approach and to

seriously explore the various alternatives that exist to fund the debt
that was incurred in the building of these roads.
  E-tolling is clearly not the solution.
  Moss Ntlha

The journalists, however, were impatient to know if OUTA was intending to seek further legal recourse to have the glaringly unfinished business of the matter of 'lawfulness' settled.

'Will it ever be settled?' I asked. I responded that we believed that a continuation of litigation and an appeal to the Constitutional Court would be a futile exercise. For now, any plans to litigate would be left to if and when the first person was prosecuted for non-payment of e-tolls. For it would be at this stage, we believed, that the courts could no longer duck the merits of our case. We also stated that we didn't want to risk going to the Constitutional Court in this climate to find against the judgments of the review as we also stood the chance that the Constitutional Court might have killed any possibility of a collateral challenge later, if indeed they ruled against OUTA on the merits.

We had every right to continue our fight, and fight on we would. We remained resolute, but going forward, our time and stress levels would not be taken up by begging society for money to fight court battles on the interpretation of administrative law. We had a new strategy to morph the organisation into a civil action space.

OUTA would continue to expose the weaknesses and unlawfulness of the e-toll policy, along with the stark inefficiencies and unworkability of SANRAL's scheme, which we predicted would become a reality if and when the scheme was launched.

This was the only tank of fuel we had left, to challenge the system's existence and hopefully we could ensure that the public's civil courage would be sufficiently heightened through this drive. Our efforts to do so through a decision of the courts had not borne the fruits we expected. But that didn't mean e-tolling would succeed. It was now up to the court of public opinion to exercise civil disobedience, the likes of which would be further vindicated not only by their disgust in the decision, but by the many errors and inefficiencies that the cumbersome scheme would unleash on the Gauteng road users.

The real contest was about to begin and we were intrigued to see if, and to what extent, the power of the e-toll decision would shift from the authorities to the people.

The e-tolls court challenge timeline

Level of court structure		Mar/Apr 2012	Aug/Sep 2012	Nov/Dec 2012	Sep/Oct 2013
	Constitutional Court (National) Braamfontein		**Appeal: Of Interim Interdict** Treasury & SANRAL successfully applies to appeal the interdict, which is successful. Con Court bench of judges sets aside interdict, but allows review to continue.		
	Supreme Court of Appeal (National) Bloemfontein				**Appeal: Of Vorster's judgment** SCA largely dismisses Judge Vorster's review of merits, but maintains OUTA's case flawed on Admin. Law technicalities & rules e-tolls to proceed. Reverses costs order.
	High Court (Regional)	**Part A: To interdict e-toll launch** OUTA applies for urgent interdict to halt e-toll launch on 30 April, pending full judicial review (Part B). Judge Bill Prinsloo grants interdict to halt e-toll launch.		**Part B: To review lawfulness of government's e-toll decision** Acting Judge Louis Voster hears arguments and rules against applicants (OUTA), with full costs of both parties	
	Magisterial Courts (Regional)				

PART THREE

- - - - - - - - - - - - - - -

Corporate executives and business owners need to realize that there can be no compromise when it comes to ethics, and there are no easy shortcuts to success. Ethics need to be carefully sown into the fabric of their companies.
  – Vivek Wadhwa

CHAPTER 17

From litigation to civil action

The OUTA committee had decided that assisting the first person to be summoned for non-payment was the only option now available to us, if indeed we wanted a court to hear and deal seriously with the merits of our case. But that might be months or even years away from now. What were we to do between now and then?

The overturning of the costs order by the Supreme Court of Appeal was a significant issue in that it allowed OUTA to live on. Had we been forced to pick up our opponent's legal costs, we would have remained indebted to their legal teams forever and a day. We most certainly would have been forced to close shop, and with the demise of OUTA, its strong voice and opinions would have been muted, and OUTA's very necessary role going forward would have ceased to exist.

While it was extremely tempting for the OUTA committee to pack up and go home, we simply couldn't and we didn't. Despite the fact that every one of us was 'e-tolled out', and the call to drop the fight and move on with our lives was screaming loudly in the back of our minds, by doing so, not only would we have lost the opportunity to have Judge Vorster's shocking costs order overturned, or his interpretation of the merits set aside, but we would have also reneged on our responsibility to society. We would have opened the door for SANRAL to proceed with a far lesser challenge on its hands.

Three of the business organisations that made up a significant part of our membership (SAVRALA, the Retail Motor Industry and SATSA) had all indicated that their boards were in favour of calling it a day with OUTA for different reasons.

In SAVRALA's case, it was a matter of government pressure or the potential loss of government business being brought to bear on its individual members. Government entities conducted significant fleet-related leasing and rental business with SAVRALA's members and it was no secret that pressure was exerted on them either to resign from the body or that SAVRALA should distance itself from OUTA. SAVRALA made it clear that while it was in favour of the demise of e-tolls, its members needed to distance themselves from OUTA.

The Retail Motor Industry and SATSA had recently undergone changes at their respective CEO level and their new leadership was not in touch with the intricacies of the case. They had other matters on their plates and their boards, too, had indicated that since OUTA's loss in the Supreme Court, it was time to pull back.

I recalled a *Mail & Guardian* report by Charles Molele that featured government pressure on SAVRALA's members and in particular on Avis, some eight months earlier on 22 March 2013. Titled 'E-Tolls, no remorse, no business', the report reflected that an official who headed the Office of the Deputy President had said that Avis had to distance itself from e-toll opponents or suffer the consequences.

The newspaper accused the government of 'blackmailing' Avis Rent a Car after the Presidency moved its multimillion-rand car-hire contract to a competitor company following Avis's opposition to the e-tolling of freeways while I filled the role of chief executive. The report went on to say, 'The *Mail & Guardian* has seen correspondence between South African National Roads Agency Limited (SANRAL) chief executive Nazir Alli and senior officials in the Presidency that indicates that Avis must apologise to the government and publicly distance itself from Duvenage and the Opposition to Urban Tolling Alliance (OUTA) before it would be allowed to do business with the government again.'

An e-mail from Alli addressed to Busani Ngcaweni, who headed the office of Deputy President Kgalema Motlanthe and several senior government officials, read: 'A small addition to our list of car-hire companies that have signed up with us ... Yesterday Avis (the red people) signed up with us. However, please do not hire cars from them yet. [We are] waiting to see visible signs of remorse. It is the right thing to do. No remorse, no business.'

The newspaper report went on to mention: 'A government official, who spoke on condition of anonymity, said Duvenage's involvement with OUTA angered both the government and Avis,' and that '[a]ccording to an insider close to the falling out, Avis's new management has been under tremendous pressure from shareholders to mend relations with the government. As a result, the company has joined a list of other car-hire companies that have signed up for e-tags for their fleets, despite its initial opposition to the tolls.'

Naturally, I was pissed off on hearing about this bullying behaviour, but it was to be expected. To me, it was a clear sign of two issues that portrayed a weakness in the relationship between our government and business, which was detrimental to our country:

1. Our government leadership was behaving in an immature, bully-boy manner when it didn't get its way.
2. The weakness of corporate South Africa by forsaking its original strong belief in challenging the authorities on this unsound policy for the sake of improved short-term business and resultant profits.

It was October 2013 and with OUTA's big funding members pulling back, I was worried that the rest would follow, namely SANCU and QASA. It was important that if we were to continue to exist as a formidable force, we needed to retain a semblance of some of the original team in place.

But what about the rest of us? The directors of OUTA, Paul Pauwen, Michael Tatalias and myself, were all once employed by one of the founding member companies and were no longer with them. We had become self-employed and had contributed countless hours of personal time to the e-toll challenge.

The thought of closing shop and walking away didn't sit easy with us. We had put too much into halting this scheme to give up now.

We were grateful to QASA for standing with us and remaining part of the alliance. The need for the exemption of people with disabilities had still not been addressed by SANRAL and QASA's leadership stood strong on this issue, despite the pressure being brought to bear on them by government.

With OUTA's decision to halt the litigation process, the committee's discussion revealed that litigation was not the only methodology for challenging unjust government decisions. For if that were the case, the apartheid regime and other unsound polices that precipitated movements such as the Treatment Action Campaign's fight for citizen access to Aids treatment would never have been overturned.

We decided to hold another meeting in mid-November 2013, which would give us time to report back to our respective constituencies and give thought as to the future of OUTA.

We met again on 14 November 2013 during which our discussion conveyed common thinking that OUTA should continue to play a meaningful role in the fight against e-tolls. To do so, we needed to be a civil action group with a new focus.

Some said that with the benefit of hindsight perhaps going the route of litigation had not been necessary and was a waste of time and money. However, I dispute that notion as we should never under-estimate the impact that our court interdict had by halting the launch of the scheme on 28 April 2012. I sincerely believe that this interdict played a massive role in creating awareness of how wrong the scheme was for the country and in lifting the moral courage of hundreds of thousands who might have rushed off to purchase e-tags and thereby possibly have taken the compliance levels high enough for SANRAL to call it a success.

We also couldn't pack up because we knew what was coming. We knew that Nazir Alli, Vusi Mona and their PR team were poised to employ a plethora of media tactics to persuade the public to participate in the scheme as they prepared for the launch of e-tolls.

At this stage, our inside sources (who came to us, not the other way around), told us that the launch of e-tolls was planned for the last week of November or the first week in December 2013.

We remained convinced that the system was fraught with significant inefficiencies, which would give rise to numerous billing errors. We believed the system would not keep pace with the vast number of com-plaints or problems related to cloned number plates and low levels of road-user compliance.

We decided that our role would be to empower society with relevant knowledge and facts to the extent that it would be the people who would raise the challenge against SANRAL through their personal decisions to remain civilly disobedient – this decision being a conscientious one. Our role was to keep SANRAL honest and to challenge its question-able claims by exposing the many untruths and misinformation it was bound to express. SANRAL had a history of such behaviour and we didn't expect it to stop now.

The matter had become a psychological war against SANRAL's prop-aganda campaign. We had seen how SANRAL had been misleading the public with the number of e-tags sold in an attempt to create the impres-sion that the public were flocking to the e-toll kiosks to purchase their tags ahead of the launch.

We concluded our meeting with a position that our duty was to keep society sufficiently informed on what was really happening with the e-toll system, the real e-tag compliance levels (through research) and other important matters, such that motorists would be better informed to make their own decisions on whether or not to participate in what we believed was an unjust system.

OUTA's membership required that we convene a special meeting to address new board appointments. Michael Tatalias from SATSA had temporarily immigrated to Canada for study purposes and we needed to replace him. Jeff Osborne, who was the outgoing Retail Motor Industry CEO, was happy to fill Michael's seat, which was great for us as he came with immense experience on the matter, having been committed to OUTA's cause and formation from the outset.

Paul Pauwen and I were the other two existing directors and we remained in place.

I indicated to the team that I was happy to continue and to chair the alliance, but that after two years in this role, a year and a half of which I had been unemployed by the end of 2013, I needed to get back to work. My family had been living off our savings and I couldn't continue like this on a full-time basis any more. OUTA's leadership required new and additional energy to assist with media and public enquiries, as well as constant monitoring of SANRAL's media tactics and claims.

I therefore recommended that OUTA employ the services of John Clarke as a consultant and joint spokesperson for the organisation. John was extremely knowledgeable about OUTA's case and had joined Paul, Ari and I at the Supreme Court of Appeal hearing in Bloemfontein on 25 September 2013. John also had extensive experience in dealing with SANRAL and Nazir Alli on the N2 Wild Coast toll road matter. He was a social worker and a writer. His participation would help us tremendously in the preparation of media releases as well as attending to the numerous public enquiries that were coming through our website. John's appointment would take a lot of the pressure off me, allowing me to begin to build my career again.

Enter John Clarke

As stated earlier in Chapter 10, I had met John Clarke in my business capacity in Durban in 2011 while presenting the Avis Journey of Sustainability to a group of prominent conservation-minded leaders. It was a case study we had started to document about Avis's leading role in reducing the company's negative impact on the environment and becoming South Africa's first carbon neutral company.

Part of Avis's corporate social responsibility programme was to support the efforts of people and organisations that worked hard to conserve the country's ecology. I was convinced by John Clarke that the efforts of the Amadiba community were a genuine attempt to challenge the wrongful behaviour of a mining company trying to mine the sand dunes along the Eastern Cape's pristine Wild Coast. Their defence also included the need to thwart SANRAL's plans to construct a new N2 tolled route through the Wild Cost when all that was required was an upgrading of the existing route. Carving a new route closer to the coastline, across the Amadiba tribal and ancestral lands, just didn't make sense.

John had separately interviewed Nazir Alli and Mark Caruso of Mineral Commodities Limited, the Australian mining company that had plans to mine the titanium-rich sand dunes at Xolobeni on the Wild Coast, some 16 kilometres south-west of the Wild Coast Casino resort, as the crow flies. John's work, which is revealed in his book *The Promise of Justice*, exposes SANRAL's plans to construct a shortcut for the N2 between Port Edward and Mthatha, which appeared largely connected to the plans to unlock the titanium-rich dunes to be carted off for refining in other parts of the world.

As OUTA's case began to gain momentum and prominence, John's contact with me became more important as he shared meaningful insights and understanding of SANRAL's behaviour. John inspired me with the term 'civil courage' but hastened to explain that he had been inspired by one of his friends, Alastair McIntosh, a Scottish writer and peace activist.[16] The more John worked and communicated with me, the more I realised that we needed to bring his skills and knowledge into OUTA's cause on a more prominent basis.

John's appointment as a part-time consultant to OUTA at the end of 2013 was a great relief to me. I naturally came to know John a lot better and discovered a person who was passionate about challenging social injustices that violated human rights. He came with an abundance of in-depth knowledge of the Constitution and many years of working within the civil society space. A three-year stint with the World Health Organization's Humanitarian Action unit in Africa had taken him to many other African countries, including Somalia. He has a vast network of friends – leaders, academics and activists around the world – which provided us with a host of learning opportunities and interactions with interesting people. He was an ideal candidate for the job and I was immensely impressed with his input.

Additionally, John's writing skills were excellent but elaborate – filled with anecdotes, metaphors and quips – which often added significant length to the articles we had to write. This was my only quibble with John. Because the time available to the public to read newsworthy stories is limited, our pieces needed to be punchy, to the point and written in as few words as possible. John's style was to add more flavour and interesting scene-setting anecdotes that took up too much space for news articles. It was an interesting time for both of us as we respected each other's skills and found a happy balance in our ability to mix our respective views and input to get the job done.

John took up his role with enthusiastic determination to help OUTA fulfil its new mandate of empowering society with knowledge. With input from Erin Hommes (a committed academic) and myself, John set out to compile OUTA's compelling position paper titled 'E-Tolling at an Impasse' in February 2014. We later updated and re-titled the paper as 'Beyond the Impasse', using it for OUTA's submission in September 2014 to Premier Makhura's E-Toll Advisory Panel.

In my opinion, there is no way that I or any of OUTA's members could have continued to carry out the committee's much-needed work without John on board. Since 2013 John has become not only a trusted confidant and a friend, but also a formidable force in naming, unmasking and engaging the powers to further the actualisation of human rights in South Africa.

Upping the social media ante

Up until November 2013, our social media campaign was managed by a great and vibrant team at Coza Productions, based in Cape Town under the leadership of Ryan Christian. They had taken our social media campaign Facebook following from 2 000 to 10 000 followers between November 2012 to October 2013.

In the beginning I didn't realise how powerful Facebook was going to be for our campaign. Besides mainstream media, I thought Twitter was going to be our important channel of expression and interaction, but soon discovered that Facebook was where this kind of activity and communication was most powerful. I tried hard to convince John that he needed to be on Twitter. 'My wife thinks I should be on a higher dose of Ritalin. What's Twitter?' he replied.

John has since got onto Twitter, but finds the 160-character constraint impossible to contain his vast literary genius, so he uses it sparingly.

In September 2013 Ryan had also overseen the production of our six-minute video titled 'Gauteng E-Tolls Makes No Sense'.[17] It was a cleverly done artist's sketch of the story to a voice-over script that took me a few hours to write. The video was launched on 7 October 2013 and within four days it had 40 000 views. We were overwhelmed as we were expecting around 20 000 hits in total. Over the next month the video went viral and achieved over 300 000 views and stabilised at around 340 000 some six months later. We believe this video played a major role in increasing society's understanding of the issues surrounding the irrationality of the e-toll plan and, in turn, heightened their civil courage.

While Ryan and his Coza Productions team were great for OUTA's cause, being based in Cape Town they were a little distant from the reality and energy of the e-toll debate, which was largely a Gauteng issue. It became apparent that our social media effort needed to be managed by someone based in Gauteng who could feel the pulse and energy, and communicate the issues unfolding on a weekly and sometimes daily basis. I explained to Ryan that after working with his company for a year it was time to move the campaign to a social media specialist based in Gauteng who was already actively involved in the cause. Ryan understood and agreed.

Enter Hutchie

Rob Hutchinson had been very successful with his own anti-e-toll social media campaign – 'Proudly E-tag Free'. He sent a note to us through our website contact page wanting to know if we should discuss collaborative efforts in our mutual challenge against e-tolls. This was followed by a brief telephone conversation in mid-November 2013 and later that week we met for coffee.

I was moved by Hutchie's young and refreshing activist approach to the e-toll debate. Rob also came with a marketing background and a driven mindset that had built up a sizeable following of over 65 000 followers on his own 'Proudly E-tag Free' Facebook site.

Rob came across as a quiet and rather reserved individual, but once you got him going, the enthusiasm and ideas he could generate were great.

Two cappuccinos later, I had heard enough to be persuaded that we needed to have Rob on our team and I asked him what he thought of the idea of managing and driving OUTA's social media work. His face lit up and he was overjoyed at the mention of the idea. Rob had come to this meeting only to see how we could work more closely together, not realising that I was in search of someone of his calibre to actually take the reins of OUTA's social media efforts.

I indicated to Hutchie that I would propose at OUTA's January 2014 committee meeting that he be appointed in a consulting capacity to assist us with our social media campaign. He was bowled over by the suggestion and seized the opportunity with gusto and enthusiasm. He agreed to do some work with us from early in December 2013, just after the e-toll scheme had launched, on a pro-bono basis, until the committee ratified his appointment in January.

Within four months, by April 2014, Rob had nearly trebled our Facebook following from 10 500 to 30 000 followers.

Rob's role at OUTA was immense. He also took over the handling of OUTA's website queries, which were pouring in fast as the inefficiencies of e-tolls began to give rise to numerous complaints. This in turn took a lot of pressure off John and me as we became sucked into more and more media enquiries, press releases and reports that required OUTA's input. Rob is a Facebook marketing guru of note and I have no doubt that after OUTA, some organisation will employ him for his skills in this space.

OUTA's renewed energy

As with any organisation, its existence and the effectiveness rely on energy. People energy. We needed the right people with the right mindset and positive energy levels for OUTA to continue to play a meaningful role in the e-toll challenge. It was a role that would become more critical now than ever before, since the e-toll scheme had been launched on 3 December 2013 and the real work of exposing the predicted problems was about to get underway. The e-toll launch is described in more detail in Chapter 19.

Our view was that once the predicted problems began to emerge and clear signs of its unsustainability were evident, the irrationality of the scheme might help the authorities to make some hard and fast decisions, even if only to halt the prosecution of citizens for non-payment. If indeed only the latter transpired, then the scheme would fail anyway.

The decision to bring John and Rob on board had been the right move. Their appointments certainly imparted a new will and purpose to continue the cause.

OUTA had transformed from a grouping of business associations fighting an unjust government policy to that of a group of individual people with a common cause. The fact that SANCU and QASA were still with us remained extremely important, but the energy that directed OUTA's behaviour had now moved from what was once directed through the views of business associations to that of individuals and leaders.

John had entered the fray with such lively input and new thinking, which had the impact of spiking our energy levels once again. Every organisation needs new energy to prevent it from sinking into the trap of old-style thinking. I was certainly happy to have him on board. He lived ten minutes away from me and we would often meet to discuss and write media releases, which were extremely pertinent in the build-up and after-math of the e-toll launch. Fego's restaurant in Bryanston's Nicolway Centre became our regular rendezvous and the manager decided to put us on his special customer discount list.

And then there was John's sense of humour. When SANRAL spokes-person Vusi Mona conceded that it was having 'teething problems' shortly after the launch, John quipped, 'more a question of having false teeth than teething problems'. I cracked up.

I had been writing opinion pieces for the *Daily Maverick* for some time, and it was nice to be able to bounce these off John now that he was on board. He also had such keen and interesting opinions on other social issues that I suggested to editor Branko Brkic that John be invited to the elite Opinionista ranks. Branko read some of John's input and agreed. Not only did John become a regular contributor but he took the time to engage diligently with the regular *DM* commen-tariat to refine and clarify the issues as well as build friendships with strangers.

'People don't generally resist change. But they do resist "being changed",' is one of John's favourite aphorisms. It begs the question: so how does beneficial social, political and economic change occur? The learning I gained on this e-toll challenge journey would help me to deal with this question more easily and is a matter I reflect on in more detail in the final chapter of this book.

While I don't believe there is a silver bullet that guarantees success, I do know what guarantees failure: an attitude that uses power and con-trol to force compliance rather than authority and integrity to inspire commitment.

Compiling OUTA's position paper

When the anticipated evidence began to mount of teething problems in the operational management domain of the e-toll debacle, and anticipating that OUTA was going to be blamed for deliberately sabotaging e-tolling and creating a self-fulfilling prophecy to prove in practice what we had failed to do in court, John and I began to discuss the need to write an assessment and appraisal that would stand up under rigorous academic and intellectual scrutiny. It would encapsulate OUTA's learning to date in order to put some constructive proposals on the table to resolve the e-toll impasse.

During this discussion I had with John in December 2013, I mentioned to him the input and interesting insights that were shared with me by Erin Hommes, an academic from the University of Pretoria who I met shortly after OUTA's interdict in 2012, when I was still the chief executive at Avis. Erin called me to discuss her research about the ethics and use of ITS (Intelligent Transport Systems – e-tolling) around the world, from which she had identified critical factors that arose from both successful and unsuccessful applications. Because of the necessarily laborious and tedious process of ensuring proper peer review and academic publishing protocols, her research still needed to work its way through the academic system, but given the heat that was being generated around e-tolling, she interviewed me and shared her draft research, hoping it would generate light and put our experience into some reasoned global perspective.

John was intrigued and suggested I rekindle contact with her to discuss and obtain approval for the use of some of this interesting information. We also wanted to find out if she had established more insights into her initial research project, which had been shelved. John, with his insatiable passion for learning, soaked it up.

Now that e-tolling had been launched, our own research and insights had predicted that Gauteng's e-toll scheme had a high probability for failure in the medium to long run. We based our views on the fact that a user-pays system requires an immense positive energy and support from society in order to drive the high compliance levels to ensure success. In the numerous international examples where negative societal energy existed, a sizeable component of the users get away with not paying for the scheme, which, in turn, causes a spiralling decline in support over time and the eventual collapse of the system.

We needed to get our research down on paper and thereby formalise

OUTA's position towards the scheme with more insight, facts and research. We also needed to dispel the myth that we didn't want to pay for the freeway upgrade, or that we were a radical bunch of people whose sole purpose was simply to defy government on illogical grounds. We believed our role was a constructive one to play in transcending society's impasse on the e-toll matter, and, as such, we needed to express and explain the logic behind our cause.

Aside from the aggrieved views that SANRAL had run roughshod over society's constitutional rights with a failed public engagement process, or that its collection costs were irrationally high, we were also concerned about the practical workability of the scheme, which we could see was fraught with external and internal inefficiencies that it could not escape. The most significant of these practical challenges facing SANRAL were: (a) the ease and extent to which vehicle licence plate tampering would take place; and (b) the vast amount of erroneous vehicle ownership data being fed into SANRAL's system from the eNatis national vehicle licensing system.

SANRAL's licence plate tampering headache

Licence plate tampering was a serious problem for the e-tolling scheme and took the form of two main areas of modus operandi:

- Licence plate cloning: when someone fraudulently fits a vehicle registration number that is identical to that of a vehicle that looks exactly like their own vehicle (colour, model, etc.). The impact of this behaviour is one that lumps the rightful owner of that vehicle registration with the 'cloned vehicle's' e-toll movements (and traffic fines). This was a big problem that the car rental and fleet companies had contemplated with the scheme.

- Number plate tampering: when people deliberately swap two or more numbers or letters in their licence plate around or deface their registration plates. Defacing could be done with mud, scratching off or painting the numbers to look different, thereby having the impact of confusing the electronic vehicle licence number reader when recording this in the system. This practice essentially renders their contact details in the vehicle licence system as untraceable. Number plate tampering also has the unintended consequence of number plate cloning, but it is invariably easier for the innocent person, when challenging the e-toll movement/charge, to show that the vehicle in question (normally in the photograph) is different from their vehicle recorded in the eNatis licence registration system.

The underlying problems that had given rise to these situations are twofold:

1. There are no effective regulations and controls in place to manage the manufacture and issuing of false licence plates to the public. In many parts of the world, audit trails exist to prevent and punish the issuers of false licence plates. This is not the case in South Africa, which makes it easy for people to fraudulently purchase a licence plate of their choice over the counter.

2. There has been insufficient or ineffective police enforcement to retaliate against this growing problem of false licence plates in the region. Licence plate tampering has grown over the past decade, a behaviour expressed by those who want to escape growing number of camera speed-control systems being erected. Municipalities and metros around the country had become wise to an ability to increase their revenues by simply erecting more speed and other traffic infringement fining systems. Many road users have argued that this behaviour by the local authorities was not one that drove a genuine attempt to improve road safety, but was more aligned to unfair revenue generation and, as a result, road users have reacted by simply refusing to pay their traffic fines while others decided to defy the law by fitting false licence plates.

We sincerely believed that the e-toll system would become a catalyst to the growing problem of falsified number plates and, in effect, the road users could escape paying for e-tolls as a result of the inefficiencies of the local authorities in enforcing and administering the country's vehicle licence system.

Armed with our views that e-tolling would suffer at the hands of these and other technical challenges, and our opinion that OUTA's past work had raised the awareness of the scheme's unjust and possibly unlawful introduction (when tested against a criminal charge for non-payment), we believed that society's civil courage was sufficiently heightened to ensure low levels of compliance would be sustained long after the e-tolling scheme's launch on 3 December 2013.

We were motivated by OUTA's new lease of life as we prepared to stave off SANRAL's propaganda and remain resolute in highlighting the scheme's ills. We heightened our call for civil courage in the challenge against e-tolls and remained convinced that if society remained strong-willed and did not heed SANRAL's calls and threats to participate in the scheme, it would eventually collapse.

But would the public remain strong, or would they falter? The compilation of our position paper was very necessary and we needed to use all mechanisms of the media to have as many people read it as we possibly could.

CHAPTER 18

Media wars, propaganda and SANRAL PR blunders

From the outset, the e-toll scheme encountered public relation blunders and disasters on a regular basis. From 2010 to the end of 2012, SANRAL's chief executive officer, Nazir Alli, was the initial face and voice that defended the scheme and handled the press enquiries, with the project's chief operating officer, Alex van Niekerk, and the chief financial officer, Inge Mulder, filling in from time to time.

Aside from the fact that there had been very little public consultation on the project, Alli became notorious for dodging direct questions, and even told a journalist, who enquired about the detail of SANRAL's e-toll model, that 'you won't understand it'.

Alli had a way of coming across as a very convincing and believable person, especially the first time you met or heard him speak. However, once his friendly and becoming facade had been penetrated, my impression of him was one of an arrogant and unapproachable persona. It was this side to him that many journalists began to encounter and expose as time went on.

Government officials didn't do any better to win the public over, which was a critical requirement for the system to succeed. As far back as February 2011, as mentioned in Part 1, the transport minister at the time, S'bu Ndebele, told the public that if they don't like the tolls they should hop on a taxi, a bus, or a train.

This angered the public who already felt their opinions and concerns about the e-toll scheme were not being listened to.

Later Ndebele made another remark that I felt was arrogant in its tone: 'Plan A is e-tolling and plan B is plan A.'

A year later government spokesperson Jimmy Manyi told the public, 'Get used to it. This is not just a bad dream, it's a reality, it's going to happen.'

In my opinion, an opinion shared by many others, these incidents and statements by government officials were examples of arrogance combined with diabolical tact, not the kind of behaviour befitting an inclusive, democratic government that was supposed to care about its people.

By late 2012, I can only assume that SANRAL decided to seek new energy and tactics for its external communication process.

In January 2013 SANRAL announced the appointment of a new spokesperson: senior government 'spin doctor' Vusi Mona.

Mona was the deputy CEO at the Government Communication and Information System at the time. He would reprise his role there to take up the position at SANRAL in February 2013.

At the announcement of the new appointment, Gauteng MPL for the DA Jack Bloom said the damage to SANRAL's reputation had already been done and no amount of spin or a focused PR programme could help it.

'A SANRAL charm offensive would be like putting lipstick on a pig. A change in policy is needed and no more spin doctoring,' Bloom was quoted as saying in *The New Age* on 13 January 2013. I merrily used this metaphor 'putting lipstick on a pig' when describing government's new farcical dispensation that Deputy President Ramaphosa announced on 20 May 2015.

Vusi Mona's chequered past

Mona didn't exactly arrive at his new role with a squeaky clean imagine.

According to the Department of Communications he was born in Nelspruit, Mpumalanga and held a BA degree in English and Economics and a postgraduate degree in Education. A teacher by trade he moved into the world of journalism where his career rapidly took off.

He was the launch editor of *The Teacher* newspaper, which appeared in the *Mail & Guardian,* whereafter he became the editor of *Tribute* magazine.

He later joined the *City Press* as a features editor and within a year was appointed as deputy editor, eventually becoming the editor in 2000.

It was in this position that scandal broke around Mona. He shot to notoriety when he published a story handed to him by a former *Sunday Times* journalist, after it had been rejected by her editor. The story alleged that former public prosecutions director Bulelani Ngcuka was an apartheid spy.

This in turn led to the Hefer Commission of Inquiry in 2003, which was set up to look into allegations that Ngcuka had been investigated for being an apartheid spy and, as a result, abused his power as the country's chief prosecutor.

Mona's evidence relates to a meeting that was held in a hotel in Sandton on 24 July 2003 where Ngcuka briefed certain newspaper editors about the investigations against Mac Maharaj and the Deputy President Jacob Zuma.

The meeting was meant to be off the record. Mona told the commission he left the meeting with a sense of discomfort: Ngcuka, he thought, had abused his power and violated people's constitutional rights. After reflecting on the matter and discussing it with colleagues, he decided to reveal what Ngcuka had said at the meeting in a document sent to the chief justice, to the public protector and to others.

During the commission, Mona revealed some of the details of the off-the-record briefing by Ngcuka, something journalists are ethically bound not to do, and later admitted under cross-examination that his evidence had been untruthful in certain respects. The two faux pas left him disgraced and, in our view, with zero credibility, although some felt he had been unfairly persecuted.

The Hefer Commission found that Mona had perjured himself in his testimony, and thus found his testimony to have been unhelpful. Hefer considered recommending that Mona be criminally charged for his perjury, but took pity on him because he believed this finding would be the cause of sufficient suffering for the errors of his ways.

In late 2003 Mona left *City Press* following a conflict-of-interest investigation by his employer, Media24, into his undeclared participation in the Rainbow Kwanda Communications consortium, which won the Mpumalanga Regional Government PR contract (as reported in the *Mail & Guardian*, 10 July 2009). This added further controversy and a cloud of mistrust to his persona and dealings.

In 2007 he was appointed head of media and communication for Rhema Church before being offered a position to return to government as head of communication at the Presidency.

Having full insight into the outcome and findings of the Hefer Commission and the conflict-of-interest matter at Media24, one could take the view that it was a reckless risk for SANRAL to have employed Mona as its media spokesperson. If it wanted to present a convincing and pleasing image to society, it should probably have employed someone who didn't come with this unnecessary baggage of their past.

But, who are we to judge SANRAL's recruitment efforts and policies?

Looking back at Mona's appointment at SANRAL, our job of discrediting the e-toll scheme was made a lot easier. SANRAL's loss and, I guess, OUTA's gain.

By the end of 2012, the e-toll saga had been one of the top media stories for the previous two years and was not letting up. Mona's appointment at SANRAL certainly offered him a platform and opportunity to make good on his past, to exert a new stamp of reason and rational behaviour.

From our perspective, Mona's appointment at SANRAL sent a clear message: big guns and additional resources, backed by a recent and massive increase in its marketing budget. SANRAL was clearly intent on trying to dispel the negative sentiment linked to both the SANRAL brand and the e-tolling system, as well as to persuade sufficient freeway users to comply with its scheme.

Adverts promoting e-tolling appeared everywhere: newsprint, radio, TV and billboards. We were up against a juggernaut.

In August 2013 questions by the DA expressed a concern in Parliament about SANRAL's massively increased marketing budget. In 2010, SANRAL had spent R7 million on marketing matters. In 2011, this had increased substantially to R54 million, obviously in an attempt to counter the growing dissension around the e-toll scheme. Then, in 2012, its marketing budget was increased to R74 million and the financial year ending 2013 saw a further increase in this budget to R85 million.

The only major change in SANRAL's strategy over that period was the introduction of its e-tolls, so it was logical to extrapolate that the increase from below R7 million in 2010 to R85 million in 2013 was the result of the need for a massive campaign to coerce the public into acceptance of the scheme.

Looking back over the three-year period from 2011 to 2014, the marketing schools and journals could very well consider this situation as a case study for what could be argued to be the biggest failure and 'waste of money' campaigns undertaken in South Africa's modern times.

SANRAL and the media

SANRAL's increased marketing spend resulted in more than simply getting its messages out there.

Throughout the fracas, OUTA and other critics had received significant airtime on the emotive e-toll issue. It was a subject that sold newspapers and got the radio listeners talking. I imagine that the exposure that OUTA, COSATU, the Justice Project South Africa (JPSA) and others received through the various news portals was severely undermining SANRAL's ability to get public acceptance of the scheme. Not for any reason other than the logic and opinions we expressed, these views probably resonated better with the public than the input provided by SANRAL.

But it was a few months into 2013 that we discovered a very noticeable shift in the airtime exposure extended towards OUTA. We even had people contacting us to express similar sentiments and opinions on this matter.

The listeners of one regional radio station indicated to us that there seemed to be a clear change in strategy by this specific radio station. For a number of reasons, I won't mention its name. Up until the end of 2013 this radio station had called OUTA on a regular basis to provide input on the topic. Then, overnight, the request from OUTA to provide comment dried up and there appeared to be a noticeable shift towards being more accepting of the e-toll situation by this radio station. According to the listeners, it had gone soft on SANRAL and Vusi Mona appeared to get more airtime to explain its issues and to talk up the good side of e-tolling.

Personally, I hadn't taken notice of this development as I was not a frequent listener of this station. Its listeners were adamant and quick to point out this obvious shift to us. I then realised that it was a feasible deduction to make because our requests for quick sound bites and live interviews from that radio station had literally dissipated to virtually nothing in the space of a few weeks, yet the topic was still a highly emotive and very newsworthy one.

Was this just because of its marketing campaign?

I guess I need to be careful not to speculate. We didn't have time to run around and check this stuff. Neither do I have an intention to name this radio station as it has given us airtime in the past and the amount of airtime it afforded us improved once again in the latter part of 2014.

I must, however, add that there were a couple of radio stations that remained loyal. These were Talk Radio 702/94.7 (the Prime Media Group), RSG (Radio Sonder Grense), Power FM, Cii and others. These guys remained true to their audience.

I can also say that the airtime we received from the government-controlled television channels (SABC 1, 2 and 3 and Channel 404) and radio stations (SAFM and Radio 5) were minimal throughout 2012, 2013 and into mid-2014. For every ten interviews we did with other (private) TV broadcasters, such as e-News/e-NCA and, surprisingly, ANN7, we would do one with the government-controlled broadcasters at SABC. But, of course, we expected nothing less and it is a really sad and sorry state of affairs for me to have to say that.

Things did change, however, and in the latter half of 2014 and into 2015, SABC's 24-hour news channels (Channel 404) and Morning Live on SABC 2 conducted a number of interviews with John and me to give input on the e-toll developments. Their past sparse inclusion of OUTA from their studios dissipated and we became welcome, regular guests.

New energy for OUTA

Some ten months after Mona's full-time appointment in February 2013, OUTA's new civil action strategy was about to kick in. With John and Rob on board, we were better prepared and set up to expose SANRAL's and government's PR spin, especially now that the distractions of time-consuming litigation were out of the way.

The one issue that was a constant bone of contention for us was the number of e-tags that SANRAL claimed were in use. We consistently believed that the figures the media (and the public) were being given weren't making sense. From as early as 2011 and into early 2012, the Department of Transport was claiming increasing sales, reaching 500 000 e-tags sold by April 2012 (at the time of the interdict), despite the fact that e-tolls had not even been launched. We knew that government as well as several fleet companies had fitted tags to test the system with SANRAL, Europcar being one of them. We also knew that many tags had been issued to the leasing organisations and banks, which would eventually install and manage the e-tag process for corporate fleets in much the same way as they managed their fuel cards and vehicle mainte-nance programmes. We also noticed that many e-tags were sitting on the shelves at supermarkets and news agencies.

While we had no proof, we put this claim of half a million e-tags sold by SANRAL as sheer propaganda. We suspected that SANRAL was counting all these tags that were sitting in storage and on shop shelves as 'sold' to the public when, in actual fact, they were not affixed on the screens of vehicles that were using the freeways on a regular basis. In OUTA's view, this would be a clear attempt to create the impression that society was buying into the scheme and was a ploy designed to pressurise those 'unsure' members of the public to 'tag up'.

As things turned out, Vusi Mona's appointment was hardly the threat we expected it to be. In fact, he was rather good for our cause and somewhat damaging to SANRAL's. On a few occasions, we exposed Vusi Mona for deliberately providing misleading information about the number of e-tags sold. Mona came across to me as someone who shot from the hip without giving careful thought to how his statements might contradict questionable claims made during earlier comments. In my opinion, he didn't appear to be the slick spokesperson who was going to turn around the public's perception on e-tolling and, by the middle of 2014, one got the impression that Mona's voice was doing more damage to the scheme than good.

Four months into his new role, one of Mona's big blunders was a press statement he made on 1 July 2013 wherein he claimed huge success in the number of e-tag sales, following SANRAL's recent marketing campaign and efforts in this regard. He stated that in the six-week period from the end of April to mid-June 2013, SANRAL had sold an additional 350 000 e-tags, which was an increase in sales of more than 140%, from 250 000 to 600 000.

What utter bull, I recalled thinking as I opened my Apple Mac to type out a press statement in response to Mona's claim. The reason we could denounce his claim and the numbers he had circulated was that both the Department of Transport and SANRAL had, on a number of occasions throughout 2012 and early into 2013, reported that its e-tag sales were at volumes far in excess of the 250 000 that Mona pegged the figure at for the end of April 2013. Minister S'bu Ndebele had put the e-tag sales at just over 501 000 in April 2012 and SANRAL had put this figure at over 600 000 on a few occasions by the beginning of 2013. How could it be possible that its e-tag sales had gone from 600 000 back down to 250 000 in a few months and then back up to 600 000 six weeks later?

When the press questioned Mona following OUTA's retort of 'more misleading information from SANRAL', the response reported in the media was: 'Despite the questions and confusion surrounding SANRAL's maths, the agency is sticking to its 600 000 figure.' Of course it would. That wasn't even good spin doctoring. Sheer laziness and shoddy spokesperson, I thought. How its PR agency had failed to point that out must have been a concern for SANRAL. For us it was a case of 'too good to be true'. Blunders like this made it all too easy for OUTA to expose SANRAL's propaganda strategy.

We can only surmise that Mona went to sleep that night feeling very embarrassed. SANRAL clearly slipped up.

But, a month later, Mona was at it again. He had issued another SANRAL statement wherein it was claimed on 31 July 2013 that in order to pay the maximum cap of R450, the road user will have travelled through 301 gantries and have done an average of 2 760 kilometres during the month on the e-tolled roads.

Having seen how Mona's numbers previously did not add up, I logged onto SANRAL's website and used its own 'e-toll calculator' to verify his statement. Once again, we exposed his erroneous claims. By taking two different routes (north to south and west to east), we found that you would only travel 1 598 kilometres and use only 163 gantries, almost half the number quoted by Mona, in order to reach a monthly bill of approximately R450.

In our responding press statement we asked how it was conceivable for the SANRAL spokesperson and head of PR and marketing to get these calculations so wrong.

Instead of improving, the marketing faux pas continued. In October 2013 Transport Minister Dipuo Peters, speaking at the South African Chamber of Commerce and Industry meeting, said that e-tolls were just like pay toilets.

'Those who use a facility, you pay R1 or R2. Those toilets need to be maintained. Would you pay [to use a] dirty toilet?' Peters asked. 'Responsible citizens will pay for the open and smooth roads.'

Then President Jacob Zuma put his foot in it during a speech at the ANC's manifesto forum at Wits University, where he was questioned about the wisdom and logic of the e-tolling system that would soon be implemented. 'We can't think like Africans in Africa generally. We are in Johannesburg. This is Johannesburg. It is not some national road in Malawi,' he said. The *Mail & Guardian* reported, 'What the president meant by this has been a subject of debate on Twitter, with some claiming it was arrogant and classist.'[18]

His comments created a huge stir that resulted in more explanations as to what was really implied and apologetic remarks made to the Malawian government, which had taken the comment to imply that Malawi was a backward nation.

There is nothing like having your opponents shoot themselves in the foot, time after time. This was honey for the media who seized every obvious opportunity to comment on the emotive topic. We lapped it up, releasing press statements on a regular basis in request for responses to the never-ending faux pas and misleading comments by SANRAL or its bosses. It seemed that the only way government and its agencies could stop embarrassing themselves on the issue was simply to keep quiet.

Shortly before the 3 December 2013 launch date we witnessed more inconsistencies with the information regarding e-tag sales. At the end of November, SANRAL claimed in its media releases that e-tag sales had increased to 700 000, but when the media enquired as to the detail on the breakdown of this figure (between corporate fleets, government, public, etc.), none was provided. We didn't believe the figures, but we had no way of proving them wrong and called for transparency and exposure of the exact numbers within the system from an independent body. No such luck and SANRAL refrained from even rising to the bait, a common tactic in the spin-doctor world: 'Never entertain a response to a question you don't want to go near.' Just ignore it.

But it wasn't only in terms of figures that Mona came up short. On 15 January 2014, just over a month after the scheme was launched, he appeared one night on Radio 702 and Cape Talk to answer questions on the project. One listener called in asking about an SMS she supposedly received from SANRAL, asking her to pay the e-toll fees she owed.

The listener asked, 'How do I, as a road user, know that I'm not being scammed, because a lot of people will jump on the bandwagon and try to scam you? How do you guarantee that these SMSs are genuine and not scams?'

Mona replied: 'Very easy. Raise your IQ a little bit.'

The press had a field day and Howard Dembovsky from the JPSA was not amused, calling on Mona to resign or for the minister of transport to dismiss him 'since he clearly has no respect for the public he is supposed to serve'.

Dembovsky said Mona should have known better than openly and blatantly insult a member of the public who was asking a legitimate question. Mona replied to the call for his resignation saying that Dembovsky was simply angry about e-tolls and with SANRAL.

SANRAL was quick to issue an apology, saying it regretted the comments made by Mona, which were 'made in jest to the listener'.

'The agency is of the opinion that Mr Mona's comment is now being blown out of proportion by JPSA, as the listener has not followed up with a complaint. If the listener was offended, that was not the intention of Mr Mona,' SANRAL said.

On hearing Dembovsky call for Mona to resign, I phoned Howard to suggest this might not be a good idea. In my opinion, Mona was good for our cause as he was doing more damage to SANRAL's credibility than we could ever do in a lifetime.

Howard had a good chuckle and agreed to hold back on his suggestion that Vusi should vamoose. He agreed that Vusi was 'a masterpiece' and was probably of more value to the anti-toll lobbyists inside SANRAL than out.

Mona was full of personal attacks on his opponents. He called me a 'hustler', a 'populist', a 'wanna-be road engineer.' In May 2013, he said OUTA was like a rehabilitated smoker 'repeating the same boring list of misinterpretations and half-truths'. Again on 8 April 2015, Mona implied in a *Daily Maverick* article that I had racist tendencies, wherein he wrote:

> *Mr Duvenage, by his own admission in Busani Ngcaweni's book* Liberation Diaries: Reflections on 20 Years of Democracy, *says he grew up not being encouraged to make contact with blacks. So it might be that he is still battling with that. I am not friends with him, but I will take a call from him.*

It was a cheap shot.

For the record, I was invited to write an essay to be featured in Busani Ngcaweni's book (*Liberation Diaries*), wherein I reflected on the wrongs and challenges of being raised in all-white schools during the racist regime of apartheid, a time when our families were not encouraged to socialise with black people. This is no secret. I also reflected in that essay, however, that as a teenager I was not comfortable with the notion of racial segregation and deliberately befriended a person of colour. Now Mona wouldn't mention that, would he?

In an opinion piece on *SA Breaking News*, Mona said that whenever he hears from OUTA, his first reaction is a deep sigh followed by the thought, can they please find at least one new thing to say?

This was an interesting comment and I pondered on it for a few days, as it was a matter that I imagined others might have given thought to.

Our response to Mona's opinion was simply that ours was not a case or cause that needed reinvention or finding new things to say. The case of irrationality, inefficiency and high costs of collection, compounded by an unlawful public engagement process, were the main reasons we had started this challenge. Nothing more was required and nothing had changed, other than the mounting faux pas by SANRAL that were unfolding along the way and, of course, we would expose the ongoing misinformation and untruths it announced as and when these arose. We really did not need to go in search of a new approach or a different angle to keep our challenge alive.

Our cause and claims were consistent and if this was boring for Mona, well, that was his problem, not ours.

Again, on 16 May 2015, Mona was at his tactics of trying to discredit OUTA and SANRAL. In a *Saturday Star* opinion piece, Mona tried to denounce OUTA as a motley group made up of a 'lay theologian, a former traffic cop and a businessman on early retirement', who were merely trying to fleece money from the public and called for transparency of our books and who our funders were. The public laid into him, with 284 comments to the *IOL* online article within 36 hours. We responded by placing all our audited financial standing on our website, a matter we believe we should have done anyway, but as far as telling him who funded us (barring the DA's public announcement of their R1-million donation), we were simply not going to do that, given the history of government's bullying behaviour against its critics. Our response also pointed out the exact nature of our spending and that we never earned a cent from the public for our time.

CHAPTER 19

E-toll launch day arrives, 3 December 2013

On 20 November 2013, the minister of transport, Dipuo Peters, eventually announced what seemed to be the final e-tolling launch date.

I say 'eventually' because there had been five launch dates announced by the authorities over the past 32 months, the first one being as early as April 2011.

And if I thought the past two years had been busy, what was about to unfold in terms of media presence and availability for interviews, reading, researching and writing articles was well beyond what we had experienced to date. My full-time involvement over the two and a half years in the e-toll fight had been taxing, but now the game was on. Over the next twelve months, we needed to be quick on our feet, with tactical manoeuvres and media campaigns that would outsmart or counter SANRAL's claims.

With the e-toll launch date announced, we started receiving a lot of 'commiseration messages'. Our Facebook site had many postings along the lines of 'thanks for putting up a good fight' and 'pity you lost', 'pity you didn't achieve what you set out to do', etc.

This was very worrying for us, as we knew the e-toll scheme's ultimate test lay in its ability to work and raise the R260 million per month it required. To do so, SANRAL still had to achieve the high levels of compliance required for success, along with efficient collection processes and enforcement for non-payment. These 'messages of defeat' were worrying and we got the impression that many of the once-defiant public would now capitulate.

The fight was still society's to win as long as their civil courage remained more than lip service. The OUTA research and position paper ('E-tolling at an Impasse'), due for release in February 2014, three months after the launch, contained numerous international examples of how these systems fail due to compliance levels that drop below the 80% mark. We were confident that SANRAL would never achieve 80%, let alone the 93% mentioned in court. At the time, my gut feel estimated a maximum of 60% compliance for the scheme, at which level it would still be a monumental failure.

SANRAL was very aware of the low compliance challenge and its propaganda aims were twofold: (i) talk the system up by creating an impression of success; and (ii) make the defaulters feel very uneasy and insecure if they didn't pay through messages of threats and intimidation of possible arrest and criminal records. SANRAL needed to get the compliance levels as high as possible in the shortest time it could, and its marketing and propaganda campaign it undertook was immense.

We received insider information, prior to the minister's announcement, that the system was going to be launched on 2 December 2013.

We needed to be ahead of the game to take the wind out of its sails by letting the media know the launch date before SANRAL did. It would just have the impact of pissing SANRAL off a tad and would give the impression that OUTA was connected to the inner workings of the beast. Our press statement of 15 November mentioned that the minister would announce the launch date of the system as being 2 December 2013.

Obviously the media then turned to SANRAL for confirmation of OUTA's claim and the Department of Transport spokesperson, Tiyani Rikhotso, was tasked with the job of denying our claim, saying he didn't know where we got our information from.

Five days later, on 20 November, Minister Dipuo Peters made her announcement that e-tolls would be launching on 3 December 2013. We chuckled when we heard the date had been changed by one day because our source was very reliable. Perhaps SANRAL amended the date to prove that we were wrong, or was it to accommodate the minister's schedule? Who knows, but it didn't change the fact that we were being provided with good information volunteered by people working within government and SANRAL, much to their irritation.

In her announcement Peters made it clear that government intended to use the full authority and might of the law on those who refused to pay their e-toll fees. She said the GFIP and its funding mechanism were helping to create a better South Africa. Astonishingly, she even said that Mandela would have agreed because it was always his plan to build up the country. This emotional manipulation by way of pulling out the Madiba card, to weigh in with sentimental blackmail whenever it suited the ANC, was a worn-out ploy and no one was having anything to do with it on the e-toll matter.

The press conference at the e-toll launch announcement went on for over an hour. After Minister Peters had spoken it was Nazir Alli's turn at the mic, during which he drove the enforcement point home again, saying SANRAL would be issuing a summons to those who refused to pay their e-toll fees. This point had to be made very clear as we had no doubt that SANRAL knew the public were overwhelmingly against the scheme and would not come marching to their outlets willingly. Our opinion was that SANRAL decided to rely heavily on the fear factor as a major component to drive compliance under duress.

This intimidation tactic was continuously repeated on numerous occasions over the next few months. Vusi Mona also reminded the public that a criminal record would pose many problems when applying for finance credit, jobs and in other areas of everyday life.

*

The QuadPara Association of South Africa (QASA) had remained a critic of the e-toll scheme and immediately put out a statement saying that ironically the e-toll launch on 3 December was also the United Nations' International Day for Persons with Disabilities.

'To imagine Gauteng motorists departing for their year-end break with the South African government facing charges of human rights violations against people with disabilities is a crying shame,' said Ari Seirlis, reiterating that his members had still not been made exempt from paying e-toll fees.

OUTA also published a media release indicating that the launch of e-tolling would have significant negative consequences for the country.

'We are concerned that the executive arm of government has failed to take society into its confidence, and in the process has sown the seeds of what we fear will go down in history as a very costly failure and something that could have been avoided,' I said at the time.

But it didn't matter what we said. All our talking and court action had not halted the process. Government was determined to go ahead. All we could do now was watch the reality of a predicted unworkable system unfold. The final and ultimate hurdle for SANRAL had arrived. Could they do it?

SANRAL appeared ecstatic that finally the system it had stood so firmly by for all these years was going to go live. Alli said this now signalled SANRAL's ability to start servicing the debt of the road upgrade and he encouraged people to buy e-tags, saying it was 'the right thing to do'.

In addition to the hard-line intimidation strategies adopted in their messaging, Minister Peters and SANRAL also applied a charm offensive intended to encourage the public to buy e-tags. Their tactics consisted of the following reminders to the public:

- E-tag users qualify for a 48% discount off the standard tariffs;
- 83% of e-toll users would pay an average of less than R100 a month; and
- a significant number of 900 000 people had made the 'right decision' to purchase e-tags.

Peters urged motorists to buy tags. 'It's in your best interest that you get tagged ... We are aware of campaigns discouraging people from registering and we wish to encourage motorists not to pay attention to this,' she had said just days before the launch.

The announcement also had an immediate effect on Austrian Kapsch TrafficCom's share price, which increased to 45 euros by late in February 2014, from 39 euros at the time of the e-toll launch date press briefing. A table of the e-toll events and the corresponding movements in the Kapsch TrafficCom share price is attached in Appendix 2, which depicts an uncanny relationship to the e-toll developments in South Africa.

Within a few weeks of the e-toll launch, our concern was a growing sense of defeatism settling in. We got the sense that many road users had started to give up. The commiseration messages kept coming in. This felt like a case of a good fight while it lasted, but now that the scheme has been turned on, let's move on. This became a serious concern for the OUTA committee. The earlier research polls by Ipsos and TNS had reflected that most would remain defiant. We wondered if this was turning out to be a case of more talk and less action.

We had our work cut out for us. With no money to spend on billboards or advertising campaigns, we could only turn to social media and press announcements through the mainstream media to communicate with the public. Our early messages cautioned that just because e-tolls had started didn't mean the system was working sufficiently smoothly to achieve its goals for success. The challenge of exposing the weaknesses and inefficiencies of the scheme lay ahead.

We used messages like 'civil courage' and reminded our social media members that all the past talk of defiance now needed to be translated into action. The time for civil action was now and we were right to stand up against an unjust and irrational policy.

It was time to walk that talk.

We were further encouraged by the faith-based movements that joined the fray, asking people to take a stand against e-tolls and not buy an e-tag. The Catholic, Methodist, Presbyterian and Uniting Reformed churches, amongst others, slammed the government for not listening to the people and for the effect tolling would have on people's lives.

'We will be accused, as churches, of being unpatriotic and disloyal to government for calling for this resistance, but we cannot blindly follow what government tells us is right for our people. We struggled through, and fought against apartheid, and we will fight this too,' the churches said in a joint statement.

They called for peaceful and non-violent protest against e-tolls.

A strident voice in the anti-e-tolling campaign, who had also repeatedly spoken out against the e-toll system on a regular basis, was Howard Dembovsky, the chairperson of the JPSA. He expressed a concern that e-tolls could be launched when government had not made it clear exactly how it would collect money from those who did not pay. There was no indication how motorists would be prosecuted if they refused to pay their bills.

Dembovsky sent legal letters to various government departments seeking clarity on the threatened prosecution of e-toll transgressors. The answers he sought were never received.

It was an important question and over a year later, by 2015, it was one that had still not been fully answered.

A day or two before the gantries were turned on for payment, long queues outside the previously empty SANRAL e-toll customer care centres began to develop. People were flocking to get their tags, or so it would appear. It seemed that government's propaganda was working even though many who were signing up were doing so grudgingly. The queues, however, were also due to the long time it took for each registration. We were told it took up to two hours to register a user.

SANRAL enjoyed seeing these queues and the government-backed television broadcaster, SABC, ran visuals to show how people were standing in line at centres across the region to get their tags. 'Get your tags now, ahead of the rush,' was the message espoused by Mona and I imagined, at this stage, that Nazir Alli was reclining on his sofa with a broad smile on his face. Was everything falling into place for him at last?

The next twelve months would tell a completely different story.

When the clock struck midnight on 3 December there were no glitches, the computers kicked into gear and the electronic system was open for business. We imagined that SANRAL's plan to launch just before the Christmas mid-summer holiday break would help it to iron out possible glitches during the lowest freeway traffic period before business peaked again in mid-January 2014.

COSATU declared the day 'Black Tuesday'.

'3 December 2013 will go down in history as a turning point for the democratic state and government. It will represent the day on which our government refused to listen to the views of the people and the poor,' said COSATU Provincial Secretary Dumisani Dakile.

The OUTA committee contemplated some form of protest on launch day, but our tight resources and time constraints kept us hamstrung.

Ari Seirlis from QASA said, 'Wayne, we are planning a protest as the e-toll launch coincides with International Day of Persons with Disabilities.'

Ari has a good track record for campaigning against systems and buildings that are not conducive to free movement of people with disabilities. Advocacy and campaigning is a skill of QASA's. If any organisation could highlight the plight of its constituency under attack, it was Ari and the QASA team. They had campaigned vigorously outside soccer stadiums in 2010 that were not wheelchair friendly. The disabled were not exempt from e-tolls and, despite several attempts to have their concerns addressed by SANRAL, not much had happened.

QASA has a group of active wheelchair campaigners called the 'dirty dozen'. They are there in a flash when called on for their presence during a legitimate campaign, chaining themselves to pillars outside the head offices of many an authority. They could create a media stir when they wanted to.

Ari said to me: 'That's it. We are going to chain ourselves to a gantry on the highway, all twelve of us. Can you suggest which one will have the best visibility for us?'

I laughed and said he was crazy, but in the same breath I thought it was a marvellous idea. I was inspired by Ari's energy. However, after taking legal advice, he was persuaded not to go this route as anyone on foot (or in a wheelchair) on the highway would be breaking the law. The dirty dozen stood a chance of being arrested and Ari didn't want to risk that.

With a highway protest called off, Ari's mind remained focused on ensuring the protest went ahead and this time he spoke of doing something outside the e-toll store at the Rivonia off-ramp.

We had to keep the planning for the protest under wraps to thwart any attempt by SANRAL to block it. Suspecting that my phone had been tapped for some time now, we did all our communication through WhatsApp. I also got a message to *Carte Blanche* and a number of the media to witness QASA's protest message on launch day at SANRAL's e-tolls kiosk in Rivonia.

'E-tolls has paralysed us,' QASA declared on its posters. The dozen wheelchair-bound protestors first went into the store and tried to register for a disabled exemption e-tag, saying that SANRAL had indicated this was possible, but of course they were turned away. During the protest, which had now moved into the car park, the group set an old dilapidated wheelchair alight. Pictures of the wheelchair on fire became the image of the day and were splashed across TV screens and newspapers alike.

Their message to government and SANRAL was loud and clear: 'e-tolls will burn the disabled community.'

The height of the PR wars

Public relations was an important part of the campaign from both parties' point of view. Obviously, the success of the e-toll user-pays system would depend on the number of people who purchased and fitted an e-tag and then kept their account with SANRAL paid up. The more who fitted e-tags, the greater the scheme's chance of success.

In the event that the people refrained from tagging up, SANRAL would have a tough time in collecting the funds. We knew that any attempt to issue summonses for criminal prosecution of hundreds of thousands of citizens, would attract too much negative publicity and ramifications for the ANC during the forthcoming national and regional elections in May 2014.

While SANRAL was talking up the e-tag numbers, our hunch was that society was standing its ground and that more people would abstain from purchasing e-tags than those who would. We also knew that a sizeable volume of the e-tagged vehicles on the freeways belonged to government, corporate and car rental fleets.

It wasn't until the eventual launch of e-tolling on 3 December 2013 that the moment of truth would arrive, to enable OUTA to expose SANRAL's misleading claims. Once the scheme had launched, we had the opportunity to prove our claims of an unworkable system through the predicted advent of four main issues:

- High public defiance that would produce a sizeable shortfall in the required compliance levels for success.

- High billing error rates would expose the system's inefficiencies and problems that would plague it.
- A high likelihood existed that the authorities would be unable to enforce the non-payment of e-tolls.
- Consequently, the low levels of revenue generation would see the system fall well short of its required and initially targeted revenue stream of R260 million per month, in order to service the bonds and e-toll collection costs incurred by Electronic Toll Collection.

Within a week of e-tolls being launched, SANRAL's propaganda machine was hard at work by claiming that over 950 000 tags were 'out there' to create the impression that society had generally accepted the situation. Every now and then it added more to its numbers.

We were sure that this claimed number of tags sold was misleading, but up until the launch, we had no idea how to prove our point. However, that was about to change now that the system had been turned on.

'The only way we can tell is to physically count the number of e-tags fitted to windscreens,' I suggested to John Clarke and Rob Hutchinson on the day that e-tolling was launched. It was safe to assume that those who had e-tags would have installed them as indicated by SANRAL in the installation instructions, on the windscreen, preferably around the rear-view mirror area. This made the e-tags easily identifiable and visible from the outside. I ran the idea of a physical count past another committee member, Rob Handfield Jones, who agreed that the logic was indeed correct.

Prior to proceeding with an e-tag counting exercise, I did two things:

1. I conducted some high-level calculations to establish what it was that we could expect and what we were trying to prove.
2. I then made contact with research experts at TNS and Market Research Management to establish the sample sizes and methodology required to ensure our planned research was sound.

Past media statements by SANRAL had suggested there are roughly 3.5 million registered cars and trucks in Gauteng, excluding trailers, caravans, etc. SANRAL had also stated that roughly 2.4 million vehicles make use of the freeways every month and if one were to take a rolling three-month average, this figure climbs to around 2.8 million due to infrequent users and out-of-towners making use of the freeway on the odd occasion. There were also roughly one million regular (almost daily weekday) commuters that made use of the GFIP highways.

From these figures, if we assumed that SANRAL's claim of 900 000 tags was accurate, now that the system was turned on, we could expect to divide that number into 2.4 million and witness around 38% of the vehicles using the freeway with e-tags visibly displayed on their windscreens.

The research experts indicated that the accuracy of our research would be improved if we followed these rules:

- All counting methodologies need to be consistent.
- Counting at off-ramps or on-ramps is better than on bridges over-looking the freeway as the cars would be stationary or moving slowly enough for easy identification of those vehicles with e-tags.
- Use notepads, pens and counters, clicking every time a tagged car is spotted and, when reaching a total count of 100 vehicles, note the number of 'clicked' (e-tagged) counts and record this number.
- Continue to do this for a few hundred vehicles at various intersections and at various times of the day.
- When in doubt as to the nature of an object in the windscreen that appeared even partially like an e-tag, or an obscured e-tag, give the benefit of the doubt to SANRAL and count it as a tag.
- Be accurate and true to yourself because if another independent research company goes into the field within a short space of time to verify your methodology and numbers, you don't want to be embarrassed by making false claims. We were told to 'err on the side of caution'.

And so it was that on 5 December 2013, we hit the freeway interchanges and intersections. At times we moved in pairs, where one counted at the on-ramp and the other at the off-ramp to the freeway. At other times, we counted the vehicles on the most congested (slowest moving ramp) on our own. Once we reached around 300 vehicles counted, we would get in our cars and move on to another off- or on-ramp. We did this repetitively at different times of the day between 5 and 10 December 2013, the first week of the launch of e-tolls.

I must say that while I was expecting SANRAL to be overstating its claims, I never expected the extent to which it was. We also realised that SANRAL's claims of 950 000 tags must have included those for government vehicles that might have been based out of town. So, while its

number might be right, what was more important was the actual rate of
e-tag penetration on the Gauteng freeways.

I was expecting around 30% of the vehicles we counted to have e-tags,
which was down from SANRAL's estimate of 35%. You can imagine our
surprise when our numbers tallied less than half that – at a paltry 15%.
At first I thought our count was wrong. John, Rob and I met for coffee
early on 6 December to discuss what we thought might be wrong with
our numbers. We couldn't find anything wrong with how we did the
counting and so we hit the road to do more counts. At 15% usage, we
extrapolated that around 360 000 vehicles of the 2.4 million were tagged.
This was a far cry from SANRAL's claim of 950 000.

Our re-counts produced the same results. I then asked that we do more
counts on 12 and 13 December before the factories and business slowed
down for the Christmas break. Once again our count came in at a similar
number, slightly lower at 14%.

On pondering our numbers, we deduced the following:

- That our methodology and the numbers we had counted were fairly
  accurate.
- That there were probably still a number of fleet and government
  vehicles that were not yet tagged and that, at best, once the fleet
  owners had caught up with fitting their e-tags to their vehicles, we
  could expect this number to climb by 10% to between 25% and
  30% by the end of January.
- This would mean that SANRAL was definitely exaggerating its
  claims, as we estimated that between 680 000 to 720 000 freeway
  users were tagged or about to be tagged.

According to us, SANRAL was providing the public with misleading
numbers. We suggested it was probably counting every e-tag that it had
issued, including those in stock and on shop shelves. For all we knew it
was including tagged government vehicles in Mpumalanga and Limpopo,
but these were of no consequence as they were not generating revenue for
the e-toll system. What mattered was how many of the 2.4 million vehicles a month using the Gauteng freeways were being driven with e-tags.

We also realised that a fair number of people would have decided not
to get e-tags, but would nonetheless pay their manually posted bills, or
go into the e-toll centres, or online to settle their bills. But we also knew
that these people would be in the minority, as it made no sense to pay
a higher bill through tedious tracking and payment methods when the

convenient and cheaper option of getting an e-tag was available to those who decided to pay. People paying without a tag would not do so for long.

Many asked why we were doing these e-tag counts. The answer was simply to counter SANRAL's propaganda. By publishing our own research, we were inviting SANRAL to dispute our numbers. If it failed to allow an independent person to verify its accurate data, then our numbers became the credible source and we had the upper hand with every right to dispute SANRAL's claims. Its integrity would be questioned. We had nothing to lose and everything to gain through our e-tag counting exercise.

Our plot worked exactly as we expected and SANRAL never rose to our bait to allow journalists to compare our data with that in their systems.

Instead, SANRAL castigated us by saying 'OUTA is making wild allegations that have no factual basis'. Mona claimed that SANRAL did not need to use sampling as it had the actual numbers of e-tags taken up through its customer service centres and bulk distribution outlets, which was an accurate number.

'For the record, 920 310 e-tags have thus far been taken up. Approximately 600 000 of these are individual account holders and more than 200 000 are key account holders,' SANRAL said in a statement on 17 December 2013.

I smiled, knowing that we had the upper hand for as long as SANRAL didn't allow access to its actual numbers. Hints of the inconsistencies came in statements such as 'approximately 600 000 are individual account holders'. If it had the exact number of e-tags issued at 920 310, what was so difficult about providing the exact number of individual users?

We conducted a second round of counts from 29 January 2014 to 6 February, by which time business was back in full swing in Gauteng. Our counts now showed that the number had increased to 29% of vehicles with e-tags. This was in line with what we had expected and while it was worrying in one sense, the penetration rate was still very low – too low to sustain the system. But it was climbing. We envisaged that by now, six weeks into the scheme, most of the people who had decided to tag up would have done so, although SANRAL's intimidation tactics might still drive that number up to 40% or 45%. I was now confident that an e-tag penetration rate of 50% was looking out of reach for them.

Our media statements were aimed at heightening civil courage by telling the Gauteng freeway users that if they were un-tagged, they were in the majority. It was an uplifting message to stay strong. It appeared to be working as the rate of increase after March 2014, from our counting, was slowing down.

'I sense that Mr Mona is projecting the wish of his own subconscious thinking again, not an honest and transparent engagement with reality,' said John Clarke in our 19 February 2014 press release.

Towards the end of February 2014, Mona put out another release saying SANRAL had surpassed its milestone of one million registered users and that more than 1.2 million e-tags had been taken up. Our e-tag counts had extrapolated the 'real' figure to be around 35% by the end of February, which meant that around 850 000 vehicles were tagged, some 30% below SANRAL's claims.

The propaganda war was heating up. By March 2014, SANRAL had unleashed a barrage of advertisements on radio, TV and the press, claiming that less than 83% of the e-tagged road users would pay less that R100 per month, and thanking the R1.2 million e-tagged customers for doing the right thing.

The media loved every minute of it, not only the great revenues from SANRAL's advertising campaigns, but the incessant volume of news on the emotive topic.

While our campaign of *reassurance* and *stay strong* was being pumped out to an estimated 100 000 followers through various Facebook and Twitter platforms, we could sense there was still a high degree of trepidation creeping in from the public.

Our Facebook site and e-mail portal through the website had become inundated with questions, most of which were along the lines of: 'What to do? The bills are mounting, do we pay or not?'

Between January and March 2014, SANRAL's intimidation and threats of criminal prosecutions were plaguing everyone's minds: 'Pay your e-toll bills if you don't want a criminal record,' said SANRAL, in full offensive mode and applying a stern and threatening drive.

To some degree, its campaign was working. The stress levels of the public and within OUTA's committee were on the rise. We kept having to remind ourselves that our international research showed that compliance at under 80% to 85% spelled failure. Three months into the scheme and SANRAL was only one third of the way there. But we also knew that once it crossed the 50% mark, this would be a big milestone. We had to stick to our guns and use every opportunity we could to dispel SANRAL's misleading claims and intimidation.

We also reminded ourselves that a similarly heavy-handed government communication campaign backfired on the Hong Kong authorities in the mid-1980s when they had failed to obtain public acceptance of their e-toll scheme.

OUTA's social media campaign was running at full tilt throughout the first four months of 2014 and Rob Hutchinson spent many a sleepless night and early morning sifting through and responding to hundreds of comments. Howard Dembovsky of the JPSA had also mounted a heated campaign against SANRAL for its misleading and slanderous quotes by Mona.

But a new dynamic was brewing. The silence was deafening from a once vocal sector of the anti-e-toll camp – COSATU. Its call for the 'mother of all protest marches' made at the beginning of 2014 never transpired. Additionally, the church entities had taken their foot off the gas. The OUTA committee was feeling rather alone in the e-toll wilderness.

A changing landscape – signs of trouble for SANRAL

By the end of May 2014, once the election results had raised the possibility that the e-toll issue had put a massive dent in the ANC's support in the region, things started to change. We got a sense that the e-tag penetration growth rate had tapered off at around the 40% to 45% mark. Was our relentless media and social media campaign, in conjunction with the election results and the political dynamics, starting to pay off?

During an interview on 28 February 2014 on Talk Radio 702, SANRAL's Nazir Alli told John Robbie that it was on track with its targets. In fact it was slightly ahead, he said. When I heard that I thought, you have obviously lowered your targets by a substantial amount, Mr Alli. Well below your court papers' suggestion of an achievable 93%. It was clear that SANRAL had now devised much lower ramp-up targets of around 30% in the earlier months, which enabled it to claim it was 'ahead of its game'. It was clear to us that SANRAL was trying to either impress the minister of transport or themselves by suggesting the ramp-up targets were all on track. We knew that in order to succeed, these systems needed to achieve a far higher level of compliance within a short space of time from the outset.

Another important boost to our campaign happened on 13 February

2014, when a Kapsch TrafficCom internal 'informant' based in Austria came forward and provided us with inside information on the real e-tag numbers. This gave us confidence that we were right and that SANRAL was indeed misleading the public. Our moral courage was once again uplifted and we knew we had to be relentless in our challenge of every bit of misinformation we uncovered.

In March we got further confirmation that we had been right all along when Minister of Transport Dipuo Peters responded to parliamentary questions by stating that the number of e-tags fitted to vehicles making use of the Gauteng highways was 'between 23% and 28.6% as at 1 February 2014'.

Peters's reply also contradicted SANRAL's press releases on the number of e-tags fitted in individual vehicles. The minister said there were 912 049 e-tags issued, but only 51% of that number (468 388 – the actual number she quoted) were fitted into vehicles belonging to private freeway users. The balance was for government and corporate vehicles.

SANRAL had once again been caught out in a misrepresentation of the truth because, on 17 December, its media statements reported Mona as stating approximately 600 000 of the 920 310 e-tags sold were in use by private freeway users.

This is the beauty of the Internet and modern-day information filing. History will always expose deceit, especially in a situation of massive information flow such as this. The more one fabricates the 'truth' the more that fabric unravels and one gets horribly caught up in one's own deceit. This had happened on many occasions for SANRAL. Its numbers never added up and our claims of their misleading propaganda were, we believe, vindicated.

We pondered over whether SANRAL's intention was simply to keep the scheme alive for as long as it could in the hope that e-tolls might become accepted by the majority of people over time. Even so, the scheme was doomed.

CHAPTER 20

SANRAL's migraine begins

▬ ▬ ▬ ▬ ▬ ▬ ▬ ▬ ▬ ▬ ▬ ▬ ▬ ▬

As early as a few weeks after the e-toll launch date, mid December 2013, and the complaints had started rolling in. Billing took place every seven days and within two weeks motorists started receiving their e-toll bills in the post.

The problems we predicted began to unfold.

Many Gauteng citizens were on their summer vacation when they started receiving threatening text messages on their cellphones from the Electronic Toll Collection's (ETC's) Violations Processing Centre (VPC), informing them that they owed money for use of the freeway, and that if payment was not forthcoming, penalties and possible criminal prosecutions would take place.

The public were far from impressed.

SANRAL made sure its message was clear, right from the start: pay up or be prepared to suffer the consequences. In our opinion, its campaign was clearly positioned to intimidate motorists into compliance as it sought to coerce people to fit e-tags.

'We appeal to law-abiding citizens not to be misled by those who support lawlessness. It is important to note that not paying your toll fees is not just a traffic offence, but a criminal one,' said SANRAL's spokesperson Vusi Mona in December 2013.

With so few people tagged up at the start of the scheme, SANRAL knew its administrative problems were insurmountable unless it managed to convince the motorists to comply, and quickly. The vehicle ownership information in the e-toll system relied on the eNatis system. Unfortunately for SANRAL, eNatis was far from accurate, and without a high level of reliable data relating to vehicle ownership and billing details, a significant portion of SANRAL's invoices failed to reach the vehicle owners.

SANRAL had also made use of other databases, such as the metro traffic fines system, to link vehicle registration numbers to names, addresses and cellphone numbers. This lead to people receiving phone calls from the ETC call centre agents informing them they owed electronic toll collection money and trying to convince motorists to give them personal information such as e-mail and postal addresses to make billing administration easier.

One of the first complainants was Cornelia van Niekerk from Fines-4-U, a highly successful traffic fine management company, which received 32 phone calls in one day from the ETC violations centre. Van Niekerk's company manages traffic fines for the fleets of more than 80 companies, for which she is listed as their respective company's proxy in the eNatis system. She certainly had nothing to do with their e-toll accounts, yet she was being harassed by ETC for weeks.

Van Niekerk explained to the SANRAL call centre agent that these bills had nothing to do with her. But the calls kept coming. She was furious and started to record all the calls.

In one of the phone calls, a call centre agent apparently told Van Niekerk that she has an e-toll bill of more than R2 000. Each time the agent attempted to encourage her to register 'her' vehicles on the e-toll system, which would make the process easier for both SANRAL and 'her' company, and each time Van Niekerk explained that she had nothing to do with these vehicles. She was only responsible for managing their traffic fines where she had registered her name on the PayMyFines website as their proxy. It was clear to Van Niekerk that SANRAL's system was using information from the PayMyFines database, a matter which SANRAL had earlier denied. This website was owned by TMT Services (Pty) Ltd, a South African company owned by Kapsch TrafficCom, which, in turn, was the 85% shareholder of ETC.

It was clear to Van Niekerk that the SANRAL call centre agent did not update the system by removing her details linked to these various company vehicles as, a few weeks later, Van Niekerk started receiving piles of e-toll invoices – meant for her customers – through the post. Her post became so cumbersome that the post office had to deliver the mail in a van as the postman could not carry all of it.

It took a lawyer's letter from Fines-4-U to halt SANRAL's use of her personal information from the PayMyFines database.

This same problem was being experienced by other companies and people whose names were entered as the proxy for companies with fleets.

It was not long before the eNatis anomalies and the related problems for SANRAL started to filter into its handling of unpaid accounts. In reality, SANRAL did not have the correct postal or residential addresses, names or contact numbers for the owners of a significant number of the vehicles. Howard Dembovsky and others had estimated the information error rate in eNatis (and therefore in SANRAL's system) to be as high as 50%, making it extremely difficult for ETC's e-toll invoicing and revenue collection process to function with the required efficiency.

These issues began to unfold as numerous complaints to the press, OUTA, SANRAL, the Public Protector, the National Consumer Commissioner, HelloPeter and many other channels began to surface. Social media were having a field day.

People were receiving calls about cars they had never owned, or which they had sold years previously, or which had been written off in accidents. Many were receiving calls from SANRAL asking them to pay for e-toll routes that they never used.

One parent revealed that his ten-year-old child had received an SMS on his phone telling him to pay his e-toll bill, while another received an SMS from SANRAL, requesting payment of an overdue bill of R612.12 on his deceased father's cellphone. The son had kept his father's cellphone to manage his father's estate and affairs since his death, which had happened over a year ago. He said he did not know whether to laugh or cry.

There were also numerous cases of people in other provinces getting bills, even though they had not driven in Gauteng, which began to raise the problem of cloned number plates, a matter which, back in 2011, the car rental industry had warned SANRAL would become a bigger problem due to the e-toll system. Naturally, SANRAL down played our concern at the time.

A woman who lived in Durban, KwaZulu-Natal, received e-toll bills and was also contacted by the police and told her car had been spotted at crime scenes. The car's licence plate turned out to be a cloned registration of her vehicle as the woman had never travelled in Gauteng.

The Star newspaper decided to do an exposé on the cloned vehicle licence plate problem and sent out a team of journalists to find out how easy it would be to buy a number plate of one's choice. The paper found that at different sites all over Johannesburg all you had to do was write down your registration number on a piece of paper, pay the requested amount of between R150 and R350, to receive two number plates of your choice. This was causing a nightmare for the Johannesburg metro police whose four-person vehicle number plate investigation unit faced an impossible task of dealing with this growing problem.

The complication with cloned licence plates, and e-tolls, is that the real owner of the vehicle licence number is the one who is prejudiced by SANRAL's system. The onus is on the rightful owner to complete an affidavit and fill in a dispute or 'representation' form, which needs to be stamped by a commissioner of oaths and dispatched to SANRAL's queries department by registered mail. SANRAL (or the ETC), in turn, would assess the incorrect charges and *decide* if a refund would be processed or not.

Here are the onerous instructions on the dispute form:

a. *This form must be completed in black ink and posted by registered mail to the following address: Private Bag X164, Centurion, 0046 or can be personally submitted at any e-toll customer service centre.*

b. *The completed form must be submitted to and signed before a Commissioner of Oaths on presentation of the original VPC e-toll Tax Invoice if applicable.*

c. *A copy of the completed and signed form and supporting documents must be kept for your own records.*

d. *Receipt of the application will be acknowledged within 21 days, failing which it must be re-submitted by posting it by registered mail to the address given above or resubmitting it at an e-toll customer service centre.*

Even the taxi operators, who were supposed to be exempt from e-tolling, were facing problems with the system. Taxi operators who did not have the requisite permits, which many had been struggling for years to get from the Department of Transport, could not get the promised exemption.

We heard of hundreds of people receiving invoices for the small amount of R5.00, printed on four pages in colour and delivered by post. With the postage cost at R3.00, plus the administration and variable expenses, it appeared that SANRAL had not even got the basics right. We even received examples from people who received invoices with a zero balance. Basic inefficiencies of this nature were unfathomable and filled the media's pages with content that many found amusing. Someone commented that 'if the system is as good as SANRAL professes it to be, why then are there so many basic errors?'

Even motorists who had registered with SANRAL found out their personal details weren't safe. *ITWeb* – a respected publisher of information security and IT matters – discovered a serious vulnerability in the e-toll online account management pages.

It revealed that the e-toll website had been breached and attackers had gained access to customer data.

ITWeb's story led to Minister Dipuo Peters blaming 'media houses' for SANRAL's poor performance record. The minister told Parliament that these media houses were hacking the system, disrupting its operations and sabotaging its workings.

It wasn't long before SANRAL's e-toll system hit the top spot on complaints site HelloPeter. It appeared that SANRAL did not even monitor the site because there had been no moves on its behalf to try to engage with unhappy customers. A few weeks later there was some engagement in the form of a cut-and-paste message that read, 'Thank you for your query. It is receiving attention. SANRAL will revert with a response.'

By 12 December 2013, less than two weeks after launch date, there were 61 complaints on the site, the number of which kept on growing as time went on. The complaints ranged from bad attitude, to lack of feedback, to broken e-tags and billing queries.

Those who complained about problems with their e-tags were met by an angry online group who said they deserved the aggravation of dealing with SANRAL for having bought an e-tag in the first place. Anyone who was remotely positive about the system was met with harsh criticism.

In most of the cases motorists said that when they called ETC and SANRAL, they were told the onus was on them to prove they had not used the system. SANRAL's response was to urge people to pay first and then lodge a query with them.

The thousands of complaints painted a picture of a system in crisis within its first month of operation. Of course, this was denied by SANRAL, with Mona saying that the complaints were being conflated by e-toll opposition entities. SANRAL was adamant the system was functioning well, and there were only a few glitches.

'We assure members of the public that we take their concerns seriously and are making every effort to deal with those that are valid,' said Mona. He said in the *Pretoria News* on 11 January 2014 that no system was foolproof, and there were not a large number of complaints.

At that stage, within a couple of weeks, OUTA had already received between 600 and 700 complaints from motorists and the volume was growing.

In a media statement on 26 January 2014, SANRAL said the number of complaints was not large compared to the nearly one million accounts that had been registered for e-tolling. Mona said that when comparing these figures, it was misleading to say the system was not working. In our opinion, this was a classic case of denial.

The public didn't appear to agree with Mona's view, and the anger continued to mount.

Anthrax scare

On 21 January 2014 SANRAL's Central Operations Centre was evacuated after an envelope was delivered with a white substance inside. The Tshwane Hazardous Material Unit was called in, resulting in the shutdown of electricity and evacuation of the building. The powder was found to be harmless.

Three days later the whole exercise was repeated again when another envelope arrived.

'SANRAL is extremely worried about the impact this kind of behaviour is having on the people who work at the centre,' said Nazir Alli in a press release. 'Most of them are first-time workers and relatively young. Whoever is not happy about a government policy has appropriate channels to express their dissatisfaction.'

By the end of the month the Hawks had made an arrest. It turned out that the sender of the envelopes containing the white powder was an employee of one of SANRAL's service providers.

We were naturally worried about the anthrax scares as this was not the kind of backlash we wanted to take place. When this kind of behaviour creeps in, or if people start to burn down gantries, as some had threatened to do, then I believe the cause of resistance begins to backfire and society becomes the loser. We hoped the authorities would nip this one in the bud very quickly. The fact that MEC Ismail Vadi laid some of the blame for the anthrax scare at our feet was also an unfortunate statement on his behalf.

Zuma raises a concern

A few days later even SANRAL couldn't deny the complaints were a problem after President Jacob Zuma publicly raised concerns about incorrect billing.

Suddenly the organisation's whole attitude to the crisis did a 180-degree about-turn.

On 5 February 2014, barely two months after the launch, SANRAL acknowledged what the president had said and stated it was taking the complaints very seriously. Alli said some of the problems emanated from incorrect data on the eNatis system and cloned vehicle number plates. It also said that more than 50% of motorcycles didn't have number plates.

Voilà! At last, the concerns and unintended consequences of the scheme that we had constantly spoken of were now being echoed by SANRAL. These were the important problems and issues that SAVRALA had warned SANRAL about in 2011.

As expected, SANRAL tried to play the situation down. 'SANRAL is well aware of the challenges and apologises to road users for any inconvenience caused. A system of this magnitude was always going to have its teething problems but these are not insurmountable,' said Alli.

For at least three months after launch date the complaints rolled in thick and fast. It started to become a pleasant headache for us, as OUTA was never geared to receive complaints en masse. OUTA's team consisted of only a few full-time active people and we were simply unable to respond to the hundreds of queries received on a daily basis at that stage.

We wrote to the National Consumer Commissioner and said that SANRAL was behaving out of line, particularly in terms of its attitude of telling complainants to pay up and that the onus was on the motorists to go through the onerous process of proving their invoices had been incorrectly charged. The commissioner released a statement to indicate his concerns about SANRAL's billing process and that these had to be addressed.

We tried to answer every single e-mail that we received at OUTA, but we couldn't keep up. Enter Brian Williams. Whew!

Brian managed IT solutions company Compliance Verification Solutions (Pty) Ltd, and contacted us to assist with the development of an online portal where complaints could be automated and sent directly to SANRAL, with a logging and dispute management tool for the users to verify that these complaints were properly logged with SANRAL.

He designed the portal such that people could complain to SANRAL through the portal on OUTA's website by using SANRAL's reference number, which appeared on the bill. This way, SANRAL couldn't obtain access to complainants' telephone numbers and/or e-mail addresses, which had often never been recorded on SANRAL's system. Our aim was to make it easy for road users to lodge complaints to SANRAL while securing their privacy. By doing so, in the event that any of these people were summonsed for non-payment, they had a valid excuse in that they had a record of lodging a dispute regarding their bill to SANRAL, which, in turn, had done nothing about rectifying the matter.

The use of OUTA's online complaint portal climbed rapidly with 657 complaints logged in the first two weeks of February 2014. A month later in March, some 3 854 complaints were logged and thereafter, the use of our portal began to taper off. Many, we suspected, had decided not to even bother complaining as the furore about the e-toll problems was widespread and well documented in the press.

SANRAL either couldn't cope with them or did not want to address complaints that were directed through an OUTA portal, so it put in place an automated response to every enquiry: 'In compliance with the POPI Act (Protection of Personal Information) we are not allowed to respond to these complaints through this portal.'

We checked with Brian, whose business was focused on information compliance and verification, and he expressed his opinion that SANRAL's reaction and response to this initiative was wrong. Our process exercised no transgression of the POPI Act and in fact supported it by not disclosing to anyone the information that was shared by the complainant.

Naturally, SANRAL's automated response added to the decline of use. However, some continued to log their issues, encouraged by us to do so, as this was sufficient proof that their respective billing disputes with SANRAL had been made.

Mounting bills cause trepidation

Throughout the first half of 2014, the public remained concerned about their mounting e-toll bills and thousands were in two minds about whether to get a tag or not. We then communicated in a press statement, as well as messaging our social media followers, that it made no sense to pay SANRAL the higher penalty rate of three times that of e-tagged users. If indeed the road users were to pay for the use of the freeways, they should register and purchase an e-tag. It was a case of encouraging people to get an e-tag if they were going to pay and, if not, to then exercise civil disobedience by conscientiously objecting to paying for the system completely.

Even those who had taken the time to get an e-tag and register their vehicle into SANRAL's system were getting incorrect bills. Compliant e-tagged users started to complain to OUTA and kept us informed of the system's woes. By mid-2014, the anger and frustration expressed by the motorists was at an all time high.

*

Obviously, there were a lot of people who were compliant and got an e-tag. They didn't want the hassle or risk of falling foul of the law. In many such instances, SANRAL's intimidation tactics had been the catalyst to many a 'tag-up' decision made under duress. As a result, the e-tag penetration rate was increasing and who can blame these citizens? The thought of just one night in a South African jail and a criminal record was a frightening one for even the most burly of people.

We could 'hear' the fear in the comments on our Facebook page and all we could do in response to them was paint a picture of reality: 'based on the fact that over 1.5 million people were non-compliant, what were the chances?' We believed that if we could get the majority of the freeway users to look beyond the threats and to be morally courageous for the right reasons, then the system's demise through low compliance was inevitable.

The more SANRAL threatened the South African motoring public, the more we exposed the irrationality of their plans and said that OUTA would be in court to defend the first person prosecuted. We sketched various scenarios that illustrated the difficulty of applying the law equally to all defaulters.

We posed one real-life scenario by asking which judge would seriously criminalise a single, hard-working school teacher and single mother for not paying her e-toll bills? We added to the scene by depicting her as living in a low-cost housing settlement and not being connected to the Internet. She also lived nowhere close to a SANRAL e-toll customer centre, and yet she made use of these freeways to commute each day in her own car to teach her pupils on the other side of town. Furthermore, her weekends were taken up by getting her own children to sports events and church. She would have had no time or money to visit distant e-toll service centres, or to pay for something she felt justified in rejecting.

We felt that any judge, faced with such a scenario, would be hard pressed to give this person a criminal record. We knew the scheme would be extremely difficult to enforce, if not impossible.

LEFT: SC Alistair Franklin (left) and SC Alfred Cockrel during the interdict hearings of April 2012.
(*The Star*, Antoine de Ras)

BELOW: Paul Pauwen (left), Wayne Duvenage (centre), Marc Corcoran and an unidentified supporter outside the Gauteng North High Court, following the successful interdict of the e-toll launch on 28 April 2012.
(*The Star*, Motshwari Mofokeng)

ABOVE: Yusuf Abramjee (left), Wayne Duvenage (centre) and Paul Pauwen at the press conference in Hatfield, following the interdict of the e-toll launch on 28 April 2012.
(*The Star*, Motshwari Mofokeng)

RIGHT: Wayne Duvenage in the Constitutional Court gallery in August 2012. (*The Star*, Dumisani Sibeko)

ABOVE: Vusi Mona (left), head of communications at SANRAL, alongside Alex van Niekerk, the chief operations officer and project manager of the GFIP e-toll operations at SANRAL. (*The Star*, Boxer Ngwenya)

BELOW: Acting Judge Louis Vorster, who presided over Part B of the review from 26 to 28 November 2012. (*The Star*, Chris Collingridge)

ABOVE: Ismail Vadi (left) and Nazir Alli en route to the High Court during Part B of the review hearings. (*The Star*, Thobile Mathonsi)

RIGHT: Minister of Transport Dikobe Ben Martins was appointed in June 2012 and remained in this post until July 2013. (*The Star*, Thobile Mathonsi)

ABOVE: Minister of Transport Dipuo Peters was appointed in July 2013. (*The Star*, Thobile Mathonsi)

BELOW: Deputy President Kgalema Motlanthe (left) and Wayne Duvenage at the Union Buildings in 2012. (*The Star*, Siyabulela Duda)

ABOVE: Kevin Louis (left), John Clarke (centre) and Howard Dembovsky at an OUTA press conference. (*The Star*, Itumeleng English)

BELOW: Dr Trish Hanekom (left), with Professor Muxe Nkondo (centre left) handing over the E-Toll Advisory Panel report to Gauteng Premier David Makhura. Gauteng MEC for Transport Ismail Vadi looks on (right). (*The Star*, Motshwari Mofokeng)

ABOVE: The public defiance becomes brazen.

BELOW: Ali Gule was present at every rally with his famous placard. (*The Star*, Paballo Thekiso)

ABOVE: Zwelinzima Vavi leads the anti-e-toll march in Johannesburg on 30 November 2012.
(*The Star*, Paballo Thekiso)

LEFT: Ari Seirlis, CEO of the QuadPara Association of South Africa, outside the Supreme Court on 25 September 2013.

LEFT: Ari Seirlis and others demonstrating outside the Rivonia Road e-toll customer service centre on launch day, 3 December 2013.

BELOW: Bikers Against Tolls during a drive-slow protest ride.

ABOVE: Carola Trummer (left) and Cavey Parker, two faithful Bridge Banner Brigaders.

RIGHT: Bridge protests were a regular sight on the e-tolled roads.

ABOVE: Taxi operators march on the M1 North during the e-toll taxi strike in November 2014.
(*The Star*, Matthews Baloyi)

BELOW: Cavey Parker over the N1 e-tolled freeway. (*The Star*, Paballo Thekiso)

ABOVE: Mmusi Maimane, leader of the DA, has been very critical of the e-toll scheme. (*The Star*, Masi Losi)

BELOW: A group of DA protesters outside the Constitutional Court in August 2012. (*The Star*, Phill Magakoe)

CHAPTER 21

Whistle-blower/informer confirms OUTA's opinions and research

▬ ▬ ▬ ▬ ▬ ▬ ▬ ▬ ▬ ▬ ▬ ▬ ▬ ▬

There are certain things men must do to remain men.
– Captain James Tiberius Kirk in *The Ultimate Computer*

Heroes come in all shapes and sizes and sometimes they stay hidden, a shadow sticking to the darkness that nobody even knows exists.

Whistle-blowers and informers are so often the unsung heroes of society. They are the underground weapons that keep democracy alive and kicking. They see something wrong, and instead of keeping quiet, they secretly or overtly provide information to those they believe can do something to right the wrong. And so often, it changes their lives for the worse.

These are men and women who take a huge risk and they know it. Their jobs are on the line if they are discovered giving information and they stand the chance of being persecuted or even prosecuted. But for the good of society they take those risks. Without them, society is impoverished.

There were a number of whistle-blowers who helped OUTA along the way and their input heightened our courage. They gave us much-needed information to confirm our convictions, our speculation and our estimations. In short, without their input, we might have held back on many of our media statements. We might have doubted our guesstimates and views. Our tactics would have been weaker. Our claims, which heightened society's courage and civil action, might not have been aired.

I must point out that in every instance of information that was provided to OUTA from people within SANRAL, Electronic Toll Collection (ETC) or Kapsch, we never solicited or went hunting for their input at all. These people volunteered of their own accord to provide us with information, which was often very helpful to our cause.

One of OUTA's very special whistle-blowers was a person who

introduced himself to us a James Tiberius, taking the pseudonym of the fictional character of *Star Trek*'s Captain Kirk, the youngest Captain in *Starfleet* to receive command of a vessel, the USS *Enterprise*.

He communicated with us at a time when the heat was on, two months after the e-toll system was launched. This was when people were queuing to tag up under duress, and while we had an idea of the e-tag penetration rate, we were never completely sure. We were in a space of doubt as to whether our messages that gave people strength to stand their ground were actually working or whether we would ever win this war of words.

I must say that it was at this stage that I secretly began to doubt if the compliance levels would remain low enough to pull it off. I started to question myself as to whether our stance was the right one to take. That maybe we were being unpatriotic. Would sufficient people remain defiant? Perhaps the system would eventually work and we would be left standing alone, a bunch of losers who ought to have been supportive to government's decision and not challenged the scheme.

Then Captain Kirk's message arrived, in time to snap me out of my worries and give us hope and clarity that we were firmly on the right path. He confirmed that our e-tag counts and assumptions were spot on. Most importantly for me was his confirmation that we were absolutely right and justified in our challenge of the scheme. In his opinion, the scheme was poorly managed and handled in a shocking manner by an arrogant organisation under the leadership of Nazir Alli.

Kirk confirmed the system's inefficiencies and how unprepared SANRAL was to launch. This feedback had the effect of 'brightening the light' within our strategy and we were assured by Kirk that OUTA was not an organisation clutching at straws. We were on track and correct in our approach and reasoning to challenge SANRAL.

It was a Thursday morning in February 2014, 11.22 am to be exact, when the e-mail from James Tiberius pinged into the OUTA 'Contact Us' e-mail box. At that time, all incoming mails were received on John Clarke's laptop.

'Dear OUTA. It took me some time to decide if I should ever do this or not,' it read. 'However, I have decided to act personally, and not as a representative of who I work for – which would be Kapsch TrafficCom Ag (Austria).'

The message immediately caught John's attention, and he read the rest of the mail with eagerness.

'I worked on the e-toll system in Gauteng in 2011, 2012 and 2013.

What an experience working with SANRAL and their representative agent: Tolplan. And not a good one! Their arrogance ... staggering. Only to be topped by their inability to listen to any form of advice,' the e-mail continued.

The 'captain' went on to tell us that the idea and design of the e-toll system was based on a national system of tolled roads and not just a regional one. He said that the real costs of the system came from the operations centre, which hosts one of the largest storage arrays in the southern hemisphere.

'The system is designed to toll thousands of kilometres, not only [GFIP's] 185 km. The decision to scale this way is to be found in a SANRAL executive decision based on future speculation about expansion, mostly in the Western Cape and KwaZulu-Natal,' he wrote.

James Tiberius (or JT as he was later referred to as) said this idea of a grandiose plan was opposed by Kapsch because it drove up their risks, but its hands were tied as the contract was already signed. He said Kapsch wanted to be more economical, but 'SANRAL were suffering delusions of grandeur, due to the World Cup being hosted at that time. Everything had to be big.'

We later referred to the Midrand centre as the *Starship Enterprise,* the mother ship that would have its reach felt right across the country.

JT explained that his company, Kapsch TrafficCom, was not allowed to take part in any public relations or marketing activities.

He also said Kapsch was incurring unrealistic performance penalties for not achieving certain deadlines, but these were more as a result of the inefficiencies of a grander system sought by SANRAL. Kapsch was between a rock and a hard place and continued on without too many complaints against SANRAL, believing the company should see the project through in the hope that it would recover its losses in the long run. At the time of JT's communication with us, Kapsch TrafficCom was losing a lot of money on the project.

JT went on to say, 'I know from a personal conversation with a very, very senior person at KTC (Kapsch) Austria, that in 2012 he wished the deal had never been signed, but that pulling out would cost him R10 plus billion in penalties, which he could not really afford to write off without [culling] 1 500 jobs, plus the 800 people in South Africa.'

John read the mail a couple of times and wondered if this was indeed true or not. Was it a scam? he thought, before he sent it on to me with a comment, 'Check this mail out, Wayne. What do you think?'

Like John, I too was sceptical. If indeed it was true, it was a massive confirmation for us and if JT was willing, maybe we could get more information from him. Everything he said made sense and confirmed our thinking. In just one e-mail, JT had given us enormous insight into the relationship between SANRAL and Kapsch, which sounded far from healthy. If true, it would be an immensely positive confirmation for OUTA's work and would help us to focus our strategy going forward.

And yet we couldn't help but think this mail and the JT character might be a trap. He could very well have been someone from within SANRAL hoping to win us over, confiding just enough to gain our confidence and then later embarrass us. Perhaps the plot was aimed at infiltrating the OUTA committee to learn about our strategy, our strengths and weaknesses.

Our minds were racing.

We agreed to ponder over the mail and we met for breakfast the next morning to discuss how to handle our response to Captain Kirk. We were excited as the mail certainly did add some intrigue to the situation. If it was a scam, how were we to proceed? How could we establish his credentials? If he was for real, how could we get him to open up and give us more valuable information?

We decided to treat him as the real thing, but not to allow ourselves to be compromised until we were sure of his position, sincerity and credentials. We also searched the Kapsch TrafficCom website to check the various members of its senior management team in an attempt to work out who he could be.

Our reply to James Tiberius opened up a string of correspondence that would last several months. He turned out to be the real thing and senior enough in the ranks to give us the truth and absolute facts. He became invaluable in telling us the exact number of e-tags that had been sold, which confirmed that our e-tag counting exercises were extremely accurate. He even helped us correct some of our draft press releases.

Eventually he revealed his true identity to us, but forever more we will know him as James Tiberius.

On 28 February 2014 we had just heard Nazir Alli being interviewed by John Robbie on Talk Radio 702. He had given some figures on the amount of money SANRAL was bringing in from e-tolling, which we found highly suspect.

We sent the information to JT and he gave us some new information, filling us in on what was really happening.

We prepared a media statement that said: 'Mr Alli said that the system was performing well and thanked "the over one million users of the roads who had registered" and that SANRAL had now received "over R300 million, exceeding our target of R200 million".'

I realised Alli was playing with words. His sentence was taken as a monthly figure, where in fact, it could only have referred to the full first three months of operation and if so, SANRAL's targets were extremely low and its performance was dismal.

We described in the press release that we were receiving privileged information from a confidential source, which contradicted Alli's figures. James Tiberius confirmed our suspicion that while there were 1.2 million e-tags logged on the system as issued, there was no way all of those e-tags were in use. They were, as we suspected, issued to shops, their outlets, large fleet leasing and bank customers, government fleets, etc. Many of these 1.2 million e-tags were in cupboards, in storage or on shop shelves. They were not linked to specific vehicles in SANRAL's e-toll system, nor were they attached to vehicle windscreens.

In fact he told us there was only a 21% e-tag penetration rate by the end of January and that based on 2 387 565 vehicles passing through gantries in that month, only 501 389 vehicles were fitted with e-tags. This was powerful information. Not only did it confirm our counts but it confirmed that JT did have access to the information we needed.

We were relieved to be receiving inside information from such a powerful source and we cautiously shared this information, albeit still at a delicate stage of the interaction, with the OUTA committee members.

'The problem with the e-toll system is not "teething problems" as Mr Alli says but "truth decay",' we wrote in our press release. This was one of John's favourite quips at the time, as we challenged SANRAL to tell the truth about the number of e-tags in use.

The captain read our press release and suggested that we remove the exact e-tag figures to help protect his identity.

'If you quote such precise numbers, this will not be helpful and will cause ETC to lock down and become very paranoid,' JT suggested.

We listened to him and wrote a second draft of the media statement, using instead the figures SANRAL had previously given:

The e-tolling system was designed on the assumption that 2.3 to 2.4 million vehicles used the freeways. With only half of that gross number now 'registered', it would mean that for SANRAL to have

received revenues amounting to 'around R300 million per month'
as claimed, the average monthly bill per registered users would be
approximately R230 per month.

This is in contradiction to SANRAL's earlier reports that 83%
will pay less than R100 per month, and that 10% will pay between
R100 and R200 per month, 2% will pay between R200 and R300 per
month and only 0.59% will pay between R300 and R450 per month.
Based on the above, if their reports were anywhere close to being
reliable, the maximum cash inflow would then have been only R108
million per month. However these numbers referred only to users
who had bought e-tags.

James Tiberius speculated that there could be some creative accounting taking place or, he said, the figures could be correct considering heavy duty vehicles, which are not capped at R450 per month.

'Trucks are the hidden "cash-cow" of any large-scale tolling system,' he told us.

The captain then revealed that the two-year delay in the start of e-tolls had cost Kapsch 'more money than all the profits that could ever have been made in the eight years of contractual operation in the most optimistic of situations'. He said that the Austrian company was paid for system performance and not revenue collected. This performance was based on things such as the availability of each gantry, speed with which transactions were processed, trip-reconstruction time, speed of processing violations and speed of verifying potential incidents.

He said that SANRAL had anchored into the contract that any legislative changes would be at its (ETC's) expense.

'I guess you remember all the legislative changes made in the last two years. So, we had to pay for all those changes,' James Tiberius wrote.

'The project is a disaster for us ... right now, we only want to prevent any more damage.'

In March 2014, JT told us that the gantries were dysfunctional for two years: 'They were lucky they had legislative problems – the systems would not have been fully or reliably operable prior to 2013 as a lot of infrastructural issues (e.g., power) at the gantries and many distribution points and satellite centres were unresolved.'

Up until a month into our communication with JT, I left the correspondence to John, while he copied me in on all interactions.

By the beginning of March we decided that it was time for me to enter the engagement with the captain.

'I must say I am both intrigued and happy that we have met you (even if only electronically for now),' I wrote. 'There is no doubt that our challenge to halt this ill-conceived plan is a hundred times bigger than we envisaged it to be and any sane person or organisation would have called it off by now, but I guess we do not have the luxury of sanity within our opponents on this one,' I continued.

I asked James Tiberius if Kapsch could not see that this contract was sliding out of control.

He replied saying the company was not entirely happy with how everything went, but they are a business and pulling out of a contract is not an easily considered option as it would be more damaging to them from a financial and a reputational perspective. It would also cost a lot of jobs.

He pointed out that Kapsch TrafficCom is a publicly listed company with shareholders, and management would have to prove that pulling out of such a major contract was a legitimate and prudent decision, or else the public prosecutor in Austria would investigate for misappropriation.

He revealed that by the end of March 2014, the e-tag penetration was climbing and stood at 35% at that point in time.

'This is being interpreted by management as a sign that acceptance is being gained,' JT said.

That statement really worried us.

He went on to say that it was now being discovered that eNatis had low-quality data and that a sizeable number of vehicles were being driven without number plates, or with plates and numbers that were unidentifiable. He said that SANRAL was introducing a pitch to the authorities '… that e-tolls is going to help clean up a number of ailments that have been plaguing South African motoring'. We, however, were aware that this would not be possible and that, in fact, e-tolling was a catalyst for the false and cloned licence plate problem, being driven higher by people trying to circumvent the scheme. It was becoming a big challenge for the metro police.

JT added, 'However, they [Kapsch management] are not blind, stupid and stubborn – if the situation changes, or new information comes to light, they can re-evaluate their position.'

I wrote back to James and told him that we believed the increase in e-tag uptake was not a sign of the greater acceptance of e-tolls, but rather the tail end of those who had succumbed to SANRAL's intimidation and threats. I told him that we believed the growth rate would not peak much beyond 45%, and even if it reached 60%, the system still remained doomed.

I also explained that the eNatis system would take years to rectify and the situation regarding the cloned number plates was getting worse and not better. This was a serious problem that SANRAL could not control.

We decided at this point to make public our interactions with JT, along with the valuable input we had received from him. We explained our intentions to him and he had no objection, other than to ask that we exercise caution not to speak of the detail that would expose him. He did, however, indicate that he would stand by his convictions and that he had plans to move on in a few months' time anyway, so if indeed he was discovered, it would not be a doomsday situation.

By now, John had revealed some of what JT had told us through a complaint affidavit that was lodged with Public Protector Thuli Madonsela. We pondered as to who we should give the story to. Stephan Hofstatter of the *Sunday Times* had previously carried a great exposé on SANRAL,[19] as had Angelique Serrao over many months. At the time, John was dealing with a journalist from the *City Press*, Lloyd Gedye, on another story, so he happened to bounce it off him to test his interest in running the story. Lloyd was extremely keen and he approached his editor of *City Press* newspaper, Ferial Haffajee, to sense her appetite for an exclusive, long as the story was prominent and we vetted the text.

When the story broke, SANRAL denied all the allegations that James Tiberius had made.

The story was written as an exposé of John's complaint to the Public Protector. We sent the captain the link in an e-mail we titled: 'Hope you have your defensive shield set and ready for warp speed.'

James Tiberius was not happy with the story, believing that the paper had sensationalised parts of the input and that his words (from our mails) had been quoted out of context.

I agreed with him and stated that we were also concerned with elements of the report, but explained that the interpretation of the information disseminated had remained factual and accurate as we understood it to be.

'Nonetheless, I believe the process that is unfolding is to be expected and we need to remain focused,' I wrote.

I hoped that the breaking story wouldn't alienate JT and that he would remain in support of our fight.

Within a day of the report appearing, due to the manner in which one or two aspects were written, the Kapsch TrafficCom directors were able to deduce who the whistle-blower was inside their Austrian ranks. He was summoned to the office of the head honcho, Georg Kapsch, was read the riot act and was given little choice but to leave the organisation. He chose to resign with immediate effect.

JT's communication with us ceased. We were worried that the story had indeed created more problems for him than we had envisaged. However, after the dust had settled and he had packed his things and considered the consequences of our mutual actions, he reconnected with us and agreed that he would carry on engaging with us.

Thank goodness, I thought and breathed a sigh of relief. These situations have a knack of backfiring and turning nasty, but JT was a wise and level-headed man with the courage of his convictions. He also highlighted that in his view our best approach was to continue attacking 'SANRAL's laughable public engagement' process as this remained an all-important element that had given rise not only to its constitutional failure, but was the reason why people were fed up since SANRAL had never given them any of the necessary opportunities to impact on the e-toll decision.

He also revealed that in his opinion, senior management at Kapsch felt that SANRAL's communication policy was a nightmare.

Things went quiet for a while because James Tiberius changed jobs and there was not much more he could help us with from that point on. However, we kept him updated and informed him of the latest developments as we saw them unfolding.

In an e-mail discussion we had with JT in November 2014, he said it was clear that the level of acceptance had indeed stagnated and even regressed, making the system commercially unviable.

He also indicated that Kapsch TrafficCom was undergoing significant changes, with many people leaving, both of their own volition and because of retrenchments. He felt it was a shame because he had hoped to improve things at Kapsch, 'but the inability of managers whose job it was to think strategically to see what is plainly [wrong] in front of them was quite an eye opener.

'But despite the conflict of ethics, I had a fantastic time in South Africa and I miss it dearly and I really enjoyed working there,' JT said.

I am confident that OUTA's efforts were given a massive boost by JT's input and we are forever indebted to this brave man for his ethical approach to the situation.

In flew Icarus

While JT's input was significant for OUTA, there were others. One pos-sibly even as brave and significant for us as Captain Kirk was someone we dubbed Icarus.

Icarus worked in the ETC system's IT department in Midrand and decided to make voluntary contact with us via e-mail back in mid-2012, during the height of our legal campaign.

We gave him the code name Icarus after the son of the master crafts-man Daedalus in Greek mythology who ignored his father's instructions not to fly too close to the sun, lest his wings made from feathers and wax should melt and he would come crashing to the earth.

As I indicated earlier, we used code names from time to time, or switched to WhatsApp communication, as we were concerned that our phones may have been tapped by those who we were probably in search of input about our strategy. We had to do all we could to keep our informers' identities safe.

We couldn't believe the detail and volume of information Icarus was providing us with. His flight was indeed very close to the 'hot sun'. When we asked for more information, he did his best to source it for us.

Marc Corcoran and I met with him at various locations, at which ses-sions he kept us abreast of the numerous problems that SANRAL (ETC) was having in developing and testing various critical systems. The mes-sage was that throughout 2012 and into 2013 there were continuous fail-ures related to critical systems testing. These processes were essential for the system's ability to succeed through to the enforcement and pros-ecution stage. The various failures made us realise the system was far from ready to launch, despite SANRAL (through their lawyers) stating in court that they could launch within two weeks of the interdict being set aside in September 2012. We were reminded of the Treasury's senior counsel, Jeremy Gauntlett's, claim of fiscal Armageddon and Marc had a quiet chuckle as what had since transpired was SANRAL's inability to launch until over a year and three months later, and even then, the sys-tems were still incapable of producing accurate invoicing. In our opinion the claims made in court were farcical to say the least.

Icarus's input was of further value to us at the time in that it reassured us that our thinking was correct and minimised our need to speculate on SANRAL's readiness. He also confirmed SANRAL's misinformation and other information about the system's shortcomings. In addition, we learnt of SANRAL's need to more than double its server size and storage capacity in December 2012. This indirectly signalled to us that SANRAL had realised that its expected compliance levels were not going to be as high as anticipated and, as a result, it needed to store more information for longer periods if it were to have any hope of managing the enforcement process. Indirectly, SANRAL's actions were acknowledgment that things were not going the way they had expected. More wind in our sails.

Other whistle-blowers also provided us with information about the level and extent of corruption that took place during the road construction process, which is why we were happy with the Competition Commission's findings on the matter (more about this in Chapter 24). OUTA and other critics have on numerous occasions called on both the SANRAL board and the minister of transport's office for an independent commission of enquiry into the GFIP construction collusion as we believed that society had overpaid substantially for this project.

Whistle-blowers are critical to the work undertaken by civil society. Non-governmental organisations (NGOs) that seek to hold government accountable for the efficient use of taxpayers' money rely on their input and everything should be done to heighten their efforts and protection.

Were I to give advice to potential whistle-blowers, I would ask that they do not hold back. When in doubt, if your information is factual and substantive, be brave, but be responsible and be careful. Do your utmost to assist in bringing those who behave out of line back into line. But do so without jeopardising your life or your future. Easier said than done, I know.

Whistle-blowers and informers, we salute you.

A message for our president

Dear President Jacob Zuma. Please be serious about tackling the scourge of corruption. You are on record as wanting to root out this cancerous behaviour that plagues our society, yet you pay mere lip-service to this absolute need. I say this because there are vast amounts of evidence that corruption is taking place every day, costing us billions of rands every year, throughout all levels of government and business. Yet we see so few, if any, real cases of people being brought to book.

Were I in your shoes, I would use tax payers' funds to support the assembly of the top local and international private and forensic investigative teams into a body that would tackle this problem head on.

I would ensure that they remain independent and report to a body of representatives made up of people with standing in civil society, business and government.

I would give them special powers and dedicated courts to do their job with zero interference. They would have access to modern equipment and WikiLeaks-type information portals at their disposal. But they too would undergo regular polygraph tests and be scrutinised through checks and balances to ensure they do not become a law unto themselves.

Then I would read the riot act to public servants and deny both them and their family members any rights to conduct business with the state. Anyone caught doing so would not only be dismissed, but could face criminal charges.

This massive corruption-fighting entity would represent public money so well spent that it would, in effect, save South African society from the gross wastage that happens every day under the very noses of the authorities that are supposed to protect us from this evil. Its costs would be more than covered – a thousand times over – by the saving of lost taxes and public money that is squandered every day.

In addition, I would treble the Public Protector's budget and ensure that she was able to do her work efficiently and with great effect.

It's never too late to fix a bad situation.

CHAPTER 22

Complaints and research add strength to OUTA

Despite thousands of complaints received from the public, information from whistle-blowers, public outrage and low levels of compliance, SANRAL and the Department of Transport appeared not to be bothered. They appeared blinkered to the reality and chaos around them, behaving in a manner that depicted an attitude of 'we can do what we wish'.

COSATU's strikes could bring the city centre or the freeways to a standstill, but SANRAL seemed to remain unfazed. It simply batted the efforts of OUTA, COSATU, political parties and the public at large aside and forged ahead regardless, possibly believing that all would fall into place at some stage.

Its behaviour made us more resolute as we dug in and vowed to mount more pressure to keep the civil courage high. In our opinion this was the only way the system would grind to a halt – by taking the decision away from the authorities and placing it in the hands of the people.

Lodging a complaint with the Public Protector

A month after the system's launch, in January 2014, John decided it was time we lodged a complaint with the Public Protector. Thuli Madonsela had a reputation of a pit bull when it came to fighting for the rights of society. If anyone wouldn't be scared to look objectively at a project like this one, it was her. She was someone we thought would not shy away from conducting a necessary investigation and would not be intimidated by government.

There would be two complaints lodged with the office of the Public Protector. We decided not to lodge the complaints in OUTA's capacity as we had recently come out of a long period of adversarial litigation with SANRAL. We were aware that the Public Protector might treat this complaint as another desperate attempt by OUTA to get at SANRAL, after failing to do so in the courts. Effectively, it was about highlighting the issues and asking the Public Protector to delve into SANRAL's behaviour, which we believed was not in the best interests of the public. We thus agreed that it would best be lodged by John Clarke in his professional capacity despite his close link and association with OUTA.

The first was a 10 000-word submission that was anecdotal in nature, based on 1 349 complaints received from the public through the OUTA portal during the first six weeks of e-tolling. The complaint was formalised into ten statements of grievance.

These were summarised as:

- Dishonesty in reporting on the sales of e-tags in order to give the impression that the system was functioning according to plan and for failing to be honest to users that there had been security breaches after the SANRAL IT systems were hacked.
- Sending inaccurate messages to people, which is an abuse of authority and power.
- Discrimination against alternative users of the highways by not allowing them to take advantage of discounts, payments through Internet banking or providing them with documentation for normal accounting purposes.
- Unfairly penalising alternative users with exorbitant tariffs if they do not pay their e-toll bills promptly.
- Maladministration of the databases and mismanagement of the IT systems.
- Obtaining personal information by violating people's right to privacy.
- Discourtesy to people seeking redress and explanation for errors and problems that have arisen from internal problems.
- Failure to give complainants access to information.
- Failure to provide reasonable and transparent justification for decisions taken by the authorities with respect to public money.
- Failure to provide advertised discounts for users who have bought e-tags and have signed SANRAL's terms and conditions, due to system errors.

Deputy Public Protector Advocate Kevin Malunga received the complaint, promising to resolve it quickly.

We also asked the Public Protector's office to intervene on behalf of the public to get SANRAL CEO Nazir Alli, Gauteng MEC for Roads and

Transport Ismail Vadi and Director-General of the National Department of Transport Mawethu Vilana to respond to the complaints, to investigate and make substantive findings and recommendations on them.

'It was our hope that at the very least, the Deputy Public Protector would intervene to impartially mediate in that conflict, which neither the State nor the dissenting citizens wanted,' John wrote.

John used a few select voices of the people in his complaint, which depicted just a small portion of what we were witnessing every day.

The first story we highlighted was of a woman we called 'Rosa'. She lived in Vosloorus and worked at O.R. Tambo Airport as a cashier. She related to us that of her R5 300 salary she pays R2 200 per month on petrol. With the commencement of e-tolling she faced an additional daily cost of R47 a day just to travel to work and back, before the e-toll rates were capped.

Rosa refused to buy an e-tag because she was vehemently against the system.

'I want to be the first person to be charged in court as a criminal, so I can tell my story. Then everyone will know what is wrong,' Rosa said.

Rosa's story was a moving one and she represented the plight and sentiments of thousands of poor to middle-class citizens who were living close to the edge of poverty.

Rosa's decision of non-compliance with the system was legitimate and would be one that any magistrate would be hard pressed to regard as acting with criminal intent.

John explained to the Protector that this user-pays system relies on a situation of 'all users' to pay, and anything less than 80% to 85% of road users contracting with SANRAL would be problematic for the sustainability of the system. We then explained that by our counts, the extent of compliance was well below half that level and was not expected to rise much higher than 50%.

John also pointed out that motorists had a right to privacy and access to information but this had been compromised at least three times according to *ITWeb*.

'SANRAL says it takes the security of road users' data very seriously but has yet to take users into their confidence about the potential security holes in their systems. IT journalists have raised concern about "three separate security issues relating to the road agency's online systems [that] have been brought to its attention over the past few months",' he told the Protector.

Even ex-employees of the system questioned the system. A former senior executive who worked for ETC and close to SANRAL had this to say about e-tolling: 'The current e-tolling debacle raises many concerns, not only the issue of levying a toll and how much that toll should be; not only about Alli and his desperate tactics to make the albatross fly, but about the procurement and approval processes in state-owned entities. How can we have come so far and spent so much on a system that is obviously inappropriate for the South African application? What abject failure of common sense has brought us to this point?'

This comment was just one example of a member of the public that was resisting the system, John explained in his complaint.

Even the church objected to the system. The complaint included part of a sermon by church leader Reverend Dr Martin Young who suggested civil disobedience was justified. The reasons for the reverend's opinion were:

- It was morally objectionable for users to be threatened and harassed to pay for e-tolls, especially since SANRAL acknowledged that the information upon which the charges were based was often dated, full of errors and inaccurate.
- The jobs created in the collection process did not justify the additional collection charge, especially since a large portion of the revenue left the country to the profit of foreign shareholders.
- Producers of goods that were transported on the e-tolled roads would pass on the additional e-toll costs incurred onto the price of goods, thereby increasing the cost of living for consumers everywhere.
- No reasonable alternative routed and public transport options were provided to people who could not afford or chose not to travel on the e-tolled roads.
- Given that the role of the state is to protect the most vulnerable and disadvantaged of its citizens, the exemption of private minibus taxis and bus operators from paying e-tolls was grossly immoral. These industries have made it extremely difficult for government to regulate them, and the taxi industry has become notorious for being a law unto itself. The taxi's were in many instances unroadworthy, driven by unlicensed drivers, and as a result contributed to a sizeable volume of road deaths.

It was a heartfelt complaint that asked the Public Protector to listen to the views of the people.

Shortly after submitting it we started our communication with the whistle-blower from Kapsch TrafficCom, James Tiberius.

As a result of his input, we told the Protector's office that we had new information and the Deputy Public Protector advised us to draw up a separate complaint with the information that the informant had supplied us with.

The information involved key issues of the scope and scale of the project, communication with the public, e-tags and vehicle licence number category revenue streams and botched billing.

This complaint went further than asking the Protector to intervene on the public's behalf. It alleged dishonesty, maladministration and violation of good corporate governance against the SANRAL board of directors and executive staff.

In the second complaint, John focused particularly on e-tag sales. By now we had the parliamentary reply by the minister of transport, which indicated the information James Tiberius had given us and our own e-tag counts of around 29% at the time were correct and that SANRAL was being disingenuous in its marketing campaign by playing with words. To state that over one million users had registered with the system was clearly untrue.

We also questioned how much money was actually coming in versus money that was invoiced. We indicated to the Protector that we did not believe the revenue was enough to make the system viable in the medium to long term.

'With regards to the funding and bond issue, is this an investment you would put your savings in? Feel a little pity then for the nation's civil servants who are funding the debacle by way of the investment of the GFIP funds via the Public Investment Corporation,' John wrote in his complaint.

When SANRAL heard that a complaint had been made at the Public Protector it issued a statement saying it welcomed the complaint and would cooperate fully with any legitimate investigation.

The intention of this complaint was twofold. Firstly, to get the Public Protector's office to conduct an in-depth investigation, but secondly, we also knew that it would help to send a message to society at this critical stage to ignore SANRAL's intimidation and threats, to be strong and not give in to the pressure of purchasing an e-tag. This was the start of our 'be strong' campaign. The civil disobedience programme could bring the system to a halt and it was too soon for the public to falter. They needed to remain strong.

About this time in January 2014, I had received a return call from a postgraduate student at the University of Pretoria's Department of Information Sciences, Erin Hommes, whom I had got to know after a meeting we had at my Avis office in 2012 shortly after our successful court interdict that halted the scheme's launch.

Erin told me that she and Dr Marlene Holmner had gone on to complete her earlier research conducted on Intelligent Transport Systems (ITS) around the world, looking at why many of them had failed and what made the successful systems work. This international research had largely shown that if the public did not buy into or support these systems, they ultimately failed to be sustainable. Many of these systems were halted prior to launching because sanity had prevailed in the minds and thinking of the authorities in those instances. They could see the writing on the wall, unlike the case here in South Africa.

In 2012 Erin had filled me in on the initial content of her findings, but passed this information on to us as her paper had not got the nod to proceed from her professor at the time. I was disappointed that she hadn't or couldn't proceed with this valuable research.

Naturally, I was excited that academia was conducting such research on the subject as this would also help us to understand some of the deeper issues and gain insight into why the Gauteng system might fail or succeed. But when Erin informed me back in 2012 that her research had been called off, I asked her, 'What are we to do with the great information you have already uncovered then?'

'Because I am not using it, I grant you the permission to do so. It's yours now,' she said.

It was very informative and meaningful information that largely pointed to why SANRAL's e-toll scheme was doomed to fail. Until our renewed contact in January 2014, I had used these earlier insights gleaned from Erin in many of my talks and feedback sessions, along with the odd press release. But we needed to have the essence of academically backed literature on the subject.

So, you can imagine our excitement when Erin informed us, almost eighteen months later, that the research was now complete and about to be published for public consumption. This would add gravitas to our argument.

OUTA's research and position paper: 'E-tolling at an Impasse'

We informed Erin that we were compiling a comprehensive research position paper of our own and would like to quote the work that she and Dr Holmner had done, to which she agreed.

Our 15 000-word paper 'E-tolling at an Impasse'[20] was published and distributed electronically at the end of February 2014, with its main thrust and argument being that as a funding mechanism the Gauteng e-tolling decision had not been researched thoroughly enough, nor tailored to the social environment, political climate and economic context that it depended on for its viability.

The research showed that internationally, many schemes were not launched by their respective authorities (Manchester, Edinburgh, Hong Kong and others), when they could see that the scheme did not enjoy the overwhelming support of the society wherein it would be applied.

It also showed that in instances where the ITS schemes had been launched, when more than 20% of users default in payment and are not justly sanctioned, the system begins to head for trouble. This happened in Portugal's (SCUT) e-tolled freeway system,[21] which became problematic at 19% non-compliance, and a similar experience occurred in Texas. The paper points out that SANRAL's initial compliance target of over 93% (as indicated in responding papers by SANRAL during OUTA's court challenge) had been abandoned and it hoped to make up the costs through 'Alternative Category' users who pay higher punitive tariffs. Yet SANRAL had failed to contemplate what would happen if the non-e-tagged 'Alternative' users failed to pay and were not (or could not) be prosecuted accordingly.

Hommes and Holmner identified eight success factors that are critical for any e-tolling (ITS) venture to be successful.

The first point is that public support needs to be extremely high with strong advocates promoting acceptance.

This was not the case with Gauteng's e-tolls, the public support of which was so low that, at its best account, around 45% of freeway users were tagged by May 2014, many months after implementation.

The second point is that forces opposed to the scheme must be weak.

Aside from OUTA's opposition, the Gauteng e-toll scheme has been heavily opposed by COSATU, the South African Chamber of Commerce and Industry, Business Unity SA, the Southern African Catholic Bishops' Conference, the South African Council of Churches, the Southern African Faith Communities Environment Institute, the Black

Management Forum, the South African Local Government Association, the QuadPara Association of South Africa, and other civil society organisations. Eventually, even the ANC's Gauteng leadership denounced the scheme.

The third point is that tangible comfort factors must be immediately felt to create confidence.

Anyone sitting in peak-hour traffic on the highways, often in gridlocked traffic, would know the decongestion on this highway has not eased enough for motorists to be satisfied. It was a short-lived benefit.

The fourth point is that alternative public transportation systems should be adequate and reliable.

According to the Gauteng City Region Observatory, a partnership between the city of Johannesburg, the University of the Witwatersrand and the University of Johannesburg, only 10% of commuters make use of bus and train services while 42% make use of the minibus taxi system and 42% use cars. The Gautrain serves around 45 000 commuters a day, which is only 12% to 15% of the daily road commuter traffic between Pretoria and Johannesburg, and less than 3% of the total Gauteng commuters.

The fifth point is that the pricing matrix should be simple and the billing system user-friendly.

The thousands of complaints that flooded in after e-tolls launched is testament to the fact that the billing system is not user-friendly. The tariff changes for different users and the discount and penalty structures all make for a very difficult and confusing payment scheme and rate structure.

The sixth point is that the soundness of the technology and data needs to be extremely reliable.

Nazir Alli himself admitted that 'the database has let us down'. Motorists getting wrong bills, people never having used the road before being billed and cloned vehicles popping up everywhere are testament to the fact that the data was not the most reliable.

The seventh point is that environmental benefits and costs must be monitored and managed.

With the amount of paper being used up to send people long invoices, environmental wastage is a definite question motorists have about the system.

The eighth and final point is that a single agency with unquestioned legitimacy and authority should be responsible for implementation.

When the Gauteng Freeway Improvement Project (GFIP) was first built

SANRAL was regarded as a strong and credible agency. However, since the launch of e-tolling, the public perception of SANRAL has weakened significantly. SANRAL's credibility has certainly been compromised by the misinformation and lack of transparency that has been exposed in the media over the past few years.

Our report cited Hommes and Holmner's research, which explained how ITS had been successfully introduced in the three cities of London (the Inner City Congestion Charge), Stockholm (the Congestion Charge) and Singapore (the Road Pricing Scheme). In all these cities there were common characteristics that made them successful, none of which can be found in the Gauteng system.

First of all, these cities had a well-developed and reliable public transport system before the user-pays system was introduced. Secondly, the primary reason for introducing the ITS was to reduce congestion, so there was no charge outside of peak traffic periods. Thirdly, these schemes were therefore primarily introduced to manage travel and traffic behaviour and not to fund road upgrades. Fourthly, the revenues from the collection process were used to further improve public transport and finally, but most importantly, there were extensive prior public engagement programmes and strong, transparent and participatory leadership was exercised to gain public trust and support.

Our report looked carefully at why we say the fuel levy would be the best option to pay for the road upgrades. The easiest answer is that there are no additional collection costs for admin and operations of the collection process, compared to over R1 billion per annum in the case of e-tolls. SANRAL argues that since the national fuel levy would have to be applied uniformly to all motorists on a national basis, non-Gauteng motorists would be unfairly paying towards the upgrade for roads they do not use.

We argued that this does not take into account the fact that the entire country stands to benefit from a more productive and efficient Gauteng economy. The Organisation for Economic Co-operation and Development (OECD), in a 2011 report, states that the Gauteng region contributes 34% to South Africa's GDP. In addition, 52.2% of national research and development takes place in the province. As a result 75% of Gauteng's tax contributions to the Treasury flow from this region for the benefit of other provinces.

Our report also spoke about international examples where road expansion did not ease congestion for long, but instead, over time, these wider freeways in the absence of alternatives simply increased the number of cars on the road, a well-researched phenomenon known as 'induced congestion', which has already taken place in Gauteng, some four years since the freeway upgrade has been completed.

We quoted an unusually wise comment on the subject from the minister of transport at the time, S'bu Ndebele, who told Parliament in October 2011 that this (induced congestion) would be the case with GFIP, wherein he stated:

> *The key assumption of the 2007 feasibility study was that the GFIP project would reduce congestion. In my considered view, and in retrospect, the original feasibility study did not sufficiently weigh up international evidence suggesting that freeway expansion often does not – in the medium term – resolve congestion challenges, and often induces greater demand.*
>
> *It also failed to consider alternative solutions to congestion – improved public transport provision, moving more freight onto rail and a curb on urban sprawl. The project's benefits to road users may, therefore, unfortunately not be forthcoming.*

Our comprehensive document 'E-Tolls at an Impasse' would be re-written a few months later, with more updates, and titled 'Beyond the Impasse'[22] to be lodged as OUTA's submission to Premier David Makhura's E-Toll Advisory Panel assessments in June 2014.

The Advertising Standards Authority rules against SANRAL

Four months into e-tolling and after our e-tag counts had been verified through the minister of transport in Parliament in March 2014, I contacted Steven Haywood, a member of the public who had successfully complained to the Advertising Standards Authority (ASA) about the city of Johannesburg's use of the slogan 'A world class African city' and had won his case, although the appeals tribunal later set this ruling aside. He came across as an active citizen who took the time to challenge the authorities on spurious and dubious claims.

On contacting Steven, I acknowledged his positive activism and asked him if he wouldn't mind taking up another challenge and lodge a complaint to the ASA about SANRAL's questionable and misleading claims that 82.83% of the road user's average monthly cost of e-tolls would be less than R100 per month and only 1% of road users would pay more than R400 per month. Once again, I felt that if OUTA brought the complaint, it might be seen as more antagonism towards SANRAL, but coming from a member of the public, they might view it differently.

Steven was happy to do so as long as we assisted him with the input and research/arguments he needed to provide, which we keenly did, helping him to substantiate, in his opinion, that SANRAL's claims were out of line with his calculations. SANRAL was challenged to explain and substantiate with clarity how it arrived at these numbers.

The ASA ruled in Steven's favour only because SANRAL didn't bother to get back to the ASA on time with its response. In fact the ASA bent its own rules by extending the time required for SANRAL to respond, at SANRAL's request, and again it failed to submit its response on time. The ASA then instructed SANRAL to remove its misleading adverts. A week or so later, in June 2014, SANRAL rushed in with a lawyer's letter to the ASA, coupled with letters of verification of its 'facts' from its auditors as well as its advisers, Tolplan. The ASA generously decided to accept SANRAL's late response and forwarded these to Steven, requesting him as the complainant to respond to SANRAL's reply.

Again, we assisted Steven and provided him with the arguments and facts to counter SANRAL's claims, and again the ASA ruled against SANRAL. This was a massive blow to SANRAL's ego and made for great media content for many of the scheme's critics.

Another objection raised against a SANRAL advertisement came from Rob Hutchinson of Proudly E-Tag Free (and also OUTA's social media consultant). He objected to SANRAL's radio advert thanking 'the people and organisations that have taken up 1.2 million tags for the Gauteng e-roads'.

His complaint was that SANRAL had never provided any proof of the number of e-tags sold, and until they did so, this was a misleading advert.

The ASA ruled that the information from SANRAL on the number of e-tags sold 'appears to be unsubstantiated' and that the claim was misleading and in contravention of the code.

SANRAL was also ordered to withdraw this advert as the ASA stated that SANRAL had failed to substantiate its calculation.

The ASA warned that if SANRAL continued with its current pattern of failing to substantiate advertising claims it could face further sanctions.

SANRAL responded that it would no longer flight e-toll adverts that the ASA had labelled as misleading, and spokesperson Vusi Mona used the opportunity to spin a way around the misunderstandings, in that when SANRAL speaks about e-tag sales, it does not refer to registrations. Registrations in the system referred to all registration, including non-tagged vehicles and those exempt from payment. It appeared obvious to us that he was playing with words once again. We crowned Mona as the country's captain of spin.

These rulings were a big victory for society, and SANRAL's tarnished integrity took more heat from the blowtorch of the anti-toll lobbyists.

All of these actions, successes and media releases were adding more courage to citizen defiance and kept SANRAL against the ropes, explaining its behaviour or simply failing to respond to the allegations and negativity. By May 2014 it appeared the tide was turning in our favour, as SANRAL's growth in e-tag compliance levels appeared to be tapering off.

CHAPTER 23

A blow to the ANC's election results

When President Jacob Zuma had signed the e-toll bill into law in September 2013, giving a thumbs up to proceed with the launch of e-tolling, there was a sense of disbelief from the public. It was just months before the most hotly contested elections in South Africa's democratic era and it was widely known that every political party, barring the ANC, had voted against the bill.

Zuma's signing of the Transport Laws and Related Matters Amendment Bill was regarded by many as a major strategic error on behalf of the ANC. Most had speculated that he might withhold the signing until after the elections. But, it seemed the president was willingly to take a calculated risk to save SANRAL, who were desperate to get the tolling scheme operational and could not afford another credit downgrade.

The big question on everyone's lips: was the e-toll issue serious enough to divert enough votes away from the ANC in Gauteng?

The Democratic Alliance, the ANC's biggest political rival thought so, and it capitalised on every inch of public animosity against the ANC to gain votes in the national and provincial elections due to take place on 7 May 2014. E-tolling was one of its major pre-election rallying points, along with President Zuma's Nkandla homestead scandal.

The DA attacked e-tolls from every angle and made sure the public was aware that e-tolling had been approved by the ANC and the ANC alone.

The DA's campaign started in earnest in 2013 when it erected a few eye-opening billboards across Johannesburg that read: 'E-tolls. Proudly brought to you by the ANC'.

Nobody knew at first who had put the billboards up. Some even speculated that perhaps it was OUTA.

The DA let the speculation and social media talk continue for a few days, allowing the rumour mill to spread the billboard's message as far and wide as possible before admitting to erecting the billboards. This was a clever, thought-provoking, mischievous marketing ploy, which fired the first salvo in the tit-for-tat political marketing wars that characterised the energy of the 2014 elections.

The DA's Mmusi Maimane said the billboards were 100% accurate. 'E-tolls were conceived under the watch of an ANC minister, supported by an ANC executive in Gauteng, passed into law by an ANC majority parliament, and signed, sealed and delivered by an ANC president,' Maimane said at the time.

The ANC was furious and Transport Minister Dipuo Peters called the action of the DA cowardly.

But the DA made it clear that this was just the start of their campaign. A week or two later Maimane unveiled another billboard that read: 'A vote for the DA is a vote against e-tolls'.

But, the party did not stop at advertising to spread their message. It went all out to find as many holes in the e-toll saga as it could.

DA MPL Jack Bloom made it clear that the party was looking forward to the elections in May 2014.

'The e-tolls will be a fiercely contested election issue that will cost the ANC badly. The DA will campaign strongly in 2014 for the e-tolls to be scrapped,' Bloom said.

Maimane was announced as the DA's premier candidate for Gauteng. The slickly dressed, well-spoken politician soon became the political face and voice of e-toll opposition in the province. When his premier candidacy was announced, Maimane made it clear what his objectives would be: 'As premier I will make [these] jobs my top priority, stop corruption in government and fight against the unjust taxation of Gauteng residents through e-tolling.'

The DA was not alone in attacking the road payment system to try to win votes. Julius Malema and the Economic Freedom Fighters (EFF) also added their voice to the election fight. The EFF's approach was more aggressive, calling for the physical destruction of the gantries. 'We are going to destroy e-tolls physically. We can't remove them emotionally,' he said outside the SABC buildings during a protest march. 'If that is incitement to violence, police must come and arrest us.'

Publicly the ANC went on the offensive, but there was a lot happening behind the scenes.

Some of the Gauteng-based ANC branches were expressing frustration with the damaging impact the e-toll decision was having on the electorate. The Liliesleaf Farm branch asked Nazir Alli to attend a meeting to explain the e-toll decision and why the scheme was necessary. Its members wanted him to try to convince them why the e-toll decision was the best payment mechanism chosen.

I received a request for some input to be provided to a senior and well-respected member of the Liliesleaf Farm branch of the ANC, in order that he be clear on our thoughts and opinion on this same question. Obviously, I was not invited to attend the session, but the same person (and others) gave me some insightful feedback on what transpired at that meeting.

Nazir Alli essentially provided the ANC Liliesleaf Farm branch with a high-level overview of the e-toll mechanism, but, according to the source, soon changed the thrust of his speech to one of a political nature, denouncing the DA's views and opinions on the matter. One of the members then reminded Alli that he was talking to a very solid ANC group of people who had no intentions of defecting to the DA. He was reminded why he was there and that they wanted answers to their question: 'Why was the e-toll decision taken and why was it better than the alternatives available?'

They wanted to see the numbers. Apparently, Alli sensed their frustration with him. He was not providing them with the facts and the numbers they required. Alli was then asked to halt his input and return at a later stage, when he was ready to provide them with the feedback they sought, in order to convince them as to why they should support SANRAL's e-tolling decision.

He never took the opportunity to return.

On receiving this feedback, we got a sense that there had been a significant shift in the thinking of ANC supporters in the Gauteng region. They were asking very meaningful questions and one sensed that they understood the negative impact that e-tolling would have on their region's electorate. They had reason to be worried.

The Black Management Forum speaks out

The Black Management Forum (BMF) is a significantly powerful association of high-powered and politically connected business people that promotes the growth of black leadership and equity growth in business.

In 2012 Tembakazi Mnyaka was the chairperson of the BMF in Gauteng. She also happened to be the chairperson of SANRAL. Government spokesperson Jimmy Manyi was also part of the BMF. So it was obvious that during her chairperson the BMF expressed a pro-tolling position.

In September 2012 I was invited by the BMF's Pretoria branch to participate in a discussion/debate about OUTA's stance on e-tolls. I was told it was going to be a debate because Tembakazi Mnyaka would also be present. This is great, I thought, as up until that time there had been no public debate between OUTA and SANRAL on the matter. We were keen for this session as it would mean that we could pose some hard questions that SANRAL would need to answer in a live forum.

Shortly after I arrived at the venue I was welcomed and seated while we awaited the arrival of more delegates before the session got underway. Ten minutes later Tembakazi arrived with Koos Smith, the chief operations officer from SANRAL. I greeted her and Koos and watched as a sense of discomfort began to permeate her demeanour. She then had a private discussion with the facilitator of the evening's event and, a few minutes later, I was politely asked not to participate in the debate. I wasn't surprised at the request. Without arguing, I expressed my concern to the convenor that I had taken the time to be present at the invitation of the management of the BMF. I indicated that one-sided debates are a farce and will do no favours for the delegates of the BMF, and that this kind of behaviour was worrying.

The facilitator was extremely embarrassed and apologised, expressing that Tembakazi was the chairperson of the BMF and had insisted that I may not be given a platform to speak. The facilitator's hands were tied.

I quietly left the room.

The next day, I received a call from the event organiser who apologised profusely for the debacle that unfolded. He told me the BMF delegates were also angry on hearing that I was asked to leave and demanded an explanation as to why I was not allowed to talk. Apparently, they accused SANRAL of trying to hijack the debate and expressed disappointment with its behaviour.

Personally, I believe this incident was a catalyst that saw Tembakazi being removed from the position of the chairperson of the BMF in Gauteng at its December 2012 board appointment elections. She was replaced by Modise Moiloanyane as the chair and very soon thereafter the Gauteng branch of the BMF released a press statement that expressed its serious concern about the e-toll decision, indicating that it was not in favour of the scheme.

You can imagine our surprise when reading the statement. What a turn of events, I thought and wondered why this had happened. Many of the members of the BMF were powerful men and women, with both political and business clout. This was an important development and we needed to understand it.

I quickly tracked down the newly elected chairperson, Modise Moiloanyane, and requested a chat over coffee. He obliged and we agreed to meet at Thyme on Nicol coffee shop in Sandton on 19 December 2012. What a refreshing discussion. Modise filled me in as to what had transpired and why the BMF leadership, who were generally anti the e-toll debacle, couldn't denounce the scheme until their board elections had seen to the removal of Tembakazi as their chairperson.

On hearing about my failed presentation to the BMF meeting in Pretoria, Modise indicated that he would set up a slot for us to present to the BMF delegates again. True to his word, an invitation to address its members in Bedfordview took place in April 2013, which was met favourably and with some great questions, answers and insights shared. The position taken by the BMF gave us hope that there was moral courage being expressed in the business world on the issue. But why was it black leadership that was taking this stance and not the generally white-controlled elements of leadership in the trucking and motoring industries? Something was amiss.

At this same meeting at which Lot Ndlovu was in attendance, Lot was asked to give his input to the e-toll scheme, since he was its chairperson between 2006 and 2011, something I was not aware of at the time. Lot was also a past president of the BMF.

Lot stood up and gave his input, which indicated that he had raised concerns about the e-toll decision and its seemingly inadequate public engagement programme, and was not surprised by the current public outrage. This was very interesting information to the OUTA members present at the BMF meeting. We expressed a desire to discuss this input with Lot after the meeting. Unfortunately, we did not meet with him and we later learnt that he was very ill with cancer and passed away five months later on 22 August 2013.

Political alignment

Despite the fact that we had no political affiliation to any party whatsoever, we could understand why people thought we were aligned to the DA. Firstly, our committee at the time was virtually all white and all male and, without thinking about it when we formed our brand name in March 2012, the 'A' in OUTA stood for 'Alliance'. Many took this to be associated with the same word in the 'Democratic Alliance'. Perhaps if we had used the word 'Association' it would have negated this thinking somewhat.

Nonetheless, when the DA made a donation of R1 million to OUTA in early 2013, to enable us to take our case to the Supreme Court, this further heightened suspicions that we were linked to this party. SANRAL's regular allegations in this regard added more fuel to a non-existent political fire for us.

We did, however, have some discussion, some open and other private, with many political parties, COSATU and other civil action organisations. We never always agreed with many of these organisations' policies and principles, but on the matter of e-tolls, we were united in almost every respect.

The ANC also needed to ease the growing tension within their political ranks on the topic, and so they called Nazir Alli to ANC headquarters in Luthuli House to hear his input and reaction to the burning issue that had been picked up and used as a sledgehammer by various opposition parties.

Alli quickly tried to deny that his tolling scheme would affect the ANC negatively in any way during the polls. He briefed the ANC's National Executive Committee and other high-ranking officials. It was reported afterwards that Alli warned them that the financial health of other state-owned entities was interlinked with the fortunes of SANRAL.

'I don't think it [e-tolls] was a major concern – they just wanted to hear it from the horse's mouth so to speak ...,' Alli said in a press interview.

The ANC deputy president, Kgalema Motlanthe, tried to rationalise the scheme's importance to subdue the growing anger amongst the general public. He urged motorists to understand that decongesting Gauteng highways was the reason behind e-tolls and he said SANRAL was one of the best-managed state utilities in government. He went on to list the positive effects of the system, which he said included improved lighting, signage and traffic flows that were enhancing road safety.

But his words fell on deaf ears and very few paid attention to his input. Motlanthe was a respected politician, but it was widely speculated that he would be exiting the political arena after the elections. His words did not have quite the power they had had several months earlier.

But not everyone was convinced the hotly contested road taxation method would have an impact on the election results. Political analyst Professor Stephen Friedman of the Centre for the Study of Democracy did not think e-tolls would affect the ANC because most anti-tolling lob-byists were mainly from the middle class.

'If you look at middle-class suburban people who are protesting, obvi-ously this has reinforced views that government has it in for the middle class, that government wants to take money from middle-class people, to line the pockets of politicians,' Friedman said in *BusinessTech* on 3 December 2013.

So, when elections rolled in on 7 May 2014, nobody was quite sure what would happen in Gauteng.

It turned out that the ANC would still lead the province, but it had lost a significant number of votes compared with the previous term. The ANC was only able to obtain 53.6% of the vote in Gauteng, which was significantly down from 64.4% in the previous elections of 2009. This was the biggest decline the ANC had ever experienced and the one com-mon denominator in the Gauteng decline was the topic of e-tolling.

ANC Secretary General Gwede Mantashe immediately downplayed the e-tolling issue as a major factor in the decline in the ANC's provincial vote count.

He used the opportunity to encourage people to participate in the scheme. He said that people must 'stop whingeing and pay up'.

'If you talk about pressing issues [in Gauteng], you talk about e-tolls. It's a misplaced debate, an emotional debate. It doesn't talk to the work-ing class because no [other] province has the same infrastructure as Gauteng,' Mantashe told Lebogang Seale from *The Star* newspaper.

But despite Mantashe's words there were mutterings in the ANC that e-tolls had played a bigger role than the party had yet to admit.

OUTA immediately issued a statement. We said that as much as the ANC executive wanted to downplay the almost 11% decline in votes, it was largely attributable to forcing e-tolls onto a public who did not want to pay for something on which they had not been adequately consulted.

Within a few months of the elections, the ANC in Gauteng admitted that the e-tolling issue had indeed hurt them, and they realised it was time to start doing something about it.

The newly elected ANC Gauteng leadership knew very well that the local elections were less than 22 months away and if e-tolling was still around at that time, it might very well be the death knell for the party in the Gauteng region.

Gauteng Premier Makhura was about to announce a new effort to deal with the e-toll impasse.

CHAPTER 24

Gauteng freeway construction costs and collusion

In the five years since the public first became fully aware of the e-toll saga in 2010, questions have repeatedly been raised about possible collusion and questionable business behaviour surrounding the project.

Many questions were raised about the ethical nature or otherwise of elements within the project, things that may pass the legal acid test, but which are nevertheless viewed by the public as wrong.

While many points were raised, the real 'smoking gun' was the revelation that the costs of the construction of the roads were hyped up through business collusion.

From the beginning of 2011 the people wanted to know who all the beneficiaries were, linked to both the e-tolls and the road upgrade projects. Who were the trustees and directors of the many suppliers to Electronic Toll Collection (ETC)? Did ETC have full say on who their suppliers would be without interference from SANRAL? On the road construction side, what were the details in these tenders and why had the road construction cost estimates escalated so much?

Trying to follow the money became an obsession with investigative journalists who were keen to dig deeper and deeper into the project. It started with how much money ETC and its majority shareholder, Kapsch TrafficCom, would potentially make out of the deal.

Next there were questions around just how much of the money went into Black Economic Empowerment companies with the revelation by *City Press* that Moss Mashishi had sold his majority stake in his BEE-rated company to Kapsch TrafficCom.

His company, Matemeku Investments, became the main BEE shareholder through 51% ownership of TMT Services and Supplies – the South African partner of ETC joint venture.

But Mashishi and other shareholders of TMT sold 57% of the company to Kapsch for more than R70 million, *City Press* revealed.[23]

Soon, the questions went further than the company that had won the contract to manage the e-toll system; it delved into road construction and the many subcontractors.

In 2011 *The Star* newspaper looked at the cost per kilometre of GFIP road built and compared it to the cost of a similar road in the United States of America. At the time, the paper found that it cost around R91 million per kilometre to upgrade the road.

Nazir Alli vehemently defended the agency and sought to blame the high cost on journalist Angelique Serrao's maths by saying she got her figures wrong because she did not know the difference between miles and kilometres. At the time *The Star* based the figures on the fact that it cost R16.9 billion to build the roads. Later it came out that the cost was R1 billion more than this, escalating the price per kilometre to around R100 million per kilometre – far more than the cost in other countries to build a road. Everyone wanted to know how it was possible for the price to be so high.

It came as no surprise then, in 2013, when *City Press* (21 July 2013) revealed that tender rigging took place in 2006 and 2007 for the construction of the roads. This emerged from testimony by construction bosses during a Competition Commission tribunal.

It was here that details emerged of a road-construction cartel, which met in 2006 and agreed to divide up contracts between them. This suggested that the costs of road construction had been inflated through collusion.

This would partly explain why the cost estimates for the project ballooned from R6.4 billion in 2006 to R11.8 billion in 2008, to R16.9 billion in 2011 and R17.9 billion in 2012. On top of this, the additional costs for the e-toll system (such as gantries, technology, etc.) and other incidental overruns came in at R2.5 billion, which escalated the full price to R20.6 billion.

The affected roads included national roads such as the N1, N2, N5, N12 and N17, amongst others. The collusion also involved the GFIP and the Bayhead Khangela Bridge Project.

According to the *City Press* report, the construction firms that were at the meeting were WBHO, Basil Read, Grinaker-LTA, a subsidiary of Aveng, and Concor, which was acquired by Murray & Roberts later in 2006. Also present were smaller construction players Raubex, Haw & Inglis and Rumdel.

Raubex's chief executive officer, Rudolf Fourie, said in his testimony that the company regretted its acts of collusion.

'What we did was wrong,' said Fourie. 'This will not occur again.' He said the collusion ceased in mid-2007.

'The World Cup brought this kind of action into play,' said Fourie. 'It was not only stadiums that were built in this country; there were substantial road networks upgraded.'

At the tribunal SANRAL representatives said they were 'disturbed and outraged by the collusive conduct of the construction companies in question'. I remarked, 'Well, what else could they say?' Sadly, SANRAL's lack of urgency in dealing with the matter and going after the collusive companies did not display its 'outrage'. By May 2015, SANRAL had still not publicly announced in detail its decision to take corrective action against these perpetrators.

Competition authorities fined construction groups, including Murray & Roberts, WBHO, Group Five and Aveng, altogether R1.46 billion for colluding on more than 300 projects worth R61 billion. It was a tiny percentage of the gross overcharges that had been earned by these companies, hardly a slap on the wrist.

Soon after the news had emerged of the road construction cartel, OUTA's press releases called for an independent investigation into the matter and asked that SANRAL explain in detail what it was going to do about it. With little response by SANRAL on its action going forward, OUTA sent a letter to SANRAL's chairperson of the board, Tembakazi Mnyaka,[24] on 11 June 2014, asking her to answer questions around the construction collusion and for SANRAL to give us feedback. We asked when it would be filing a civil suit against the cartel members and whether it would lay any criminal charges against the construction companies.

We also asked why, when SANRAL had been queried in the past about the high cost of road construction, the response had been in essence that 'the GFIP construction costs were above board'.

We wanted to know if an Independent Certifier was appointed to ensure the project remained within budget and if not, why this practice was not applied on the GFIP project.

We called for the details on the extent of the collusion and asked why motorists should have to pay e-toll fees towards roads whose construction costs had been inflated by companies through fraudulent activities.

We wondered how it was possible that SANRAL, which is supposed to be an expert at road construction pricing, allowed such collusive behaviour to go unnoticed or unchallenged at the time of the GFIP tender process.

All OUTA received in response from SANRAL to their letter to Mnyaka was a one-page letter from its attorneys, Werksmans, pretty much telling us to mind our own business and that SANRAL was addressing the matter.

By the time 2015 arrived, two years after the Competition Commission had brought the issue into the open, SANRAL announced in limited detail on 27 January that it intended to take serious action against the collusive tendering companies.

Business Report published an article that said that SANRAL was quantifying damages it may have suffered through the collusion in order to determine whether it had a civil case to recover any loss or damages. What had kept them so long? we wondered. This is the kind of statement one expected of SANRAL back in 2013.

Vusi Mona said in the article that he believed SANRAL was the only government agency that had declared its intention to recover money from private sector companies involved in the collusion. As if this statement now makes them our heroes, I thought.

Mona said as far as criminal charges go, they would go to the National Prosecuting Authority to decide who to prosecute once a Hawks' investigation had been finalised.

Ed Jardim, a Murray & Roberts spokesperson, said the company had been cooperating with the police and had been communicating with SANRAL, but not about any civil damages claims.

Amanda Wightman, Basil Read's chief financial officer, said the group had not had any engagements with SANRAL about any civil damages claim that might be lodged against it.

The media article gave some of the figures regarding what each company had been fined and for which projects. Of these, Murray & Roberts was fined R309.4 million, some of which was for its work on GFIP.

Stefanutti Stocks settled 21 prohibited practices and was fined R306.89 million for its work on GFIP.

WBHO settled 11 cases and was fined R311.28 million. One of the cases was for GFIP.

In OUTA's opinion, these amounted to a pittance in the greater scheme of the transgressions. We had wanted to hear more and to sense an urgent and strong statement to appease the public that everything would be done and no stone left unturned to retrieve 'their money' back from the collusive tenderers. In the meantime motorists were still paying for e-tolls at bloated rates due to inflated construction company prices.

This was wrong.

On 25 November 2012 a *Sunday Times* front-page investigative story by Stephan Hofstatter[25] revealed that while South Africans pay out for the country's toll road network, a group of powerful players continually reap the spoils of lucrative tenders from SANRAL.

The paper revealed that deals appeared to benefit an 'old boys' network, specifically the company Tolplan, which has done feasibility studies on tolling roads, as they adjudicate on tenders and get engineering work on the same roads.

Alli responded to the *Sunday Times* saying SANRAL did not have a cosy relationship with anyone.

Yet, the same companies appeared to get numerous tenders. These allegations made by the *Sunday Times* were very powerful and extremely damning for SANRAL and its connected entities.

On 27 May 2011, *The Star* also revealed that Tolplan did the initial feasibility studies for the Gauteng open road tolling scheme, along with its costing analysis. In addition, it conceptualised and set out the engineering framework for the project. Tolplan was also in charge of the tender process to operate the toll roads and managed the building and operation of the gantries.

It was these feasibility studies undertaken by Tolplan that were part of the decision that open road tolling was the best option to pay for the building and maintenance of Gauteng's freeways. SANRAL said it did not believe there was a conflict of interest in awarding a contract to a company that did a feasibility study. Really?

SANRAL said that no private sector company had any influence 'to significantly affect key strategic decisions taken by the SANRAL executive and their board'.

In May 2012 *ITWeb* wrote about which companies and individual people would benefit from e-tolling. The Public Investment Corporation, which is a government investment fund, acquired R17 billion of bonds in SANRAL, specifically for the GFIP bonds.

According to the article, some of the contractors for the project were Tsebo Holdings, which is 15% owned by Nozala Investments and 15% by Lereko. Nozala is headed by Salukazi Dakile-Hlongwane, a trustee of ANC front company Chancellor House, and Lereko is owned by former environment minister Valli Moosa and Chancellor House trustee Popo Molefe.

Another company named by the media was Gijima, which is 35%

owned by well-known ANC backer Robert Gumede. Gijima was awarded a multimillion-rand contract to design and run the entire IT system for the project, said the DA's Jack Bloom.

Bloom also said that there was a link between Swedish companies involved in the Arms Deal and the Austrian company Kapsch TrafficCom, which is the leading shareholder in the ETC consortium.

The Swedish part of Kapsch holds 40% of ETC. It was previously part of Swedish manufacturing company Saab Aerospace, which sold 28 Gripen jet fighters to South Africa.

Even construction of things such as the median lighting project of the freeway was questioned.

In 2013 *The Star* wrote that the street lights along much of the Gauteng e-toll network were spaced much closer together than originally planned in 2008 or reflected on the tender. Less distance between masts meant that more lights, more cables, more poles, maintenance and electricity would be used. More spend with the supplier.

The Star revealed that of the three tenders submitted, the company with the highest offer was accepted instead of the cheaper options.

The original light masts were planned to be 68.8 metres apart, but electrical engineers working in the street-light sector measured the distance between the lights and reportedly found them to be 45 metres and 55 metres apart.

Ascertaining the freeway construction costs

In 2013 and 2014, I had sought to obtain input from the South Africa Institution of Civil Engineers, to ascertain a calculation of what the GFIP costs ought to have reasonably been. This would then help the public understand the extent of the collusion and/or maladministration surrounding the freeway construction. Try as I may, they were reluctant to assist us. I sensed it was a case of not wanting to go against SANRAL, which was regarded as a significant supplier of contract work to its members.

Nonetheless, in early 2015, we managed to track down a highly experienced road construction engineer who had recently retired and who had both the first-hand experience of road construction project pricing on SANRAL's jobs and the moral courage and time to look into the calculations for us. To cut a long story short, by using the technical information available on the project (number of lanes resurfaced and newly constructed, distance of each, bridges and flyovers, etc.), and inserting the 2009, 2010 and 2011 pricing elements and cost pressures at the time, he projected that the GFIP project should not have cost SANRAL (and therefore society) more than R10.8 billion. In areas where he did not have the exact costs, I asked him to err on the side of caution and insert the highest costs applicable at the time.

It would appear, then, that we have therefore overpaid for the GFIP project by R7.1 billion, or 66%. If that is not gross enough to suggest that an independent commission of enquiry should be undertaken on the matter, then I don't know what else is needed. We have called for one on several occasions, but no reaction from the authorities has been forthcoming.

In OUTA's opinion the smoke around the entire project was thick from the outset and despite assurance from SANRAL that nothing untoward had taken place (prior to the collusion being exposed), there was a lack of transparency and an unwillingness to explain and divulge all matters therein. All SANRAL could state was that its books are scrutinised by the auditor general. It has received an unqualified audit report for the past six years, which SANRAL says confirms its reputation for working within the appropriate legislative prescriptions.

But, in the mind of the public these questions persist. Many government departments and private businesses are audited and yet, after their clean audits have been signed off, corruption and maladministration are still found to have taken place. There are loopholes to every system and it appears that the auditor general is not necessarily looking to expose these. The public are not fools.

SANRAL's leadership said it was not an easy decision to hold companies that were involved in collusion responsible. We were puzzled by this statement. How is it not an easy decision to go after those organisations that inflated the construction costs of the very GFIP that the public refuse to pay for? It is our opinion that if they don't, the debt that society is expected to repay becomes an odious one and the public may very well have a right to reject paying e-tolls as a direct result thereof. In fact, until this issue is meaningfully resolved on behalf of society, through an independent commission of enquiry authorised by the authorities, and *all* the money is clawed back, the public have a responsibility and a strong argument not to pay e-tolls, no matter what the tariffs on offer.

SANRAL is on record to say, 'Many of the construction firms implicated have been working closely with SANRAL for decades. We built strong relationships and together we successfully delivered on the projects that brought South Africa its current world-class national highway network.'

SANRAL's company secretary and risk officer, Alice Mathew, said in an opinion piece on 17 February 2015 that the extent of the damage to the public purse had been calculated and SANRAL had appointed independent legal experts and economists to make these determinations. SANRAL would now pursue the issue through legal processes. Said Mathew:

> For SANRAL, it is absolutely vital that we maintain our credibility as a custodian of the money from taxpayers and corporate investors. They must have complete confidence in our ability to manage our resources, prevent fraud and root out any forms of corruption.
>
> Risk management is a way of life at SANRAL. It emanates from the strategic direction given by the Board, permeates through the executive management and into an operational approach where every single employee is a risk manager within his or her own work environment.

But what is the amount that SANRAL and its legal experts and economists have calculated? Why the secrecy? In the same week, OUTA submitted a response to SANRAL's employee, Alice Mathew, seeking answers to an array of questions on the matter, calling once again for an independent investigation.

OUTA's reply in an article, penned by John Clarke and myself, titled 'Can SANRAL find the road back from nowhere?' stated:

> It's not just for our sake that we have called for such an investigation, it is for the sake of the public and for SANRAL's good name. Because the reality is, until the public is reassured through an independent body that everything was above board, there will never be trust in the project or in SANRAL again. And that can only mean a death knell for any future projects that require the public buy-in.

We said it was a pity that Mathew's statements came ten years too late and it was a pity they were not from the previous chief financial officer, Catherine Smith, who claimed to have resigned in 2003 because her professional and personal conscience could not permit her to continue to lend her professional reputation to a management style that was placing SANRAL and public money at extreme risk.

We urged Mathew to spur the agency into a gallop and not to leave the unlawful conduct of the construction companies so long that it falls outside the prescribed legal time frames on the GFIP matter. SANRAL needed to force them to pay back the estimated several billions of rands, which the construction cartel had overcharged.

We went on to say:

> While the SANRAL board compiles the charge sheet, herewith some further questions that OUTA expects to have answered:
> - What was the best cost per lane kilometre that SANRAL was able to achieve in its many road building projects around the country in 2007 for (a) resurfacing of an existing road surface for a sizeable project and (b) for newly constructed roads?
> - How does the GFIP project weigh up to those benchmarks, before you add in the anomalies (skills demand and material supply shortages) which may have impacted on the GFIP price?
> - Why did the SANRAL board not initiate a thorough and independent investigation into the numerous questions surrounding GFIP's inflated construction pricing as far back as 2011 when these questions were raised?
>
> While we have read the explanations of the many bridges, median lighting and interchange improvements, the fact that SANRAL allowed this project to come in at around R100 million per kilometre (excluding the e-toll infrastructure), under their experienced noses of road construction pricing, is outrageous. Any road construction engineer worth his salt and courage will tell SANRAL that it was grossly overcharged. If minimising risk is indeed at the heart of what SANRAL practises, why then did SANRAL's risk and pricing management systems not detect the construction price collusion prior to the Competition Commission's exposure of the same in 2013? What has the board deduced in this regard?
>
> Additionally, would it not be wise for SANRAL to list the entire number of complaints laid with and through its whistle-blower process during the entire GFIP process, the value of each transgression listed, what action was taken and what the outcomes of these cases were?
>
> Having had several discussions with a number of road engineers on the costs of the GFIP construction costs, there is unanimous opinion that SANRAL has overpaid for this freeway by a significant

amount and that at worst, this project should not have cost SANRAL more that R10.8 billion, excluding the R1.8 billion related to the e-toll infrastructure expenditure. If that were the case, we have overpaid by some R7.9 billion for the road construction element, equating to [a significant] overspend. How could this possibly happen under the nose of the nation's road construction experts?

For as long as SANRAL wants to remain the chief investigator in this matter, the public will never believe the outcome and the idea of a class action by society may need to be contemplated in order to tackle SANRAL and its board members for the neglect that could possibly have occurred on the matter.

Until the writing of this book, I have not had wind of the decision for absolute transparency and an open invitation for external, independent road construction economists to scrutinise the numbers provided by SANRAL. We need absolute transparency and open books on this matter. Nothing less will suffice.

OUTA's response to Alice Mathew (which we also e-mailed directly to her) went on to explain that the e-toll system did not have a snowball's chance in hell of surviving in the long term and that the SANRAL board should seize this opportunity to rectify and re-ignite public faith in SANRAL's ailing brand.

We closed that response by saying:

There is no reason that the tender collusion scandal cannot commence a new era of transparency, accountability and meaningful participation by all stakeholders in the decisions that SANRAL makes. The only challenge [SANRAL has] is one of being able to eat the humble pie on offer.

PART FOUR

So it's been kind of a long road, but it was a good journey altogether.
   – Sidney Poitier

CHAPTER 25

The tide turns against e-tolls

Aside from the slow e-tag uptake and low revenue, due to public resistance, there were a few political events that unfolded from June 2014, some six months into the scheme's operation, that added fuel to SANRAL's already imploding e-toll plan. It was a period that marked the beginning of the end for the scheme's chances of success.

Let me start by saying that if all went according to SANRAL's original plan, it needed to get the scheme to generate around R3.2 billion per annum, that is, an average of R260 million per month, in order to be successful. Some quieter holiday months would obviously deliver lower revenues (December, January and April), while others would be higher, but on average around R260 million per month was required by SANRAL.

These were the numbers provided by SANRAL in its court affidavits in April 2012 to service the e-toll bonds taken up by the Public Investment Corporation and the Electronic Toll Collection (ETC) collections process (which came in at over R1.2 billion per annum, as per the tender). Naturally, annual tariff escalations would also kick in down the line and this is when the real profits of the scheme would begin to pay off for SANRAL, the ETC and its suppliers. As with any user-pays schemes of this nature, the level of defaulters needed to be curtailed, and SANRAL put this at 7% in their court documents in April 2012. Its leadership appeared to sincerely believe and argued in court that it would achieve around 93% compliance in order to generate the average of R260 million per month.

The question was: how quickly would SANRAL be able to ramp up the collection process to reach the required revenue levels? In order to achieve sustained success, these user-pays schemes expect to start out with high levels of compliance from the outset. The longer it takes to achieve a level of 80% plus compliance, the greater the chance of failure over time, as the scheme faces the danger of fallout by compliant users who become fed up if the authorities are unable or unwilling to apprehend the sizeable portion of non-payers. The obvious question on our minds was: at what level of income could SANRAL convince the authorities that it was achieving reasonable success?

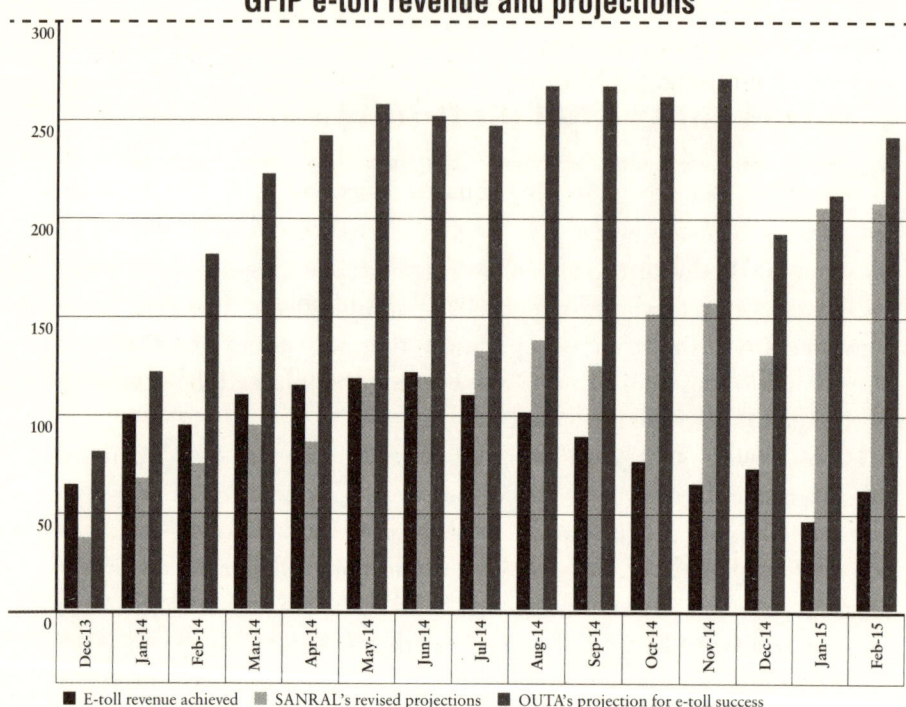

GFIP e-toll revenue and projections

■ E-toll revenue achieved ■ SANRAL's revised projections ■ OUTA's projection for e-toll success

We were about to find out and, in our opinion, for as long as we were able to claim that the scheme had more road users in defiance than in payment, the stronger the case for the scheme's ultimate failure.

In cities and regions where Intelligent Transport Systems (ITS) – electronic tolling schemes – have been successfully implemented, compliance levels generally achieve a vast majority of users paying for the scheme within the first few months of start-up, usually as a result of excellent public engagement and acceptance campaigns, long before the scheme is launched.

Portugal's SCUT e-tolled freeway scheme, launched in 2011,[26] became problematic when an average of 19% of the freeways users failed to pay for their use of the roads. At 81% compliance, the scheme was having problems of non-sustainability, as it became unviable for the authorities to chase and apprehend those who were not paying their e-toll bills.

The graph above shows SANRAL's GFIP revenue stream generated between December 2013 and February 2015, and its low (revised) targets to depict early success. It also shows OUTA's opinion of projected revenue estimations required for the scheme's success.

Column 1 (Black bars. Source: SANRAL)

Column 1 shows the actual e-toll revenues achieved over the first fifteen months of e-tolling. By May and June 2014, SANRAL's e-toll income had peaked at what OUTA termed as 'saturated penetration', outside of enforcement. Whilst SANRAL depicted this achievement as being ahead of 'target' by June 2014, this only equated to around 45% of its required and originally stated target of R260 million per month. The impact of 'three blows' that heightened the public's resistance against SANRAL's e-toll scheme are described below, but OUTA maintains that aside from these three setbacks, the scheme's success was always questionable. It was OUTA's view that the revenue levels achieved by June 2014 were around the maximum penetration the scheme would achieve, and over time this would have tapered off.

Column 2 (Light grey bars. Source: SANRAL)

Column 2 shows that SANRAL's 'revised' forecast was well below its original and required goal of R260 million per month. We believe these revised targets were a self-deceiving recipe for disaster. While these targets gave SANRAL (and their bosses at the Ministry of Transport) a sense of successful achievement, in reality, this rate of ramp-up was far too slow and ran the danger of losing the support from those who were paying. Additionally, the rising bills for those not paying reaches a point of no return as their unpaid bills eventually become too large to settle. Which is why, by June 2014, when SANRAL could see its penetration rate had tapered off, it had planned to play their last card, that of prosecutions against non-payers.

Column 3 (Dark grey bars. Source: OUTA)

This is where we believe SANRAL's compliance levels and revenue generation ought to have been in order to achieve sustainable success. In OUTA's opinion, the necessity for SANRAL to reach R260 million per month within the first six to nine months of operation was essential for the scheme's success. It stands to reason that if SANRAL could not achieve the required levels of revenue and compliance early on, it would struggle to do so going forward.

*

By June 2014, income had tapered off and OUTA believes that SANRAL knew the scheme was in serious trouble. With its back against the wall and no intention of giving up this soon, SANRAL had no option but to create a picture of success. It upped its propaganda to talk up its 'success' of growing e-tag sales and targets being achieved, yet in reality, these still fell way below the original required target of R260 million per month.

We had to work hard to counter its propaganda by exposing the real picture of an erroneous system that was failing, and falling well short of its required revenues for success. We put it in simple terms: more people were not paying than were. We were even accused of waging our own propaganda war by Stephen Grootes on Talk Radio 702's *Midday Report*. We admired Stephen's balanced reporting of the debate. Our retort was that in the absence of SANRAL being totally transparent with the actual percentage of e-tagged versus non-tagged gantry transactions, our information and research were the only facts on the table.

Despite our confidence and delight that SANRAL's penetration rate had reached peaked at around 45% by June 2014, the unfolding of a few prominent events between June and October 2014 was music to our ears. Each one of these events dealt a serious and significant blow to the scheme's compliance levels, and within a few months the rate of compliance took a serious dive. The knife was in and twisted at each turn, which had the SANRAL board wincing and pondering what next could be done to salvage the situation.

Blow #1: Makhura announces the E-Toll Advisory Panel

Shortly after taking office, in his State of the Province Address in June 2014, Premier David Makhura announced that a panel of fifteen people would be constituted to assess the socio-economic impact of e-tolls in Gauteng. Some of the panel members named at the time were: Muxe Nkondo (appointed as the chairperson), Patricia Hanekom (the panel's secretary), John Ngcebetsha, Vuyo Mahlathi, Luci Abrahams, Fiona Tregenna, Anna Mokgokong, John Sampson, Lauretta Teffo and Chris Malikane.

The panel would be tasked with inviting input and proposed solutions from various stakeholders, organisations and residents to move beyond the clear impasse. The panel would then submit its findings and recommendations to the premier who, in turn, would suggest recommendations to the National Executive for consideration.

'While we shall not promise easy solutions and claim easy victories, we must make it clear that we cannot close our eyes to the cries of the sectors of our population who are severely affected by the cost of travelling in the province,' Makhura said in his speech.

Compared to what the previous premier, Nomvula Mokonyane, had said in her State of the Province Address, Makhura's statement on the e-toll matter was profound. Mokonyane, on the other hand, had simply thanked people for buying e-tags and had spoken of a good scheme that was very necessary.

Makhura's announcement was the best news that the anti-e-toll lobbyists and the Gauteng motorists had heard in years. It certainly injected hope into OUTA's ranks and hinted that a concerted effort in search of a solution would transpire. We were cautiously optimistic though, hoping that this was not just another talk shop experience of high hopes and promises without real movement or action. We had already been through two dismal government-induced solution-seeking talk shops in the past, namely the GFIP Steering Committee in 2011 and the Inter Ministerial Committee in 2012.

What gave us confidence was that Makhura had been on record in his denouncement of the e-toll scheme as far back as 2011, when he was a member of the ANC's Gauteng Provincial Executive. We also sensed that he was concerned about the political implications of the e-toll decision, which he and his party had clearly observed and admitted was a blow to the ANC in Gauteng's regional elections held in May 2014. Makhura knew that in the not too distant future, the local government elections would be held in 2016, and his party might suffer severe losses if the e-toll scheme's noose was still hanging around its neck by then. The people were angry and something had to be done.

The DA immediately called the move a public relations stunt and pointed out that e-tolls were governed by national legislation and there wasn't much a provincial government could do about a national decision. Makhura replied in *The Star* on 11 July 2014 that Mmusi Maimane was a 'political cynic'. As it turned out, the DA was correct. The advisory panel did eventually propose that e-tolling should remain in place as the major funding mechanism to settle the GFIP bonds.

However, whatever political wrangling was taking place, OUTA believed that Makhura's announcement of the E-Toll Advisory Panel's formation would put paid to any further e-tag sign-up. In addition, many who were paying their e-toll bills under duress would contemplate not paying and begin to default on their accounts, especially if OUTA's claims that most people were still not paying for the use of the freeways were accurate.

This was the period that we upped our media PR campaign and worked with the Bridge Banner Brigade to send messages to the motorists that their civil courage was paying off and that standing strong was the right way to go.

Blow #2: The minister sets aside plans to prosecute e-toll defaulters

It was July 2014, and seven months had passed since e-tolling had been implemented. Still the majority of freeway users had not fitted e-tags and SANRAL's compliance levels were edging closer to the 50% mark.

Since the start of the scheme, SANRAL spokesperson Vusi Mona had insisted that not paying e-toll bills was a criminal offence. The threat of being summonsed, and possibly even prosecuted or fined, still hung over the heads of many motorists who had remained resilient and not paid their e-tolls. The public were confused and concerned by what this would mean. Would people be given criminal records, fined or even sent to jail if they did not pay?

As far back as 2012, Transport Minister Dikobe Benedict (Ben) Martins had said that SANRAL would use the Criminal Procedure Act to make sure people paid their bills. Howard Dembovsky of the Justice Project South Africa was quick to point out that e-tolling fell under the jurisdiction of the Administrative Adjudication of Road Traffic Offences Act, where fines were levied for those who did not pay the tolls, so why bring in the Criminal Procedure Act unless it was to threaten people into complying with the system?

'The criminal courts system is already clogged and unable to deal with existing traffic matters timeously,' said Dembovsky. 'Introducing what could conceivably be hundreds of thousands [of] ... summonses and cases into [the already overcrowded courts] ... can only be described as completely impractical.'

SANRAL issued a statement in response to Dembovsky saying it would be using the Criminal Procedure Act and that anyone found guilty could be punished with imprisonment for a period not longer than six months or a fine or both.

Towards the end of June 2014 we received reliable input that SANRAL was planning to start prosecution procedures against those who had not paid their bills. Two weeks later the National Prosecuting Authority (NPA) announced that it had assigned two prosecutors to work with SANRAL in bringing the e-toll offenders to book.

Dembovsky said the NPA and SANRAL would create a situation where the courts and jails would be filled with 'artificial criminals', many of whom could not pay the sums of money SANRAL demanded from them. He said the two prosecutors would have to prosecute over a million people as the law had to be applied equally and fairly to all transgressors, something that was virtually impossible to do.

While we knew that SANRAL, or rather the NPA, simply couldn't apply the law equally to all 1.5 million estimated e-toll 'defiers', we gathered that SANRAL's tactical plan was to provide the NPA with around 50 'best chance' cases for a successful prosecution, from which the NPA would select between five to ten cases to begin with.

We believed, as we supposed did SANRAL, that this action alone, and the publicity surrounding these prosecution hearings, would have had a significant impact on the scheme's compliance level. Under such circumstances, a sizeable number of defiant citizens would have jilted their anti-toll stance and rushed off to pay their outstanding bills, tagged-up and become compliant with the scheme.

We had many questions on our minds about this development: how many defiant road users would capitulate? What levels of compliance would they be able to achieve under this new development? Would the NPA be able to pull off these prosecutions? Who would they choose to prosecute? Would their cases be successful or not? Would the government seriously allow this process to proceed?

We anticipated that if SANRAL could drive the compliance levels up to 60% and a revenue generation of roughly R160 million or higher per month, they would have convinced both themselves and their bosses that this was enough to keep the system alive and fighting. In our minds, achieving anything under 80% would have still been a failure. At 60%, it would have merely meant the fight and negative energy against the scheme would have been protracted, with running stand-offs between SANRAL and its policing/enforcement teams over time. The situation would have become messy.

In order to prevent SANRAL's threats of prosecution from sinking in and having the impact we were worried about, it was important for OUTA to announce that we would provide the legal support and pay the legal bills for the first person who was summonsed to court for non-payment of e-tolls. This, we said, would become the test case that would set the precedent for future rulings. This is ultimately where we believed our past court claims of the system's unlawfulness, impracticalities and the irrationality of the scheme would be heard, without the threat of being ambushed by technicalities of administrative law.

We named our new drive the 'Rule of Law' campaign[27] and called on the public to heighten their resolve to help OUTA by donating money towards this probable court challenge, which would force the courts to eventually hear our arguments. We estimated the need for around R3 million to launch this defence. But we also knew that we would have a difficult task in calling for more donations towards another legal challenge, on the basis that we had lost our case in the Supreme Court and many believed the final legality of the e-toll decision had been ruled on.

Shortly after the NPA's announcement to begin with prosecutions in July of 2014, the public were up in arms. Many questions arose as to how this would be possible, both in public and through the political channels, which eventually pressurised Transport Minister Dipuo Peters to respond to these plans. The minister wisely decided that any plans to prosecute e-toll offenders would be called off until the billing errors had subsided and the scheme's problems were under control.

'She believes there are still a number of outstanding issues that need to be resolved, particularly those that affect the users of the roads, including inaccurate billing,' said the Department of Transport spokesperson Tiyani Rikhotso.

The minister also told Parliament she was extending the payment grace period to 51 days as opposed to the previously gazetted seven days, in order to allow motorists to qualify for the standard tariffs without suffering the high punitive penalties of the alternative tariffs. A sense of sanity was starting to prevail. The playing field was changing, but the scheme was not being abandoned. Mixed signals of a failing system were starting to emerge.

As it turned out, the minister's statements about amended tariff and payment grace periods failed to materialise or be gazetted for several months. We got the impression that the scheme's long-term survival was not being taken seriously. The energy and effort that SANRAL and the authorities used to have to address their challenges was waning.

The announcement by the minister to halt any prosecutions was probably the most severe blow to the scheme. The inability to enforce merely meant that the laws that enacted the scheme had no teeth and there were zero consequences if the public did not pay their e-toll bills. The scheme was now seriously becoming a lame duck and, with the added effect of the recently announced E-Toll Advisory Panel by Premier Makhura, the e-toll scheme's compliance levels started to tank very rapidly.

Once again, the opposition forces and pressure against e-tolls were heightened.

COSATU, which had been relatively quiet on the e-toll matter for several months, came back into the fray and held a protest (go slow drive) that blocked the freeways on Saturday, 18 October 2014. This protest culminated in an action of burning e-toll bills and tags in front of SANRAL's offices east of Pretoria.

Blow #3: The Gauteng Regional Congress of the ANC slams SANRAL and the e-toll decision

The ANC in Gauteng and its alliance partners the South African Communist Party, COSATU and the South African National Civic Organisation immediately rallied together to support Makhura's decision to conduct a look into the socio-economic impact of the scheme on the region.

Those in political circles said the ANC in the province had no choice but to oppose the road payment scheme if it wanted a chance of being re-elected in Gauteng, Tshwane and Ekurhuleni in the forthcoming local government elections of 2016.

In October 2014, the ANC in Gauteng held its provincial conference. Immediately the big discussion point was the e-toll decision. It quickly became clear that the Gauteng ANC would denounce e-tolling and would propose that the fuel levy or other feasible alternatives be used to fund the freeway upgrade instead.

Paul Mashatile was re-elected as ANC Gauteng provincial chairperson and while delivering his address to delegates, he launched a scathing attack on SANRAL, saying it was not running the country and that SANRAL must not behave as if it were the government.

'It's not that I don't like SANRAL, but they must know their place. Government agencies don't run the country, the ANC does … SANRAL cannot tell us what to do. We tell them what to do,' Mashatile said.

The conference was filled with controversy. Media reports emerged that President Jacob Zuma deliberately snubbed the provincial conference because of the party's stance on e-tolls. The provincial ANC had formally invited Zuma to attend and deliver the keynote closing address. But instead, the deputy president stood in for him on the Friday and ANC deputy secretary general Jessie Duarte delivered the closing address. Zuma denied the speculation, insisting he was not angry with the province for turning against e-tolls.

'SA is a democratic country and the leadership of the ANC in Gauteng has every right to state their views and that of the membership of Gauteng with regard to what the government is doing, including displeasure about e-tolls in their current form,' the president said in a statement. 'We cannot suppress the Gauteng ANC from expressing their views on this matter, in fact we welcome the feedback.'

Makhura also indicated that he had consulted with Zuma before going ahead with the review panel.

Yet Zuma's no-show at the Gauteng ANC conference continued to fuel speculation of a growing rift between the Gauteng and national leadership within the ruling party. There were rumours that e-tolls had split the ANC's top six, with the secretary general Gwede Mantashe and his deputy Duarte at loggerheads. Mantashe had reportedly earlier blamed the same Gauteng leadership as being the originators of the e-tolling plan. It was all becoming rather confusing.

What emerged from the conference, however, was a strong rejection of e-tolls in the province by the ruling party's elected regional leaders. Was this to be the final blow and death knell to the scheme's sustainability in its current guise? We believed it was.

In an interview with Lebogang Seale from *The Star*, Mantashe said that 'if you dig deep, you will not find me involved in any state of e-tolls, okay. You will find Paul Mashatile, (former Gauteng MEC) Ignatius Jacobs and Gaps (Khabisi) Mosunkutu at the heart of planning this new technology. How is it ours now?'

Mashatile lauded the infrastructure in the province, saying it was only in Gauteng that you can get a Bus Rapid Transit (BRT) system bus and catch the Gautrain.

'That doesn't make me the darling of e-tolls, okay,' Mantashe said.

He insisted that the Gauteng government should own up to the fact that e-tolling was its initiative.

'It is disingenuous of the leadership of the same province to disown that issue and want to apportion blame to somebody else. They must own up if they want to correct it. But they must not do that at the expense of blaming somebody else,' he said.

Within a week of Mantashe's interview being published, Mashatile said it was never the idea of the ANC in Gauteng to toll the roads, but a decision made by SANRAL. He made these statements during Premier Makhura's E-Tolls Advisory Panel's hearings.

Mashatile said that e-tolling was negatively affecting higher education students who own cars, small emerging businesses, as well as households. The ANC painted a picture of a province faced with possible revolt if e-tolls were not scrapped.

There was no doubting that the Gauteng ANC's rejection of the e-toll plan and the strong words issued by their chairperson, Paul Mashatile, had dealt the e-toll scheme a serious blow, which triggered a substantive decline in its revenue stream and compliance levels.

*

When one combines the effect of these three major events, all within a short space of four months during mid-2014 – adding in the backdrop that SANRAL had not been successful in driving the compliance level beyond a paltry 45% – the scheme's compliance levels were decreasing. This was a disastrous situation for the scheme and SANRAL's credit ratings.

The OUTA committee certainly believed this was the beginning of the end for the e-toll scheme. Consequently, we did not believe it could ever be considered as an effective mechanism to fund urban road infrastructure development in South Africa and SANRAL has no one but itself to blame for this development.

CHAPTER 26

Premier Makhura's E-Toll Advisory Panel hearings

Premier David Makhura's E-Toll Advisory Panel hearings took place in a boardroom at the plush Gautrain offices in Midrand. The large windows soaked in the view of the Gautrain's Midrand Station across the road, the R27-billion iconic public transport infrastructure that caters for less than 3% of Gauteng commuters. There was both a sense of pride in gazing at the evidence of another modern, large transport infrastructure project, while challenging the mechanism chosen by government to fund another.

Society is aware of the inefficiencies and questions surrounding the Gautrain decision, which have proved true in that five years after its launch, this modern public transport scheme continues to be bailed out to the tune of R500 million per annum. The same situation has applied for decades in the case of South African Airways, which receives regular bailouts from government to the tune of up to R5 billion per annum, making both of these entities a failure when it comes to user-pays schemes. Their continuous bailouts, and those of many other state-owned entities, constitute a schizophrenic approach to the user-pays principle, as espoused by the South African governing authorities.

On the left side of a large table in the main boardroom sat the review panel members. Not all of them could make it every day, but at least eight filled the seats at different times. A constant feature was the chairperson, Muxe Nkondo, and Dr Trish Hanekom. The E-Toll Advisory Panel would be in the offices for two weeks as, day after day, various organisations came forward to give presentations.

Opposite them were seats for the different members of society who would be presenting to the panel. The room was air-conditioned, and the large comfortable leather chairs were a pleasure for the panel members who were seated for long hours throughout the numerous daily presentations.

Kicking off on 27 August 2014 was labour, followed by business organisations, civil society and transport stakeholders before the hearing moved out to different areas where various communities could make their voices heard. This was followed by political parties and members of the legislature and finally, after their initial snub of the process, the Department of Transport and SANRAL were drawn in at the end to give their side of the saga.

One after another, each organisation and individual came forward to denounce the e-toll scheme, sending a clear message that the panel should heed the voice of the people who believed the project was a menace to society.

On the first day Dumisani Dakile, COSATU's Gauteng secretary, brought up the point of corruption and collusion in the construction of the roads.

He described e-tolling as the 'most immoral project this country has undertaken after the arms deal'.

Dakile warned there would be consequences for the ANC if they didn't listen to the people about this issue.

'It doesn't help to be like an ostrich and stick your head in the sand. This is a ticking time bomb,' he said. 'The people of Gauteng are cross. They do not want this thing. If the people are not listened to, the premier in four years will be governing with opposition parties.'

Dakile also spoke about the contract to administer e-tolls being given to a foreign company.

'At an ideological level, this thing amounts to privatisation [of our roads], and privatisation to a foreign company,' Dakile said.

The Justice Project South Africa began the second week with a warning that e-tolls would create thousands of artificial criminals because SANRAL planned to arrest and fine motorists who could not pay. This was something neither the courts nor jails could handle and society could not afford to be giving people criminal records simply for not being able to pay for using the roads.

'Essentially what is currently looming is a situation where a high volume of people will have to be prosecuted by the NPA on behalf of SANRAL. At present 1.3 million people have not paid, meaning they all stand a chance of being prosecuted,' said chairperson, Howard Dembovsky.

He warned that this was a looming socio-economic disaster.

'You will see people hanging themselves from these lovely gantries of ours,' Dembovsky said.

The Road Safety Campaign's chairperson, Ali Gule, added some humour to the presentations, winking and smiling at Hanekom. He said that while he welcomed the public consultation, this came too late and was almost like a memorial service for the e-tolls because soon they would be buried. He said e-tolls would cause job losses – 'the load-shedding of labourers'.

He also warned the ANC in Gauteng that it would lose votes in 2016 over the issue.

'If you don't take care of your spouse, you will let another guy in; 2016 (the municipal elections) is just around the corner,' Gule said.

OUTA was invited to present in the second week, along with other civil society organisations. Having learnt so much about the scheme's ills, its gross inefficiencies and SANRAL's questionable conduct around its public engagement process, we had a lot of important information to share with the panel, and needed to include as much as we could in our two-hour presentation. I asked Adrian D'Oliveira, OUTA's junior counsel team member, to join us at the hearings to summarise OUTA's legal challenge, and to explain why the courts had not decided on the merits of whether e-tolling was legal or not.

OUTA's presentation and research was ring-bound into a 45-page book titled 'Beyond the Impasse', providing a comprehensive overview of our opinion on the entire matter. We included in our submission the following aspects, facts and views for the panel to consider:

- Research of international case studies (featuring the work of academics Erin Hommes and Dr Marlene Holmner), which highlighted the many reasons for Intelligent Transport Systems (ITS) failure, all of which were prevalent in the Gauteng e-Toll scheme.
- We provided figures on e-tag penetration rates and exposed SANRAL's misleading propaganda, which indicated its behaviour of attempting to create a false impression of success.
- The enormous costs of the collection process, estimated at well over R1.2 billion per annum, for a scheme that only required R2.1 billion per annum to finance the bonds, was considered as being grossly irrational.
- We explained why the fuel levy was the cheaper and more equitable solution, due to its zero cost of administration, 100% compliance and, most obvious of all, the fuel levy was a current policy and funding mechanism in use by government and SANRAL to conduct road infrastructure development.

- We gave examples that highlighted the main issues related to more than 11 000 e-toll complaints we had received, let alone the tens of thousands that SANRAL itself and the National Consumer Commission must have received directly from the users.
- We included a detailed account of all the grounds that gave us, and the public at large, the right to oppose the system:
  - from SANRAL's meaningless and rather dismal public engagement process;
  - to the questions around Minister Radebe's lack of meaningful consideration of the collection costs;
  - and the absence of Minister Radebe's consideration of the fuel levy as a more viable and better alternative;
  - along with the lack of public transport and route alternatives.
- We explained the phenomenon of 'induced demand' and resultant congestion within a few years, as a result of wider roads, but in the absence of alternative transport options.
- We also questioned the weak economic arguments of the 8.4:1 benefit-to-cost ratio, as posed by SANRAL, which was based on questionable research in 2007, and which had not been substantiated since the road construction was completed in 2011.
- We expressed our concern at SANRAL's seeming lack of responsibility and accountability to detect and address the significantly high road construction charges, which gave rise to an odious debt to society.

In closing, we asked that e-tolling be suspended and stakeholders be invited to meaningfully engage to seek a solution that would have the best outcome for society at large.

'It is never too late to halt the journey down a dangerous path and embark along a safer and more prosperous route that garners the support of one's people. Persisting and pursuing with the current e-toll scheme will further drive a wedge between our government and its people,' I told the panel, as we closed our submission.

The Automobile Association's submission focused on the pressure being placed on municipal roads because people were driving through the suburbs in order to try to avoid the highways. The AA head of public affairs, Marius Luyt, said this use of municipal roads ultimately led to more road deaths.

He said that motorists used 19% of their disposable income on transport to get to work, which was high compared to other countries where it was closer to 14% on average.

Sello Rasethaba from the National Black Business Council referred to a study from Germany, which showed that when tolls were introduced on freeways, trucks moved onto secondary roads and damaged them.

Marc Corcoran, speaking on behalf of SAVRALA, raised its members' concern over the user-pays principle being applied in Gauteng, when the province provided the most towards the GDP of the country, and got very little in return.

He also asked why other transport services such as the Gautrain and Rea Vaya were subsidised by non-users nationally, but not the roads.

'There is a disconnect there,' Corcoran said.

He also highlighted what a problem the administration of tolls was for vehicle renting companies, saying the industry had spent R18 million on preparation costs.

The Road Freight Association (RFA), which was at first against e-tolls in 2012, but did an about-turn in 2013 when the tariffs for the trucking categories were capped, now gave reasons why the freight industry was suffering under e-tolls and preferred that the system was retracted.

The RFA said customers were refusing to pay e-toll bills, and operators could not recover costs, meaning they would lose between 9.2% to 16.8% of their net profit. These costs meant that trucks were being forced to use secondary roads, which were never designed to take on that kind of weight. The association said e-tolls was making the conduct of business in Gauteng more expensive and operators were moving to cheaper areas.

In their presentation, the RFA said that over the last five quarters the road freight industry had shrunk by 4 000 vehicles, resulting in the loss of 9 315 jobs, and the industry could not afford further cost increases.

The lone voice in favour of the road payment scheme during the initial phase of hearings was the Consulting Engineers of South Africa, whose members made money constructing the roads, the Gautrain and the 2010 stadiums.

Godfrey Ramalisa said the organisation had a membership of 505 firms, which employed 23 500 staff and generated an annual income of R20 billion.

Salome Sithole of the transport liaison committee of Consulting Engineers of South Africa said that as a consultant, he had to advise government on the best models to use. He supported e-tolling, saying it was the best way to pay for the roads because the road infrastructure backlog of R149 billion would only increase. The third engineer, Wally Maine, said the fiscus was stretched and a road could not compete with critical social needs.

He used Eskom as an example of what could happen if we didn't pay for road infrastructure.

'We don't want to go the way of the Eskom model where they need R200 billion to get us out of a mess,' Maine said.

They were lone voices in a sea of discontent.

The minister of transport denounces the panel's work

Right in the middle of the presentations, the minister of transport went on radio, clearly angry with the news filtering out of what was being said at the hearings.

In an interview on Talk Radio 702's Midday Report with Stephen Grootes, Minister Dipuo Peters said the panel had nothing to do with her and that there would be no review of the user-pays principle.

Peters said that when Premier David Makhura spoke to her about the panel, he said it was a socio-economic analysis of the whole GFIP.

'But, unfortunately for me, that panel seems to have taken a life of its own,' she said angrily. 'The user-pays principle is not under review.'

Peters had clearly distanced herself from Makhura's E-Toll Advisory Panel's work. The disconnect between national and provincial government over the issue was apparent, and most people wondered if the panel's process would really have any say or impact on the future of e-tolls. It was, after all, a national government decision and the upper echelons of government showed no signs of letting go.

In mid-2013, I discovered that Minister Peters and I had a mutual friend in Abeda Motlekaar, the branch manager of Avis in Kimberley. It was Abeda who set the wheels in motion for a personal off-the-record discussion with the minister, which eventually took place at her personal residence in Pretoria on Friday, 31 January 2014.

It was a meeting that focused mainly on listening to each other's points of view. She seemed to acknowledge some understanding of where we were coming from, but publicly she was vehemently against any e-toll opposition. With memories of S'bu Ndebele's previous departure from this same role, I guess the minister had to toe the line. I found the minister difficult to comprehend and nothing changed in our mutual positions after our talk. The minister carried on releasing press statements in favour of tolls, throughout the panel's hearings process. The panel continued its work despite criticism from the minister.

We were concerned by what Minister Peters had said. Statements like the one she had made depicted a government that was out of touch with its people.

'Why on earth would the ANC give their blessing to the Gauteng premier's initiative if indeed the minister appears to be intent on rejecting the pertinent and valuable information expected to come from this exercise,' I asked in a press release.

Soon after the minister's statements, SANRAL announced on 2 September 2014 that it would not present to the panel because it answered only to the minister of transport.

SANRAL's acting board chairperson, Dudu Nyamane, said it did not take instructions from any political party, but only from the minister and the legislation governing the agency.

He said he had sent an eight-page communication to the premier before the hearings.

'We took a proactive step and communicated our position on this matter. We also requested an audience with the premier to understand his position and exchange views on how, together, we can address the challenges of funding road infrastructure without it being at the expense of social infrastructure,' SANRAL said in a statement.

Some felt these statements by national government and SANRAL were an attempt to undermine the work of the panel and for the public to believe they were wasting their time in attending the public meetings that were being organised across the province.

Makhura sent out a statement in return saying the provincial government would still proceed to make its recommendations based on the findings of the advisory panel.

'The outcome of the panel will be taken seriously and the recommendations in the panel's report will be acted upon. Going to the panel to express your views is important to let the panel know how you are affected,' Makhura said.

Panel chairperson Muxe Nkondo also tried to reassure the public saying there was no reason to doubt the seriousness of its work.

Nkondo said they were trying to set up a meeting with SANRAL and the Department of Transport to hear its side of the debate.

The panel moved out of the Gautrain offices and organised weeks' worth of meetings all around Gauteng for the public at large to give their input.

Again, the evidence was clear of an angry society, frustrated at having e-tolling shoved down their throats when they never wanted it in the first place.

In the West Rand taxi drivers said their e-toll exemptions had still not been processed. Without the exemptions, the taxis would have to pay toll fees like everyone else. Graham Fritz from the South African National Taxi Council western region said it had about 10 000 members, and about half had registered with SANRAL, but none had got exemption.

Soon afterwards a *Gazette* announcement was issued, giving taxis another year to get e-tags for e-toll exemptions, which would mean nearly two years would have passed since launch date before all taxis were exempt. More signs of an unworkable system.

At the public hearings, the opposition to e-tolls continued.

Members of the public and local businesses spoke about the high unemployment in the area, saying the extra cost was not affordable for them.

In Orlando, Soweto, residents told the panel that they 'just don't get it, these politicians. They're driven around in state cars and don't know what it's like to be burdened with additional e-toll bills.'

One small business owner said he was being badly affected. He said that if one of his vehicles makes R6 000 a month, close to R1 500 goes to e-tolls. An NGO worker expressed a similar observation, saying the organisation's increased transport costs were putting financial strain on them.

Once the public hearings were completed the panel moved on to hear the input of the city of Johannesburg and the various political parties.

Thabiso Thakali from the *Saturday Star* reported that the city of Johannesburg had said that in its opinion tolls would diminish the emerging middle class, and dampen its impact on the economic growth of the city. The city said 40% of this class of people lived in Soweto and worked in the northern parts of the province.

The DA's submission looked at the financial impact the road payment scheme had on the poor, saying the demand on consumers was concerning, while the EFF took the opportunity to attack the premier and the ANC.

EFF leader Mgcini Tshwaku said the panel had not been set up by Makhuru to eradicate e-tolls, but to win over Gauteng voters ahead of the 2016 local government elections.

In its submission, the ANC in Gauteng said that it had engaged with people during its election campaign and it found that people continually expressed their unhappiness with the costs associated with the e-tolls, that they paid their taxes and that the public transport system was not sufficient.

'As the leadership of the ANC in Gauteng, we cannot be insensitive and inconsiderate to the grievances of our members, supporters and the wider community,' the ANC said.

And just when it seemed as if the panel had consulted everyone, an about-turn took place as both the Department of Transport and SANRAL came forward, just days before the panel was meant to complete its work at the end of November, to say they would be making submissions.

A sly ploy, I thought. Now that they have had the time to analyse everyone else's input, they come running in at the end of the process to have their say.

Dipuo Peters told *Business Day* that they would face the panel to 'clear the distortions' made by those opposed to e-tolls.

But things went awry almost from the start of their input. When the representatives of the Department of Transport took their seats before the panel, the minister almost immediately threatened to withdraw after a legal expert on the panel said he would reserve some of his questions for Nazir Alli to 'take him on'.

'I don't think we came here for those type of things,' said Peters, adding that if that was the approach then she would not go ahead with the presentation.

As an apparent stab at the provincial government, Peters said in her opening remarks that the decision to toll Gauteng's roads was made by the Gauteng provincial government.

The dagger was dug in deeper when later the department quoted Paul Mashatile in 2006 when he was Gauteng finance and economic affairs MEC.

'Other mechanisms of optimising provincial revenue which are currently being explored include the tolling of existing and future freeways. This will allow us to raise private sector funding for the maintenance and construction of high order roads,' quoting what Mashatile had said at the time.

The Department of Transport's presentation also included mention of the reduction in traffic congestion, that public transport had been exempted and that government had made numerous concessions in terms of the tariffs – 'a clear indication that this government cares for its people and has listened to concerns raised by them'.

The minister then referred to the court judgments, saying there was a creeping tendency to disregard the courts.

Once again we were disappointed with Peters's statements. She was clearly going on the offensive and accusing e-toll critics of spreading lies and half-truths, and we knew the courts had never really decided on the merits of whether tolling was legal or not. We believed we still had every right to defy an unjust policy.

After her opening address, Peters said that government had learnt lessons from the e-tolling system, which were not to implement any project that has not been accepted by all. A tad late for that statement, I thought at the time.

Then the minister made a major blunder in her maths, one that led to widespread criticism the next day. She discredited the fuel levy as a solution.

'If the panel is of the view that the fuel levy would cover the costs of the tolled roads it should be able to tell people that the average fuel levy will be increasing to R3.65 a litre,' Peters said.

What? Where on earth did Peters get that figure from? It's a gross exaggeration, I thought, as I tapped on my Apple's calculator app.

John and I quickly compiled a press statement to show how absurd this figure was. If an additional R3.65 per litre were added to the fuel levy, an additional R84 billion would be generated into the tax pot every year.

The capital cost of the freeway upgrade in Gauteng was R18 billion, which means the amount of R3.65 per litre, as suggested by the minister, would be able to finance almost five new GFIP projects – every year, in cash.

Our calculations showed that an increase to the fuel levy to pay for the capital costs of the road upgrade over twenty years, including the interest, would be catered for by an additional ten cents in the fuel levy.

It was clear the minister was conflating all road upgrades and backlog projects throughout the country into the R3.65 per litre figure. But why would she say this when the discussion was supposed to be focused solely on GFIP funding? We think she was badly advised by SANRAL on what to say, or maybe she misheard their advice. Whatever it was, she got it horribly wrong.

During its submissions, SANRAL estimated the current infrastructure backlog on the entire country's road network at R197 billion. Just a year prior in August of 2013, Nazir Alli was quoted as saying this figure was R149 billion.[28] An extra 32% in one year?

Why do these people constantly change the figures to suit them? I thought. This was precisely the conduct we witnessed by the authorities during the court process, ever-changing numbers to suite a different emphasis or story each time.

To further expose how outrageous these new inflated numbers were from the minister's comments, we calculated that even if the fuel levy were to be increased by an amount to cover the entire road infrastructure backlog (of Alli's new amount of R197 billion), the increase to the fuel levy would still fall far short of Peters's figure. The fuel levy would in fact need to be increased by around R0.96 per litre, which would raise sufficient revenue to fund the required capital bonds of approximately R445 billion over twenty years.

'It is this kind of misinformation and gross exaggeration that leads to further mistrust in our government,' I said. 'Statements like these are intimidating and we sincerely believe the minister's office is being misled by whoever is advising her on these figures. This also raises concerns that the minister might not be taking the necessary time or seeking expertise to challenge SANRAL on their claims and calculations. Quite frankly, this is becoming an embarrassing situation for the minister and the country.'

It wasn't only OUTA who noticed the mess government was landing itself in. In an opinion piece *The Star*'s executive editor, Brendan Seery, who has been analysing the statements made on e-tolls for years, also noticed that the R3.65 per litre figure would pay for the entire country's backlog road network.

'Right through the implementation of the Gauteng Freeway Improvement Project and the e-toll mechanisms, SANRAL has produced a tsunami of incorrect facts and figures, misleading calculations and arrogant obfuscation,' Seery said.

'It has been extremely difficult, even for those with a mathematical bent, to cut through all the waffle, hot air and deception.'

Seery then went on to look at the actual increase that would be needed to pay for GFIP, which he worked out was an increase of less than 15 cents a litre. He again asked why the roads cost so much to build in the first place. It cost around R100 million to build 1 kilometre of GFIP road when at the time it cost around R50 million to build a similar road in the United States.

*

But, the cringe-worthy moments were not yet over. SANRAL was up next.

The first thing the roads agency did when it sat before the panel was blame the panel for negatively affecting the agency's final bond auction for the year.

'Investor confidence in SANRAL has been negatively impacted by the uncertainty created by the Gauteng government's decision to set up an e-toll review panel,' the agency said.

SANRAL sought to raise R500 million, but only R415 million was allocated.

I found it quite absurd that SANRAL could blame everyone else but itself for the mess it was in. Time and time again, their woes were either placed on OUTA's, or COSATU's, and now Premier Makhura's head.

In a similar way to that used in court, where SANRAL warned that if the project did not proceed with haste, an economic catastrophe would ensue, SANRAL was now telling the panel that all it would take to sink the state-owned entity was one more credit downgrade, which would mean the Treasury would have to fork out the R40-billion debt.

The chief financial officer for SANRAL, Inge Mulder, said the agency had been downgraded four times. Shame, I thought. What is she implying? Is SANRAL not accountable for its almost entirely self-inflicted financial mess?

Alli said the bulk of the money SANRAL raised went to the upkeep of the national roads and that delaying maintenance would only increase the costs between six and eighteen times more.

Then came the statement by SANRAL's transport economist, Dr Roelof Botha, which was so shocking that even the composed members of the panel took exception to his words.

Botha had come out previously in favour of the e-toll scheme, saying he was an independent economist.

Botha told the hearing that the e-toll system benefited the poor and those who used public transport because it saves them money and travel time.

He said people in the bottom income quota should not participate in the debate.

'People who use public transport or those who don't pay income tax must *shut up* on the e-toll debate,' Botha said.

Panel member John Ngcebetsha said he did not like Botha's tone.

Alli leapt to Botha's defence saying the 'opinions expressed by a presenter are no different from opinions expressed by detractors', but he said it appeared that e-tolling detractors 'get a lot more space' to express their opinions.

Botha later retracted his words, although Alli never apologised for defending them. But alas, the cat was out of the bag and the outrage at

Botha's words was enormous. After that blunder I'm not sure anyone heard anything more about what SANRAL had to say. Despite the many damage-control media statements that SANRAL released in an attempt to defend its stance, Botha's faux pas had done more harm than any e-toll detractor ever could.

During the uproar, John Clarke called Radio 702 and challenged Botha to a public debate on his statement that 'e-tolling benefited the poor'. Botha initially accepted to do so publicly on radio, but he decided to back down when we called him to set the date and venue. The debate has never happened.

In ending its presentation panel, chairperson Muxe Nkondo said SANRAL had been strong on communicating the economic impact of e-tolls, but the panel also had to look at the social impact of the system. He also commented that both SANRAL and the Department of Transport could have communicated more effectively to avoid widespread public unease over e-tolls.

'Perhaps we should ask what we could have done to avoid the current outburst. You've been good at going through the policy and legislation and, in terms of the broad thrust (of SANRAL's presentation to the panel), it is very impressive.

'Yet, we have a collective outburst that does not work well with your economic analyses and your narrative, and we're trying to account for that,' *Engineering News* reported Nkondo as telling Alli.

The advisory panel only had a few weeks left to compile its report and the late submissions by SANRAL never deterred its output, which culminated in its report being handed in on time to the premier on 30 November 2014.

Journalists, who had been invited, were made to stand outside for hours when the report was handed over. Makhura came out later and said he would be consulting with the province about the details of the report before it would be made public. *The Times* newspaper reported that it had been leaked that the report went against e-tolling. But, until the end of 2014, nothing had been confirmed.

The people of Gauteng waited in anticipation to hear the final outcome. This was when they would see if the premier could be true to his word. Would he lobby hard with the National Executive of the proposals of the report? Would the report still advocate for an e-toll element within its suggested solution despite the overwhelming rejection thereof? Would society be any closer to finally being rid of this imposed burden?

CHAPTER 27

The signs of failure are obvious, but government won't let go

▬ ▬ ▬ ▬ ▬ ▬ ▬ ▬ ▬ ▬ ▬ ▬ ▬ ▬ ▬

It always seemed obvious to us that SANRAL's lack of transparency in keeping the scheme under wraps until the last minute would fail to garner the support of the people. This would inevitably mean that, over time, compliance levels would remain below the levels that society would deem it to be effective as a user-pays scheme, and in time, e-tolling would fail. It would fail because it simply would not be able to service both the construction debt and the collection process.

The system had begun to show outward signs of failure and unworkability a lot earlier than we had anticipated. Like the proverbial house that we all knew had not been built on a solid foundation, the cracks were now there for all to see, and from long before the system was even launched, they were rapidly growing wider.

The first major crack in the system's foundation was the enforcement mechanism. Initially, SANRAL had relied on the fact that the Administrative Adjudication of Road Traffic Offences Act (AARTO) would be in place, but it wasn't. Recent announcements in May 2015 by the Department of Transport have again spoken of the need to get AARTO operational, but it has been eight years since the first announcement of its imminent readiness. Up until May 2015, this meant that the scheme would have to rely on the criminal courts and criminal charges laid against the public who refused to pay their e-toll bills. This flaw saw SANRAL and the Department of Transport running back and forth for three years, from 2010 to 2013, trying to address and plug the holes in the regulatory environment, revising the bills on numerous occasions and still never getting this right.

The second massive flaw in the system was its reliance on data provided to it from the country's national vehicle licence system, eNatis, which was and remains fraught with inaccuracies.

A third significant instability for the scheme was the potential for the public to run roughshod over the system by tampering with their licence plates, be it swapping two numbers around, or cloning another similar car's licence or simply defacing the numbers. It is that easy to fool the Automatic Number Plate Recognition technology used by the e-toll system and, sadly, people will do this because the road traffic enforcement process is very weak in South Africa.

These factors alone would always challenge the scheme's viability. But when one throws in a disgruntled society that feels justified in defying the scheme, its foundations begins to crumble. What might have been a good idea with the use of sound technology had simply failed to live up to the expectations that SANRAL had dreamt of.

Seven months into its operation, the scheme's compliance levels were in decline and a few months later, by October 2014, news had emerged that Electronic Toll Collection (ETC) was retrenching some of its staff.

COSATU Gauteng Secretary Dumisani Dakile said more than 1 200 were being retrenched, although this seemed a bit high to us. The entire ETC set-up never had more than 1 600 staff, so 1 200 was excessive for now. But, to be sure, it would need to get to those numbers in due course.

Jamie Surkont, chief executive of ETC, said the contract called for a reduction of staff and the closure of temporary structures and service centres once a steady phase of the project was reached. 'Once the registration phase was over they needed less staff,' explained Surkont, who said they had taken 560 temporary staff and put them on contracts.

The spin was rather amusing. A '*steady state or phase* of the project now achieved'? The system's rapid revenue decline was about the only steady state that was evident, so the closure of offices made sense to us. In essence, we saw this as a significant downsizing and restructuring of the system. The start of an implosion perhaps?

Nobody was coming in to register and people had long given up on trying to figure out how to pay their e-toll bills.

There were numerous cases of people having gone to one of these outlets to pay their account only to be told they were seven days too late and their bills had already been sent to the Violations Processing Centre and now could no longer be paid there. The public could not fathom the often inexplicable information they were being given and simply started to give up on the system. The e-toll stores stood empty and we assume ETC could no longer afford to keep them open.

One customer even paid a compliment to SANRAL on 3 October 2014 for the removal of their kiosk. Compliments for SANRAL on HelloPeter were extremely rare. It read: '*I want to thank SANRAL for removing your kiosk at the Brightwater Commons. The mood in the centre improved dramatically since the SANRAL outlet does not confront shoppers at Brightwater Commons – Thank you – well done.'*

Unreliable e-toll data

Another crack in the system, which reared its head in November 2014, was that of the reliability of the scheme's information and data accuracy, a matter that was revealed in a court of law on a totally unrelated matter.

The president's son, Duduzane Zuma, was the subject of a hearing in a culpable homicide inquest after Phumzile Dube died when Zuma's Porsche and a taxi collided.

Shain Germaner of *The Star* reported on the case. At one point in the process the court requested that data from the traffic cameras and e-toll gantries be gathered to help calculate an average speed of both vehicles. But the Johannesburg metro police failed to provide the traffic camera footage and the e-toll data was revealed to be grossly inaccurate and incorrect.

What emerged was that the e-toll footage indicated its date and time stamp to reflect the vehicles to be travelling on the highway after the time that the accident actually had happened. The minibus was shown to be on the highway when it was in fact stationary at the accident site. The gantry data also seemingly created 'fictional trips' seven hours later when the vehicles were not on the road.

SANRAL spokesperson Vusi Mona defended the data. 'The data is accurate: there is nothing wrong with it,' he told *ITWeb*.

But the proof was in the court, and according to the prosecutor it was definitely wrong.

If basic information of this nature was incorrect, what did it say to the integrity of the entire scheme? Why would anyone trust their e-toll bills under such circumstances? It was a mammoth condemnation of the system's accuracy and indicated that the scheme was in fact a failure insofar as correct information was concerned.

E-tagged customers begin to de-register

Then, in December 2014, the truth about just how few people had actually been paying their e-toll bills emerged.

The Freedom Front Plus's Anton Alberts asked the minister of

transport how many registered Gauteng e-toll users had deregistered
since 1 January 2013, how many registered e-toll users there were at present, and how many use the e-toll roads but have not registered. He also
asked what amount of money e-tolling has received since it went live on
the 3 December 2013.

The minister replied that as of 30 September 2014 (ten months of operation), 93 292 accounts had been deregistered and there were 1 254 502 active
accounts registered on the system, while there were approximately 2.5 million users of the Gauteng Freeway Improvement Project (GFIP) per month.

The most interesting part of the response was just how much money
had been brought in by the system.

In total R994 765 564 was paid, less than one-third of SANRAL's initial target of R3 billion plus per annum.

At these income levels, one wonders if SANRAL is able to cover the
e-toll collection costs for the ten months in question, let alone anything
going towards the tarmac.

With the scheme's declining revenues emerging, people felt certain
that the e-toll panel review report commissioned by the Gauteng premier would provide the logical advice – to abolish the system. Anyone
who had been following the panel's hearings knew that very few of the
presentations were in favour of the system and that civil disobedience
was crippling the scheme.

Makhura's E-Toll Advisory Panel report

It therefore came as a shock when Premier David Makhura did finally
announce the findings and recommendations of the E-Toll Advisory
Panel's report. Instead of advising that e-tolls be scrapped, the report
said they should be kept, but with a few amendments:

- The removal of a few gantries, which were located close to poorer
  areas.
- Reduced rates, taking the cap from R450 to between R230 and R300.
- The extra funding to cover the reduced income from the e-toll
  scheme should be generated in a hybrid approach, with some of the
  money coming from added car licence fees, a regional fuel levy and/
  or a national fuel levy.
- A suggestion was mooted that a R120 surcharge would be added
  to annual car licence fees in Gauteng, increasing the vehicle licence
  costs by over 40%.

- There was also a suggestion that every motorist be forced to get an e-tag and when a car is purchased, it has to have an e-tag inside.

As it turned out, on 20 May 2015, Deputy President Cyril Ramaphosa announced a new dispensation on the e-tolls matter. Some of these recommendations made by the panel were taken on board, while others were not. I reflect on the new tactic by government later in this chapter.

In every element of the hybrid funding proposal suggested by the panel, e-tolling remained the main component of revenue generation, nothing less than 50% thereof. It all sounded as if e-tolls were here to stay and motorists would have the added burden of paying more on every aspect of owning a car.

So to us at OUTA, after all the promising signs throughout the panel's work, the final report was disappointing. Offering a few e-toll discounts and increasing costs in other areas were a far cry from finding a solution that would ease the burden of this system on motorists.

At a press conference on 15 January 2015, Premier Makhura announced that having received the E-Toll Advisory Panel report in December, he would now release the report and its recommendations to elicit further input from society and a stakeholder engagement forum to be held within the next month.

I had attended a previous press conference at the Gauteng provincial legislature's offices and never gave two thoughts as to why things would be different this time around. I was keen to receive a copy of the report and to hear Makhura's responses to the journalist's questions. But when I got to the entrance of the building in President Street, the security guard took one look at me and informed me that I was not allowed into the building.

I watched Mia Lindique of Eye Witness News and Max Gebhard of the *Financial Mail* walk in through the security metal detection device, and questioned why I wasn't allowed the same privilege. The security guard merely said that he didn't know who I was, or why I was not allowed on site, just that my photograph had been shown to him and he was instructed not to allow me in.

Mmmm, so this was the manner in which government's critics were being dealt with, I thought. And here I was, under the impression that the process fostered by the newly elected premier was one of improved transparency and engagement. Disappointed, but not perturbed, I turned back to the cosy coffee shop around the corner to follow the Twitter feed of the discussion inside the building. In fact, with the journalists' excellent account of things on social media feeds, I realised that I needn't have bothered attending the session in the first place.

On hearing about the issue of being turned away, I was humbled to receive a call from Premier Makhura later that evening to apologise for the manner in which the incident had been handled. I was impressed and thanked him for his call and apology. Certainly, his behaviour was far more engaging and conciliatory than I had come to expect from the heads of SANRAL.

The report that the premier handed out was still not the final decision. The premier said he would consult with society and Deputy President Cyril Ramaphosa before a final decision would be announced.

It was anticipated that the decision would be disclosed in Makhura's State of the Province address, held on 23 February 2015. But alas, it was not to be and the speculation was that the decision would be announced two days later, during Finance Minister Nhlanhla Nene's speech.

Instead Makhura called for motorists to exercise patience while he negotiated 'major financial relief' on the payment of e-tolls. He did not give details, although increases in the fuel levy and car licence fees were again mentioned.

Opposition parties were not impressed, wanting a final decision to be made and making it clear they would not be happy unless that decision was to completely scrap e-tolls. They accused Makhura of having lost the battle to scrap e-tolls.

The DA said the hybrid model was a thin disguise to force motorists to pay in one way or another. MPL John Moodley said the increased transport costs would slow down economic growth, harming job creation.

Finance Minister Nene's budget speech on 25 February 2015 also insisted e-tolls were here to stay. Nene said measures would be taken to improve compliance and enforcement. The minister indicated government was determined to stand behind SANRAL and in press briefings before the budget there was talk that more tolls could be added at a later stage. We were informed that Ramaphosa had been tasked to work with the two spheres of government (national and provincial) and, using input from the advisory panel and SANRAL, he was to come up with a practical solution to the e-toll impasse.

After these announcements OUTA put out a press release, which again pressed our point that the state can at best force only a reluctant and small minority to comply and pay the tolls. No government can force the majority to cooperate on an unpopular and unjust scheme.

Still hoping that there was a chance government and civil society could work together on this issue, we wrote to Deputy President Ramaphosa, hoping that he would pay attention and listen to the voice of civil society. We had hoped that he would be keen to hear input from some of the scheme's ardent critics, despite the fact that he might have read our submission to the advisory panel.

In the letter, we indicated to Ramaphosa that we were extremely disappointed with the panel's recommendations largely because, despite all the correct reasons it listed for society's justified rejection of the e-toll scheme, it had proposed that the 'failed' scheme remain a major part of a hybrid funding mechanism. I further expressed our frustration that the panel's interactive process had raised expectations, which had now been dashed:

> We had hoped there would be a breakthrough whereby government and civil society would at last find a way of 'Walking Together' on this matter, notwithstanding other recent disheartening events of Marikana, Nkandla and other scandals. These have left concerned citizens feeling not only disillusioned and depressed, but angry, which in turn will have a negative impact on SANRAL's e-toll ambitions by driving further resentment and heightened refusal to pay e-tolls as a means of protest and defiance.

I reflected on our many concerns with the proposals from the hybrid model, which we believed would lead to even higher unnecessary costs for motorists and society at large, who were being heavily taxed as it was.

Holding a new stick over the public

On 20 May 2015, Deputy President Cyril Ramaphosa announced what he referred to as a 'new dispensation' with a host of changes to the e-toll scheme. Flanked by Minister of Transport Dipuo Peters, the premier of Gauteng, David Makhura, and Minister of Finance Nhlanhla Nene, Ramaphosa set out to appease the public with a number of pleasantries, carrots and a new stick, in an attempt to breathe life into the e-toll system.

First the carrots

The message from Ramaphosa was aimed at convincing the public that their calls had been heard, aided by the findings of Makhura's E-Toll Advisory Panel's engagement, which was conducted during the latter half of 2014. Ramaphosa commented:

> *Among other things, the panel found that:*
> - *The implementation of the Gauteng Freeway Improvement Project and e-tolls has benefited the economy and the people of Gauteng through a better quality road system, reduced travel time, improved fuel efficiency, reduced vehicle operating costs and improved logistics efficiencies.*
> - *There is general acceptance of the user-pays principle.*
> - *It was, however, found that in its current form, the e-toll system placed a disproportionate burden on low- and middle-income households.*[29]

No one disputes the first point. The freeway upgrade most certainly produced improvement to the free flow of traffic in the region, at least for the first five years after its completion.

It's the second point that continues to be used to throw a misleading slant into what the government says about the e-toll decision, 'a general acceptance of the user-pays principle'. Who doesn't agree with a statement like that? But making this statement implies that roads are like electricity or like taking a flight to another city. It also completely ignores the fact that the fuel levy is an application of a user-pays principle, and a very efficient one at that when it comes to road users contributing towards the cost of road infrastructure.

And it is in the third point mentioned above, 'in its current form, the e-toll system placed a disproportionate burden on low- and middle-income households', that the new dispensation has done virtually nothing to alter its impact on the low- to middle-income households. I say this because, in reality, while the input sounded magnanimous, the reduction in the tariffs was virtually meaningless and not much really happened.

Ramaphosa went on to say:

> *To ensure the e-toll system is equitable, affordable, sustainable and more efficient, Cabinet has approved the following major improvements:*
> - *Public transport remains exempted. This applies to buses and taxis with operating permits.*

Essentially, however, there is nothing new here. This exemption has been applied since the start of e-tolls and no one is disputing the rationale for public transport exemption, although, as I indicated earlier, there is a question mark placed on the classification of minibus taxis as official public transport. And SANRAL's initial plans did not include a 'free ride' for taxis. In my opinion, it was on realising that this industry is notorious for blockades of the freeway if their concerns are not dealt with that authorities changed tactics here.

More concerning, however, has been the management of this process. On 28 April 2014, five months after the launch of e-tolls, SANRAL's press release claimed that 46 000 taxis (around 42% of Gauteng's estimated 110 000 taxis) were registered for e-tolls in Gauteng. 'We want to thank the South African National Taxi Council for the principled stand it took in support of e-tolling and for encouraging its members to register,' Vusi Mona said at the time.

Despite these claims, in September 2014, I decided to walk through several very busy taxi ranks and found only two taxis with an e-tag, out of 425. The taxi drivers and operators I spoke to were relatively oblivious to the scheme. Yes, they knew about e-tolls, but they weren't applying for exemption, saying 'the associations are handling that nonsense'. I wonder what will change in this regard going forward.

> ■ *A single, reduced tariff will apply to all motorists. As an example, the current standard tariff of 58c per kilometre for light motor vehicles will be reduced to 30c per kilometre. This single tariff will apply to all motorists within a vehicle class whether they have an e-tag or not.*

The e-toll tariff for tagged vehicles was always R0.30 per kilometre for light vehicles, so the new proposed tariff of R0.30 as the best rate available was unchanged. Previously, the e-toll tariffs were very complicated, with a Standard rate for non-tagged users at R0.58 per kilometre (that is, almost double if paid within seven days), or an Alternate User tariff of R1.74 per kilometre, almost six times the e-tag rate if someone missed their deadlines and was not registered with the e-toll system.

OUTA estimated that by the first quarter of 2015, only 20% of freeway users were compliant and virtually all of SANRAL's Gauteng e-toll revenue came through the lowest e-tagged rates applicable at R0.30 per kilometre. In other words, hardly anyone was paying the Standard or Alternate rates, which were essentially introduced to persuade the public to register with e-tags from the outset. It was a tactic that essentially backfired.

Consequently, when Deputy President Ramaphosa announced a reduced tariff from R0.58 to R0.30, we regard this as a misnomer. He could equally have said that the rate had been reduced by 83% from R1.74 per kilometre to R0.30 because that is actually the applicable tariff being ignored by the majority of the road users, and it is the tariff at which the majority of unpaid e-toll bills are being charged.

> ■ *The monthly cap has been dramatically reduced. Users of light motor vehicles will not pay more than R225 a month. This is half the current monthly cap of R450 a month. Revised caps will also be introduced for other vehicle classes.*

This is a disingenuous offer. SANRAL's own advertisements, which ran throughout the first six months of 2014, indicated that 93% of the freeway users would pay under R200 per month at the e-tag rate. Thus reducing the cap from R450 to R225 per month only really means something to less than 7% of the Gauteng freeway users.

> ■ *There will be no charge for infrequent users who make less than 30 gantry passes a year. If a user exceeds 30 gantry passes in a 12-month period, they will be liable for the usual charges.*

This appears to me to be another red herring to deflect attention from the failed Day Pass mechanism for infrequent users. The Day Pass rate, which was a R50 flat fee, was aimed at giving people passing through the region (no more than once a month) a so-called good deal. R50 would buy them sixteen gantry movements in a day. I doubt that more than a few hundred of these Day Passes were sold in the first year of operation. Yet there would have been several thousands of infrequent vehicles passing through the region each month. Replacing the Day Pass with 30 free gantry movements per annum for infrequent users is an attempt to appease these users, who had largely ignored the scheme in the first place.

> ■ *E-toll fees that are currently outstanding will be discounted by 60%. Users will have six months within which to settle their debts dating back to December 2013 at the discounted tariff. This does not disadvantage users who have been paying e-tolls all along.*

I can speculate that the fine print attached to this offer will be a condition by SANRAL that road users need to update the e-toll system with their details, thereby making them a part of the system. What makes this offer disingenuous is that a 60% discount offered on a rate charged at R1.74 per kilometre will net SANRAL a windfall in revenue. It would be effectively earning R0.70 per kilometre from those who have ignored the scheme to date. This is even higher than the Standard Tariff of R0.58 per kilometre.

In my opinion, the real question is, why would I want to pay 40% of a bill that I deem as not mine in the first place? I for one, along with thousands of other people, believe the scheme has been introduced unlawfully and, as such, the offer of a 60% discount to all who believe it is their right to defy an unjust scheme is meaningless.

■ *There will be a monthly cap on the penalty for accounts in arrears. All users who do not pay tolls within the required 30 days will be obliged to pay double the toll tariff. To protect users from incurring high amounts of debt, this will be capped. In the case of light motor vehicles, for example, the monthly cap for accounts in arrears will be R450.*

It appears that SANRAL has only now learnt after all these years that if people in power exert unreasonable pressure through exorbitant punitive rates (such as the 600% Alternative tariffs), the greater the pushback generally will be against unreasonable punitive measures. But in my opinion, this new offer has come far too late and people will not be convinced.

And then came the stick!

When people in power seek to coerce their subjects, the effectiveness of these tactics will be weighed up by those to whom they are directed. The public will not only evaluate how effective these measures might be to bring them on board, but they will ask questions such as: 'Why now?' and 'What were you going to do with all the extra money you sought in the first place?'

In my opinion, the authorities run the danger of a greater loss of integrity when seeking to introduce supposedly reduced tariffs a year and a half down the line. Questions are being asked as to the logic and reasons behind these tactics, especially when the substance of the offers is revealed to be lacking. I believe a heightened resolve for continued civil disobedience will be justified.

Ramaphosa got to the part that spoke to the new enforcement mechanism:

- *Settlement of e-toll fees will be linked to motor vehicle licence renewal. To further simplify the process and ensure better integration of road management systems, motorists will need to settle any outstanding e-toll fees before vehicle licence discs are issued.*

This statement silenced the room and gave an indication of government's new plan for e-toll enforcement. Low compliance is the government's biggest hurdle with e-tolling. Until now, the scheme had relied on the Criminal Procedure Act for those who refused to pay. But this was never a plausible option for the authorities, a matter that OUTA had predicted, causing the scheme's policies and its legislative boundaries to be deemed as illegitimate.

This time around, government had chosen a new and seemingly effective tool. However, the plan appeared to lack the deep testing and scrutiny required for its implementation. Within hours of the announcement, social media was abuzz with whether or not this tactic was compliant with the country's Constitution or if it was in line with the Protection of Personal Information (POPI) Act. Queries began to mount from the insurance industry, used vehicle sales and many other sectors.

The threat to withhold vehicle licences resulted in a startled reaction from the public. A number of OUTA's followers began to post messages on our Facebook page along the lines of 'Now what?' and 'This time around we're screwed. Aren't we?'

On hearing and reading the public's messages of trepidation and anxiety shortly after Ramaphosa's speech, I recalled similar reactions at the time of the e-toll launch in December 2013. At that stage, anxiety amongst the Gauteng motoring public was at an all-time high. Some people decided to tag up under duress in order to allay their fears of being arrested or slapped with a criminal record. Thankfully, the majority of Gauteng freeway users remained steadfast in their defiance and the system's compliance levels remained low.

In the wake of these new threats of withholding vehicle licences by government, we sensed the levels of civil courage by Gauteng motorists become more intense than when the scheme was launched. The level of public frustration appeared to be mounting against a government argu-ably out of touch with its people.

The questions that began to arise from this planned new enforcement process fell into three areas:

1. Can the government carry this off? Will its systems be able to integrate between the Road Traffic Management Corporation's (RTMC) eNatis system and that of ETC as well as the Post Office, other licensing outlets and vehicle sales dealerships? As it is, the scheme is fraught with numerous errors and its biggest challenge is its administrative processes.

2. Will the government be allowed to do this from a legal perspec-tive? What about the transgressions of the POPI Act, about to be promulgated? Does this plan pass the muster of the Constitution? As far as OUTA is concerned, the legality of the e-toll decision has yet to be tested. Currently, there are serious questions surrounding the lawfulness of e-tolling and, as such, it remains to be seen if non-payment of e-tolls may be allowed to interfere with other laws, such as the issuing of vehicle licences.

3. Finally, even if points 1 and 2 above are hurdles that SANRAL is able to clear, will the authorities actually implement this policy, understanding the many potential risks and unintended conse-quences that could arise from it?

Immediately after Ramaphosa's speech, the speculation and scenario planners, along with the legal fraternity and the insurance houses, were sharing their thoughts on the matter. OUTA set out to engage with vari-ous organisations and business entities in order to highlight the issues at stake for government and society, as well as their possible need to chal-lenge these latest developments in court.

OUTA will always be guided by the collective minds of the committee, but also by the views expressed by the general public (through numerous, credible polls) and by our social media followers.

Understanding the logic of alternative solutions to e-tolls

Let's face it, OUTA must not ignore the possibility that an amended e-tolling offer might be a credible option to consider. The landscape is an ever-changing one and every time a new suggestion is made, it needs to be evaluated in terms of its ramifications and repercussions. Each time, however, the guiding principle OUTA uses to assess the best option available is: when given a choice of funding mechanisms or tax options available, it is the one that best meets the needs of the public in terms of efficiency, lowest cost to society and ease of implementation, together with the highest levels of compliance that should be chosen. Unless, of course, there is a very compelling reason to select a mechanism that is less effective.

What makes the fuel levy a worthwhile option to fight for?

It is important to note that the fuel levy is a direct user-pay tax on the motoring public. It is also one that was initially introduced by the apartheid government in the 1970s in order to raise taxes directly from motorists, which was allocated to a road-building fund. Later, the ring-fenced requirement for roads and transport was removed, thereby allowing the fuel levy to be used to alleviate other pressures applied to the Treasury's allocation needs.

The fuel levy of today has become an ever-increasing and lucrative tax for the authorities to tap into. It has been generally motivated as a 'tax on the rich' because vehicle owners are regarded as being on the wealthier side of the fence. The graph below shows how much the fuel levy has attributed to the national coffers over the past twelve years.

It is interesting to note from this graph how the income to the South African Revenue Service (SARS) from the fuel levy will have increased by some 250% over twelve years, from 2004 to 2016, whilst over the same period, the volume of fuel pumped has only increased by roughly 36%, representing an average of 11% year-on-year increase in the fuel levy rates applied to motorists since 2003/2004 (excluding the Road Accident Fund).

The arguments for the use of the fuel levy as a funding mechanism are:

- The fuel levy attracts zero administration costs, compared to costs in excess of R1 billion every year to administer the collection of e-tolling revenues.
- There is a 100% compliance level with the fuel levy. Aside from the few battery-powered vehicles on our roads, petrol or diesel is used to power all road transport in South Africa. By contrast, e-tolling could only generate around 45% compliance by mid-2014 and even

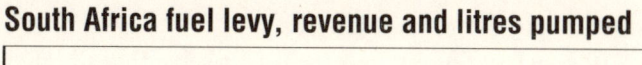

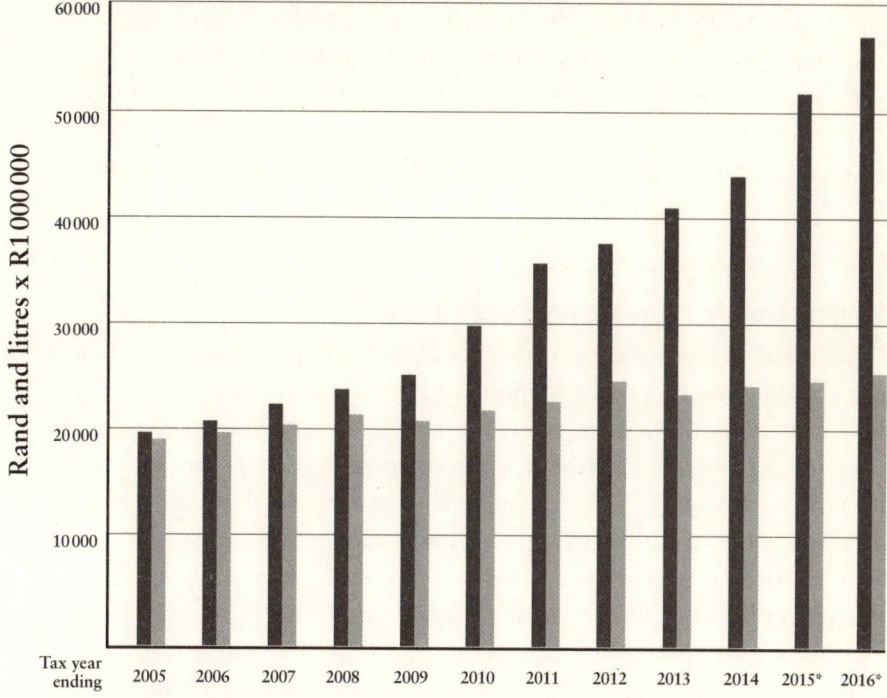

South Africa fuel levy, revenue and litres pumped

Rand and litres x R1 000 000

Tax year ending	2005	2006	2007	2008	2009	2010	2011	2012	2013	2014	2015*	2016*

Source: SARS & SAPIA *2015 & 2016 are estimated projections by OUTA, based on litre sales projected & fuel levy tarriffs.

Average fuel levy applied	R1.07	R1.10	R1.13	R1.19	R1.17	R1.38	R1.66	R1.69	R1.74	R1.90	R2.17*	R2.34*

Fuel levies indicated are an average for the tax year based on litres sold in calendar ending 3 months prior. *OUTA estimate

■ Fuel levy revenue (rand)   ■ Fuel sales volume, petrol & diesel (litres)

under the new dispensation it is expected to fall far short of the required compliance levels of 85% or higher. OUTA speculates that SANRAL will be lucky to achieve a level of even 50% compliance under the new licence renewal enforcement mechanisms suggested with the new dispensation.

■ The use of the fuel levy is currently in existence as government policy to fund road infrastructure. By contrast, e-toll regulations and policies have been rewritten and gazetted on several occasions since 2009, and are still not complete or effective in achieving the intended aims.

■ The GFIP bonds only require approximately R1.9 billion per annum to finance over 24 years, including interest. This is equivalent to approximately R0.10 per litre in the fuel price.

- The fuel price has risen by roughly R1.15 per litre since the advent of the GFIP construction in 2008, that is, twelve times higher than required to fund the GFIP bonds over 24 years.
- In 2015, the fuel levy will bring in R27 billion more revenue than it did in 2008, enough to pay for almost two extra GFIP projects every year, in cash, if indeed the GFIP project was not subjected to inflated prices from construction collusion.

Vehicle owners: Government's cash cow

While there is a correlation between car ownership and wealth in South Africa, the level of taxation applied to vehicle ownership is extremely high. There comes a time when the ability to continue with excessive taxation on motorists reaches a point of saturated tolerance. This is the point where the cost of vehicle ownership in a nation that relies on vehicles (due to poor public transport infrastructure) becomes out of sync with the perceived benefits derived and resistance from motorists begins to develop. The backlash against the e-toll decision is one such indicator of frustration expressed by motorists in South Africa, suggesting that we might have reached a peak of tolerance for government's abuse of the motoring public.

Vehicle ownership in South Africa is also currently subject to the following taxes:

1. Import/excise duties
2. Vehicle (carbon) emissions tax – roughly an additional 2.5% on the car value
3. Tyre taxes – R2.30 per kilogram on replacement tyres
4. Fuel levies – over one-third of the retail price of fuel per litre of 95 unleaded petrol in Gauteng is made up of:
   a. R0.33 – Gauteng Zonal Differential
   b. R2.54 – from April 2015
   c. R0.04 – customs
   d. R1.54 – Road Accident Fund (RAF)
   e. R0.10 – inland demand levy
   f. R0.01 – inland pipeline levy
5. Vehicle licence fees – average of R595 per car in Gauteng per annum and now
6. Tolled roads

When we weigh up all the options available to government, we fail to understand why the authorities are not making use of the most efficient tax collection mechanisms on the table, or why they cannot accept that no matter how hard they try to disguise the e-toll scheme – the nature of its inefficiencies, the high costs of administration and its overall irrationality – it will never be favoured by people, even at half the price.

On every occasion that the government has sought input from the public, in over 95% of the submissions made, society would have chosen to go with the fuel levy over e-tolls. We fail, therefore, to understand how Deputy President Ramaphosa and Premier Makhura's advisory panel can claim that they have heard the people on the e-toll matter.

CHAPTER 28

Looking back: What have we achieved?

- - - - - - - - - - - - - - - - -

Life can only be understood backwards. But it must be lived forwards.
– Soren Kierkegaard

Having chatted about the e-toll saga with so many business and political leaders, friends, colleagues and members of the public, how I wish life could be understood forwards and lived backwards – the opposite of what Kierkegaard said two centuries ago.

Nevertheless the essence of the struggle of any leader is to live one's life forward and try to inspire others to do the same, and hope that when it comes to looking back it will all make sense. Doing so now, even though there is still much more living that needs to be done, I am confident that I now understand better the key fundamental issues at stake in our country today.

The key learnings I have taken from this long journey is the significant need for citizens to hold their political leaders and governing officials to account for their performance and controls of public spending. They are after all public servants, i.e., their role is to serve the public who have entrusted them with the tax revenues so diligently earned. Policies that make no sense to the people must be ignored.

With that understanding emanating from the last four years of my life, the simple question I now have is: for the greater good of our nation, how do we live in the future, so as to ensure there is a radical change in public accountability today?

With the benefit of hindsight, it is interesting to ponder on how different the situation might have been, had a number of matters been handled in other ways. I explore a few of these here.

What if #1

What if the minister of transport at the time, Jeff Radebe, had genuinely and seriously applied his mind and more time to the e-toll plan presented to him by SANRAL in 2007 and 2008?

One wonders what might have transpired had the minister made the effort and taken the time to obtain a second opinion from a team of independent external experts and advisers tasked with seeking feedback to the following agenda:

a. Are the proposed costs of the freeway upgrade reasonable and in line with fair and recent market costs? In other words, what should the construction costs of the freeway upgrade be limited to, so that we don't create a situation of odious debt to the public?

b. Is the proposed e-toll method of extracting funds from society to fund the upgrade the best option available in terms of efficacy, cost, efficiency, value and workability?

c. Has SANRAL done its homework on two fronts: (i) Has it genuinely sought the consent of the people, which is important for the buy-in and workability of the scheme? And (ii) What are the lessons from around the world? Where have similar schemes failed and do we have similar or worse conditions that might challenge the scheme's success here in South Africa?

d. And, finally, was the scheme and its planning conducted in line with our constitutional values, more pertinently with those espoused in Chapter 10, section 195, to which state entities need to comply?

Personally, I believe that an honest evaluation of the above would not have taken long, but the answers would have provided the minister with sufficient insight to place reasonable doubt on the scheme's potential for success.

More so, an introspective assessment of SANRAL's motives and behaviour on the e-toll matter might have been enlightening if only the minister had taken a hard and closer look at the overall extractive nature of this state-owned entity.

I, for one, am convinced that a need exists for our country's leadership to institute a thorough, independent and professional look at the mechanics and reasons behind all the toll concessions throughout the country.

For if they do, this exercise will more than likely reveal that society is on the receiving end of many a bad deal, almost each and every time. Before we get onto the subject of the fuel levy, I believe we are paying far too much for our tolled roads, both in costs of construction and in toll fees.

But will our current minister order such an investigation? I doubt it.

My guess is that the extractive behaviour of the political elite is more than likely intertwined with SANRAL's irrational behaviour and they certainly don't want any auditing people digging deep into their affairs. If indeed this is not the case, then why not conduct the independent investigation? There is more than enough reason to do so, even if one just takes the GFIP construction collusion and SANRAL's slow pace to act as the only reasons needed.

What if #2

What would have happened if OUTA had failed to secure the urgent interdict that halted the launch of e-tolling on 30 April 2012? Would OUTA's members have fought on or thrown in the towel? And had OUTA pulled out, would society's moral courage to challenge the scheme have faltered at an early stage, allowing SANRAL to proceed with its ill-conceived plan, albeit with a lot of shouting and societal discontent? Would another group have stepped in to play OUTA's role?

I can't bear to think of the mess that would have transpired had the scheme been launched back in April 2012. As it was, some eighteen months later and in the midst of vastly amended regulations during that time, the scheme's subsequent launch was still a mess and, to all its intents and purposes, has failed.

I am convinced that, had SANRAL achieved a half-reasonable compliance level of 60%, the authorities would have limped on, applying aggressive tactics to force more individuals into the scheme over time. The new dispensation proposal by the deputy president on 20 May 2015 is another attempt to seek acceptable levels of compliance, whatever that might be.

What if #3

I often wonder what would have happened if Judge Vorster had *not* slapped OUTA with its opponents' legal costs in December 2012, when he ruled against us in the judicial review of the e-toll case.

Had we only been left with our own legal costs to bear, I have no doubt that OUTA's committee would have voted to halt all further action and to probably close down. I recall at that stage, we were all knackered, having lost in two courts with mounting legal bills and fading public funding support. Our appetite to fight on was at an all-time low. However, with Judge Vorster's costs order slapped in our faces, estimated at an additional R20 to R25 million linked to the government's legal costs, we really had no option but to appeal the judgment.

Appealing the costs order also gave us the opportunity to question Judge Vorster's shocking judgment on merits of the case and this also played into our hands.

As it turned out, the Supreme Court of Appeal (SCA) largely set aside Judge Vorster's ruling on the merits, amending the outcome of the case to one based on administrative law, wherein it could not condone the lateness of our application. In effect, the Supreme Court's ruling was a 'backhand compliment', as John Clarke, who always searched for the paradoxes and ironies that make life interesting, described this development. Effectively, the SCA allowed the question of the lawfulness of the e-toll decision to remain in play and therefore it could be contested at a later stage, if and when a member of society should be required to defend his or her non-compliance with e-toll payment in a court of law. This was a massive outcome for OUTA and society at large.

Looking back, I believe SANRAL's lawyers could have advised it better on the costs order against OUTA. They must have known that we had a strong chance of overturning the costs order and they must also have known that we couldn't afford this judgment and would have no option but to come back to appeal it.

However, if Nazir Alli had been shrewd, a conciliatory and well-meaning approach could have done wonders for SANRAL's case and the public's attitude towards it. Consider what might have transpired had Alli suggested to the judge (via his legal team) that the costs order should *not* be handed down to OUTA, i.e., that each should pick up its own costs. Even more magnanimous, were he wise, he might have considered that SANRAL would settle OUTA's unpaid/outstanding legal bills (at that stage a mere R2.5 million). Just imagine what that dynamic would have presented? It would most certainly have removed SANRAL's most ardent critic from the equation going forward and painted an entirely different picture on the matter.

It is my guess that Alli's desire to drive OUTA into the ground blinded his ability to consider such a tactical approach available to him. For him it was about slapping OUTA with everything possible. 'Make them suffer' is what I imagined his instructions to his attorneys were.

There is a great lesson in this example for people in authority. Sometimes during adversarial situations, using one's might and power has a lesser impact than a conciliatory one. At times, applying a more subtle and humane tactic to a situation will give you all the power you need to resolve or end the conflict. A helping hand to lift an opponent off the deck might just do wonders that a powerful legal team could never achieve (though the lawyers will caution your thinking in such instances).

Instead, OUTA raised itself from the canvas, dusted off its gloves and became even stronger, urged on by the audience of a growing supportive public who were sitting in the gallery and wanted nothing more than for OUTA to survive and fight on. And fight on we did, becoming a tactical opponent and a festering thorn in SANRAL's side for the next few years on its urban tolling project.

What if #4

Many often suggest that with hindsight, even if OUTA were not around, the scheme would have failed. The question arises, what might have happened if OUTA was not formed or did not do the work it did, or never interdicted the e-toll launch?

We have stated on numerous occasions that the e-toll scheme was always going to be imbued with massive administrative and enforcement challenges and would become unworkable. So why did we not just step back and watch it collapse, thereby saving all the expensive legal costs?

Well, hindsight is an exact science, as they say, but even so, the challenge was much more than just the unworkability of the scheme.

However, the scheme's degree of unworkability had a converse correlation to the level of compliance. And there was a tipping point at which high enough compliance levels (I estimate that at 60% to 70%) would have satisfied the authorities that the scheme was alive enough to allow it to labour on, albeit on life support.

It is also important to note that the interdict obtained by OUTA was a massive signal to the public that they had the power to halt this scheme.

Had most of society been none the wiser to the underlying issues that gave rise to their justified civil disobedience on such a large scale (which I believe the initial interdict did for many), the scheme might very well have enjoyed a sizeable majority of people tagging up.

So, I guess the questions are:

Did OUTA play a role in exposing SANRAL's ongoing misinformation, the irrationality and high costs of tolling, the real e-tag penetration rates, the Advertising Standards Authority rulings against SANRAL, along with its failed public engagement process, etc. (the list goes on)?

And might a greater understanding of these aspects have heightened civil courage sufficiently to defy the system?

On both counts I say absolutely.

I do not doubt that the Nkandla scandal, Eskom's woes, SAA's continuous bailouts and the auditor general's exposure of wide-scale abuse of taxpayers' revenues added fuel to SANRAL's fire. Middle-class South Africans were getting fed up with their taxes being wasted and here came SANRAL with another irrational road tax. It was an easy target for a tax revolt. E-tolls gave the people a chance to show a finger to government. A case of 'come fetch the money … if you can'.

And so it was that, as with any administratively challenged policy that lacks the willing support of the people, the process is prone to become meaningless. Today, despite the revised enforcement processes and a planned reliance on a future attempt to have AARTO in place, the e-toll policy will more than likely rmain a lame duck. Not the metaphorical lame duck either, but a real duck that was actually lame after stepping on a land mine.

Do we feel vindicated at the stance we took?

Absolutely, without one iota of a doubt. It was patently clear to all at OUTA and society at large, as far back as 2010, that the scheme was a farce, and the more the authorities tried to defend their decision, the greater the fiasco that developed.

From the beginning, when I learnt that SANRAL actually believed the scheme would be easy to implement and that its initial suggestion of 93% compliance was achievable, I realised how out of touch with reality the SANRAL board must have been.

It further irked me that SANRAL's leadership believed that 27% of revenue being channelled toward the administration and management of collection costs was acceptable. Yes, they claimed it was 17%, but they conveniently omit the Transaction Clearing House (TCH) costs where all the default debt piled up. They argued that the TCH process would be self-funding through the higher penalties charged. Sadly for them, this debt remained uncollected, and not much will change under the new dispensation.

While in my role as the chief executive at Avis, I was further irked by the expected rise in number plate cloning problems, which we were sure would transpire (and which did). The fact that SANRAL's procedure placed the onus on the rightful vehicle owner to prove that the false movements were not his/hers was very unreasonable. It certainly was one of the few factors that made me livid enough to say, 'Damn it, they cannot be allowed to get away with this nonsense.' Licence plate cloning remains a serious problem for the scheme, even more so now that e-tags are no longer required.

As a result, we sit here today, five years after the start of the public uproar and at the time of finishing this book, with a very shocking decision still in play, limping along with less than one in five road users subscribing to the scheme, being mainly drivers of corporate and government vehicles, and I seriously doubt if government's new enforcement plans will have the desired impact on society's willing acceptance of the scheme.

Personally, I am grateful for the experience I have gained during the e-toll saga. The cause has helped me to understand that in adversarial conflict, when the opportunity for dialogue is lost or prevented, the two opposing perspectives often become so entrenched that reality is lost somewhere in between.

I also learnt that when you feel the reality of the situation might be blurred, it becomes necessary to check in with the audience, the onlookers, the people on the outside. Not with your colleagues, for they too might be a tad high on the same juice from which you drink. In the case of e-tolls, it was to be the public that gave us the most honest opinions, but only if we invited them to do so. In such situations it is imperative to ask the questions directly, bravely and honestly. Don't ask to seek the answers you desire.

I discovered the power of honest, constructive criticism during my days at Avis, when we conducted 360-degree leadership energy reviews. These are sessions where one's boss, peers and direct reports are invited to provide anonymous feedback and a review of one's energy, impact and influence on people (in various scenarios). As daunting as it is, it becomes a major source of personal reflection and growth, if you enable it.

In taking this practice into the space of active citizenry, I have often sought criticism for my judgements and opinions expressed. I took seriously the critical responses and comments to my opinion pieces and articles written. I also read each and every article of attack on my persona by Vusi Mona and others, looking deep and hard at possible learning and growth opportunities that might lie therein. I didn't dwell too long on Mona's name-calling and attempts to discredit me.

Looking back, I remain convinced that what we have done and continue to do is right.

Our perseverance has paid off.

CHAPTER 29

Government's reluctance to let go

It is my speculative opinion that the authorities have refused to throw in the towel on the failed e-toll debacle for the following reasons:

(1) By conceding, they admit they got it horribly wrong. I sense they will experience this as a massive blow to their egos, when it ought not to be. Maybe it's because they might see this as a win for active citizenry, not a pleasant situation for our government, which faces many more future challenges that require urgent redress.

(2) Another reason is that while there is still a revenue stream at hand, even at well below their R260-million target, the paltry income is still a significant flow of funds into ETC's feeding trough, much of which flows to the hungry local companies that provide the security services, cleaning contractors, caterers, stationery suppliers, IT people, consulting services and others. The cash pipe might not be the size of the fire hydrant they were hoping for, but I guess a domestic garden hose will do. And limp on it will, for as long as there are compliant, fearful companies and government departments directing revenues towards the hungry, ill-conceived scheme.

(3) Considering the logic of all the options open to government and the stand-off that has transpired, there appears to be some underlying reason(s) at play, which makes it difficult to turn back and reconsider available alternatives. Why or what these may be, will be the subject of ongoing speculation by the public.

Extractive institutional behaviour

A book I recently read shed more light on the issues relating to the e-toll saga, as well as the many other challenges and failing situations in South Africa today. It is a book that Judge Dennis Davis makes reference to in his talk titled 'Social Justice Initiative', which he gave to a small group of people in May 2014. The YouTube clip of Judge Davis's talk was shared with me by my colleague, John Clarke.

I had previously met with Judge Davis in 2013, during a debate on his eTV show, *Judge for Yourself*. Judge Davis is extremely astute and highly respected – someone with a deep grasp of the underlying legal and socio-economic dynamics that impact societal behaviour.

In Judge Davis's talk, he shares his concern for the damage done to the fabric of society as a result of a lack of support given to civil society entities, whose role it is to tackle the extractive nature of our government's behaviour. His talk certainly enlightened me as to the nature and manner of SANRAL's extractive behaviour as a state-owned entity.

The theme of Judge Davis's talk is premised largely on the book titled *Why Nations Fail: The Origins of Power, Prosperity and Poverty* (by Daron Acemoglu and James Robinson). I downloaded the book and soaked up its interesting and insightful opinions on why South Africa was doomed to collapse under the apartheid regime and why it is once again a nation that is performing well below its full potential.

Authors Acemoglu and Robinson provide a fascinating historical account of why some nations prosper and others fail when it comes to the economic growth and levels of prosperity experienced by their respective citizens.

The reasons, they say, are not the result of cultural differences, geographic considerations, economic policies or value systems, as many have argued in the past, but rather due to the nature of their institutions. More directly, success or failure depends on the political institutions that determine their respective economic institutions.

The authors theorise that political institutions can be divided into two kinds – '*extractive*' institutions, in which a small group of individuals do their best to exploit the rest of the population, and '*inclusive*' institutions, in which many people are included in the process of governing and hence the exploitation process is either attenuated or absent.

Acemoglu and Robinson show how and why every time there are examples of growth and improved prosperity in a nation, region or area of the world, it has been when the political forces have chosen not to dominate the people at the expense of a few, but rather, to be inclusive of the wishes and well-being of their populace.

Their view clearly state:

> Nations fail today, because their extractive economic institutions do not create the incentives needed for people to save, invest, and innovate. Extractive political institutions support their economic

institutions by cementing the power of those who benefit from the extraction. Extractive economic and political institutions, though their details vary under different circumstances, are always at the root of this failure.

The grand e-toll extractive plan

On the e-toll issue, I sincerely believe the authorities were sold the idea of a grandiose plan, which had all the trappings and trimmings of lucrative revenue streams that were extractive by nature. The scheme was sold on the idea that it used modern-day, efficient technology that had been successfully applied around the world (nothing wrong with that), yet they overlooked its application, efficacy and workability in the context of the environment in which it was expected to operate.

I believe that SANRAL must have been aware that a fully inclusive and engaging approach to seek society's endorsement for the e-toll plan was never going to be easy. Instead, its extractive mindset became mistakenly blinded by the notion that if it persuaded the governing authorities to amend the regulations to suit its needs, its ability to enforce compliance through fear as opposed to commitment would result in users falling into line and tagging along.

I also believe the political leadership of the Department of Transport (and many of our current government departments for that matter) find it difficult to question and challenge the executives of state-owned entities, such as Nazir Alli and his highly qualified engineering teams, or their 'specialist' advisers such as those at Tolplan. What certainly looked good to the authorities on paper might have also blinkered their judgement of the practical challenges facing the scheme.

But, ultimately, I believe it was the lucrative potential of a R3 billion plus e-toll collection revenue stream per annum that was hard to ignore. A scheme of this nature needed many suppliers, contractors and consultants, all of whom would be able to tap into the lucrative e-toll administration and management process. Furthermore, the government's own pension fund, managed by the Public Investment Corporation, would also enjoy the fruits of the scheme by funding the capital bonds at healthy interest rates, and backed by government. A healthy risk-free investment indeed.

Additionally, the freeway upgrade construction cost, which has been estimated at R7 billion overcharged, was another indication of the extractive behaviour, whereby SANRAL virtually 'allowed' these gross overcharges to take place under their watch. SANRAL knows very well the costs and benchmarks of road construction expenses and this overspend on GFIP was not slight, or even significantly large. It was gross.

The South African government's general behaviour – extractive by nature?

Looking back on the past two decades of our nation's history, I have come to realise that e-tolling is just one example of many that display the signs of extractive institutional thinking and policy-making, expressed and supported by the general political leadership of South Africa.

Few will ever doubt that colonialism existed as an extractive policy for the enrichment of political leaders in far-off lands. However, Acemoglu and Robinson provide numerous examples of how countries are able to break the shackles of extractive policies of colonialism and become inclusive in their independence, thereby generating wealth and prosperity for their citizens.

Following the colonialist interventions, South Africa's independence sadly did not see a transition towards an inclusive mindset. Instead, our nation's freedom from colonialism merely switched to another form of extractive behaviour under the apartheid regime, which was selective in its inclusionary policies based on racial classification. Apartheid was an evil extractive policy, one that ruined the lives of millions and almost brought our nation to its knees.

Despite our citizens' ability to break the shackles of apartheid, barring a brief and extraordinary transition to new-found freedom under the incredible leadership of Nelson Mandela, our recent history and the past decade, in particular, have been fraught with numerous examples of an extractive mindset.

This is clearly evident in hundreds, if not thousands, of examples of political leaders or their families and cronies being at the receiving end of tenders and state-awarded contracts and unnecessary projects, at the expense of the people and taxpayers' money. Even the ruling ANC party's investment company, Chancellor House, enjoys the fruits of their risk-free investments in companies that are awarded state-owned entity tenders and contracts.

For too long now, millions of South African citizens have been spending their hard-earned money on services that should be supplied by the state. Those who can afford it spend more money on private medical facilities, schooling and security because they simply cannot trust or depend on these services being reliably supplied by their government.

Even many within government leadership prefer not to make use of public schooling and medical facilities because they too probably distrust their very own colleagues' capabilities of delivering reasonable services. Instead, many governing authorities tend to send their children to private schools while protecting their properties by employing private armed response teams and heaven knows which state-run hospital they will go to should they or their family members require medical attention in a life-threatening emergency.

It is, however, the poor who suffer at the hands of poor government service delivery. They have no choice but to put up with the state's failure to provide acceptable standards and quality of education, health and other basic services.

Institutional failure is perpetuated through numerous political appointments of incompetent and underqualified people in public service departments, often because of who they know and not necessarily because they are the best qualified persons for the job at hand. All too often, they will serve the extractive nature of the political regime. The excessive costs and resultant losses at the expense of the taxpayer have become a source of endless frustration to the South African taxpaying society. As a result, the nation's prosperity weakens.

A failed state on the horizon?

One doesn't need to look far to note how many a key state-owned entity has failed or is in a shocking economic state as a result of extractive thinking and behaviour.

I don't need to beat the tarnished drum of Eskom's collapse or the continuous ailing health of South African Airways, the Post Office or others. And now, even our once proud SANRAL is on the brink of another credit rating's downgrade, to its lowest levels yet – that of junk status, unless of course the state is able to provide a temporary finance solution. It might, however, be that the recent dispensation's bailout from the Treasury and a new enforcement stick will stave off that downgrade for a short while.

These are just some of the major national state entities experiencing ongoing economic and performance decline, year after year, often requiring multibillion-rand taxpayer bailouts.

I make these statements with concern, as I take no pleasure in seeing the demise of these once-flourishing organisations, which employ thousands of talented and passionate people. Engineers, technicians, administrators and employees who do their best to keep the lights on, the wheels turning and the services ticking over. They take no pleasure in working for failing institutions.

Every year or so, each new or existing politically connected appointee to these state-owned entities promises to sort its problems out, but they seldom do. If these entities were stand-alone businesses in the private sector, liquidation would have long since prevailed. However, they continue to exist through the taxpayers and the Treasury's helping hand, flying in the face of government's user-pays mantra.

Had the right leadership and competent management expertise been injected into these entities, with an inclusive approach to doing business and shutting out the extractive interfering political forces, they might very well be profitable. Until then, high costs and inefficient policies and processes will continue to drag them – and the nation – down.

One wonders what the current situation at Eskom would be, were it managed in a manner that sought the best outcomes for the citizens of the nation. Would the new power plants at Medupi and Kusile have been built in time at the initial one-third of the current cost of these projects? Would Eskom's coal purchasing contracts be less costly? Some say Medupi and Kusile might not have been built at all, but instead been replaced by independent and green energy power generation, significantly cutting our energy costs and averting the nation's suffering from ongoing load shedding. I imagine that corporate governance rules would have prevented the ANC's investment arm of Chancellor House or its connected businesses from benefiting from any investments into these projects.

Is the behaviour at SANRAL any different? When reading the *Sunday Times*'s front-page story of 25 November 2012, I sense we have a serious problem within this state-owned entity, where questionable relationships have been allowed to develop over many years, not only in the tolling concessionaire projects, but also in the road construction industry. Since the Competition Commission exposure of the collusive practices, which drove up the price tag of GFIP, SANRAL's ambivalence and vacillation on the road construction collusion issue raises many questions. At the time of printing the first edition of this book, over eighteen months has elapsed since the Competition Commission approved certificates for SANRAL to pursue civil claims against these companies. Yet no detailed plan in this regard has been shared with the very people who are expected to pay for these roads. And even when such plans do eventually arise, SANRAL might be reluctant to allow the scrutiny thereof by an independent team of experts, who will need to unpack the issues that SANRAL's critics seek answers to.

The N2 Wild Coast Consortium and the Cape Winelands preferred bid consortium are further cases that illuminate the picture. The Cape Winelands toll road includes consortiums that previously participated in the Gauteng construction collusion activities. In March 2015, the Supreme Court found it implausible to keep the 'commercially sensitive' and financial information of these Western Cape toll-road tenders out of the public domain. The people have every right to know about these schemes, which they are expected to pay for.

Our question is why was there such silence from SANRAL's (acting) chairperson and the minister of transport over this issue?

It would appear to me that SANRAL's ever-changing board members and the numerous ministerial appointments at the Department of Transport are simply unable to deal with the growing list of challenges and serious concerns emanating from SANRAL. They seem paralysed by Alli's technical expertise instead of being mindful of the real need for inspirational, accountable and transparent leadership required to take SANRAL out of the quagmire it is currently sinking into.

Looking forward

Despite my many concerns about the state of the nation, I am encouraged and upbeat about the possibilities and future of South Africa. I am mindful that when writing and expressing my concerns I run the risk of dragging not only my psyche but that of others into the doldrums of despair. That we mustn't allow.

But we also cannot adopt an ostrich mentality or remain mute in the face of the atrocities that are happening every single day in this country of ours.

We can't dwell on the past, but learn from it we must. It is the role of everyone who cares about our nation's future to do something about it.

Thus I no longer worry about what might transpire from government's plans to keep the e-toll scheme alive. The decision to implement it was flawed and that is now history. The e-toll cash cows are too lean to survive. Government can cling to its mantra that the user-pays e-toll system is here to stay, in the same way as a lone pair of underpants sticks to the inner drum of a tumble dryer in a high-spin cycle. The people remain unconvinced by government's e-toll decision, the rationale thereof or their attempts to beat them into submission.

A government out of touch with the people's reality

What needs to happen now is a concerted effort to hold our public leadership to account for all the gross shortfalls perpetuated by them at all levels of government.

I yearn to hear the South African government ruling party's executives making statements that genuinely reflect their desire to 'appoint the best people to lead and manage our state-owned entities, with a vision to make these organisations thrive with maximum efficiency and aimed at achieving the best outcomes for the people of the nation'.

I yearn for the public sector's understanding that ethics are indivisible. That we can't have one set of ethics at the private level and another at the public level. Or one set of moral values and principles during elections and another between elections. Or one standard for the wealthy residents of urban Gauteng and another for poor rural peasants in the Eastern Cape and homeless squatters of Lwandle.

I yearn for the day that we stop relying on the courts to keep government honest, a situation that merely perpetuates 'lawfare', wherein truth often becomes, if not a casualty, then a permanent hostage. For it is only when 'bite' is needed that the courts should play their role in dispensing justice and creating good order in society by ensuring absolute equality of all – be they presidents or paupers – before the law.

I yearn for a rise in the number of active citizens who use social media to maximum effect in constant vigilance, not only to bemoan the lack of government ethics, but also the ethics of big business and civil society institutions, be they religious, sporting, environmental or cultural organisations, by challenging them to be true to their purpose.

We have seen enough to know that the extractive behaviour that permeates our state-owned entities will have far-reaching negative consequences for the prosperity of South Africa. 'Business as usual' must now be challenged, and, to this end, society can no longer afford to sit back and watch the rubberstamping of questionable research, inflated proposals and contracts being awarded to connected business with multiple middlemen involved. If the citizens and ethical business organisations of South Africa are unable to mobilise a mindset of highly active, constructive and participative civil action forces, then we must all begin to worry.

Where to from here?

Let us assume for now that the yearning for a ruling party and government leadership to change their ways will not be a reality in the short to medium term. What can and should the taxpaying public do to hold government to account for the unnecessary losses and corruption that bleeds the nation to death?

There are two areas where I believe society can become more organised and demanding of an effective change that would lead to improved prosperity in South Africa: firstly, business/industry associations and, secondly, civil society action groups.

Business and industry associations

The world is filled with business/industry/trade associations. These organisations are generally founded and funded by businesses that operate in a specific industry. They exist for lobbying and general industry interest purposes. Most industry associations are non-profit organisations that are governed by laws to ensure they are directed by officers who are also members of the association and may not conduct anti-competitive practices.

Under normal circumstances these entities generally do good work, but in abnormal situations they tend to protect their members from attack, be it new legislation that may damage the industry's profit returns or reduce standards that threaten the industry or its members' existence. Prior to healthy competition regulations, these associations were often extractive, collusive and monopolising by nature. Today, they have the potential to serve a greater purpose.

South Africa has numerous business associations, some well managed and with good influence over their members, while others are weak and serve little purpose to their members.

Examples of industry associations include:

National Association of Automobile Manufacturers in South Africa
    (NAAMSA)

South African Dental Association

Airline Association of South Africa
Federated Hospitality Association of South Africa
Retail Motor Industry
South African Insurance Association

Then there are associations that represent a conglomeration of business/ industry associations, such as the South African Chamber of Commerce and Industry and Business Unity South Africa (BUSA), where many and diverse industry bodies gather to lobby government on wide-ranging issues and topics that impact on the nation as a whole.

Three stages of industry association maturity are:

(1) Self-interest associations: While not transgressing anti-competitive regulations, these associations exist to protect the interests of their members, keep membership conditions tight and do not actively promote a healthy competitive environment. They stick to their own industry issues and do not generally drive transformational change.

(2) Inclusive industry associations: These exist to promote competitiveness and high industry standards. Industry associations in this space project mature thinking in that they drive transformation in their respective industries, being inclusive towards assisting new or smaller entities to participate and become successful. At this level, these associations drive healthy competition and improve industry standards.

(3) Inclusive and externally innovative associations: Much like the inclusive associations in (2) above, these industry associations exist to bring about improvements and change, not only within their respective industries, but also for the improvement of prosperity and trading conditions beyond their boundaries. These innovative industry associations are the champions of good business practice for the people, by getting involved in general business regulatory matters, legislation and policy setting, that has a positive impact of improving the prosperity for the country as a whole, and not only for their members or shareholders.

It is when business enables its industry associations to operate in the third stage of maturity that a nation's prosperity evolves and improves. Sadly for South Africa, most of our business and industry associations do not operate at this level. For it is at this level of maturity that industry

associations operate to ensure that government policy adoption is conducted not only in the interests of its members, but also of society as a
whole. Associations operating at this level will question and challenge
the squandering of taxes by the public service and get involved in structures that add value to government policy-making.

Below are just three of a number of taxes that, in my opinion, should
not have been allowed to be introduced. Big business should have fought
harder to protect society from the introduction of these taxes, or at least
they should be vehemently challenging them today.

The Plastic Bag Levy (Tax) of South Africa

Introduced in mid-2004, the purpose of the plastic bag tax was to generate funds and create jobs for lucrative waste recycling programmes.
These would be instrumental not only in cleaning up the environment,
but also in creating jobs for manufacturing and recycling of plastic bags,
etc. It was also predicted that this new tax would impact on consumer
behaviour by reducing the number of plastic bags used.

To date, barring a small initial dip in plastic bags usage in the beginning,
consumer behaviour has not changed. Neither have the recycling and job
creation initiatives transpired. All that has happened is millions of additional rands are generated from the sale of plastic bags each month, the
profits of which flow between the retailers and government's coffers.

While I, for one, admire the good work conducted by the Consumer
Goods Council of South Africa, I hope they might make a call to the
authorities to suggest a timeout on the plastic bag levy. No matter which
way they look at it, the Plastic Bag Tax is a waste of time and money for
society and we could well do without it. We could also do with greater
citizen action by using recycled bags.

The Vehicle Emissions Tax

The tax was introduced in 2006 to tax cars at R90 per gram of CO_2
emitted above 120 grams. Obviously, the more CO_2 emitted from less efficient engine technology, the higher the emissions tax. At best, one might
argue that the intention was to change buyer behavior (to purchase lower
emission vehicles) and to get manufacturers to produce cleaner burning
engine technology. The latter, however, was an ongoing result of vehicle manufacturers working to reduce emissions due to higher fuel costs
anyway.

The result of the tax did not elicit a change in buying behaviour. The economic conditions and consumer preferences saw the vehicle buying patterns change. The vehicle emissions tax was also never ring-fenced and used for cleaner vehicle energy projects as is done in Europe through the collection of such taxes. All that happened in South Africa is that the tax generates an additional R1.5 billion per annum into government's coffers.

Personally, I feel that NAAMSA did not put up a good fight to halt the introduction of this tax. Instead, it ensured that all its members were more or less equally impacted by the introduction thereof. Today NAAMSA should be fighting to have this tax abolished but I believe it probably won't. The regulations that impact on the lucrative local content and export programme incentives are too big to risk by the ruffling of government's feathers.

The Tyre Recycling Tax

Introduced in early 2012, the Recycling and Economic Development Initiative of South Africa (REDISA) was commissioned to manage the country's used tyre waste, estimated at over 200 000 tonnes a year. REDISA was set up to collect the waste tyres from all tyre fitment outlets around the country, including stock piles unaccounted for, and then to use these in various recycling processes and for fuel and other energy needs.

The initiative envisaged was a noble one, reducing tyre waste being dumped at landfills, thereby reducing environmental and health problems for the country. In addition, as with the plastic bag tax, the tax was to create jobs and drive a new recycling initiative. A levy of R2.30 per kilogram of new tyre sold would be applied and passed on to the coffers of REDISA, a new private structure entity.

Unfortunately, while the Retail Motor Industry did challenge the introduction of this tax in court, it lost and the initiative was given the green light to proceed. Some three years later, despite all the good talk, not much has happened and all indications are that millions of rands generated are merely pouring into the salaries of individuals who manage the board of a highly ineffective tyre recycling initiative.

*

In all three of the above cases, business associations are allowing the continuation of irrational extractive taxes that do not offer any real benefit

to society. These are taxes that increase the extractive nature of our policies and institutions in South Africa, making our country poorer, not
richer, for them.

Some will argue that they feed the national budget anyway, so why
worry? The problem is that not all of these taxes reach the Treasury coffers and then there is the question of taxes being squandered, on which
the Treasury should focus more, and less on trying to fill its coffers.

Will business seriously challenge the carbon tax?

The next grossly extractive tax being planned for South Africa by the
Treasury is that of the general carbon tax, that is, a tax planned to be
applied to all businesses that use energy derived from fossil fuels (coal-fired
electricity and or petrol/diesel). The revenue generated from the planned
carbon tax will feed directly into the coffers of the government and will
not be ring-fenced to drive green energy initiatives in South Africa.

Some believe a carbon tax will get businesses to change their energy
consumption habits. I say not at all, especially in this day and age. The
mere fact that Eskom is becoming so expensive and inefficient is doing
the job of having businesses reduce their energy use and seeking alternative energy sources. The introduction of a carbon tax will simply be
an expense passed on, making it more expensive to live and consume in
South Africa. Government will enjoy the additional proceeds to keep its
bloated salary bill satisfied. It will also cost business and government billions of rands a year to administer and the only happy entities (besides
government) will be the auditing companies, which will largely provide
the calculation and verification services for the carbon tax. This one
must not be allowed to happen.

Business associations should be challenging the South African government on the continued existence of these taxes in every way possible.
Yet they don't. Instead, they kowtow to the authorities whom they know
will make the business regulatory environment more difficult if they are
challenged in such a manner.

Industries that fear government become weaker

This is precisely what happened with the e-toll tax, whereby SAVRALA
members were heavily leant on by the governing authorities and eventually the association's members were instructed by their bosses to pull

back on the e-toll challenge, so much so that the leasing members largely disbanded the association. Today, SAVRALA is considering dropping the 'LA' element and redefining itself as SAVRA, the South African Vehicle Rental Association. As such, it will no longer accommodate the needs of its leasing cousins.

This action will bring a smile to the face of SANRAL and the governing authorities and will no doubt see those businesses placed back on the various government fleet tender lists. But sooner or later, when the need arises, the leasing industry will have to reorganise itself. And, I imagine when it does, boldly written into its constitution will be a paragraph on 'treading lightly when it comes to challenging our friends in government'. It will take new and bold leadership within the leasing industry to break its current 'business as usual mould' again.

I sincerely believe that corporate South Africa can strengthen its respective industry associations by beefing them up with strong leadership to avert the dismal result of weak administrators who ineffectively represent the collective industry and society's needs.

The fact that BUSA is not the strong and robust arm of business representation at the National Economic Development and Labour Council, and at other government interfacing levels, is a sad situation indeed. While discussing this matter with a member of Business Leadership South Africa in 2012, the members confirmed their concern about a weak united business front at BUSA at that time. Perhaps it has got stronger today, I'm not sure.

In saying this, I do not suggest for one minute that big business is the silver bullet or should bear the brunt of criticism for our dire situation. Neither are they squeaky clean or blameless for many of the problems that we face today. All I am highlighting is that big business has immense power and can do much more to protect society from government's extractive abuse. It is, after all, the business sector that collects and pays over the PAYE, VAT and corporate taxes to the South African Revenue Service.

Civil society action

Civil society action groups have a meaningful role to play in keeping a watchful eye on the work of government institutions. But active citizenry can very often be driven from a negative or destructive position. This happens when society's frustrations become vented through loosely banded groups of citizens and individuals who often make decisions based on unsubstantiated information. Their actions have the potential to be expressed in an overt and often destructive manner or quietly and covertly through the withholding of taxes and non-payment of services.

Overt and destructive forms of active citizenry generate a visible expression of anger in order to highlight the plight or views of disgruntled citizens. Often a showdown of force between citizens and the government policing units sparks the unfortunate death of innocent citizens. The tension, however, very seldom abates, until the authorities address the desires of the people, which they invariably do succumb to.

Covert defiance generally takes the form of a tax revolt, in one guise or another.

The nature and danger of tax revolts

Modern-day tax revolts are not always visible, but when they become organised overt expressions by a group of citizens who simply stand defiant against the authorities by openly claiming their right to minimise their dues to the taxman or public service authorities, the stage is normally set for a courtroom or enforcement showdown.

Tax resistance also takes place through the non-payment of local taxes that society is able to test the boundaries on. They are easiest to conduct where cumbersome administration and poor enforcement processes are involved, such as the payment of traffic fines (a lucrative municipal revenue stream that has little to do with road safety), vehicle licence fees, e-tolls and others.

Poor administration and the inability or lack of desire by the authorities to enforce transgressions leads to dwindling local tax revenues. This, in turn, leads to the authorities' application of substantive increases in these taxes, which engenders greater defiance, and so the vicious circle goes.

The tax revolt becomes bigger and more entrenched when communities and individuals begin to defy payment for services, which ought to be easily addressed by the authorities in order to enforce compliance. This is evident in our current refusal by many citizens to pay their electricity bills or rates and taxes. For obvious reasons of political interference (such as keeping the peace with a voting constituency), municipalities and metros are prevented from taking action and the behaviour spreads like a cancer to other suburbs and regions.

But it is when provisional taxpayers and businesses start to question and challenge why their taxes are being squandered by poor public service administration, that the Treasury's problems begin. This is when the public form class action suits and stand in defiance of government by withholding taxes.

I would certainly not like to live in a country where a full-scale tax revolt begins to unfold. We must do all we can to avoid this situation. But doing so will take strong business and civil action leadership to whip the public sector into healthy, competent shape again, by holding our civil servants to account.

I'm not sure if government realises its need for an organised, healthy and active civil society.

The need for organised civil society interest groups is actually in the best interests of both government and its citizens. Without these organised platforms, through which both society and the government are able to engage with each other, unnecessary and extractive behaviour by both public and private entities goes unchallenged.

Civil action groups act as watchdog entities that help government to remain honest and true to its mandate of serving the people. Any mature government should welcome this state of affairs unless, of course, this same government does not want its own leadership's extractive behaviour to be exposed and challenged. This is more likely to describe the situation and behaviour of our public leadership today who say that there is a Public Protector in place to fulfil that role. Yet when the Public Protector is effective, they ignore its instructions and make it difficult to perform. How stupid is that?

The power of social media

Today's world of activism is very different from that of the past. It is a connected world where people share their frustrations, experiences and thoughts for a common purpose. The Internet and social media are now a reality, which is feared by an authoritarian extractive leadership weary of the power of a disgruntled and united society. Fortunately for OUTA, modern-day social media platforms were here and played an important role in its challenge of the unjust e-toll tax. An effective social media campaign within a healthy free press environment, promoted by our nation's strong Constitution that aids the freedom of speech, were all paramount to the success of our campaign.

This doesn't mean that OUTA had a free ride or that government didn't make our lives difficult. But there is no doubt that if OUTA's case had been fought just one decade earlier, in the absence of a connected society, or under restrictive conditions as applied in a country like China, we would not have achieved the necessary communication levels and flow of information so vital to our cause.

I must also express my concern that we tend to over-use social media to vent and complain. Of course venting will happen, but we need to turn the vast amounts of negative energy into a positive channel for more action and positive words of encouragement.

Organised civil action

We have many civilly active organisations throughout South Africa and it is my belief that many are doing a sterling job, but there are also many that limp along, sucking up donor funding and not achieving their goals.

The successful ones are those whose leaders are passionately committed to driving their respective causes. They are the morally courageous who are up for both the challenge and the adversity that comes with their work. The likes of Right2Know and Section27, the Treatment Action Campaign and the Institute for Accountability in South Africa come to mind.

We need more of them.

Subsequent to OUTA's formation, we received numerous requests to challenge bigger national issues.

Our committee has often discussed a potential need to transform OUTA into a larger, more organised institution to oppose the many situations of unjust or unnecessary taxation of society. Going down this road might see OUTA breathing life into a bigger organisation aimed at addressing a wider scope for civil action, and holding political leadership to account.

The debate in the world of civil activism is, however, often centred on effectiveness, scalability and size. Some believe that larger entities have greater power and ability to raise the necessary funds to tackle the issues at hand, while others believe that smaller entities are more effective and focused in tackling their respective matters.

Enter the notion of a People's Parliament, or the People's (own) Public Protector

In the early 1970s twelve intellectuals and scientists published *Limits to Growth*, a revolutionary book based on early computer simulations and projections. They had formed a special group that met regularly to discuss the future of both society and the planet. They called themselves the Club of Rome. Their work was revolutionary at the time and did much to generate global awareness of our need to start managing the planet as a valuable and limited resource.

There is a real temptation to set up a similar Club of Active South African Citizens, to analyse and stoke the fires, debate and take action to propagate the likelihood of a more prosperous growth for South Africa. As much as I see the need for this in our society, I also have many questions about whether it will work.

Would it spark the public's participation beyond its current realm of Facebook or armchair activism? Would it encourage big business to play its part? Will a heightened awareness for stronger civil action witness taxpaying members of society taking part in human protests, camping on the lawns of the Union Buildings, or outside Parliament, to demonstrate their defiance of poor government leadership?

And who will run or manage a centralised and powerful civil action group?

There are many passionate South African citizens who have the time and should do this work. There are many retired, semi-retired or unemployed people with outstanding leadership skills, some wealthy and others not. There must be hundreds of citizens that could get involved, to drive a meaningful civil action campaign. But will they?

It's about one's passion for the cause and the giving of one's time. They will need to have the expertise, the legal brains, the communication acumen and the leadership skills to do this exciting work. Their future and that of their children is at stake.

Such an entity's existence would probably dovetail with the work of the Public Protector and other, effective entities such as Corruption Watch, Right2Know, Section27 and other well-intentioned institutions.

Civil activism driving 'current democracy'

Civil activism generates the energy that feeds a new form of democracy, one that holds government and politicians to account for their performance between elections. Some call it 'current democracy', making use of the various mechanisms such as referendums (made easier today with modern communication processes), blogsites and other live platforms to announce, debate and vote on current socio-economic and governance issues.

The fact that the vast majority of citizens of voting age have a cell-phone is a marvellous opportunity to tap into.

Current democracy has the ability to shift the political power away from extractive behaviour towards performance-based outcomes that deliver the best results for society and the communities being served. It moves power back to the people and is a mechanism that could be ped-dled by civil society, even if the political authorities may not want to embrace it. If done correctly, the political leadership will have no option but to embrace this new movement. You can bet your last rand, though, that the state's intelligence services will be listening and watching its every move. But that should not deter its work.

Under such a civil action and/or political dispensation, citizens are encouraged to become more organised and active in driving and dealing with meaningful issues that enable a shift from the current herd-driven, low-performance malaise of corruption and rampant cronyism to a new level of intelligent and honest action required of public leadership.

I caution, however, that we should be careful not to fall into the trap of thinking some central body needs to be formed in order to create this energy. If we believe this, we may seek to become like the government, facing the same issues it now has to deal with, power vested in a few, which has the ability to destroy effective and active democracy.

The key is to spark the thought process among citizens, spreading knowledge and civil courage to disobey stupid rules. We need to pro-mote the view that by working together, people are more powerful than they think and that society should look at supporting self-organised and effective groups that form spontaneously.

Someone once asked Hugh Glenister (during his challenge to keep the Scorpions intact), 'What are you trying to achieve?' His reply was, 'To light the match, if the fire takes then I am on the right track, if it does not, then I am as mad as many say I am.' Hugh's actions certainly lit my flame.

It would appear to many that the fight and demeanour that the ANC displayed in its earlier vision to serve the people, some two decades ago, has come full circle. The ruling party, once passionate fighters for lib-erty, have become just like their National Party forebears, abusing their power in a display of disrespect towards the taxpaying citizens of South Africa. The public's desperate desire is to have their hard-earned rev-enues used more efficiently, to build a more inclusive and prosperous nation. Instead, they continue to witness numerous examples that speak of the exact opposite: an extractive and decaying nation being plundered by many within the ranks of public leadership.

It is my sincere belief that organised civil action can and must create the necessary energy to deal with the extractive decay and putrid behaviour of some of our current public leadership. It is important to note that not all those in power are out of line. But there are many. Far too many for our country to afford.

An uncontested idea is not worth anything

There are vastly more failed ideas and innovations than successful ones. Some had huge merit, but it would appear that the most successful ideas (which become a reality) are the ones whose innovators responded constructively to their critics, who effectively helped to play a part in the improvement of the idea.

Thus, the question is, how might SANRAL have dealt differently with OUTA? What verdict will the judgement of history hand down? I know that Nazir Alli believes that history will vindicate him. I, of course, believe that history will vindicate OUTA, even though this civil action movement might not be around forever.

Either way I am less interested in being proved right as I am concerned about the squandering of public money that has been spent on 'lawfare', when the bones of contention might have been better picked clean and discarded through constructive dialogue and the use of effective alternative dispute resolution mechanisms.

Thoughts about my own future

'Are you going into politics?' is the question I am most frequently asked in recent times. The simple answer? Not likely. I don't regard myself as a politician. I don't have the patience for all the protocol and waffle, moving at a snail's pace to get stuff done.

'How about a full-time activist?' Well, at least I can say I've got the T-shirt. Maybe not a large T-shirt, like the ones that Jay Naidoo or Mark Heywood wear. In reality though, I have been a reluctant activist. If I could have jumped off this train earlier, I probably would have. But, I hate quitting on a job or challenge, especially one that I have partially instigated and, even more so, when there is a bright light at the end of the tunnel. I firmly believe in sticking it out. Yes, there was immense joy and learning over the past three years of my life, heading up the OUTA challenge, but it also came with its price. Now for me, it's time to move on.

Would I participate in another civil action body or challenge, or a People's Parliament? Maybe, however, if indeed I do continue to play a full-time role in a civil action movement, I would need to earn a living from it. There is only so much time and effort that one can put into this work, with no income derived therefrom. My time and my life needs to be more directed by what is best for my family and me going forward.

Will I go back into the car rental industry that I enjoyed for so many years? Not likely. Been there, done that. I need new pastures, ones that I can grow in.

Currently, aside from my role as chairperson of OUTA, I am having a great time unleashing my pent-up entrepreneurial energy, developing a new business in the area of service and leadership excellence. If there is one area of my career that I enjoyed and learnt the most from, it was working with a team of great executives and taking the Avis service excellence and internal culture change programme to new heights, on a sustainable and meaningful basis.

This experience has been the basis of a new consulting business, eXcentris, which I have recently set up with a few good people. I am happy to see where eXcentris will take me, or rather, where we will take this new business to. I am also exploring new business/equity ventures that make sense, while at the same time I conduct business and motivation talks on the two passions in my life: service excellence and active citizenry.

At heart, I am an entrepreneur and South Africa has opportunities and people like no other, in which and with whom I intend to explore, grow and share. Despite my frustrations and our nation's challenges, this country is still a great place to be, but imagine …

Just imagine if we could tempt our political leadership out of their extractive mindset and into a new inclusive psyche that creates the platforms and environments to foster growth, productive employment, healthy competition, administrative efficiency and maximised prosperity for all its people.

No one would be able to touch us.

Now is the time to make it happen.

Notes

------- ------- ------- ------- ------- ------- ------- ------- ------- ------- ------- ------- ------- -------

Chapter 1

1 IPress release, 'OUTA Files Legal Application to Halt E-tolls', 23 March 2012.
2 Ibid.
3 Ibid.
4 Ibid.

Chapter 2

5 www.ibtimes.com/2014-soccer-world-cup-brazil-predicts-revenue-20-times-over-south-africas-2010-experts-skeptical (accessed 7 May 2015).
6 Ramos Mabugu, Hélène Malsonnave, Véronique Robichaud and Margaret Chitiga, 'Fiscal Imbalances and Intertemporal CGE Modelling', www.ff.co.za/.../270-chapter-3-fiscal-imbalances-and-intertemporal-cge (accessed 7 May 2015).
7 Statistics South Africa Census, 2011 data.
8 www.timeslive.co.za/politics/2015/03/03/gauteng-spends-55-of-2015-budget-on-employee-pay (accessed 7 May 2015).
9 This figure of around R375 billion was supplied in discussion with South African economists.
10 'Assault on Gauteng's Asphalt', *Mail & Guardian*, 31 October 2005.
11 Chapter 12 of the Constitution, clause 195 spells these out.

Chapter 5

12 www.youtube.com/watch?v=-mc93qnSRQM (accessed 7 May 2015).

Chapter 6

13 oldgov.gcis.gov.za/speeches/view.php?sid=16829 (accessed 8 May 2015).

Chapter 8

14 GFIP Steering Committee Report.

Chapter 13

15 www.theportugalnews.com/news/dead-loss/28626 (accessed 7 May 2015).

Chapter 17

16 Author of *Soil and Soul, People vs Corporate Power*. The term 'Civil Courage' was first used by the king of the amaMpondo in a media statement that John helped him draft in 2010 after he was deposed, thanks to the inspiration John got from Alastair McIntosh who wrote to offer consolation. John relates the remarkable story in a chapter that appears in the *New South Africa Review* 4, titled 'amaDiba Moment: How Civil Courage Confronted State and Corporate Collusion', published by Wits

University Press.
17 www.youtube.com/watch?v=4hNYrcU5Hh4#t=11 (accessed 7 May 2015).

Chapter 18

18 mg.co.za/article/2013-10-22-zuma-dont-think-like-an-african-pay-up-for-e-tolls
    (accessed 7 May 2015).

Chapter 21

19 www.timeslive.co.za/local/2012/11/25/taking-their-toll-how-a-cosy-club-dominates-
    sa-s-toll-road-empire (accessed 7 May 2015).

Chapter 22

20 www.outa.co.za/site/wp-content/uploads/2014/02/2014-02-27-Etolls-at-an-Impasse.
    pdf (accessed 7 May 2015).
21 www.theportugalnews.com/news/dead-loss/28626 (accessed 7 May 2015)
22 www.outa.co.za/site/wp-content/uploads/2014/09/2014-09-01-OUTAs-submission.
    pdf (accessed 7 May 2015).

Chapter 24

23 152.111.1.87/argief/berigte/citypress/2012/03/12/CP/6/p6%20tollsturnSide.html
    (accessed 7 May 2015).
24 www.outa.co.za/site/wp-content/uploads/2014/08/OUTA-Queries-to-SANRAL-
    Board-2014-06-09b.pdf (accessed 7 May 2015).
25 www.timeslive.co.za/local/2012/11/25/taking-their-toll-how-a-cosy-club-dominates-
    sa-s-toll-road-empire (accessed 7 May 2015).

Chapter 25

26 www.theportugalnews.com/news/dead-loss/28626 (accessed 7 May 2015).
27 www.outa.co.za/site/wp-content/uploads/2014/08/Rule_of_Law_Campaign_V7.pdf
    (accessed 7 May 2015).

Chapter 26

28 www.infrastructurene.ws/2013/08/20/south-africas-infrastructure-needs-
    intervention/ (accessed 7 May 2015).

Chapter 27

29 www.thepresidency.gov.za/pebble.asp?relid=19746.

Acknowledgements

Wayne Duvenage

This book is a culmination of personal experiences, but it also draws and reflects on the writings, work and action of many journalists and members of the public whom I would never be able to acknowledge, but whose input has inspired all of us at OUTA.

Acknowledging journalists might not be right, as this may suggest some degree of favoritism being show towards OUTA. However, the truth is that I found the level of professionalism of South Africa's journalists very high, fair and true to their profession, almost all of the time.

To Andrea Nattrass of Pan Macmillan who agreed to publish and assisted with the structure of the book, I am ever grateful. The decision around the timing of writing and releasing this book was a challenge. Andrea's skills and insights were valuable in the regard. I realise now there is no best time to finalise a book on a subject that is drawn out over a long period of time and has not yet reached its conclusion.

To Angelique Serrao who did the writing, recording and transcribing of many hours of discussion, along with assisting in the structure of the story, I say a big thank you. Angelique's intricate knowledge of the story was also extremely important in the writing of this book, as she was a leading investigative journalist at _The Star_ newspaper at the time the e-toll saga began to unfold in 2010. Angelique's work played a significant role in highlighting and exposing the issues that society wanted answers to.

My thanks also go to the editor of _The Star_, Kevin Ritchie, who gave permission for Angelique to work on the book and for us to use copyrighted images in the book.

Also to Valda Strauss our editor who helped us to get it all in shape – thank you.

To my wife, Helen, for her extreme patience, reading, checking and never-ending support. You are my rock and sounding board for so much in my life. And then to our children for their support and understanding and the lost hours of family time, taken up by this cause.

My parents, Arthur and Bee, who have done so much throughout my life and made it all so real. Looking back, I needed nothing more than what you gave, and yet you still gave so much more in your very different ways, right down to this chapter in my life.

Then there were the OUTA directors and committee members, all of whom were extremely important to the process and governance of the organisation and its work. While they appear in the book, I mention the following people again, who sat at one time or another on the OUTA committee and extended sound advice and input at our meetings: Paul Pauwen, Michael Tatalias, Jeff Osborne, Clif Johnston, Ari Seirlis, Marc Corcoran, Nick Tselentis, Rob Handfield Jones, Tracey McKay, Mokesh Morar, Howard Dembovsky, Rob Hutchinson and John Clarke.

In particular, thanks to Paul Pauwen, Marc Corcoran, John Clarke, Rob Hutchinson and Ari Seirlis for their outstanding work and effort on OUTA's many matters, as well as for personal support and upliftment. To Sharon Clarke, who was ever-patient and supportive, despite John's lost family time during the cause. John, your input, proofreading and spokesperson role took a massive weight off my shoulders and your positive energy was of immense benefit towards the cause. Ari Seirlis, you are simply an inspiration.

A separate mention of thanks to Howard Dembovsky (JPSA) and Rob Handfield Jones (Driving.co.za), who challenged SANRAL and the Department of Transport on a number of issues.

To Bikers Against Tolls for the many demonstration rallies and the platform you shared with OUTA.

Pieter Conradie, Kelvin Buchannan, Rebecca Thompson and Brent Williams, the CEO at Cliffe Dekker Hofmeyr attorneys. This formidable team took a massive load off OUTA's plate and we are grateful for your professionalism and support. But, more importantly, it was the decision by CDH to donate back to OUTA by writing off a substantial amount of outstanding debt, and the many hours given for free and at reduced rates, running into millions of rands, that we are ever grateful for.

To Adrian d'Oliveira, our junior counsel member of the team, I can't thank you enough for your additional advice and support you gave us beyond the call of duty when we needed your input at presentations and meetings with influential people. Your free time and input is much appreciated.

To Alistair Franklin, Alfred Cockrel and Mike Maritz, the three senior counsel on our team at one time or another, I pay my sincerest thanks. Solid advocates who fought hard and did a brilliant job in our corner all the way.

To the many other members of organisations and associations that fought ahead, alongside and behind OUTA along the way, you made the cause so much stronger. To you we are extremely grateful:

Gary Ronald, spokesperson of the Automobile Association until 2013.

Jason Fivas, a passionate member of the public who kept us in the loop with his many theories and intense communications with various authorities on the e-toll matter.

Ali Gule, a member of the public who was present at every rally and outside the courts with his placards.

Somadoda Fikeni for sharing your wisdom and attending our Freedom Day talk in 2014, despite a dismal public turnout.

Zwelinzima Vavi and Patrick Craven filled the positions of secretary general and spokesperson of COSATU at the height of the e-toll challenge, until their resignation from the powerful trade union movement in March 2015. Both Zwelinzima and Patrick played a very vocal, pivotal and participatory role in raising COSATU's voice about the wrongs of e-tolling. They organised and were ever-present at rallies, debates and discussions on the topic.

To those in politics, from both the Democratic Alliance and the Freedom Front Plus, I say thank you to Ian Ollis, Mike Moriaty, Jack Bloom, Manny de Freitas and Anton Alberts for playing your part and asking the pertinent questions in Parliament.

Azar Jamine for his contribution and work conducted in assessing the economic viability and providing sound opinions on the e-toll decision, and for the Foreword he has provided to this book.

To Yusuf Abramjee and Talk Radio 702 for the Lead SA award. Yusuf's speech at the November 2012 public hearing in Pretoria was a powerful message to the authorities and his assistance at OUTA's media gathering on 28 April 2012, following the interdict of the e-toll launch, was much appreciated.

Brian Williams who did great work in setting up the automated complaints portal on OUTA's website.

Yoav Techlet and Deon Schwarbsky for the initial support and work done on building our website and getting the platform right for our social media campaign.

Ryan Christian of Coza Productions for the great work and support on our social media programme in 2013 and arranging the artist and production of the OUTA YouTube clips that went viral.

Mike Roussos and Mike Deeb of the Catholic Church who did so much work in getting the Peace and Justice Conference to take a stand against the government on its e-toll decision.

Kevin Louis & Associates Attorneys for so much work and support.

Rotary Club of Benoni Aurora for their Paul Harris Fellow recognition of the work done by OUTA.

Advocate Paul Hoffman of the Institute for Accountability in Southern Africa for his input and assistance in our applications for funding from potential donors.

Hugh Glenister for his wisdom, sound advice, and the generous donations towards the cause.

Mark Heywood for your sound advice and support.

I'd like to acknowledge the almost 13 000 individuals and families, along with the over 400 businesses that helped OUTA to raise almost R12.5 million to fight South Africa's biggest publicly funded legal challenge against a government decision. Despite the fact that we didn't get the final rulings we sought, the messages that came out of this legal challenge were powerful. This extent of active citizenry has been incredibly moving, without which OUTA would not have concluded its work.

Finally, to the roughly 1.5 million users of the Gauteng freeways who held out and refused to comply with the policy of e-tolling, we salute and acknowledge your courage. Your active citizenry has provided the authorities with food for thought about the might of citizen power.

Angelique Serrao

For Wayne: thank you for giving me the opportunity to help tell your story. Your courage, refusing to back down on what you believe in and your unwavering ethics are to be admired. Your kindness, and the numerous muffins, which got me through all those early mornings, will never be forgotten.

For all the boys in my life: my amazingly understanding husband, Thomas, who did more than his fair share of babysitting to get me through the long writing and editing sessions. My two greatest loves, Sebastian and Daniel, who are my constant inspiration. And my brother Olivier, my rock, whose advice always gets me through.

To my mom, who always believed in me and made me so strong. I wish you could be here to hold this book. I miss you every day.

To my editor at *The Star*, Kevin Ritchie, who allowed me to embark on this new journey. For your care and advice every step of the way and for allowing us use of the photos taken from *The Star*'s archives. Without you I would never have been able to do this.

To my colleagues at *The Star*, both past and present, who helped me pitch and write e-toll stories. I must have sounded like a broken record at times. Thank you Jillian Green, Louise Flanagan, Mojalefa Mashego, Shain Germaner, Brendan Roane, Lebogang Seale, Moegsien Williams, Makhudu Sefara, Gill Gifford, Shaun Smillie and Janet Smith, who all worked on this story with me in one way or another over the past five years. Not forgetting photographers Chris Collingridge, Bongiwe Mchunu, Antoine de Ras, Itumeleng English and Paballo Thekiso, who waited hours outside of court or at protests to get the perfect shot, and who tried so many different ways to make a gantry look appealing.

Thank you also to all of those people who kept on feeding me information, and granting me those much-valued exclusives. Howard Dembovsky, Neil Campbell, Jack Bloom, Gary Ronald, Marc Corcoran, Paul Pauwen, and all those whose names never appeared for a reason, but I know who you are. I hope your trust in me paid off.

In particular, a big thank you to BtT. I hope one day we can meet.

And last, but far from least, thank you to Mandy Wiener for your encouragement and advice, to editor Valda Strauss for all that hard work polishing thousands of words, and to publisher Andrea Nattrass who believed in me. I can never tell you how much that has meant.

An open letter to Environmental Affairs Minister Edna Molewa

‒ ‒ ‒ ‒ ‒ ‒ ‒ ‒ ‒ ‒ ‒ ‒ ‒ ‒ ‒ ‒ ‒

August 2011
Attention: The Honourable Ms Edna Molewa
Minister of Environmental Affairs
South African Government

Dear Ms Molewa

OPEN LETTER: CARBON TAXATION POLICY SETTING

We imagine that by now your respective departments are assessing and analysing the inputs provided by various stakeholders to determine the best route forward for the introduction of a prosperous 'carbon taxation' policy into the South African environment.

At Avis, we understand the urgent need to address the required reduction of greenhouse gas (GHG) emissions on a global scale. The time to introduce an effective carbon tax policy which deals with this huge challenge cannot come soon enough. The intention of this open letter is not meant to be tutorial, condescending or forthright on this matter, but rather is aimed at providing a view from the perspective of a business that takes climate change and global warming seriously. In doing so, we respectfully propose a few suggestions for consideration when formulating SA's carbon taxation policy, which should be a gift to the world if its design does not undermine the true purpose for which it is intended.

While we believe there will have been significant and meaningful input provided by business and environmental experts on this matter, we hope and trust that these will have featured the following issues and hereby request that these be taken into account:

    1. Global warming and climate change are global issues. With this in mind, we urge that the structure of a South African carbon tax

policy does not oppose or conflict with instruments put in place by the UN Framework Convention on Climate Change (UNFCCC), the Clean Development Mechanism (CDM) and other recognised voluntary carbon reduction standards, which have the greatest potential of addressing global warming.

2. The SA government must be encouraged not to introduce a carbon tax scheme which is aimed solely at bolstering the national fiscus and thereby effectively becoming just another source of government revenue, without directly addressing the environmental issues for which they are intended. A truly effective structure of carbon taxation policy setting should be aimed at becoming 'tax or revenue neutral' to the fiscus while providing punitive consequences to carbon-intensive operations but reducing the financial burden on those who emit below a given threshold.

3. Should there be a surplus carbon taxation revenue stream (deliberate or not), these funds should be earmarked and ring-fenced for local clean energy production, sustainable development and job creation from which all South Africans should be able to benefit into the future.

4. Consideration should be given to the exemption of businesses that subscribe to the UNFCCC's CDM and who are thus net carbon-neutral by their direct participation in both mandatory and voluntary carbon trading schemes. This enables companies to meet their corporate social investment objectives as well as having the comfort that their funds are ring-fenced to address sustainable development where it's needed most. Failure to do so would effectively be a double taxation for these businesses, which may then be encouraged to disengage from carbon offsetting and the deserving communities being the biggest losers. This would be a sad day. In light of this, one trusts that there will be an incentive for SA companies which are or wish to be 'carbon neutral' – be this through local or global emissions reduction projects – to qualify for SA carbon tax exemption.

At Avis, we are serious about reducing our impact on the environment and have introduced a comprehensive sustainability program which includes intensive water and other waste recycling, along with our carbon neutral position and energy reduction programs. We support the notion of a carbon taxation strategy by the government, but only if the process therein is transparent, efficient and effectively geared towards the direct reduction of carbon emissions in a manner that will produce the highest benefit for our planet.

We wish you every success in the setting of the policies that will guide responsible carbon taxation in South Africa, trusting that this will become a model policy for the world, a policy that will be designed not to enrich the general fiscus and 'government coffers', but rather to fill the 'life coffers' of our one and only planet.

Kapsch TrafficCom AG share price and e-toll events

Kapsch TrafficCom AG, based in Vienna, is listed on the Austrian Stock Exchange. Its core business is the provision of high-performance, Intelligent Transport Systems (ITS). Despite having many projects and 30 subsidiary representative offices around the world, there is an uncanny relationship and movement of its share price to the activities and performance of the South African e-toll project, managed by ETC, of which Kapsch TrafficCom owns 85%. The graph below illustrates the South African e-toll events in relationship to the Kapsch TrafficCom share price.

Kapsch TrafficCom AG share price (euros) and the events of Gauteng's e-toll

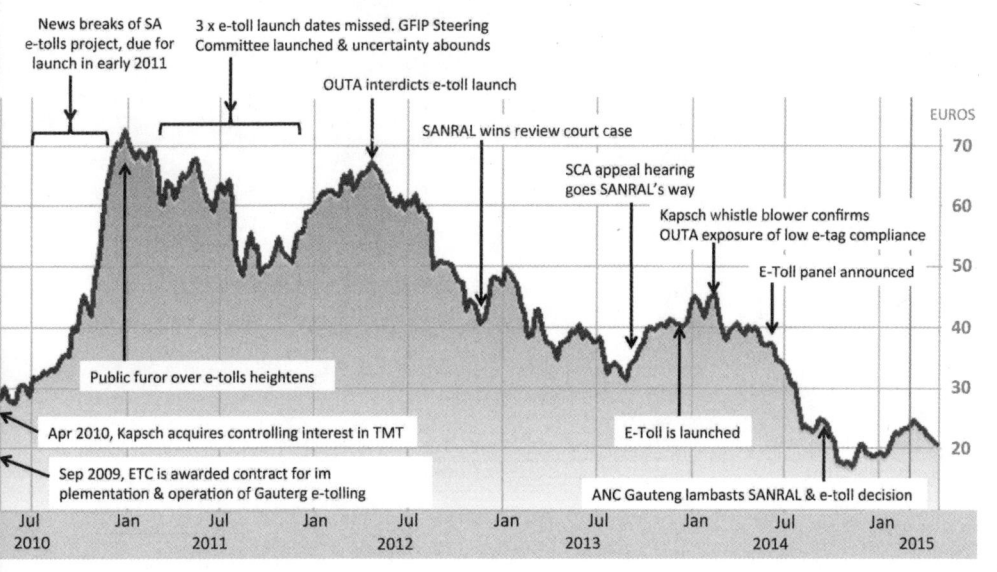